29. 4. 1991

THE RECORD SOCIETY OF
LANCASHIRE AND CHESHIRE

FOUNDED TO TRANSCRIBE AND PUBLISH
ORIGINAL DOCUMENTS RELATING TO THE TWO COUNTIES

VOLUME CXXV

The Society wishes to acknowledge with gratitude the assistance given towards the cost of publication by

Cheshire County Council
Lancashire County Council
Greater Manchester County Council Residuary Body

ISBN 0 902593 20 X

Produced by Alan Sutton Publishing Limited, Stroud, Gloucestershire
Printed in Great Britain

ACCOUNT OF MASTER JOHN DE BURNHAM THE YOUNGER, CHAMBERLAIN OF CHESTER, OF THE REVENUES OF THE COUNTIES OF CHESTER AND FLINT, MICHAELMAS 1361 TO MICHAELMAS 1362

Edited by
P.H.W. Booth and A.D. Carr

PRINTED FOR THE SOCIETY
1991

CONTENTS

In Memory of Alec R. Myers
(1912–80)

GENERAL EDITOR'S PREFACE

Over the past twenty years or so, a resurgence of interest in the history of Cheshire (represented, for instance, by the publication of the first volumes of the *Victoria History of Cheshire*) has drawn attention to the lack of satisfactory texts of the county's medieval records. Perhaps surprisingly, the Record Society itself has hitherto published few contributions in this field. It was in response to a perceived lack of adequate access to the records which form the starting-point for any attempt to study medieval Cheshire's political, social and economic history that P.H.W. Booth proposed in 1977 that the Society should embark on a programme of publishing texts from the major categories of Cheshire records in the Public Record Office. In choosing the Chester chamberlain's accounts as the subject-matter of the first such volume, he aimed to reflect the rise in academic standards and expectations since the Society's publication, in 1910, of R. Stewart-Brown's edition of a selection of fourteenth-century accounts. In 1978 A.D. Carr agreed to collaborate in this project by producing the sections of the text and related notes concerning the county of Flint, for which the chamberlain of Chester was also responsible.

This volume, however, aims to do far more than provide the definitive text for the student of the palatinate's finances in the year 1361–62. Using this document as a base, the substantial introductory chapters offer insight into the history of fourteenth-century accounting and auditing practice; taxation and revenue-raising, especially in relation to the policies of the earl of Chester, the Black Prince; the special status of Cheshire as a county palatine; the workings of the county's administrative and legal systems; the maintenance of public order, with special reference to the mythical 'great Rebellion' of 1353 (the subject of a concluding appendix); and the careers and factional rivalries of the Cheshire gentry. The Flintshire sections provide parallel insights into the government and administration of that county, including details of the rôles played by the local leaders of the Welsh community and their relationships with the Cheshire authorities. A further contribution to the general history of the region in the fourteenth century is furnished by the biographical notes on over 150 Cheshire and Flintshire persons whose names appear in the account.

Record Society subscribers and other readers will be aware that this volume, as its number indicates, was originally intended to appear in 1986/87. The constant pressure of other commitments, and the prolonged spell of illness of one of the joint editors, have led to the Society's recent volumes appearing out of their scheduled numerical sequence. The General Editor would like to take the opportunity to apologise for any confusion or frustration which these unavoidable delays may have caused, and to venture to suggest that the quality of this text and translation, and the range and depth of the accompanying notes, amply repay the time and care which have been expended in their production.

ACKNOWLEDGMENTS

The editors would like to record their thanks to Nêst Roberts, Carol Robinson and Joan Squires for help with typing part of the edition. Valuable assistance has also been given with various historical and technical points by Dorothy Clayton, the late Brian Harris, Simon Harrison, John H. Harrop, Philip Morgan, Brian C. Redwood, Alan Thacker, Andrew Thomson and Andrew Tonkinson. The General Editor of the Record Society, Peter McNiven, has afforded patient help and encouragement well beyond the call of duty, without which this volume could never have been produced. The University of Liverpool Research Development Fund gave financial assistance with the research costs. The text and translation are Crown Copyright, and are published here with the permission of the Controller of Her Majesty's Stationery Office.

EDITORIAL NOTE

The text of the chamberlain's account for 1361–62, edited in this volume, is based on a transcript of Public Record Office SC6 772/3, the more complete of the two surviving copies of the account. It has been corrected and supplemented, where appropriate, by reference to SC6 772/4. The copies are subsequently referred to as 772/3 and 772/4. Variant readings have been recorded in the text footnotes. Both copies of the account are sewn chancery fashion, and the start of each membrane is marked in the text: for 772/3, the membrane numbers are put in angle brackets – ⟨m 1⟩ – those referring to 772/4 in chain brackets – {m 2d}. Membrane numbers appear in roman type for the beginning of each membrane, and subsequently in italics at the head of each page of the text. The small portion of the text which is missing from the damaged head of membrane one of 772/4 – that is parts of sections **1** and **2** on the face of the membrane, and parts of sections **27** and **28** on the dorse – is printed in italics. Marginal notes are also printed in italics, but additionally enclosed in round brackets. They are placed at the head of the section or entry to which they refer.

In the transcript of the text all abbreviated words have been extended when there is no reasonable doubt of their form. Capital letters have been employed as in 772/3. As is usually the case with fourteenth-century clerks, it is not always possible to distinguish *c* from *t* when followed by *i* and a vowel. Consequently, the transcript has adopted the usage suggested by the modern English word derived from the Latin original. Thus, *solutionis* has been preferred to *solucionis*, and *nunciorum* to *nuntiorum*. Words or letters about which the transcriber was uncertain, because of damage to the records, are enclosed in square brackets. In the cases where there is some doubt about the extension of words which are legible, they have been enclosed in round brackets. Place-names which are suspended have not been extended, and the suspension is indicated with a final apostrophe. Welsh personal names have not been extended either, and marks of contraction and suspension indicated with apostrophes. In the phrases used for the dating of letters *dat'* has been left suspended, except where the context makes it clear that it is a noun, since it could otherwise be read either as a past participle (agreeing with *litteras*) or as the indeclinable *datum*, as is the case with its use in title deeds.

The translation of the text is literal, but not slavishly so. 'Beforesaid', 'aforesaid', and 'said' have been commonly omitted when they are not required to help the meaning. Dates are first given in their original form (day of the week, feast day, and regnal year), and followed, in brackets, with the modern form (date of the month, and year of Grace, employing the historical year beginning on 1 January). Place-names which are not surnames are translated into their modern forms; where there is no modern form, they are printed in italics.

xi

English and Welsh Christian names are translated into their modern forms; English surnames are left as in the text.

For ease of reference, both text and translation have been divided into numbered sections (e.g. **4**), which have been further subdivided, where necessary, into entries (e.g. **4.5**).

Terminal dates are expressed in two ways. Those separated by a dash (e.g. 1371–72) refer to accounting years which run from one Michaelmas to the Michaelmas following. Where a diagonal stroke is employed (e.g. 1371/72) the term refers either to an accounting period which does not both begin and end at Michaelmas, or to any other period of time which straddles two historical years.

LIST OF ABBREVIATIONS AND WORKS CITED BY SHORT TITLE

B.B.C.S.	*Bulletin of the Board of Celtic Studies*
B.P.	Black Prince
B.P.R.	*Register of Edward the Black Prince, preserved in the Public Record Office* (1920–33)
Bennett, *Community, Class*	M.J. Bennett, *Community, Class and Careerism: Cheshire and Lancashire Society in the Age of Sir Gawain and the Green Knight* (1983)
Booth, *Financial Administration*	P.H.W. Booth, *The Financial Administration of the Lordship and County of Chester, 1272–1377*, Chetham Society, 3rd series 28 (1981)
C49, C53	Public Record Office reference numbers
C.C.R.	*Calendar of Close Rolls*
C.F.R.	*Calendar of Fine Rolls*
C.P.R.	*Calendar of Patent Rolls*
C. Chart. R.	*Calendar of Charter Rolls*
Cal. Anc. Corr. Concerning Wales	J.G. Edwards, ed., *Calendar of Ancient Correspondence Concerning Wales* (1935)
Cal. Chanc. R. Var.	*Calendar of Various Chancery Rolls, Supplementary Close Rolls, Welsh Rolls, Scutage Rolls, preserved in the Public Record Office . . . A.D. 1277–1326* (1912)
ChAcc	R. Stewart-Brown, ed., *Accounts of the Chamberlain and other Officers of the County of Chester, 1301–1360*, R.S.L.C., lix (1910)
CHES	Public Record Office reference
Cheshire in the Pipe Rolls	R. Stewart-Brown, ed., *Cheshire in the Pipe Rolls, 1158–1301*, R.S.L.C., xcii (1938)
Chet. Soc.	Chetham Society
ChRR	*Calendar of Recognizance Rolls of the Palatinate of Chester* in *35th Annual Report of the Deputy Keeper of the Public Records* (1875)
D.K.R.28	*Calendar of Deeds, Inquisitions and Writs of Dower, Enrolled on the Plea Rolls of the County of Chester. -Edward 3* in *28th Annual Report of the Deputy Keeper of the Public Records* (1867)
D.K.R.32	*Duchy of Lancaster: Calendar of Rolls of the Chancery of the County Palatine* in *32nd Annual Report of the Deputy Keeper of the Public Records* (1871)
D.N.B.	*Dictionary of National Biography*

del.	deleted
E41, E368, E372	Public Record Office reference numbers
EC	J.P. Earwaker, *East Cheshire* (1877–80)
E.H.R.	*English Historical Review*
Econ.H.R.	*Economic History Review*
FMA(1)	A. Jones, ed., *Flintshire Ministers' Accounts, 1301–1328*, Flintshire Historical Society, 1913
FMA(2)	D.L. Evans, ed., *Flintshire Ministers' Accounts, 1328–1353*, Flintshire Historical Society, 1929
Fasti xi	John le Neve, *Fasti Ecclesiae Anglicanae 1300–1541*, xi: *the Welsh Dioceses*, comp. B. Jones (1965)
intl.	interlineated
J.C.A.S.	*Journal of the Chester Archaeological Society*
J.R.U.L.M.	John Rylands University Library of Manchester
Jnl Flints.Hist.Soc.	*Journal of the Flintshire Historical Society*
Jnl Medieval Hist.	*Journal of Medieval History*
Jnl Mer.Hist.& Rec.Soc.	*Journal of the Merioneth Historical and Record Society*
List of Sheriffs	*Public Record Office, Lists and Indexes IX, List of Sheriffs* (reprinted 1963)
Morgan, *War and Society*	P. Morgan, *War and Society in Medieval Cheshire, 1277–1403*, Chetham Society, 3rd series 34 (1987)
N.L.W.	National Library of Wales
Nott.Med.Studs	*Nottingham Medieval Studies*
om.	omitted
Ormerod	G. Ormerod, *The History of the County Palatine and City of Chester*, 2nd ed. revised and enlarged by T. Helsby (1882)
R.S.L.C.	Record Society of Lancashire and Cheshire
Record of Caernarvon	H. Ellis, ed., *The Record of Caernarvon*, Record Commission (1838)
rep.	repeated
SC1, SC2, SC6, SC11	Public Record Office reference numbers
Sharp, *Contributions*	M. Sharp, 'Contributions to the History of the Earldom and County of Chester, 1237–1399', Manchester Ph.D. thesis (1925). 2 vols. – Vol. 2 is an Appendix.
Somerville, *Duchy of Lancaster*	R. Somerville, *History of the Duchy of Lancaster, Vol. 1, 1265–1603* (1953)
T.H.S.L.C.	*Transactions of the Historic Society of Lancashire and Cheshire*
Tout	T.F. Tout, *Chapters in the Administrative History of Medieval England* (1920–33)
Tran.Caerns.Hist.Soc.	*Transactions of the Caernarvonshire Historical Society*

Trans.Denbs.Hist.Soc.	*Transactions of the Denbighshire Historical Society*
Trans.Hon.Soc. *Cymmrodorion*	*Transactions of the Honourable Society of Cymm-* *rodorion*
U.C.N.W.	University College of North Wales
V.C.H.	*Victoria County History* (of Cheshire unless other- wise stated)

Note: Since the beginning of the publication of this volume, the Public Record Office has recommended standard formats for the citing of its manuscripts, some of which differ slightly from those used here, e.g. SC6 772/3 would now be cited as SC 6/772/3.

INTRODUCTION

I. THE PUBLICATION HISTORY OF THE CHESTER CHAMBERLAINS' ACCOUNTS.

In 1910, this society published, as volume 59 of its series, what was then the earliest known group of Chester Chamberlains' Accounts. A few of the society's members had provided the money to employ W.K. Boyd, record agent of R. Stewart-Brown, the society's secretary, to make transcripts of documents in the Public Record Office class 'Ministers' and Receivers' Accounts'. This is one of the so-called 'Special Collections' of documents artificially brought together from a number of different classes, and it now has the call number SC6. Stewart-Brown had first become interested in these accounts when he was collecting material for his book on the history of the Wirral Hundred Court, published in 1907, in which he claimed 'to be the first to make any extensive examination of the Cheshire Ministers' Accounts for historical purposes', and he stated that Boyd had 'taken great trouble and interest in making extracts for me from (them)'.[1]

The 1910 volume consists primarily of translated extracts, largely of the material relating to Cheshire, from 23 chamberlains' accounts and related documents (SC6 771/1–23), together with reasonably full translations of two account rolls from the 'Divers Ministers' Accounts' series, that is of those Cheshire officials who were on an administrative level below that of the chamberlain. The first one, SC6 783/15, contains accounts for 1349–50 as follows:

 1. Sheriff of Cheshire
 2. Sheriffs of the city of Chester
 3. Bailiff of Northwich town
 4. Bailiff of Middlewich
 5. Forester in fee of Wirral
 6. Forester in fee of Delamere
 7. Escheator of Cheshire

The second, SC6 783/16, contains accounts for 1350–51, that is of the same officials as in the previous year, but adding to them:

---

1 *The Wapentake of Wirral: A History of the Royal Franchise of the Hundred and Hundred Court of Wirral in Cheshire* (1907) p. vii.

8. Farmers of the Dee mills
9. Keeper of the Dee passage
10. Constable of Chester castle
11. Gardener in fee of Chester castle
12. Bailiff of the manor of Frodsham
13. Bailiff of the manor of Drakelow

The 23 documents edited by Stewart-Brown as 'chamberlains' accounts' are listed as numbers 2 to 24 in the first part of Appendix 1 (pp. 196–207). Of them, only eighteen are, in fact, chamberlains' accounts, and they relate to various years between 1301 and 1360. Twelve cover a single financial year (from the morrow of Michaelmas to the Michaelmas following), two more than a single year, and four only part of a year. Of the remaining five, one is the *visus* (view) of a chamberlain's account (that is, an interim account, taken part-way through the year), and two are files of 'particulars of receipt', or detailed lists of revenues to be charged on chamberlains' accounts. The final document does not relate to the chamberlain at all, but is the account of a different, short-lived official, called the 'receiver in Cheshire in Flintshire', for 1342–43.

Judging by the pains he took to justify the enterprise in his brief introduction of fifteen pages, and the fact that finance had to be specially solicited for the transcript, Stewart-Brown must have felt that he was taking a considerable risk in publishing these records. It appeared, with his name as editor, as *Accounts of the Chamberlains and other Officers of the County of Chester, 1301 to 1360*. The title is misleading, as is the short version on the spine (*Cheshire Chamberlains' Accounts, 1301–1360*), since the chamberlain of Chester had responsibility for two counties, Cheshire and Flintshire, and there is some material relating to the latter county in the volume.

Three years later, in 1913, Arthur Jones, of Birkbeck College, London, edited a volume for the Flintshire Historical Society entitled *Flintshire Ministers' Accounts, 1301–1328*. The title page has no series number, but the spine has the legend *Flintshire Historical Society*, III. It is similar to Stewart-Brown's work in that it consists of translations of the Flintshire portions of nine of the chamberlain's accounts, between 1301 and 1328, but it differs in that it is preceded by a much more substantial introduction, of 50 pages. Jones tells us that he had had access to Boyd's transcripts for the first three of the accounts (1301 to 1304), but goes on to say that he checked them with the originals. It is not clear, therefore, whether Boyd had been instructed to give up transcribing Flintshire material in detail after the first three rolls, or whether Jones decided that if he had to check with the original accounts, he might as well construct a completely new transcript for the remainder.

Fifteen years later, in 1928, a volume of translations of the Flintshire sections of twelve more accounts was published. It appeared as volume II of the Flintshire Historical Society's new Record Series. It was edited by D.L. Evans (later Sir David Evans) of the Public Record Office, and is entitled *Flintshire*

Ministers' Accounts, 1328–1353. Again, it has a long introduction, this time of over 70 pages. Unlike Jones's volume, but like Stewart-Brown's, this edition includes other documents, as well as chamberlain's accounts. In addition to extracts from the 1342–43 receiver's account, there are four translated 'Divers Ministers'' accounts, this time of Flintshire. They are for 1349–50 (SC6 1186/4), 1350–51 (SC6 1186/5 and 1186/6), 1351–52 (SC6 1186/7 and 1186/8), and 1352–53 (SC6 1186/9 and 1186/10). The 1349–50 roll consists of the following accounts:

1. Bailiffs of Hope
2. Ringild of Hopedale
3. Receiver of Hopedale
4. Bailiffs of Ewloe
5. Bailiffs of Flint town
6. Bailiff of Coleshill
7. Bailiff of Caerwys
8. Bailiff of Bachegraig
9. Bailiff of Faenol
10. Bailiffs of Rhuddlan
11. Bailiff of Mostyn
12. Constables and sheriffs of Flint

The later accounts are similar, except that 2 and 3 drop out. From 1351–52 onwards there are accounts of the raglot and escheator of Englefield, and the constable of Rhuddlan castle, and for 1352–53 an account of the constable of Hope castle is added.

In addition, Evans published two examples of the Flintshire material from the 'great rolls of debts', for 1351–52 (SC6 783/19 and 784/1) and 1352–53 (SC6 784/2). The 'great roll', which comprises a compendium of uncollected revenue in both counties, is attached to the Divers Ministers' accounts for Cheshire.

Finally, in 1938, a full transcript was published, without translation, of a newly-discovered chamberlain's account for the period 7 February to Michaelmas 1301. It had been deposited, with other Wynnstay manuscripts, in the National Library of Wales in 1934, and was issued as an appendix (pp. 193–216) to Stewart-Brown's edition of *Cheshire in the Pipe Rolls, 1158–1301*, volume 92 of this society's publications. On this occasion, the transcript was made by the editor. There is a brief introduction of four pages, but, unlike Stewart-Brown's 1910 volume, there is some annotation to the text, which is followed by four pages of notes.

When volume 59 was published by the Record Society, Stewart-Brown expressed the hope that 'when the interesting nature of these rolls becomes better known, the members of the Society, as a whole, may be willing to provide the necessary funds for further volumes'. (p. 1). As far as Cheshire was concerned, that hope was not fulfilled, and during the following seventy years or so only one further account was published. Part of the reason for this may have been that the original edition was inadequate by the standards of the time, and conceals much of the interest of the documents that it purports to promote. There is a sharp contrast between its merits and those of the two Flintshire volumes. Stewart-Brown came near the end of the great line of gentlemen-antiquaries, whose contributions from the sixteenth century onwards to the study of Cheshire's history must not be under-estimated. The rather short-sighted editorial policy of the Record Society in its early decades – no elaborate introductions or critical apparatus – was designed for that milieu. One only has to compare volume 59 with, say, James Tait's magnificent edition of the *Domesday Survey of Cheshire*, or his two volumes of the *Chartulary of St Werburgh's Abbey*, published by the Chetham Society in 1916, 1920 and 1922, to see the difference that training in critical methods of documentary research could make.

Perhaps Stewart-Brown was compelled, by the need to justify the enterprise, to put too many accounts in one volume. In order to do that, Flintshire details had to be omitted from all but one of the accounts 'as not being within the scope of the society'. Furthermore, as we go through the accounts and compare them with the originals, we can see that more and more material was left out, as the notes in Appendix 1 demonstrate. The principles of selection are difficult to understand. For example, it is hard to see why the master mason and carpenter of the earldom, and the wages paid to them, should have been omitted from the accounts in the 1350s (pp. 166, 229, 235), or the payments to the soldiers leaving Cheshire for France in 1355 (p. 231). Also, there are far too many serious errors in the translation, particularly in the figures. If the test of a published text, translation or calendar is that it should be sufficiently reliable, and organised on such consistent principles, that consultation of the originals is only rarely necessary, then volume 59 is a failure. It might be thought to be labouring the point here, if the volume had not, of necessity, been relied on by most historians of Cheshire – both professional and amateur – since its publication.

The two Flintshire volumes are of a very different standard from the Cheshire one. Arthur Jones had been a pupil of both James Tait and T.F. Tout at Manchester University. As we have seen, Tait contributed much to Cheshire's historiography, while Tout interested himself in the medieval records of Flintshire. D.L. Evans was an assistant keeper in the Public Record Office, who subsequently rose to be its head (then called Deputy Keeper), and was skilled in the twin sub-sciences of palaeography and diplomatic. As Stewart-Brown's volume had appeared first, it is understandable, if regrettable, that both Jones and Evans decided to edit only the Flintshire portions of their accounts. However, they did include the Flintshire material in its entirety, without making excerpts, as Stewart-Brown had in the case of Cheshire, and their level of accuracy is much higher.

What also marks out the Flintshire volumes is the quality of their introductions. Arthur Jones's is, in effect, an essay in medieval Flintshire history, and he gave special attention to the county's social structure. Evans was able to build on

Jones's introduction and had the great advantage, denied to Stewart-Brown, that by the time he came to edit his volume, the riches contained in the Black Prince's Register had become accessible. Although Part Three, the Palatinate of Chester volume (1351/65), was not published until 1933, the typescript of the superb calendar had been produced by Evans's colleague, M.C.B. Dawes (whose assistance Evans acknowledged in his preface to the accounts) some years before. It was utilised by Margaret Sharp, T.F. Tout's daughter, when she was completing, in the mid 1920s, her magisterial Ph.D. thesis on Cheshire administrative history. Evans, therefore, since Jones had already provided a general introduction to the county's history, was able to concentrate in his introduction on some important aspects of Flintshire's history in the mid-fourteenth century, such as the trial of the bishop of St Asaph, the financing of the Hundred Years' War, the effects of the Black Death, and the organisation of lead-mining at Holywell.

The publication of further Chester chamberlains' accounts was suggested to the late Professor A.R. Myers by P.H.W. Booth in September 1970, and arose out of a thesis on which the latter was working on the financial administration of thirteenth- and fourteenth-century Cheshire. The project was then put on one side for a number of years, while the research and the thesis were completed. At this early stage, the idea of publishing a single complete account was favoured, in both text and translation if possible, and with full annotation. That for 1361–62 was chosen since it was the first (almost) complete chamberlain's account to survive after the last in Stewart-Brown's volume.

In 1978 the project was taken up seriously again, when the Council of the Record Society agreed, in principle, to support a programme of publication of Palatinate of Chester records over a period of years. This seemed feasible, because the establishment of the Victoria History of Cheshire, with the late Brian E. Harris as editor, in 1972, and the setting up of the Medieval Cheshire seminar by Liverpool University in 1974, had helped to stimulate a continuing interest in research into the history of late medieval Cheshire. All those who had become involved in that work were only too aware of how valuable the uniquely-rich Palatinate records were, and there was much support for the idea of publishing different classes of the records at particular periods, both to illustrate and set forth their value, and to enable them to be used properly.

The publication of the 1361–62 chamberlain's account only became possible when A.D. Carr, of the University College of North Wales, Bangor, agreed in 1978 to collaborate with P.H.W. Booth in the venture, and take responsibility for the final form of the Flintshire sections of the account, and for the relevant notes. During the following half dozen years, the project made steady, if slow progress. The original transcript had to be corrected by collating the two versions of the account, and noting variant readings. Other classes of Palatinate records had to be combed by both editors for the purpose of writing notes to the translation and biographies of those mentioned in the account. Nearly all the research has had to be done in the Public Record Office, London, and during much of the time the financial and political pressures on those working in Universities made such work more than usually difficult.

With the publication of another Account of the Chamberlain of Chester it might be thought foolhardy to echo Stewart-Brown's expression of hope of some eighty years ago, that its appearance might stimulate the publication of other volumes of Palatinate of Chester material. There was some excuse in the years before the First World War for the failure to build on the first editor's enthusiasm for these records. Now there is none, and published work has made it clear that the late medieval records of the Palatinate of Chester provide a source of unparalleled richness for the history of both Cheshire and Flintshire. If the present-day interest in local and regional history is more than superficial, then surely more of these records must be researched and made available for use.

II. ACCOUNTS AND ACCOUNTING METHODS OF THE EARLDOM OF CHESTER IN THE FOURTEENTH CENTURY

The account of the chamberlain of Chester for 1361–62 comes from a group of thirty-one accounts (and related documents) connected with the chamberlain's office between 1301 and 1374.[1] All but one of them are in the Public Record Office, in that unfortunately constructed special collection called 'Ministers' and Receivers' Accounts', which now has the modern call number SC6. It is tempting, therefore, to treat them as an archival unit: that is, a group of documents created by the administrators who produced them, drawn up to a consistent pattern, and capable of being directly compared with each other. This is not the case. First, the accounts under discussion were produced by three distinct administrations with different procedures and accounting methods. The first was that of Edward of Caernarfon (earl of Chester from 1301 to 1307), the second Edward of Woodstock ('the Black Prince', earl of Chester from 1333 to 1376), and the third the royal exchequer (through which the earldom's accounts were audited between 1327 and 1331). No complete account for a full year survives for the earldom of Edward of Windsor (1312 to 1327), and those which do suggest that at that time the earldom accounted through the royal exchequer. The second point to make is that the accounts were originally kept in at least two, possibly more repositories, as will be seen below.[2]

The fourteenth-century chamberlains of Chester were administrators who had little scope to make independent decisions. When there was an earl of Chester (1301/1307; 1312/27; 1333/76) they were subject to the control of the earl's central administration, based in London. When the earldom was in the king's hands – that is, between the earl's accession as king and the creation of his son as earl of Chester – the supervising authority was the royal government. During the childhood of the earl the royal government continued to exercise administrative control. So, during the whole of Edward of Windsor's earldom (1312/27), and the first part of that of the Black Prince, (1333/46), the earl's personal authority appears to have been nominal. It is not surprising, then, to find that the administrative procedures and accounting methods employed in the earldom's administration in the fourteenth century were heavily influenced by those of the royal exchequer. After all, the officials who had ultimate control were either

---

1   See Appendix 1, List of Chamberlains' Accounts, 1301 to 1374.
2   For a general discussion of the forms of account used in the earldom of Chester at this time see P.H.W. Booth, *The Financial Administration of the Lordship and County of Chester, 1272 to 1377*, Chet. Soc., 3rd ser. 28 (1981), Chapter Two.

former exchequer officials themselves, or had aspirations to hold high office in the king's government in the future.[3]

The account, which survives in two contemporary versions, is a product of the administrative procedures devised by Peter Gildesburgh in the mid-1340s for the English and Welsh estates of the Black Prince at the time when he was assuming adult responsibilities. Gildesburgh had learned his trade in the foreign accounts department of the royal exchequer, which had responsibility for the financial administration of the king's landed property. It has been shown elsewhere that Gildesburgh's system was designed to be highly centralised, and relied on long-serving professional administrators who were minutely supervised in their work.[4] Of the sixteen surviving accounts from 1347 to 1374, one of which is a half-yearly 'view', twelve were rendered by one man, Master John Burnham (or 'Brunham') the younger, and at least another twelve of his are missing. Three of the accounts, for 1360–61, 1361–62 and 1370–71, survive in two versions.[5]

During this period, the chamberlain functioned at the middle level of a three-tiered system of financial control and accounting:

1. First level: receiver-general
2. Second level: receiver
3. Third level: bailiff/reeve

The terms given here are those normally found in large lay estates of the second half of the fourteenth century. Money was collected and transferred from officials at the third level, typically manorial bailiffs or reeves, to the receiver at a regional centre. The receiver, in turn, made regular payments or 'liveries' to the receiver-general at headquarters. Each level produced accounts, because each official was a *minister computans* – that is, was bound to render a formal account for the money he had received and paid out. This was not, though, a chain of responsibility. Account was rendered not to the official at the level above, but to representatives of the lord's council, called 'auditors', who were empowered to hear and approve the accounts of all the estate's accounting officials.

So, the chamberlain of Chester, as 'receiver' of the two counties, Cheshire and Flintshire, which constituted the earldom, received periodic liveries of money from the third-level officials. These liveries appear in the first half of the chamberlain's account as part of the 'issues' (*exitus*) of various types: sections **4** to **6, 11, 17** and **18** relate to the third-level officials of Cheshire, **19** to **22** to those of Flintshire. On the account for 1361–62 Burnham himself made twelve liveries

3   Ibid., pp. 26–29.
4   Ibid.
5   See below, Appendix 1.

to Peter Lacy, who served as the prince's receiver-general from 1346 to 1371. They appear in section **41**, and are listed in accordance with Lacy's acquittances, between 14 May and 28 November 1362. The largest was for £764 12s. 8d. (18 October), the smallest £17 (19 July).

Accounts for the third level were kept in four groups from 1353: 1. Divers Ministers of Cheshire,[6] 2. Divers Ministers of Flintshire,[7] 3. Macclesfield ministers,[8] 4. the St Pierre account.[9] There is no surviving account of the receiver-general for 1361–62. It is normally the case with large, lay estates at this time that few, if any, from the first level have survived, rather more from level two, but most from level three. Only part of the revenue which appears in the chamberlain's account consisted of liveries from level-three accounting officials. A considerable proportion of it, including the various fines paid by instalments (sections **8, 12, 13, 14, 15, 23, 24, 25**), the prises (**9**), and the fee of the seal (**16**) was paid directly to the chamberlain in the Chester exchequer without going through another account. Also there were officials who, although they collected and paid in revenue, were not bound to render account themselves, only through the account of another.

For example, in the foot of Richard Done's account for Delamere forest in 1361–62, it can be seen that he made a livery of £17 4s. 0d. to the chamberlain.[10] It represented a payment of the issues of the farm of the agistment and pannage of the forest 'by the hands of' Henry Torfot and five others. That livery appears in the charge of the chamberlain's account (**5.7**) with similar wording. Clearly, the farmers of the agistment had paid the money directly to the chamberlain in the exchequer of Chester, although the livery was accounted for in Done's account. In the larger bailiwicks, such direct payments by non-accounting, subordinate officials were common.

The earldom of Chester's accounts for 1361–62 were audited in Chester during March 1363.[11] This was a time of change at the centre of the Black Prince's administration. Sir John Wingfield had died in the summer of 1361, having been the manager of the prince's estates for some ten years.[12] Wingfield had come to the prince's service after a career with the earl of Salisbury and the elder Sir Bartholomew Burgherssh. Both were close associates of the king, and Burgherssh had been master of the prince's household during his childhood. Wingfield was no office warrior, though: he fought at Crécy and Poitiers, and won fame in the latter battle through his capture of the Sire d'Aubigny. His undoubted military and administrative talents would have marked him out for

6 1361–62: SC6 785/9 **WR** and 785/10 **QR**.
7 SC6 1186/21, 22, 23.
8 SC6 803/5 **WR**, and 803/6 **QR**.
9 None survives for 1361–62. That for 1360–61 is SC6 783/10.
10 SC6 785/9, mm.1, 1d.
11 SC6 785/9, m.4.
12 His last act to be recorded in the Black Prince's Register is dated 8 July 1361 (*B.P.R.*, iv. 390).

the very highest offices in the kingdom, had he and his master lived long enough.[13]

His career offers a striking contrast with that of his predecessor. Peter Gildesburgh was a financial clerk of the old school, who had begun at the bottom of the ladder in the king's exchequer, from where he had been seconded to the prince's wardrobe – the household financial department – and then climbed to the top of his master's financial affairs in the years before the Black Death.[14] The replacement of such clerical officials by laymen, such as Wingfield, was becoming usual as the fourteenth century wore on, and a literate laity – at least at the higher social levels – could be taken for granted.

It was while Sir John was fighting at Poitiers, that John Delves deputised for him in England and thus appeared as his likely successor. Delves first comes to notice in the employment of the earl of Arundel, as his under-sheriff of Shropshire in 1348.[15] Arundel had been appointed justiciar of North Wales for life in 1334, and in 1348 Delves became his deputy (lieutenant) in this office as well, and thus joined the Black Prince's administrative service. He took on the lieutenant-justiciarship of Chester in addition, in 1353.[16] He had a thorough legal training, since, in addition to holding the two judicial posts already mentioned, he also acted as the prince's attorney in prosecuting *quo warranto* pleas in North Wales in 1348, and may have served as a puisne justice of the court of common pleas at Westminster in 1364 and 1365.[17] Clearly a lawyer/administrator of this type was well placed to shine during a time when the minute enforcement of old and new rights over subjects and tenants, and the exploitation of the financial proceeds of courts of justice of all types, was the way of ensuring that the prince's landed revenue did not fall in the decades following the Black Death.

There had also been a change of personnel among the auditors. Although the veteran William Spridlyngton is recorded in entry **45.13** of this account as 'one of the auditors of the accounts of the prince's ministers', he appears to have given up active involvement in the job not long after February 1363 and did not, therefore, audit this account.[18] The prince had already attempted, without success, to secure the bishopric of St Asaph for him six years previously, and he was to succeed in persuading the pope to provide him to that see in 1376.[19] Although Spridlyngton retained a position of great influence within the prince's

13 T.F. Tout, *Chapters in the Administrative History of Medieval England* (1920–33), v. 387; M.H. Keen, *England in the Late Middle Ages* (1972), p. 146; Booth, *Financial Administration*, p. 74.
14 Booth, *Financial Administration*, pp. 64–65.
15 *List of Sheriffs, Public Record Office, Lists and Indexes IX* (reprinted 1963), p. 118.
16 Tout, vi. 60; *B.P.R.*, iii. 125.
17 H. Ellis, ed., *The Record of Caernarvon*, Record Commission (1838), p. 151; Booth, *Financial Administration*, pp. 65–66, 74–75.
18 He was last referred to as acting as auditor on 20 February 1363 (*B.P.R.*, iv. 483).
19 *John le Neve: Fasti Ecclesiae Anglicanae, 1300–1541*, comp. B. Jones, xi (1965), 37, 40.

council until his master's death, he was obviously making the transition in the 1360s to part-time work. So, although the chamberlain's account does not furnish us with the name of its auditors, they can be inferred from the Divers Ministers' accounts as Richard Stokes (appointed in 1359) and William Cranewell, who had become an auditor as recently as October 1362.[20]

The audit that took place in the exchequer room of Chester castle in the spring of 1363 was carried out by emissaries of the Black Prince's council, employing systems of audit and account that had been devised centrally for all their master's English and Welsh estates. The type of account was unusual in fourteenth-century England, in that it was significantly different from the 'common form' (also known as the 'Westminster form') used by the vast majority of the country's lay estates at that time.[21] The major difference is to be found in the treatment of arrears, called *arreràgia*, and *remanentia*. In the common form, arrears were added into the current revenue, and liveries of money into the current expenses.

FIGURE 1

COMMON FORM ACCOUNT

1. Charge

    a. Arrears *plus*
    b. Receipts

    Sum Total

2. Discharge

    a. Expenses *plus*
    b. Liveries of money

    Sum Total

3. Balance

    1. *minus* 2. (This becomes the arrears of the following year's account.)

In the system employed by the Black Prince's estate administrators at this time, the arrears were accounted for separately from the receipts, and the liveries of money were separated from the expenses and included after the striking of the balance between the charge and discharge in a separate section called the 'foot' (*pes*) of the account. This system bears some resemblance to the 'Winchester' form of estate accounting, as used on the estates of the bishopric of Winchester, which was older than the common form. However, it was more

---

20   SC6 785/9; *B.P.R.*, iv. 328, 469.
21   Booth, *Financial Administration*, pp. 20–28; P.D.A. Harvey, *Manorial Records*, British Records Association (Archives and the User No. 5) (1984), pp. 25–41.

likely a development of the procedure of the foreign accounts department of the royal exchequer, from where it had been imported by Peter Gildesburgh.

FIGURE 2

'FOREIGN ACCOUNT' FORM OF ACCOUNT

1. Charge   Receipts

                              Sum Total

2. Discharge   Expenses

                              Sum Total

3. Balance   1. *minus* 2.

4. Joint sum of indebtedness: Balance (3) *plus* remainder of the previous year.

                              Sum Total

5. Foot   Liveries to higher level, *plus* allowances and
                              exonerations.

6. Remainder   4. *minus* 5. (This becomes the remainder for
                              the following year).

Another important aspect of accounting procedure is the relationship between the chamberlain's account and those of the four groups of third-tier officials which were audited at the same time. It would have been possible to link them by transferring the charge from the inferior accounts to the superior, as was the case with the chamberlains' accounts in the early fourteenth century.[22] With the reform of the prince's accounting procedures in the 1340s, a different method, which has been called 'transfer-livery', was adopted, which meant that the *liveries of money* in the inferior accounts appeared as *receipts* in the chamberlain's account. This explains why there are two sets of arrears in this chamberlain's account: sections **2** and **3** (called *arreragia*), and section **40** (*remanentia*) in the 'foot' of the account.

To see how this worked, take as an example the 1361–62 account of William Jonet, who served as the reeve of Shotwick manor from 1351 to 1372.[23] He made three liveries of money to the chamberlain in the foot of his account. Two, for

22 Booth, *Financial Administration*, pp. 31–34.
23 SC6 785/9, m.3.

£21 13s. 0d. and £1 10s. 0d., were of current revenue, namely that which had arisen during 1361–62. The third livery, of £3 7s. 8d., was of arrears, that is of revenue that had arisen in Shotwick before 1361–62. This third livery was transferred to the chamberlain's account, see entry **2.9**, where it appears amongst the *arreragia*. The other two were transferred in entry **5.1**, amongst the issues of manors, towns and forests. So it is clear that where money is recorded as issues or arrears coming from a third-tier accountant to the chamberlain, the figures represent actual transfers of cash and not of charge (*onus*), or liability to pay.

The account was written by a number of clerks, whom the auditors brought with them. They were paid 40s. 0d. for 'writing and duplicating this account and those of the aforesaid officials (i.e. of the counties of Chester and Flint, and of Macclesfield), and of the lands of John de St Pierre.' (entry **31.10**). This payment had been agreed in 1352, after representations made by the then auditors, William Spridlyngton and Nicholas Pynnok, to Sir John Wingfield.[24] It allowed the auditors to bring their own trained clerks with them on circuit, and made it easier to establish a central style of auditing and accounting.

As has already been seen, the 1361–62 chamberlain's account survives in two versions, (SC6 772/3 and SC6 772/4). Both are incomplete, in that part of the beginning of membrane one is missing, probably because of damage from damp to the outside of the two parchment rolls. Slightly more of SC6 772/3 survives, and it has therefore been taken as the base text, since there is no compelling reason to think, as will be seen, that either version is the original. The list of extant accounts from 1301 to 1374 shows that the nineteen which survive after 1347 originally came from two archival groups. Although the Public Record Office staff appear to have kept no note of where those records which were combined into SC6 came from, it is relatively easy to discover their provenance by looking at the original ink-stamps on the parchment. Five of the nineteen are stamped 'Exchequer: Queen's Remembrancer', and these are marked **Q.R.** in the final column of the list. They comprise those accounts which had been taken to London in the medieval period, probably by the auditors' clerks on their return from the audit. It is likely that they were kept in the archives of the prince's central exchequer at Westminster, in the custody of his receiver-general. The other fourteen were originally stamped 'Welsh Records', a designation that was later changed to 'Chester Records'. These accounts, marked **W.R.** in the list, had been kept at Chester castle, and were removed to London only in the nineteenth century.[25]

---

24 *B.P.R.*, iii. 79. In the chamberlain's account for 1350–51, 6s. 8d. was paid for the clerks writing and duplicating account rolls, etc. [omitted from *ChAcc*, p. 169] (SC6 771/17, m.7). £2 13s. 4d. was paid for the three clerks writing and duplicating accounts and other memoranda from 14 January to 18 March 1354, that is for nine weeks' and two days' work. [omitted from *ChAcc*, p. 214] (SC6 771/18, m.2d).

25 Booth, *Financial Administration*, pp. 14–15.

Accounts in the third-level series make it clear that versions were marked either 'original' or 'duplicate', although the earliest Flintshire ministers' accounts, for 1349–50, were marked 'final' and 'principal'.[26] As nearly all the chamberlains' accounts of the Black Prince's time survive in a damaged state, for only three do we have this information. The two **QR** accounts for the first and second parts of 1373–74 (SC6 772/9, 10) are called 'duplicates', as are all the **QR** accounts in the Divers Ministers of Cheshire series. The **WR** chamberlain's account for 1372–73 (SC6 772/8) is the only 'original' which is definitely known to have been such. The version of our present account which is listed first, SC6 772/3, is a **WR** 'duplicate' account, while the second (SC6 772/4) is also from the **WR** group.

This presents us with problems. If our two versions were written for the archives at Chester castle, and one is a self-proclaimed 'duplicate', then the natural assumption must be that the other, although not marked as such, must be the original. There are reasons, as will be seen, for thinking that this might not be the case. But why should two versions of an account be kept at Chester castle anyway? It would make sense for two copies to have survived in the **QR** series, since it is known that the royal exchequer had some responsibility for helping to collect the Black Prince's debts, and may have required duplicate account rolls to enable it to help with that task.[27] There is an obscure clue in a note written at the beginning of the dorse of 772/3 which can be read as either *per* or *pro Chaundos*. This might mean that an official copy of the account was made for Sir John Chandos, who had a number of important and lucrative official posts in Cheshire, for which he employed an agent, Robert Morton, **30.4**. There are other examples of Cheshire official accounts that are now in private collections.[28] If so, it is difficult to explain how the account found its way back into the treasury at Chester castle, and it has to be more likely that the note in question is merely a casual scribble, of which there are other examples on the rolls.[29]

There is no really convincing evidence that 772/3 is dependent on 772/4, and there is some reason to think that what we have is two duplicates. If so, then the original must be missing. There are three surviving versions of the Divers Ministers' accounts of Cheshire for 1359–60, two of which come from the **WR** series.[30] Unfortunately, none of the three is marked 'original' or 'duplicate'.

Moreover, it is not wholly clear what is meant by 'original' and 'duplicate' in the context of these accounts. At least two, and possibly three or more clerks were employed at the 1363 audit. As the Divers Ministers' and Macclesfield ministers' accounts are extant in a reasonably complete series from the 1350s

26 *FMA(2)*, p. 74.
27 *B.P.R.*, iv. 32.
28 e.g. *Cheshire in the Pipe Rolls*, p. 193.
29 See the marginal note to entry **13.14**, and the note following entry **14.2**.
30 SC6 785/5 **WR**, SC6 785/6 **WR**, SC6 785/7 **QR**.

onwards, it is possible to speculate as to how the various versions of these accounts were produced. In the 1350s, the 'original' appears to have been the account that was actually produced at the audit. Much of it had been written up in advance, the sums and the foot of the account are written by hands and in ink-colours which are different from its main body, and there are many amendments and additions. The 'duplicates' are fair copies, probably written carefully after the audit. The terms used for the 1349–50 Flintshire accounts seem to confirm this: the 'principal' account being the one written at the audit, the 'final' being the fair copy. However, as the 1360s wear on, the 'original' Divers Ministers' accounts are much more carefully written, and it may be that the auditors had come to allow the accountants to bring a preliminary draft to be audited, and so the 'original' could be written as a copy at the audit. There are not enough chamberlains' accounts extant for any conclusions to be made about how they were drafted. As they could only be audited after the third-level accounts, on which they were dependent, it is possible that there were always preliminary drafts of the chamberlains' accounts. In Appendix 1 it has been suggested that several accounts extant from earlier in the fourteenth century are such drafts.

It appears that the main body of each original account, whether there had been a preliminary draft or not, was written out in advance of the audit proper: that is, everything up to and excluding the 'foot', but minus the sum totals. Much could be compiled from the previous year's account, or from subsidiary documents such as *particule* (particulars) of receipts, vouchers, indentures and tallies of expenditure. As the accounting system operated on the charge/discharge principle, which meant that the accountant's receipts actually represented the revenue he was *charged* to collect, then pre-writing was relatively easy. Certain sections of the account, such as the sum totals, the 'foot' (including the liveries of money, respites, and final balance) were probably written at the audit itself.

This would account for the auditors' notes which, in those versions of an account which are known to have been 'original', are written in a different hand and different ink-colour from material which is immediately adjacent. Such are the notes *probatur* written after the sum total, presumably to indicate the auditors' approval of each section of the account and the entries contained within it (e.g. **2**). Similarly, at the end of the account is often written the note *examinatur*, or *examinatur per totum*, which may refer to the auditors' approval of the account at the beginning of the audit of the following year, possibly before the first draft of that year's account was made. The accounts also have marginal notes, often indicating action which was to be taken, and, again, in the 'originals' they are in a different hand or ink-colour, which suggests that they were written at the audit on an account which had been largely drafted in advance.

There are 35 sections in this account which might be expected to have *probatur* written after the sum – that is excluding sections for which the sum was *nichil*. 772/3 had the note after eight of them, while 772/4 has it after seventeen. On the other hand, it is only in 772/3 in which we find the note *examinatur* at the end. More important, it appears that the auditors' notes in both versions of the account were written at the same time as the body of the document.

To sum up, then, what we appear to have is two duplicate copies of the 1361–62 chamberlain's account, the original having been lost. Neither was meant to be an exact copy of the original, but no material of significance appears to have been omitted. When the clerks came to write up the duplicates after the audit, they took turns with the tedious task of copying. The same clerk's hand appears at the beginning of both 772/3 and 772/4. This clerk wrote sections **1** to **12.8** of 772/3; both hand and ink-colour change from **12.9**. The first clerk also wrote sections **1** to **13.12** of 772/4, to be succeeded by another hand in entry **13.13**; from **13.14** the first clerk's hand appears again.

So, we must think of the clerks undertaking the considerable task of producing more than one duplicate copy of each account after the audit and fitting in the work with other jobs that they had to carry out. The audit copy – either the 'original' or a preliminary draft plus the original – of the 1361–62 chamberlain's account was before them. In writing the duplicates, they could either employ this original or those parts of other duplicates that had already been written. It is possible that there were five versions of the 1361–62 account written at or after the 1363 audit: two copies for Westminster (one for the prince's exchequer, one for the king's) and three for Chester castle.

In order to see how the 1361–62 account operated, and how the expectations of the 'charge' were borne out by the reality of the 'foot', it is best to set out the figures in diagrammatic form. First, though, we have to note that the account is in reality two accounts. After the money account (sections **1** to **47**) there follows a stock account (sections **48** to **56**). This latter consists of those items of dead stock (prise wine, lead and lead-ore, and artillery) for which the chamberlain had to answer. As he was primarily a receiver of revenues in his financial capacity, this second account is little more than an appendage and does not merit further consideration here.

Chamberlain's Account, 1361–62

(Fractions of farthings are ignored.)

1.   CHARGE (**1** to **26**)

a. *Arrears* (**2** to **3**)

   i.   Cheshire £264 10s. 8d. (**2**)
   ii.   Flintshire £145 19s. 4¾d. (**3**)

b.   *Current receipts* (**4** to **25**)

   i.   Cheshire £2,231 5s. 3¼d. (**4** to **18**)
   ii.   Flintshire £567 4s. 4½d. (**19** to **25**)

Sum Total: £3,208 19s. 8½d. (**26**)

2. DISCHARGE (**27** to **38**)

Expenses

Sum Total: £807 3s. 3d. (**39**)

3. BALANCE (**39**)   (1 minus 2) £2,401 16s. 5½d.

4. JOINT SUM OF   Add balance (**39**) to the remainder
   INDEBTEDNESS   of the chamberlain's account for
                   1360–61, £708 17s. 3d. (**40**)
                   £3,110 13s. 8½d.

5. FOOT OF ACCOUNT (**41** to **42**)
       a. Liveries of money (payments by the
           chamberlain to the receiver-general) (**41**)
           £1,952 7s. 10d.
       b. Allowances and exonerations (**42**)
           £40 13s. 4¼d.

6. REMAINDER (**43**)   (4 minus 5)   £1,117 12s. 6¼d.
   The remainder (**43**) is carried forward to the following year's account,
   for 1362–63, where it is added into part 4, as above.

7. RESPITES (**45**)   £339 2s. 6½d.

8. CLEAR REMAINDER (**47**)   £778 9s. 11¾d.

    It will be seen that Burnham was charged to answer for £3,208 19s. 8½d. in his account for 1361–62. Of this, £410 10s. 0d. was arrears (£264 10s. 8d. of Cheshire, and £145 19s. 4¾d. of Flintshire). Of the current charge of £2,798 9s. 7¾d., almost exactly one-fifth applied to Flintshire (£567 4s. 4½d.), and four-fifths to Cheshire (£2,231 5s. 3¼d.) Some of this he had received as 'liveries' of either receipts or arrears from level-three officials, the rest he was charged to answer for without there being any subordinate account. He then discharged as much of that liability as possible by showing that he had either paid authorised expenses, or made liveries to the receiver-general.

    Individual items of receipt and expenditure had to be warranted in some way before the auditors could give their approval, presumably by writing *probatur* after the sum of money. As far as the receipts were concerned, those items in the account that comprised liveries from level-three accountants were warranted by the relevant level-three account, which had already been audited. Much of the remainder of the receipts consisted of fines and instalments of fines, which were warranted by the relevant rolls (such as the roll of the 1357 Cheshire forest eyre, **8**), appropriately modified by the prince's letters which had either pardoned an individual's liability, or granted an attermination. The constant reference to such letters being *penes Camerarium* suggests that he kept them in annual files, to be produced at the audit. In these files he doubtless kept 'particulars', or detailed lists of other receipts, such as exist for the chamberlains' accounts of the early fourteenth century[31].

As far as expenditure was concerned, some items had to be warranted by a voucher which had authorised the payment in advance, together with letters (or a bill) of acquittance from the recipient, to demonstrate that the money had reached its authorised purpose. Such were the ancient alms to ecclesiastical foundations (**28**), the payments of fees and wages to officials, and payments of annuities (**29, 30**). The payment of the 'ancient alms' had once been warranted by the letters of appointment of the justiciar of Chester, in which they were listed in detail.[32] By the 1363 audit the straightforward charitable gifts, some of which had been inherited from the Anglo-Norman earls of Chester, (**28.1** to **28.3** and **28.9** to **28.12**) were treated as customary, and authorised because they appeared as 'ex antiquo' payments in the previous year's account. The 'alms' which were, in effect, compensation for property which had been alienated to Vale Royal Abbey at Edward I's behest (**28.4** to **28.8**) were authorised by the king's letters of 2 July 1293, which could be found, the account tells us, among the 'warrants of account of the same 21st year'.[33]

Examples of other types of voucher are the letters of appointment of William Hulpeston (Helpeston) as master-mason (**29.9**), and the letters granting an annuity to Sir Alan Cheyne (**30.12**). In these cases not only were the original letters available, but there were official copies, on the recognizance roll and in the Black Prince's Register, to act as a further check. In both cases letters of acquittance of the person to whom the money had been paid by the chamberlain had to be produced at the audit, and cited in the account. It is clear that files of these were kept also, although none have survived from this period.[34]

Some payments did not require vouchers, as they were the running expenses of the chamberlain's bailiwick, such as the items listed as 'necessaries' (parchment, leather bags, rent of land for fulling mills, and so on) (**31**), expenses of writ-servers (**32**), prise wine (**33**), lead smelted for the prince's works (**36**), and the purchase of arrows (**37**). It is clear that although approval in advance through a voucher was not required for the auditors to allow such expenditure, the central administration was not prepared to allow it to exceed reasonable bounds. On 30 August 1359, Delves and Burnham had been ordered to stop all building work on the castles and manor houses of the earldom, except for

---

31 Appendix 1, documents 4 and 6, p. 197.
32 For example, in the writ of intendancy following the appointment of Sir Robert Holland as justiciar, to hold at farm, 1 October 1307 (*C.F.R., 1307–19*, p. 5).
33 These letters do not appear in any of the chancery enrolments, or among the chancery warrants.
34 Booth, *Financial Administration*, p. 20.

essential repairs, and clearly the word 'essential' was meant to be interpreted strictly.[35]

Although running repairs did not require vouchers, they were subject to the time-honoured device of 'controlment.' (**34**). The 'particulars', or details of the expenditure, were drawn up as an indented duplicate, part of which, the counter roll, was kept by the official with overall oversight of that work, and the other part of which was probably kept by the craftsman or a clerk of works for the particular job. Both copies had to be produced, and checked, at the audit. In cases of doubt, they could be submitted to a sworn inquest for arbitration. For example, £9 18s. 4½d. was spent on repairs to property on the earldom's manor of Frodsham in 1361–62 under the supervision of the master-carpenter, Richard de Ercal (**34.12**). An 'indented roll of particulars' was handed over at the audit, *contra predictum Magistrum Contrarotulatorem*, which means, literally, 'against the aforesaid master (Richard), as controller' i.e. after examining the counter-roll which he had kept of the work done.[36]

Works which required exceptional expenditure, such as building a new lodge in Macclesfield park (**34.5**) and the chevet under construction by William Hulpeston, the prince's master-mason, at the east end of the church of Vale Royal Abbey, needed to be warranted by vouchers (**35**). The strict operation of financial control can be seen in the case of the cost of the building-work in the inner bailey of Chester castle for the lieutenant-justiciar's accommodation (**34.10**). As the £30 assigned by John Delves for the work had been exceeded, a note in the margin orders that the matter be referred to the prince's council. Delves, of course, was not only lieutenant but also a member of the council.

The last section of the expenses part of the account is unusual. It consists of a prest – that is, a cash advance – made to the parker of Macclesfield (**38**). Prests were much used in household accounts, but are comparatively rare in those of estates, since they offended against the doctrine that prior approval was necessary for unusually high expenditure. In this case the parker received the advance because there was not sufficient money charged on his account for him to take his wages and pay other expenses.[37]

It is the *pes compoti* (the foot of the account, **40** to **47**) which makes the form of accounting employed by the Black Prince's officials at this time distinctive. In this the balance between the chamberlain's receipts and expenses – his charge and discharge – is followed by the 'dynamic' element of the account, which shows how much of his 'net charge' was collected and paid over. As can be seen,

35 *B.P.R.*, iii. 364.
36 For some earlier sets of particulars, see E 101/486/10, 12 (Dee mills, 1298/99), E 101/486/15 (Flint, Rhuddlan and Chester castles, Macclesfield manor-house, 1303/4), E 101/487/5 (Chester, Flint and Rhuddlan castles, various mills, and the enclosure of Shotwick park, 1328).
37 William Chorley's account as parker of Macclesfield for 1361–62 is SC6 803/5, m.2. His receipts consisted of £2 8s. 0d. paid for animals agisted in the park in summer, while his annual wages were £3 0s. 10d., and he had spent, in addition, £2 2s. 4d. on repairs to the park fence.

this 'net charge' – or what the chamberlain was held by the auditors to have to answer for after the discharge of *current* expenses – amounted to £3,110 13s. 8½d. (called 'joint sum of indebtedness' (**40**)). Of that, £708 17s. 3d. was remainder, being the undischarged liability from the previous year (1360–61).

Next, the account went on to record and deduct from the charge the twelve 'liveries of money' – the payments that Burnham had made to Peter Lacy, the receiver-general, which totalled something less than £2,000 (**41**). They are grouped together in accordance with the acquittances sealed by Lacy, which the chamberlain had to produce to receive allowance on his account from the auditors, while Lacy was charged with them on *his* account, as noted in the margin. The first eight indentures, for liveries totalling £1,076 12s. 9d., were sealed between 14 May and 20 August 1362. The second indenture was for an isolated livery of £9 1s. 1d. sealed on 2 June that year. The final group of three, for £866 14s. 0d. in all, were sealed between 18 October and 28 November 1362. It is likely that the dates represent the arrival of the cash in London, although it is not clear why there are two indentures for 18 October 1362. The last livery of all was made on 28 November 1362, about two months after the closing date of the account, an indication that liveries made before the account was audited – in this case before March 1363 – were not carried forward to the following year.

Section **42** follows with *allocationes* (allowances, or sums which the auditors admit should have appeared in the *discharge*) and *exonerationes* (exonerations, or sums which the auditors admit should not have appeared in the *charge*). It is easy to explain why these calculations should be made here, if it is accepted that the bulk of the original account had been written up, as far as **39**, in advance of the audit. The three examples given here are not particularly 'hard cases', but instances of delay in processing information or obtaining decisions. In **42.1**, the receiver of the earl of Salisbury handed over the acquittance 'upon the account'. This phrase presumably means during the course of the audit itself. The exoneration of part of William Trussell's fine imposed in the 1357 Macclesfield forest eyre (**42.2**) was only agreed after the case had been decided at the county court of 7 March 1363, probably during the time of the audit. The final example (**42.3**) in this section is a payment made to the justices of labourers of Macclesfield hundred which was agreed by the (lieutenant)-justiciar, chamberlain, and auditors – clearly at the audit itself.

The final adjustments of section **42** are followed by the balance which constitutes the remainder for 1361–62, the comparatively large sum of £1,117 12s. 6¼d. (**43**). This was then transferred to the account of the following year, 1362–63, as it was part of the chamberlain's charge that still had to be accounted for in the future. In part this was John Burnham's personal liability. The Statute of Westminster II of 1285 (13 Edward I c.11) had empowered the auditors of any landlord to commit a bailiff or other official to a royal prison if his account were found to be in arrears.[38] In the earldom of Chester the statute was clearly held to

---

38   T.F.T. Plucknett, *A Concise History of the Common Law*, 5th ed. (1956), p. 449.

mean the earl's prison, since there are several examples of committals to Chester castle in this period.[39] Although the personal liability of the accountant remained at the centre of medieval accountancy, the accounts came to be used by the administrators of great estates as sophisticated tools of analysis, which made an overstrict doctrine of personal liability redundant.[40]

The last two sections of the money account, the respites (**45, 46**) and the 'clear remainder' (**47**), are indications of this. They deduct from the chamberlain's remainder some fifteen items for which the auditors clearly felt there were reasonable causes for delay. Twelve out of the fifteen relate to judicial fines, and of those, ten had been imposed in the 1357 forest eyres. Fines and amercements were always difficult to collect, but these last presented the additional problem of being associated with a revenue-raising campaign which had utilised what were for Cheshire legal and procedural novelties. The total amount respited, nearly £400 (**46**), shows that the remainder was not to be wholly attributed to the normal course of the financial administration in the earldom. The 'clear remainder' of £778 9s. 11¾d., plus a half-farthing (**47**), represents the auditors' estimate of the part of the charge that remained uncollected for 'normal' reasons. High as that was, it did not result in John Burnham being even temporarily imprisoned in the castle in which he worked.

After the account had been audited, the final stage was for its remainder to be entered upon the 'great roll of debts'. This first appeared as a separate roll for the earldom in 1351–52.[41] It consists partly of 'desperate debts', extracted from accounts, but largely of a compendium of remainders of all the earldom's accounts. The Flintshire sections of the great roll for 1351–52 and 1352–53 were published by D.L. Evans in his *Flintshire Ministers' Accounts*.[42] From 1352–53 onwards, the great roll consists of a single membrane bound together with the Cheshire Divers Ministers' accounts.[43] It has been argued elsewhere that such a document only makes sense as a draft for a lost series of general enrolments of debts for all the prince's estates in England and Wales.[44] It has also been suggested that the great roll is an expanded version of an older record, called the 'pipe', which recorded difficult debts on the chamberlain's account in the early fourteenth century.[45]

D.L. Evans thought that the reason for starting the 'great roll' in the period 'immediately after the pestilence', was to try to stop the income from land declining.[46] Similarly, R.R. Davies has stated that the officials of the principality

---

39 Booth, *Financial Administration*, pp. 101–2.
40 Ibid., pp. 35–42.
41 SC6 783/19 and 784/1.
42 *FMA(2)*, pp. 91–94, 117–19.
43 SC6 784/2, mm.8, 8d.
44 Booth, *Financial Administration*, pp. 37–38.
45 Ibid.
46 'Some Notes on the History of the Principality of Wales in the Time of the Black Prince (1343–76)', *Trans. Hon. Soc. Cymmrodorion*, 1925–26, p. 79.

'were compelled to institute a Great Roll of Debts in 1351', implying that financial pressure was to blame.[47] In fact, real shrinkage of revenue did not come until much later in the century. The prince's officials instituted the 'great roll' because they wanted to know how much of the revenue in his estates remained uncollected each year, and it was natural for a vigorous, centralised administration to want to know this. It may be more than coincidence that the great roll was begun in the year that Sir John Wingfield took over the management of the prince's lands.

The 1361–62 Chester chamberlain's account stands as witness to a system of audit and accounting which was sophisticated and well adapted to its purpose. First, the account – as the record of a process, the audit – enabled the prince's administration to keep track of the financial obligations of subordinate officials, and ensure that revenue was neither lost nor spent without advance approval. But more than this, the account was a flexible means of financial control and planning. The separation of the 'foot' from the body of the account enabled the centre both to plot the flow of funds from year to year, and to make realistic estimates of the financial worth of the earldom when called upon to do so.[48]

47 *Conquest, Coexistence, and Change: Wales 1063–1415* (1987), p. 426.
48 Booth, *Financial Administration*, pp. 38–39.

III. THE CHAMBERLAIN'S ACCOUNT AND THE COUNTY OF CHESTER

When the Black Prince's auditors and their clerks arrived in Chester in the early spring of 1363 to hear and approve the accounts of the earldom for 1361–62, they found Cheshire a county which was, in many ways, a thoroughly English shire, but with significant differences from what they were used to elsewhere. Its basic structure consisted of some 460 local communities, organised in the familiar way as townships for the purposes of law and government. From a tenurial point of view, those same communities could be viewed as the manors of local landlords.[1] In society, the principal division was between the free and the unfree. On further investigation, however, they would have found that this social boundary was drawn in an unusual way. For example, one of the particulars of the account they were coming to hear was an extent of the lordship of Longdendale (**6.6**), situated in the extreme eastern 'panhandle' of the county. It had been compiled in 1360, and included the manor of Hattersley, which was held as a tenancy of the lordship. The manor was divided between two lords, Richard de Eton and Sir William Caryngton, who held the manor by military service. In addition, though, they were also bound to do three days reaping in harvest time for it, as well as three days ploughing in the spring, and other labour services, including building deer-hays, and constructing the earthworks at the mill, for their overlord, the lord of Longdendale.[2] The closest parallel to this can be found in what had become south Lancashire. There, nearly three hundred years earlier, the Domesday investigators of the land between Ribble and Mersey had found the thegns who held estates within the great royal manor-hundred of West Derby performing similar services for their lands. They were obliged to 'build the king's buildings, and make fisheries, deer hays in the wood, and stag-beats. . . . Each one of them sent his reapers to cut the king's corn for one day in August.' The commissioners had expressed their surprise at such an inappropriate mixture, by saying that the thegns performed these tasks 'just as villeins do' (*sicut villani*).[3]

Some of what made Cheshire different was, therefore, the consequence of the survival of ancient forms of social organisation, such as were found widely in the

---

1 The first comprehensive list of Cheshire townships, in the 1405 mise book, gives the number of townships in each hundred as: Eddisbury (57), Broxton (81), Wirral (69), Northwich (62), Bucklow (69), Nantwich (62) and Macclesfield (61); total: 461 (J.R.U.L.M. Tatton MS.345).
2 P.H.W. Booth and J.H. and S.A. Harrop, 'The Extent of Longdendale, 1360', *Cheshire Sheaf*, 5th ser. [98].
3 P. Morgan, ed., *Domesday Book: Cheshire* (1978), R1 (40a).

northern counties of England. They represented the persistence of Celtic institutions in Anglo-Saxon society.[4] It was not just in the hilly, sparsely settled lands of the east that such anomalies were to be found, however. In Burton in Wirral, on the bank of the river Dee, there were free tenants of the bishop of Coventry and Lichfield who paid heriots, along with their bond neighbours.[5] The payment of heriot was one of the lawyers' tests of unfree status, and the prince's auditors might have wondered how they could make sense of any division between free and bond in this county. This was not mere theoretical speculation, since, less than thirty years before their arrival, there took place in central Cheshire the most bitter and well-organised peasant uprising that the north-west of England experienced in the Middle Ages. Yet those villagers of Darnhall and Over whom the abbot of Vale Royal claimed as his bondmen, and whose obligations he caused to be recorded in such minute and vindictive detail, owed no labour services at all.[6] Back on the Dee bank, in the earl of Chester's own manor of Shotwick, there lived bondmen who did owe labour services, although they were not very heavy and rather like those of the two Hattersley landlords, but their free neighbours did none.[7] Strangest of all, John Hicson, a tenant of Shotwick, came before the manor court in September 1382, only a year after the great Peasants' Revolt, claiming that he was not free but the king's *nativus* (the usual Cheshire term for an unfree man).[8]

It is more difficult than usual to quantify the social and demographic structure of medieval Cheshire, since the county lacks the documentary 'bench-marks' of the fourteenth century, particularly the 1332/34 lay subsidy returns and the lay poll-tax returns of 1377 and 1379. Consequently, discussion of the county's social and economic history in the fourteenth century has to depend on fragmentary sources, and conclusions must be tentative. Until fairly recently, the views of H.J. Hewitt have been generally accepted. It was his opinion that later medieval Cheshire was backward, marginal and poor, in that it suffered the double penalty of being on the western side of the Pennines and on the border with Wales. This meant, so he maintained, high rainfall, unproductive cereal crops, and the necessary predominance in the county of pastoral husbandry, which in turn implied a sparse and largely poverty-stricken population. Economic development was hindered between 1272 and 1377 by the existence of large areas of forest, of deer-parks, wood and waste. Added to these disadvantages were the

4   J.H.E. Jolliffe, 'Northumbrian Institutions', *E.H.R.*, xli (1926), pp. 1–42; G.W.S. Barrow, 'The pattern of lordship and feudal settlement in Cumbria', *Jnl Medieval Hist.*, 1975, pp. 117–38.
5   P.H.W. Booth and R.N. Jones, 'Burton in Wirral: from Domesday to Dormitory', *Cheshire History*, 4 (1979), pp. 28–42 (Extent of Burton in Wirral, 1298).
6   J. Brownbill, ed., *The Ledger-Book of Vale Royal Abbey*, R.S.L.C., lxviii (1914), pp. 31–32, 37–42.
7   R. Stewart-Brown, 'Extent of the Royal Manor of Shotwick', *T.H.S.L.C.*, 64 (1912), pp. 138–40.
8   SC2 156/13.

political and military insecurity of the Welsh border in the late thirteenth century, and the oppressive and extortionate policies of the Black Prince in the third quarter of the fourteenth, which were so harsh that they brought about the 'impoverishment of enterprising cultivators'.[9]

Recent research has cast some doubt on the Hewitt thesis. It is evident from unpublished sources not employed by him that Cheshire experienced both substantial growth in population and expansion of the area under cultivation in the two centuries following the Domesday survey.[10] By the mid-fourteenth century, the production of cereals in the villages was clearly an important part of the county's agrarian economy, and there is no reason to think that crop yields were low by contemporary standards. Cattle and sheep were to be found, it is true, but large herds and flocks were confined to the uplands, such as the slopes of Frodsham Hill in the west, and the sides of Shutlingsloe in the east.[11] The increase in population and, consequently, of trade had led to the establishment by 1349 of a network of market towns and of chartered boroughs, alongside the North-West's metropolis, the city of Chester.[12] These small market and urban centres were primarily for the sale and distribution of agricultural produce, but by the later fourteenth century they were also trading in linen cloth produced in the west of the county, and woollen cloth from the central and eastern districts. In 1371 a detailed inventory was made of the stock and personal possessions of a mercer in the borough of Malpas, which is situated in the south-west of the county. It reveals that his stocks of cloth were largely of linen, with some wool. His woollen cloth came mostly from the adjoining Welsh upland areas, while the linen was very likely of local manufacture.[13] Inquiries held in the 1360s and 1370s by the sheriff of Cheshire into breaches of the Statute of Labourers reveal the presence of linen spinners and weavers in the area around Malpas.[14] Other industries included the production of leather, which the chamberlain's account reveals was presenting a problem of demarcation between the incipient trade

9 H.J. Hewitt, *Mediaeval Cheshire: An Economic and Social History of Cheshire in the Reigns of the Three Edwards*, Chet. Soc., new ser. 88 (1929). (Also published as volume cxcv in University of Manchester Publications: History Series, vi). Hewitt's view was, itself, a reaction against the older idea, originally formulated by the seventeenth-century antiquaries and topographers, that medieval Cheshire was a county marked out by prosperity, loyalty and social stability. Geoffrey Barraclough took over Hewitt's thesis uncritically, and restated it with characteristic forcefulness in 'The Earldom and County Palatine of Chester', *T.H.S.L.C.*, 103 (1951), pp. 23–57. (Also published, as a separate pamphlet, by Blackwell, in 1953).

10 P.H.W. Booth, 'Farming for Profit in the Fourteenth Century: the Cheshire Estates of the Earldom of Chester', *J.C.A.S.*, 62 (1980), pp. 73–90.

11 Booth, *Financial Administration*, pp. 93–97.

12 There has been no systematic study of either boroughs or market towns in medieval Cheshire. For the boroughs, see M.W. Beresford and H.P.R. Finberg, *English Medieval Boroughs: a Handlist* (1973).

13 There is evidence for woollen spinners and weavers in the area around Halton (CHES 19/1, mm.20, 48).

14 See a forthcoming article in the *J.C.A.S.* by P H.W. Booth.

guilds in the city of Chester (**13.1**), but which was also carried on at Halton and elsewhere in the county. In mid-Cheshire were the anciently-established salt towns of Nantwich, Northwich and Middlewich, while in Macclesfield forest both iron-mining and smelting and coal-mining were important in the first half of the fourteenth century.[15]

The unpublished evidence also suggests that the Black Death of 1349 brought about, in the long term, profound economic and social changes in Cheshire. Again, the sources are fragmentary, but they show that the first outbreak of the pestilence had occurred in the county in the early summer of 1349. There was a recurrence in 1361, and the establishment of the bubonic plague as an endemic feature meant a substantial drop in population – in some communities a reduction of between a third and a half is likely.[16] As well as the loosening of social cohesion, and long-term changes in land-tenure, this demographic decline resulted in the abandonment of considerable areas of arable to pasture, as labour became more expensive, and the faint beginnings of the reign of the dairy cow in parts of Cheshire can be discerned.[17]

Consequently, the officials of the Black Prince must have been aware, during the 1363 audit, that Cheshire was suffering a shrinkage in its economic base. The prince's officials had had to reduce some rents in the aftermath of the Black Death, and let land on what were, to the prince at any rate, unfavourable terms. Some property was already beginning to prove unlettable.[18] As about four-fifths of the revenue of the earldom of Chester originated in Cheshire, this must have been a cause of great concern. The remainder on the chamberlain's account was increasing in an alarming fashion. It had risen from £708 17s. 3d. at the end of the 1360–61 account (**40**), to £1,117 12s. 6¼d. at the end of 1361–62 (**43**). Much of this increase can be attributed to the difficulty in collecting the fines that had been imposed in the 1357 forest eyres. Some £339 2s. 6½d. of this revenue was respited at the end of the account (**46**). These eyres serve as an important link between the political, social and economic problems that Cheshire was beginning to experience in the 1350s and 1360s, and the economic growth and development that had been the county's lot in the decades immediately before the Black Death.

Forest eyres had first been held in Cheshire in 1347. A second set followed ten years later, in 1357.[19] The second eyre was originally planned to be held in 1353, during the prince's state visit to the county, but was postponed for four years. This delay was one of the concessions granted by the prince to the community of the county in return for their grant to him of the massive common fine of 5,000

---

15 See below, p. xliv.
16 Booth, 'Farming for Profit', p. 79; *Financial Administration*, pp. 88–93, 127–28.
17 Booth, 'Farming for Profit', pp. 79–81.
18 Booth 'Farming for Profit', p. 79; *Financial Administration*, pp. 97–98.
19 P.H.W. Booth, 'The End of Wirral Forest: an Anniversary', *Cheshire History Newsletter*, 12, pp. 18–20; Booth, *Financial Administration*, pp. 120, 122, 139.

marks.[20] In between the two eyres the normal Cheshire forest inquiry, the triennial 'regard of the forest' continued to be held. The forest eyre of 1347, and the subsequent regards, provoked the most serious outbreak of communal hostility and resistance to government policy that was experienced in fourteenth-century Cheshire. Objection was taken to the importation of English forest law and custom into the county, so that a major revenue-raising campaign could be coated with a thin veneer of legal form.[21] The resistance to the 1347 eyre meant that it was a financial failure, and only raised a few hundred pounds.[22] However, the two communities of Wirral and Delamere-Mondrum forests had been softened up sufficiently by 1357 that they responded to the second eyre by offering common fines of £1,000 and £2,000 respectively, payable by instalments over five years (**8.1**, **8.2**), in lieu of individual fines. Although the administration pressed very hard to get Macclesfield forest to follow suit, the community there would not agree, and so individual fines had to be assessed and collected.[23]

The Macclesfield membranes of the 1357 forest eyre roll enable us to do two things: first, to estimate the impact of the fines on the forest community, and, secondly, to relate the fines to the development of the forest landscape in the years preceding the eyre, as appears in the record of assarts and purprestures.[24] The Macclesfield forest eyre was presided over by Sir Richard Willoughby, Sir Richard Stafford, John Delves and the chamberlain, and opened on Monday, 9 October 1357. The assarts and purprestures dealt with at the eyre had been investigated four years earlier, in 1353, at a regard held by Willoughby and Stafford on Tuesday 27 August. It will be remembered that this was the year in which the eyre was originally going to be held.

The eyre roll discloses that nearly 1,050 Cheshire acres (2,225 statute) were presented as having been ploughed up for cultivation in Macclesfield forest, mostly in the fourteen years between 1333 and 1346. On the face of it, this does not appear to reveal extensive land reclamation. However, three points have to be borne in mind. First, 94% of the acreage assarted was confined to only seven local communities. Secondly, apart from Macclesfield borough and Shrigley, all nine places in which assarting was alleged were on the forest periphery. Marple and Norbury are at its northern extremity, while North Rode, Gawsworth, Prestbury, Adlington and Poynton are on the western border.[25] Thirdly, the

---

20 *B.P.R.*, iii. 113.
21 See the petitions to the prince's council in 1351 for evidence of resentment (*B.P.R.*, iii. 23–27). See also Judith A. Green, 'Forests' in *V.C.H.*, ii. 169–70.
22 £184 in Wirral forest, £178 in Delamere-Mondrum (*B.P.R.*, iii. 8–10; *ChAcc*, p. 121).
23 See the letters of 28 February 1358, by which the forest justices were urged to conclude a common fine with the men of Macclesfield forest (*B.P.R.*, iii. 298). The fine of £87 referred to in entry **8.14** was probably agreed by the tenants of the demesne townships of Macclesfield manor.
24 CHES 33/6, mm.36–41d. The editors express their thanks to Andrew Tonkinson, for generously making available his transcript of the Macclesfield section of the eyre roll.
25 Green, 'Forests', 180; F.I. Dunn, *The Ancient Parishes, Townships and Chapelries of Cheshire* (1987) (Map).

fifteen townships of Macclesfield manor were largely unrepresented, not because they experienced no clearance of land at this time, but because they had paid a common fine for forest offences (**8.14**). Finally, the prince's officials tell us that they suspected a great deal of under-recording of forest offences was going to take place in the eyre, and so we must regard the assarts presented in the roll as a bare minimum.

It is clear, then, that some places in east Cheshire were experiencing an energetic phase of landscape development in the years immediately before the Black Death.[26] For example, it was claimed in the eyre that in Robert Legh's manor of Adlington 46 houses and outbuildings (*domus*) had been constructed between 1333 and 1348, to the forest's detriment. In the same period 411 Cheshire acres (871 statute) of land were cleared there for ploughing, of which 215 Cheshire acres (456 statute) had been ploughed in 1332/33. Adlington was a medium-sized township of 3,899 statute acres, as measured by the Ordnance Survey,[27] and so in fifteen years not much less than a quarter of its superficial area had been cleared for agriculture. Moreover, this was not a remote, upland community which had never seen the plough before. Adlington had been assessed as having land for ten ploughs in Domesday, although only three were in operation.[28] In all, 116 buildings were erected in twelve forest townships. These are signs that the demand for land was still at a high level in Cheshire, and they are consonant with a population that was rising up to the outbreak of the Black Death. They were accompanied by evidence of buoyant rural industries. No fewer than 27 bloomeries, using locally-mined ironstone and timber, are recorded in the eyre roll as being in operation during the same period. The effect of this activity on the landscape can be gauged when it is realised that one iron forge, that at Dane Wood, was said to have consumed 1,000 oak trees, together with underwood, in ten years.[29]

What we see here is, in fact, the last phase of the centuries-old process of land-clearance and settlement in Cheshire. It happened in the east of the county because that was an area that was largely underdeveloped at the time of the Domesday survey. So it was that one of Cheshire's least promising land-use regions – the slopes and deep-cut valleys of the Pennine foothills – was brought into full productive use. This evidence cannot be reconciled with Hewitt's view that operation of the forest law inhibited colonisation and agrarian development in Cheshire. The elder Robert Legh and his tenants do not seem to have been deterred from ploughing up what was left of potential arable in Adlington, and they cannot have suspected that an unprecedentedly severe investigation of

---

26 CHES 33/6, m.38 (Marple), m.40 (Macclesfield borough, Gawsworth), m.40d (Shrigley, North Rode, Prestbury), m.41 (Adlington, Poynton), m.41d (Poynton, Norbury).
27 *Kelly's Directory of Cheshire* (1902), p. 9.
28 Morgan, *Cheshire Domesday*, 1:26. There was also a very large area of woodland, and a sizeable acreage of meadow.
29 CHES 33/6, m.38d.

forest law infringements would take place twenty years in the future.

On the other hand, to communities that were beginning to experience the retreat from cultivation that had already started in the 1350s, the penalties imposed in the 1357 forest eyres were clearly difficult to accept. Robert Legh's fine of £100 for past assarting and purprestures was a high one, even after it had been reduced by £20 through the prince's grace (**8.4**). The common fines agreed with Wirral and Delamere-Mondrum were of a different order of magnitude. We know nothing about how they were collected, but we must assume that the main reason the influential members of the forest communities agreed to them in the first place was that they would have a considerable say over how the burden was shared out. Delamere-Mondrum's £2,000 was massive. This forest, which did not completely cover Eddisbury, only one of the seven hundreds of Cheshire, was bound to pay £400 a year for five years. As we shall see later, the heaviest tax imposed by the prince between 1341 and 1373 only amounted to instalments of £833 a year payable by the whole county. The problem with a forest eyre, as part of a new package of taxations, was that its incidence was arbitrary, and it could fall very heavily.

It is quite possible to believe the younger Richard Munshull, a landlord with two manors – Aston-juxta-Mondrum and Church Minshull – in the southern bailiwick of the forest, when he said that the payment of his share of the common fine of Delamere-Mondrum would ruin his family. At any event, he lost possession of his lands, which were taken over by the county officials for non-payment of the fine. Part of their income was to be set aside to feed, clothe and house the Munshull family. As a result of the seizure, an extent of the two manors was made at Nantwich in June 1360. It tells us there was a manor-house at Aston, and leasehold tenants who paid 76s. 2d. a year in rent, and a carucate of demesne land containing 40 (Cheshire) acres 'each acre being worth 12d. if it could be let for sowing, but if not the herbage is worth 13s. 4d.'. In addition there was a watermill which was out of action, which could be worth four marks a year, if repaired.[30] Aston is low-lying and waterlogged, and it is not surprising to find such land not finding takers when the demand for land had begun to decline. The landlord stood to lose revenue of £4 a year from this one property, in the likely event of the reversion of marginal arable to pasture. This was an extreme case, and the prince's policies did not produce many victims of the social status of Richard Munshull. However, his policies were liable to produce economic and political victims, and there were clear social prices to be paid in such circumstances.

Geoffrey Barraclough's statement that the topographers Camden and Speed 'paint an almost uniform picture of prosperity (for Cheshire in the sixteenth and

---

30 CHES 3/34 Ed. III/3. See P. Morgan, *War and Society in Medieval Cheshire*, Chet. Soc., 3rd ser. 34 (1987), p. 84, where it seems to be assumed that each acre (rather than the whole piece of land) would be worth 13s. 4d. in herbage, which is absurd.

early seventeenth centuries), very different from the poverty of Cheshire in the Middle Ages' needs to be turned on its head.[31] What the auditors saw in 1363 was a county that was at the beginning of a transition, not from poverty to prosperity, but from arable cultivation towards pastoral. If such generalisations mean anything, then it would be easier to claim that it was Tudor and Stuart Cheshire that was 'backward', in contrast with the county in the late thirteenth and early fourteenth centuries. Cheshire's distinctiveness, at least in its economic and social aspects, was not a unique blend of geographical and political disadvantage, but the result of its sharing in a diversity that was regionally based.

Surely, though, our inquisitorial visitors must have found a very different picture of government and administration in Cheshire from what they saw in the rest of England? After all, no other county, apart from perhaps Lancashire, had anything like the Cheshire portion of the chamberlain's account. In fact, much was the same. Cheshire was a county, with a sheriff and under-sheriff, and a county court, and was divided into seven hundreds. There were areas of privileged, private jurisdiction similar to those that could be found in Derbyshire or Essex. For example, in 1365 the landlords who held the manor of Nantwich between them put in their defence to a plea of *quo warranto*.[32] They claimed the right to have a view of frankpledge in their manor court, or halmote, together with a private hundred court, a five-day annual fair, a weekly market, the tolls on the sale of salt and other merchandise, and 'pelf', or the goods belonging to a felon who had been arrested by their officials.[33]

The owners of the manor of Nantwich, a mesne barony of the earl of Chester, similar to the Lancashire baronies of the duke of Lancaster, held their land of the earl by knight-service, in the familiar fashion.[34] As elsewhere in England, this tenure was no longer used to recruit officers directly for the army, but it remained important as the source of revenue from the rights of wardship and marriage, and the county had an escheator to safeguard this income for the prince.

As far as its public law-courts were concerned, Cheshire was no less part of England than Middlesex was. The common law of England, together with parliamentary statutes, formed the legal framework within which justice was done.[35] The final court of appeal was the King's Bench, and petitions for remedies of grievances could also be made to the king in parliament.[36] In late

---

31 Barraclough, 'Earldom and County Palatine', p. 47.
32 CHES 29/70, m.18.
33 For the definition of pelf, see Sir William Trussell of Kibblestone's claim to a plea of *quo warranto*, later in the following plea roll (CHES 29/71, m.32d).
34 R. Stewart-Brown, ed., *Calendars of County Court, City Court and Eyre Rolls of Chester, 1259–1297*, Chet. Soc., new ser. 84 (1925), pp. 109–12.
35 Long ago Stewart-Brown pointed out that in both adjectival and substantive law Cheshire differed little from the rest of England, ibid., p. xviii.
36 For example, the case of Thomas Arden v. Isabel Hampton was removed from the Chester county court to the court of King's Bench by writ of error in July 1355 (*C.C.R., 1354–60*, p. 148).

1367, Edward III's prohibition of the use of foreign currency by merchants was proclaimed in the Chester county court.[37] When Cheshire's practice differed from the English mainstream, it was often because it shared, once again, a distinction that was regional, and could be found throughout the North-West or on the Welsh border. For example, local law-enforcement was much the same as the national pattern. Townships were supposed to have constables to apprehend criminals, the victims of crime were obliged to raise the hue and cry, and coroners were responsible for inquiring into cases of sudden death. Despite the claims of the lords of Nantwich in 1365, Cheshire had neither frankpledge nor tithings, just as the royal justices in eyre had found to be the case in Shropshire in 1256. Instead, there were officials called 'serjeants of the peace', whose job it was to enforce the criminal law and arrest the more serious criminals.[38] Again, they were found widely in the north and west of the country, and have striking analogues in Wales and the March.

What made Cheshire different, apart from those differences that it shared with other places in the region, was that what had originally been an ordinary English county had come to be governed as a subordinate regality. In other words, a considerable part of the royal authority was exercised by the earl and his officials. This had brought about an unusual relationship between the king and the county, the long continuance of which meant that the county community had come to regard it as part of its own liberties. In other words, a devolution of power by kings of England to earls of Chester had come to be in the interest of powerful elements within the community, so that they were ready to resist substantial constitutional change. Consequently, Cheshire was still governed differently from the rest of England, even when there was no separate earl, and the county was 'in the king's hands'. By the fifteenth century, this combination of delegated authority and a self-consciously privileged community was summed up by the phrase 'county palatine', a term which was still somewhat exotic and not officially accepted in the 1360s.

Three factors had brought this unique position about. The first was the position of power established in the county by the Anglo-Norman earls of Chester before 1237. The second was the decision of King Henry III, after encountering resistance to his initial plans to normalise the county's position, to leave its liberties more or less intact. The third was the decision by the king to grant the county to his son, Edward, in 1254, together with its 'liberties', a practice followed by most of his successors. Consequently, there was a 'royal lord' ruling Cheshire for much of the time after 1237 who was not the king. By giving their heirs both the title of earl of Chester, and the effective rule – to a

37 *C.C.R, 1364–68*, p. 404.
38 R. Stewart-Brown, *The Serjeants of the Peace in Medieval England and Wales*, (1936) pp. 66, 135; T.P. Highet, *The Early History of the Davenports of Davenport*, Chet. Soc., 3rd ser. 9 (1960); A. Harding, ed., *The Roll of the Shropshire Eyre of 1256*, Selden Society, 96 (1980), pp. xvii–xviii.

greater or lesser extent – of the county, successive monarchs gave them an independent income and experience in government, while continuing to reinforce the sense of separateness of those in the county who stood to benefit from its semi-independent status.

By the time of the 1363 audit, therefore, although King Edward III's authority over the people of Cheshire was real and undoubted, it was remote. Hardly any one in the county would have had personal experience of its effects. On the other hand, the King's first-born son – as Edward, the Black Prince calls himself in his public acts – was a 'royal lord' who had a 'royal liberty' in Cheshire, largely because he was the successor to the position of the last two Anglo-Norman earls of Chester, Ranulf III and John of Scotland. In the 1360s an ever-increasing proportion of the people of the county were becoming aware by personal experience of his regal authority, which was signposted throughout the county's government and its documentary record. In September 1368, for example, the grand jury at the Chester county court presented that a fortified bridge had been constructed over the River Dee, between Holt and Farndon, thirty years previously. It had been built by the last earl of Warenne to be lord of Bromfield and Yale. The taking of tolls from those crossing the bridge from the Cheshire side by the officials of the earl of Arundel, Warenne's successor was, said the jury, 'against the state of the earl of Chester, and the dignity of the sword of Chester'.[39] Similarly, those indicted for serious criminal offences in the superior courts of the county were accused of acting 'against the peace of the earl of Chester, his sword and dignity'.[40] The 'sword', the badge of an earl, fills the place of the crown in a normal English indictment. Each time the county court met, the earl's justiciar, or his lieutenant, held 'pleas of the crown'.[41] It was in the earl's name, not the king's, that the sturgeon caught in the River Dee in 1362 was claimed as a royal fish (**9.7**). On a more day-to-day level, those who lent or borrowed money would frequently be aware that the prince exercised preference in the collection of debts, and had to be paid before anyone else was. In 1354 it was recognised that in this area he had 'the same prerogative (in Cheshire) as the king has in England'.[42] The charter of 18 March 1333, by which Edward III granted the earldom of Chester to his infant son, stated that he should hold the earldom as the king had done before his accession (that is when he was earl of Chester, 1312 to 1327). The royal liberties which went with the earldom were included in the grant, they were not additional concessions, and therefore came from before the county was taken over by King Henry III.[43]

It was the earl of Chester who levied taxes from his Cheshire subjects between

39   CHES 25/4, m.21.
40   For this phrase in full, see the appeal of felony of robbery by John Stoke against John Holcroft in the 1353 trailbaston sessions (*Cheshire History*, 13 (1984), pp. 23–24).
41   See the plea rolls of the county court, CHES 29.
42   *B.P.R.*, iii. 152.
43   *C. Chart. R., 1327–41*, p. 300.

1346 and 1373, while they contributed to none of those granted to the king in parliament.[44] In addition, the earl took imposts on imported wine (**9.1**), granted pardons of life and limb (**13.7**), and commissioned his own justices to hold a general eyre, forest eyres, and sessions of trailbaston (**8, 15**). Perhaps the most solemn manifestation of Earl Edward's 'royal liberty' came in 1353 when, in the presence and at the request of the community of his county of Chester, he enacted legislation with the advice of his great council to change the law of Cheshire.[45]

In England the word *comitatus* can mean two different things – earldom or county. In Cheshire the two meanings were more closely entangled. So, the chamberlain's account of 1361–62 is the financial record of a shire – with receipts and expenditure arising out of government, taxation, fines in public courts of justice, and the cost of military operations. It is also the financial record of a landed estate, an earldom, with its manors, towns and woods, revenue from private jurisdiction, expenditure on almsgiving, and gifts to the dependants of the earl. Not only did the Black Prince have extensive powers, unbalanced by any other source of authority apart from the Church, but he ruled as earl of Chester for over forty years. From his assumption of adult responsibilities in 1346, the royal government of England had ceased to have any immediate concern with Cheshire. There are only five administrative orders relating to the county on the royal chancery rolls between 1350 and 1376: the 1355 transfer of a suit to the King's Bench, a commission of array in 1359 and a levy of archers for Ireland in 1361, the 1367 prohibition of foreign currency, and an order to provide William of Windsor with ships to take him from the River Dee to Ireland in 1373.[46] Because of Edward's long tenure as earl, his harmonious relationships with his father, and his succession to the royal liberties of previous earls of Chester, the crown was rarely of such little account in Cheshire as was the case at this time.

Cheshire was charged to yield £2,233 in the financial year 1361–62, that is 80% of the gross current charge of the two counties (less liveries of arrears [**2 and 3**] and less remainder [**40**])[47]. Much of the revenue only appears in the chamberlain's account of this period as summary figures, and the details have to be sought in the level-three accounts for 1361–62: Divers Ministers (Cheshire), SC6 785/9, and Macclesfield Ministers, SC6 803/5. (The account for the St Pierre lands in Cheshire for this year is missing.) It is possible to break down the

44 See below, pp. liv–lvi.
45 Booth, *Financial Administration*, pp. 121–22.
46 *C.C.R., 1354–60*, p. 148; *C.P.R., 1358–61*, pp. 324–25; *C.P.R., 1361–64*, p. 21; *C.C.R., 1369–74*, p. 520. In addition, the king confirmed by royal letters patent some of the prince's grants of annuities to his retainers. This was not so much to add extra authority to the grants, but to ensure that they would continue to be paid should the prince die before his father (e.g. *C.P.R., 1367–70*, pp. 45–46, a confirmation of a grant to Sir William Trussell the son).
47 Figures in this section have been rounded up, to the nearest pound.

revenue charged on the account for this year into five classes, to enable comparisons to be made with accounts for the early part of the fourteenth century.

TABLE 1

CHESHIRE REVENUE CHARGED ON THE 1361–62 CHAMBERLAIN'S ACCOUNT

		£	% (1)	% (2)
1.	Land revenue (**4, 5, 6, 18**)	814	35	54.4
2.	Escheats, etc. (**17**)	202	9	13.5
3.	Judicial revenue (**11, 12, 13, 14, 15**)	475	21	31.7
4.	Duties on overseas trade (**9, 16**)	6	2	0.4
5.	Extraordinary revenue (**8**)	736	33	–
		2,233	100	100

It is not really possible to produce a more refined classification than this, and it has to be admitted that there is substantial overlap between the categories of revenue. For example, all the revenue charged on the county sheriff's account is classed as 'judicial', although some of it consists of rents (the 'chamber rents')[48] and other customary payments (e.g. 'sheriff's stuth'). Also, a considerable proportion of the 'land revenue' of class 1 is made up of judicial revenue, such as the perquisites of the manorial halmotes, or of the Macclesfield hundred court. Attempts to refine the categorisation further are met with irresolvable dilemmas. If, for example, we should take the chamber rents out of the judicial revenue, how are we to classify the annual payments we find in them which were made for liberties (such as the bailiwick of Caldy hundred)? Or again, if we decide to remove the perquisites of Macclesfield halmote from the land revenue class, we have to remember that part of the money charged for this court was for licences to burn charcoal in Macclesfield forest: can this be said to be judicial revenue?

It is better, therefore, to keep to a crude analysis, while being wary of making easy comparisons on that basis. The 'land revenue' class is largely made up of

48 See *ChAcc*, p. 73.

rents, customary payments, and revenue from local courts of manor or town. Since the abandonment of direct management of demesne lands in the earl's estates after the mid 1350s, the only farming enterprise to produce revenue was the large herd of cattle kept on Macclesfield manor.[49] Class 2 consists of the revenues for which the county escheator was responsible, which arose from the feudal superiority of the earl of Chester. They were made up of reliefs, small escheats, payments for wardships and marriages, and so on. The 'judicial revenue' class is mostly the result of the fines and amercements of the county court and hundred eyre sessions, and the proceeds of the hundred courts (except for Macclesfield). The duties on overseas trade consist of the prise of wine, timber, and coal (to which has been added the unclassifiable 'issues of the fee of the seal'). Finally, under the heading 'extraordinary revenue' have been placed those charges which were quasi-taxatory. They were the fines (both communal and individual) imposed as a result of the 1357 forest eyre.

It is instructive to compare the sums charged, and their origins, with those on the chamberlain's account for 1302–3.

TABLE 2

CHESHIRE REVENUE CHARGED ON THE 1302–3 CHAMBERLAIN'S ACCOUNT[50]

		£	%
1.	Land revenue	780	61.3
2.	Escheats, etc.	73	5.7
3.	Judicial revenue	391	30.7
4.	Duties on overseas trade	29	2.3
5.	Extraordinary revenue	–	–
		1,273	100

Comparison of the accounts for the two years has been made more meaningful by giving two sets of percentages for the 1361–62 account, one of which (% 1) includes the extraordinary revenue, while the other (% 2) excludes it, and it is

49 Booth, *Financial Administration*, pp. 93–97.
50 *ChAcc*, pp. 15–37.

this second column which should be compared with the corresponding figures for 1302–3. The two tables demonstrate that there was only one really significant change in the ordinary revenue of Cheshire between 1302 and 1362. This was in class 2, the money collected by the escheator, which had risen from 5.7% to 13.5% of the current charge. This had come about as the result of a change in policy. In the summer of 1359, the prince's officials were in desperate need of money to help finance the Rheims expedition, which lasted from October that year to the establishment of peace at Brétigny in May 1360. In June 1359, the auditors and the chamberlains of North Wales and Chester were ordered to make sure that all the money due in by midsummer was collected 'in view of the prince's great need of money for his next expedition'.[51] In July, the prince pawned jewelry which had formerly belonged to the king of France to the earl of Arundel as security for a loan of £2,000.[52] Interestingly, it seems that the negotiation of that loan meant that the prince had to respond favourably to Arundel's complaint that he had been assessed to pay an unreasonable sum to the common fine of Delamere forest, and give him a pardon.[53] In August there was an unprecedented order to the receiver of Cornwall to sell wood 'as the prince is in great need of money at present'.[54] Other loans had to be negotiated, until in October 1359, the month that the prince left for France, Sir John Wingfield, who was accompanying him on the expedition, received a bond from his master, secured on the prince's estates, for 20,000 marks, the sum which Sir John had raised for the expedition's expenses.[55] It is in this context that the order has to be placed that was issued on 25 September 1359, telling the lieutenant, chamberlain and escheator to raise as much money as possible from all wardships, marriages and escheated land in Cheshire.[56]

This was not just an administrative exhortation, but, it has been argued elsewhere, an acknowledgement that the prince's financial straits required the normal source of middle-range patronage in Cheshire to be diverted to purely financial uses.[57] Financially, the goods were delivered, as the increased income charged under the escheator's heading in the chamberlain's account witnesses, but there was a cost. The legitimate expectations of Cheshire magnates that they should be able to buy wardships and marriages on favourable terms, in return for their service to the prince, would have to be disappointed. If they were not

---

51   *B.P.R.*, iii. 348.
52   *B.P.R.*, iii. 354; *B.P.R.*, iv. 312, 333.
53   *B.P.R.*, iii. 364, 389.
54   Ibid., ii. 155.
55   *B.P.R.*, iv. 326. Other loans were made to the prince by the merchants of Asti and Carignano (1,000 gold marks: 4 Aug.); Sir Ralph Neville (500 marks: 16 Oct.); the bishop of Lincoln (500 marks: 16 Oct.); a group of London merchants (£1,000: 18 Oct.); the bishop of Winchester (1,000 marks: 25 Oct.); Adam Franceys (£100: 25 Oct.); Henry Pycard (£100: 25 Oct.); William Pole 'the uncle' (250 marks: 25 Oct.); *B.P.R.*, iv. 305, 319, 321, 327.
56   *B.P.R.*, iii. 368.
57   Booth, *Financial Administration*, 78–79.

directly involved in the prince's military operations at this period, then it might be that there was no way in which their aspirations could be met, at a time when heavy financial demands were being made upon them by the county government, and landowners were beginning to feel the consequences of demographic decline.

The major difference between the two accounts can be accounted for by the fact that 'extraordinary revenue' from the forest-eyre fines, which was taxation in all but name, was being collected in 1361–62, and not in 1302–3. Cheshire had ceased to pay parliamentary taxation after 1292, and it has been pointed out elsewhere that the forest eyre fines have to be seen as one element of a new, ad hoc system of taxation that was being developed for Cheshire in the three decades after 1346.[58] A similar process was at work in both the principality of Wales and the marcher lordships where, likewise, parliamentary taxation was not being exacted at this time, and levies had to take the form of what R.R. Davies calls 'casual revenue'.[59] In Geoffrey Barraclough's view, although Cheshire saw an increase in wealth during the Black Prince's time, much was 'drained off to pay for the prince's prodigal expenditure'. This led, so he thought, to harsh and illegal methods being employed by the administration in order to exact ever-increasing amounts of revenue. 'The fines exacted in 1347, 1353 and 1357 exceeded in magnitude anything Cheshire had ever known; and the abuse of his powers by the absentee earl aroused deep-seated resentment throughout the county. The outcome was the great rebellion of 1353'.[60]

This over-simple view that the conduct of an oppressive prince provoked a violent response in a sorely-tried people has been criticised before. Also, it is based on an assumption which is at variance with the evidence, namely that the county's aggregate wealth increased throughout the Black Prince's time. As the chamberlain's account is evidence of one specific aspect of the Black Prince's relationships with his Cheshire subjects, that which could be expressed in financial terms, it will have to be considered again, and an alternative synthesis put forward. First, the 'great rebellion of 1353' has to be finally laid to rest. In this account the last instalments of the fines imposed by Sir William Shareshull at his 1353 trailbaston sessions were charged (**15**). The surviving evidence for the events of that year, the great bulk of which is unpublished, and had not been employed either by H.J. Hewitt or Geoffrey Barraclough before formulating their views as stated above, is surveyed elsewhere, and a calendar of the 1353 trailbaston roll is now in print.[61]

The notion of a revolt or rebellion in 1353 was taken by Barraclough from

---

58 Ibid., pp. 116–26.
59 *Lordship and Society in the March of Wales, 1282–1400* (1978), pp. 185–87.
60 'Earldom and County Palatine', p. 41.
61 P.H.W. Booth, 'Taxation and Public Order: Cheshire in 1353', *Northern History*, xii (1976), pp. 16–31; *Financial Administration*, pp. 116–41. The trailbaston cases are published in *Cheshire History*, 11, 12 (1983); 13, 14 (1984); 16 (1985).

Hewitt, who in turn appears to have derived it from two uncritical lives of the Black Prince which were published in the nineteenth century. They had inflated a cautious remark in Sir Joshua Barnes's late seventeenth-century *Life* of the prince, and turned it into a positive statement that a rebellion had taken place in Cheshire in 1353. Barnes, who did not actually say that a revolt had taken place, was himself relying on Henry of Knighton's chronicle, the only fourteenth-century account of the prince's visit to Cheshire in that year, which itself was compiled at least forty years after the events it purported to describe, and contains significant errors. The transmission of this myth has had such an important effect on the historiography of later fourteenth-century Cheshire that the various texts are given in Appendix 3 (pp. 212–24). For those who prefer contemporary original sources, the trailbaston roll itself can be consulted. The evidence it contains is simply not consistent with there having been any organised, armed rebellion in Cheshire prior to the prince's visit in 1353, and if it had not been for Hewitt or Barraclough, no-one who had read the original sources would have suspected that there had been any such.

On the other hand, it is true that the levies of extraordinary revenue in Cheshire from 1341 to 1376 had no precedents in the county's history. As we have seen, the county community appeared to have escaped paying any taxation at all, to either king or earl, for nearly half a century, from 1292 to 1341. During that time Staffordshire and Derbyshire had contributed to no fewer than eighteen parliamentary subsidies.[62] This means that the community of Cheshire was better-off by perhaps as much as £10,000 to £15,000 by 1341. While it is true that any community that has escaped paying taxes for a long period of time might, nevertheless, be reluctant to see the justice of being brought into line in this way, this is what the prince's extraordinary revenue campaign amounted to. This can be best appreciated by placing the various taxatory levies exacted from Cheshire alongside the parliamentary subsidies imposed from 1340 onwards.

TABLE 3

LEVIES IMPOSED ON ENGLAND AND CHESHIRE, 1340 TO 1374

ENGLAND		CHESHIRE	
1340/41	Commissions of trailbaston led to communal fines of up	1341	Sessions of oyer & terminer by Hugh Berwick et al. in

---

62 For the list of subsidies levied, see the three articles by James R. Willard, in *E.H.R.*, xxviii (1913), pp. 519–21; xxix (1914), pp. 319–21; xxx (1915), p. 723 and G.L. Harriss, *King, Parliament and Public Finance in Medieval England to 1369* (1975), pp. 270–93, 466–508; see also J.H. Ramsay, *A History of the Revenues of the Kings of England*, ii. (1925). As fixed in 1334, the subsidy payable by Derbyshire was £471, by Staffordshire £579. However, at the height of the yield of taxation on moveables, in 1290, the two counties had been assessed to pay £2,354 and £1,343 respectively.

ENGLAND

to 1,000 marks (*Harriss*, pp. 270–93).

CHESHIRE

Cheshire, fines of about £900 were payable over six years (*ChAcc*, pp. 114–15).

1346   Feudal aid, at 40s. a knight's fee, to make the king's son a knight, replaced by a fifteenth and tenth, (*Harriss*, pp. 410–16).

1346   Grant of £1,000 by Cheshire, payable over 2 years, called 'mise of £1,000' (*B.P.R.*, i. 34; *ChAcc*, pp. 67, 122, 163).

1347   First forest eyre, a financial failure (*B.P.R.*, i. 137, 157; *ChAcc*, pp. 120–21.)

1352/53   Fifteenth and tenth

1353   Common fine of 5,000 marks, payable over four years (C53/62, m.11; *B.P.R.*, iii. 115, 146; *ChAcc*, p. 213).

1357   Fifteenth and tenth

1357   Second forest eyre: common fines of £1,000 (Wirral), £2,000 (Delamere), payable over 5 years (*ChAcc*, p. 247).

1359   Fifteenth and tenth

There were no direct taxes levied in England during the peace with France, 1360 to 1369 (*Harriss*, pp. 466–508).

1368   Subsidy of 2,500 marks, payable over 2 years, and 201 marks from the city of Chester (SC6 772/5, m.3).

1371   Tax on parishes, of £50,000 (*Ramsay*, p. 258).

1372   Fifteenth and tenth (*Ramsay*, p. 263).

1373/74   Two fifteenths and tenths, over 2 years (*Ramsay*, p. 266).

1373   Gift of £2,000, payable over three years (SC6 772/9, m.2).

The use of the words 'harsh' and 'prodigal' to describe the levies imposed upon Cheshire during these years suggests that the county was treated unfavourably by comparison with other parts of England. The figures given above cannot justify that view. Indeed, what is striking is how much in step with taxation in England the various Cheshire levies were. For example, the 1340/41 trailbaston fines in England correspond to the fines from the 1341 sessions of oyer and terminer in Cheshire; likewise the 1346 feudal aid matches the Cheshire grant (or 'mise') of £1,000, the 1352/53 lay subsidy matches the Cheshire common fine of 5,000 marks, and the 1357 lay subsidy matches the Cheshire forest eyre fines of that year.

This is not surprising, of course, since the prince's military activities overseas were a subordinate part of his father's government's foreign policy. The pressure points which led up to demands for extraordinary taxation, in the years before Crécy and Poitiers for example, were the same for the rulers of both England and Cheshire. The correspondence in terms of taxation grew less as the prince took up his new role as prince of Aquitaine in 1363, and started to make financial demands upon his estates of an independent kind. Thus, Cheshire was persuaded to grant a subsidy of 2,500 marks in 1368, when England was at peace with France, and so no national taxation was appropriate. However, this was the year following the prince's victory at Najera (in April 1367), and the subsequent unexpected expense resulting from the failure of Pedro the Cruel of Castile to give promised subventions. In this case, the levy of a tax from Cheshire has its direct parallel with the notorious *fouage* that the prince exacted in Aquitaine, which encountered great resistance and led to the renewal of the war with France.[63]

It is strange, then, that at a time when actual royal control over the county was at its lowest point, certainly since 1237, the policy by which Cheshire was ruled was largely subordinate to that of the king. In fact, the lessons of the previous three centuries or so would have pointed to a quite different outcome, since the normal behaviour of heirs apparent of English kings was, at best, hostile towards their fathers, and, at worst, could degenerate into outright opposition. In this case the lessons of the reigns of Edward I and Edward II seem to have been learned, in the sense that solidarity among the royal family had become paramount, but the long-term effects were not necessarily any better.

An analysis of the expense side of the 1361–62 chamberlain's account can demonstrate similar factors at work. The discharge side of the account amounts to £807, which is 29% of the £2,800 of the gross current charge. The expenses are not divided between Cheshire and Flintshire, as is the case with the receipts, and in some cases (such as the fees of the chamberlain, the prince's attorneys, and the master craftsmen) it is impossible to distinguish the two. This is by no means all the expenditure that could legitimately be set against the chamberlain's

63   Morgan, *War and Society*, pp. 130–31.

account that year, nor is it all 'expenses' in the modern sense of the word. First, the level-three accounts, from which liveries were made to the chamberlain, have their own expenses sections, and so the sums which come from such sources are net, rather than gross. For example, on Henry Torfot's account as bailiff of the manor of Frodsham, his current charge was £13 10s. 11d. His expenses were £3 2s. 2½d., leaving a net charge of £10 8s. 8½d. He made a livery of his 'issues' (that is, out of his current net charge) to the chamberlain of £6 8s. 0d., which appears in entry **5.3** of the chamberlain's account, 'as part-payment of the same manor's issues for this year'.[64] He also made liveries of his remainder from previous years, which appears in entry **2.8** of the chamberlain's account. This 'transfer-livery' mechanism is one of the main technical differences between the accounts of the prince's majority, and those of the early fourteenth century.

Secondly, some of the items that appear in the 'expenses' side of this account are not really expenses at all. For example, most of the expenditure which is included under the annuities of section **30** is, in fact, payments of fees to the prince's retainers and servants which are charged to the chamberlain of Chester for the convenience and security of the recipients. For example, the life-annuity of ten marks collected by the prince's baker, Richard Dokesey, is taken from the issues of Macclesfield mills and oven, and discharged on entry **30.13** of the account. This could equally be regarded as Cheshire income, accruing to the prince, which he has used to pay one of his household employees.

Making the appropriate allowances, though, the amount of money spent locally, on what might be called running expenses of the chamberlain's office, does appear to be low. Table 4 sets out the discharge side of the account classified in the way the account does itself:

TABLE 4

EXPENSES DISCHARGED ON THE CHAMBERLAIN'S ACCOUNT, 1361–62

	£	% of total expenses
1. Older expenses: Alms (**28**)	61	
Fees (**29**)	155	
Necessaries and messengers (**31, 32**)	7	
Wine prise (**33**)	2	
Works (**34**)	87	39.8

64 SC6 785/9, m.6.

	£	% of total expenses
Lead (**36**)	3	
Purchase of arrows (**37**)	6	
	321	
2. Newer expenses: New fees and annuities (**30**)	350	43.3
Vale Royal works (**35**)	133	16.5
3. Prest to William Chorley (**38**)	3	0.4
Total (1, 2 and 3)	807	

The entire discharge is less than one-third (29%) of the gross current charge of the account. Of this, over half (59.8%) is devoted to the 'newer expenses' – most of which consists of assigned annuities to the prince's servants and retainers. This leaves just under two-fifths of the expenses which can be regarded as the 'running' expenses of the bailiwick, only 11.5% of the gross current charge. Perhaps the best indication of the reluctance of the administration to spend money locally is the small amount spent on works, a mere 3% of the gross current charge. A comparison of the figures for similar expenditure in the early fourteenth century will show that this was in keeping with what was considered to be normal peace-time maintenance work. A tight rein had to be kept on this aspect of the chamberlain's function, and there is no better evidence for that than the auditor's marginal note to this account which orders a referral to the prince's council of the overspend on the refurbishment of John Delves' own suite of rooms in Chester castle (**34.10**).

The two unusual items are **35** and **38**. The first is the payment to the master mason of money towards the construction of the chevet at the east end of Vale Royal Abbey. The prince had granted 500 marks to the abbey at the end of his 1353 visit, to come out of the 5,000 marks common fine granted him that year.[65] Together with the lesser gift of one halfpenny a day for life to the poor woman, Margaret de Tranemole (**30.10**), this formed part of the manifestation of the prince's benevolence, an essential political demonstration of the gracious side of his lordship at a time when heavy demands were being made upon his subjects.

---

65   *B.P.R.*, iii. 122.

It may have been received somewhat cynically, since, according to Knighton's late fourteenth-century version, the prince was said to be paying his tithe of the profits he had gained from Cheshire. In 1358 the prince visited the abbey and made new grants towards its building programme. The following year he gave the additional sum of £860 for the construction of the chevet, which was meant to be a monumental expression of his lordship, and which would also associate him with the memory of his great-grandfather, who had laid the abbey's foundation stone over eighty years previously.[66] The other payment, of an advance (or 'prest') to William Chorley, the parker of Macclesfield, has been explained as an unusual example of this accounting device, made necessary because the parker had no regular source of revenue to set against his expenses.

The chamberlain delivered to Peter de Lacy, the prince's receiver-general in London, £1,952 7s. 10d. (**41**). Unfortunately, the account does not distinguish which of that money was the chamberlain's arrears, part of the remainder of £708 17s. 3d. (**40**), which had increased so worryingly during 1361–62, and which was current receipts. This distinction is quite frequently found in the level-three accounts, and means that what have been called 'livery profiles' can be constructed. They enable us to see how each year's charge is paid off in the years that follow.[67] The figure for liveries is just what it purports to be, that is money which was handed over to the prince's central exchequer. It cannot be regarded as the 'value' or the 'profits' of the earldom of Chester. As has already been stated, those annuities which were charged to the chamberlain's account have to be regarded as part of the fiscal yield of the earldom, and there were other annuities charged to level-three accounts as well which must be interpreted in the same light. For example, John Pearson, the bailiff of Rudheath, had paid an annuity of £40 to Sir John Chandos on his 1361–62 account, before he made his own liveries to the chamberlain.[68]

Nevertheless, it is instructive to compare the sum actually transferred in this account to the receiver-general with equivalent figures for the earliest surviving full-year accounts:

1301–2	£1,013	(*ChAcc*, p. 12)
1302–3	£1,697	(ibid., p. 26)
1303–4	£1,514	(ibid., p. 45).

Once again this makes clear that what was primarily different in the financial administration of Cheshire in the Black Prince's time from that when his

66 Ibid., 309–10, 361–62.
67 Booth, *Financial Administration*, p. 162.
68 SC6 785/9, m.2d.

grandfather was earl, was not that the prince's administration was extortionate but that no taxes were paid in the earlier period, whereas Cheshire was taxed later on. This is not to say that there were no trends to be discerned in the items of 'ordinary' revenue within the county. Clearly all types of revenue were exploited energetically in order to raise the maximum financial yield during the Black Prince's mature years, as has already been seen with the management of the escheator's office. As rents proved difficult to increase at a time of economic shrinkage, there was a tendency to try to supply the deficiency by the exploitation of the profits of justice. This was certainly the case in Cheshire from the 1350s onwards, and it has been suggested that the increase of revenue from the ordinary judicial sources contributed to the ultimate decline in the prince's authority in the county, which was paralleled in the leasing of demesne lands and the use of patronage in appointment to offices.[69]

The 1361–62 chamberlain's account gives only a partial view of the Black Prince's financial relationships with his Cheshire subjects. Much of the fine detail has to be sought in the level-three accounts of sheriff, bailiffs, foresters and so on. However, this account does illustrate and provide evidence for the carrying out of financial policy by the government of Cheshire, and give clues to the social and political effects which that policy was bringing about. The entire document tells of an administrative system geared up to produce the money to pay for foreign policy. The auditors, when they met the county's officials in the spring of 1363, were examining a fiscal period of some fifteen years. They looked back to the mobilisation of the county's resources, in both men and money, which had led to the prince's great victory at Poitiers. Cheshire had continued to resource the subsequent military actions which took place before the peace was settled in 1360. After a short break, the king granted the new principality of Aquitaine to his son in July 1362, and in 1363 the prince set out to take up his new responsibilities.

Recent studies of this period of the county's history have tended to emphasise the gains to be made in such a time of foreign warfare by the ruling social group in Cheshire, who were going to call themselves 'the gentry' in future ages. According to Philip Morgan's thorough and perceptive study, 'military service was no longer an aspect of vigorous lordship, but an alternative prospect for a section of Cheshire society led by the lesser gentry who had now assumed the command of local society at war during the later fourteenth century'.[70] Michael Bennett's welcome original analysis of the cultural and social history of North-west England sees the entire region experiencing a golden age in the late fourteenth century, at a time when many local men were making their fortunes elsewhere, in England and overseas.[71]

---

69 Booth, *Financial Administration*, pp. 133–41.
70 *War and Society*, p. 139.
71 *Community, Class and Careerism: Cheshire and Lancashire Society in the Age of Sir Gawain and the Green Knight* (1983), p. 247.

Anyone who has stood in the chancel of Bunbury church before the alabaster tomb of Sir Hugh Calveley, must be aware that there were profits to be made for Cheshire men out of a prolonged war with France. Also, some of these profits were reinvested back home, after a fashion. To justify the career of Sir Hugh by the collegiate church that he built to receive his mortal remains seems reminiscent of the excuses made for the Belgian Leopold, and his pernicious government of the Congo in pursuit of 'red rubber', on the grounds of the magnificent public buildings that were made possible with the proceeds. What of those 'gentry' families who failed to benefit from the profits of war, or of those, the majority of society, who were not gentry? It is not easy to draw up a convincing profit-and-loss account which will include a whole county community.

It may be that historians have, in the past, been too anxious to lament the fortunes of war and to assume that the effects would necessarily have been disastrous. What cannot be denied, though, is that Cheshire was beginning to suffer worrying symptoms of social malaise as the 1350s and 1360s wore on, which must have been connected with the running of the war and the administrative policies which proved necessary to support it. Consider the careers of the father and son, Robert Legh of Adlington, the elder and younger. The older man appears in the account as paying the instalments of his fine in the Macclesfield forest eyre (**8.4**). The younger appears later on, in connection with a fine of 100 marks imposed in the county court, in 1362 (**13.3**). The family were a text-book example of how the descendants of a younger branch of a landed family – the Venables of Bradwall – had to strive hard to make their fortunes.[72]

The elder Robert was himself a younger son, and so needed the combination of lucrative service, profitable marriage, and a measure of luck in order to thrive. In 1331, Queen Isabella received her dower manor of Macclesfield back again, and it was probably in the ten years that followed that Legh entered her service. By 1346, he was acting as her 'principal keeper' of Macclesfield forest, and it was at the old queen's request that he was excused military service in the retinue of the earl of Lancaster.[73] He played an important role in the transfer of the manor from the queen to her grandson in 1347, and thus gained himself a new patron. From this time, until his death over twenty years later, he held the key position of deputy steward of Macclesfield – in effect, acting steward of the most important complex of lands and jurisdictions in Cheshire. In addition, he served as riding forester, justice of the three sessions of the hundred court held after the Macclesfield eyre, and justice of labourers in Macclesfield hundred. He had luck, in addition, in that his mother's nephew had decided to settle the manor of Adlington on his aunt in 1315, and he succeeded to the property on her death in 1352. It was almost certainly this that directed his attention away from Sandbach, where the family originated, to Macclesfield. It is unlikely that he

---

72 J.P. Earwaker, *East Cheshire* (1877–80), ii. 249–50.
73 See biographical notes, pp. 155–56.

could have achieved the status of deputy steward of Macclesfield, if this landed endowment had not come his way. It was around this time that he bought the wardship of Richard son of Robert de Eton from Sir Robert Holland, the then lord of Longdendale.

The younger Robert made a good marriage, to Maud Arderne, through whom he acquired property in the Stockport, Cheadle and Hyde areas in east Cheshire. His other main contribution to his family's rise was through military service. He first appeared in the Black Prince's service in 1350, and in 1355 was retained by the prince in war for a fee of £6 13s. 4d. a year. He fought at Poitiers with a contingent of archers, and was appointed the commander of the archers from Macclesfield hundred during the Rheims expedition of 1359. He was by that time called one of the prince's esquires, and was in receipt of the same retaining fee as in 1355. He acquired a wardship, as his father had done, but this time from the prince himself, thus demonstrating how patronage could confer additional benefits. He bought the wardship and marriage of Katherine Honford, a coheiress of Geoffrey Honford who had been killed in 1359/60 by order of Sir John Hyde. Hyde held property in the same place as Legh, and was a fellow-member of the prince's Poitiers army. Geoffrey Honford was probably a relative of Legh, through his mother, Sybil. After his father's death, Legh succeeded to his place in the administration of Macclesfield manor-hundred, and served as both riding forester and steward before his death, in 1382.

The two Leghs were conspicuously successful in taking advantage of the opportunities that were open to a middle-ranking family in the prince's time. The son of the second Robert, yet another Robert, was the first member of the family to acquire knighthood. He served as county sheriff at the time of the formation of Richard II's Cheshire guard in the late 1390s, and was implicated in Henry Percy's rebellion against Henry IV in 1403.[74] The most substantial 'take-off' into higher social status came with the descendants of the elder Robert Legh's second wife, Maud Norley. Largely through marriage, once again, they became the Leghs of Lyme, and very substantial landowners indeed in both mid and east Cheshire, and south Lancashire.

It is not surprising to find the first two Roberts using their local position of power to influence events in the right direction. For example, the elder Robert was accused of abusing his position as deputy steward, in the 1350s, to manipulate, to his advantage, law-suits in which his daughter-in-law's family were involved. When Robert Eton sued his erstwhile guardian for 'waste' – that is, illicit asset-stripping of the ward's property – the sheriff had to be brought in to impanel a jury of men of Macclesfield hundred, which was something that he would not normally do, and to ensure that none of its members were connected to any of the parties, or to Robert Legh.

74 Bennett, *Community, Class*, p. 170. Morgan, in *War and Society* confuses Sir Robert Legh (203, 209, 215) with 'Robert Legh the younger' (his father) (109, 111, 143).

Of much more concern was the division of Macclesfield hundred into factions, based on the two Leghs on the one hand, and Adam Mottram, William Dounes, and William Soty on the other. The formation of factions has been detected in the 1353 trailbaston roll, with two outstanding examples being the gangs led by William Stanley of Storeton, master forester of Wirral, and by Richard Done of Utkinton, master forester of Delamere-Mondrum.[75] They were both quite small landowners, who, in a county which lacked any landed families which clearly outranked and could control all the others, were prepared to use their power bases in their respective forests ruthlessly to advance themselves and their families. William Stanley's line turned out to be the most successful of all, as the Stanleys of Lathom became, by the early sixteenth century, the most powerful and wealthiest noble family in north-west England. The case in Macclesfield hundred is not as clear-cut, however. Adam Mottram was a man of small fortune, who used every opportunity to claw his way up the social ladder.[76] He appears in the account paying a composite fine for various legal and administrative offences, including the arrears of his hereditary office of gaoler and rent collector of Macclesfield manor (**12.6**).

Adam, like the younger Robert Legh, served at Poitiers. Without, it appears, any really substantial landed property. Mottram became the most active 'entrepreneur' in the sense of seeking offices and land that the prince had in the 1350s and 1360s. He made many enemies, as was, no doubt, unavoidable. One of them was Robert Foxwist, a Macclesfield forester, who played a key and unpopular role in collecting evidence in 1353 of forest offences which was ultimately to be tried in the forest eyre of 1357. When there was a complicated legal dispute over land between the two men in the Macclesfield halmote in 1352, Foxwist was able to employ his substantial influence with the prince's government to get the verdict of the court overturned. The halmote was, of course, presided over by Robert Legh the elder, as steward. After 1353, Foxwist bore the brunt of the community's hostility towards the government's forest eyre in Macclesfield and, despite the prince's gesture towards protecting him, he was eventually thrown to the wolves.[77] Mottram made other enemies, such as Thomas Fitton of Gawsworth, with whom he became embroiled in a dispute over land in 1354/55.

It was in the late 1350s that a polarisation between Mottram and the two Leghs first appeared. In 1357, there was a serious fight between the deputy steward and the hereditary gaoler in Macclesfield, in which the younger Robert Legh and others were involved, and for which they all received pardons on the grounds of their good service at Poitiers. Two years later, Adam and his partner, William Dounes, disrupted the proceedings in the Macclesfield halmote, when it

---

75 Booth, 'Taxation and Public Order', pp. 26–28, 30–31.
76 Booth, *Financial Administration*, pp. 101–7.
77 Ibid., pp. 104–5.

became clear that the jury was going to give a verdict they could not accept. The case concerned a suit between them and the tenants of Bollington, which the two men leased from William Soty (whose attorney Adam was), and which hinged on the allegation that the two men were planning to fraudulently alter the terms of tenure to their own advantage. It appears that a second affray then broke out, in which Adam was attacked and wounded by Robert Legh the younger in the halmote itself, which was being held under the presidency of his father. Also involved on the Legh side were Hamo Fitton, John de Norley (possibly a relative of Legh's second wife) and John Cotton.

Such actions by socially climbing and ambitious officials must have been worrying to the county administration, particularly as the operation of the prince's patronage, inevitable after such a campaign as Poitiers, could often make things worse. As the prince's involvement in France took up more and more of his time, the lack of a figure of power in the county to whom all could defer became a real problem. That the prince's government in London thought that Cheshire was experiencing unusually serious outbreaks of disorder from the 1350s onwards is undeniable. The 1353 state visit of the prince to the county was primarily to investigate the problem and restore order. The letter of 7 November 1353, sent to the county officials only a month after the prince's return to London, was a personal expression of his impotent anger at the continuing, violent breaches of the 'ordinances for the peace' that he had personally proclaimed when he was in Chester, and an order for exemplary punishment to be inflicted on offenders.[78]

The continuing problem was part of the reason for his second, and last, visit to the county in 1358, only five years before the audit of the chamberlain's account. This visit was much shorter, only two weeks as compared with two months in 1353. A great deal of the time appears to have been spent in sorting out the problems of the community of Flintshire. Another proclamation was issued in the prince's name, forbidding armed bands to ride to the terror of the people. Four years later, the prince's administrators were expressing concern that the proclamation was being disregarded.[79]

It was a widely-held view in England during the second half of the fourteenth century that the standard of public order was markedly deteriorating. It is difficult to come to grips with this, because of the impossibility of devising any acceptable measure of criminality to test such a hypothesis. Elsewhere it has been argued that the prince's officials' perception of the problem in Cheshire in the 1350s was firmly based. The division of county society into 'factions', or 'criminal gangs' was real, and was based on a degeneration of the prince's *dominium*, the only factor that could have resolved the situation, through the sale of office and land, the over-use of patronage, and, most important of all, the

78   *B.P.R.*, iii. 129.
79   Ibid., 307–23, 442–43.

reliance on the financial profits of judicial authority, so that the factionalisation was made worse. It has also been argued that there is a direct line of development from the armed interest groups of the 1353 trailbaston sessions, through the armed gangs said to be invading other counties from Cheshire from the 1350s onwards, to the Cheshire guard of 1397 and the last, turbulent years of Richard II and their aftermath.[80]

The 1361–62 chamberlain's account is a documentary witness to the development of these social problems. What is most striking about it is the large number of people who had become involved in a direct relationship with the prince, itself made possible because of the administrative reforms and strong, centralised government of the mid 1340s and later. The prince's council and the local officials had to spend a great deal of time in mediating the prince's authority to his people. Acceptable instalments of fines, arrears of accounts, and taxatory levies had to be agreed, sufficiently small so that there might not be too many victims of financial policy, such as Richard Munshull, but not so lenient that reluctant payers might be encouraged not to pay at all. Much of the account is concerned with instalments of this type. At the same time, there was considerable and growing pressure to call in money as quickly as possible.

The growing arrears on the account are, at least in part, evidence that the balance was shifting in a direction unfavourable to many members of the county community. Resistance to payment was clearly growing at a time when the ordinary sources of revenue could not be raised any further, and there were already signs of shrinkage. Similarly, R.R. Davies found that in parts of Wales in the fourteenth century administrative and financial policy brought about alienation between lord and subjects which led to noncooperation, resistance to payment of imposts and, sometimes, to communal violence.[81] Before long it was going to be clear that, far from the successes in the French war leading to financial benefits for all, the continuing costs in holding on to the English conquests had put continuing financial pressure on nearly everyone, pressure made worse by the need to favour particular groups and individuals in order to prosecute the war at all. Financial pressure provoked group resistance, and the lack of creatively firm government at home meant that such resistance tended to follow pathological social forms. So it was that a flowering of regional culture, and the birth of a 'gentry' who were to be the heirs to the Black Prince's authority, could take place at a time of social decay and apparently irresolvable community problems.

---

80 Booth, 'Taxation and Public Order', pp. 16–18.
81 *Conquest, Coexistence, and Change: Wales 1063–1415* (1987), pp. 410–11.

IV. THE CHAMBERLAIN'S ACCOUNT AND THE COUNTY OF FLINT

The chamberlain's account for 1361–62 reflects the differences between Cheshire and Flintshire, differences summed up by the simple fact that the former was in England and the latter in Wales. The county created in 1284 by the Statute of Wales was not a homogeneous unit.[1] The cantref of Englefield or Tegeingl and the town of Rhuddlan had been part of Gwynedd Is Conwy, while Hopedale and Maelor Saesneg had been part of northern Powys or Powys Fadog.[2] The association of Englefield and Rhuddlan with Chester had not begun in 1284. The territory between the Clwyd and the Dee had long been a debatable land; it had been occupied by the Mercians in the eighth and ninth centuries and most of it was part of Cheshire when *Domesday Book* was compiled in 1086, but it had changed hands several times since then and after its reconquest by Owain Gwynedd in the twelfth century it had once again become Welsh in speech and population.[3] In 1277 it came finally into the possession of the English Crown and it was here that the final Welsh war began when Dafydd, the brother of Llywelyn ap Gruffydd, prince of Wales, attacked Hawarden on the night of 21 March 1282.[4] When the war ended four new marcher lordships were created in north-east Wales and the county of Flint was made up of the lands which remained in Edward's hands after this had been done.

In some ways the new county was a Welsh extension of the earldom of Chester, and this is reflected in its records. The chamberlain of Chester answered in his account for both counties and the series of accounts of divers ministers begins in 1349–50, as does that for Cheshire.[5] As in Cheshire, the highest court was the justiciar's sessions, held by the justiciar of Chester at Flint or Rhuddlan; in 1361–62 sessions were held in the county on 20 December, 4 April, 8 August and 19 September.[6] Because Flintshire was governed from Chester its medieval judicial records are among the best preserved for any part of Wales, the series of plea rolls being almost continuous from 1283 to 1830.[7]

1 For the text of the Statute, often incorrectly called the Statute of Rhuddlan, see Ivor Bowen, *The Statutes of Wales* (1908), pp. 2–27; see also T.F. Tout, 'Flintshire: its History and its Records' in *Jnl. Flints. Hist. Soc.*, i (1911), pp. 5–38 and C.R. Williams, *The History of Flintshire* (1961), pp. 89–90.
2 Williams, op. et loc. cit.
3 J.E. Lloyd, *A History of Wales from the Earliest Times to the Edwardian Conquest*, 3rd ed. (1939), i. 242; *Domesday Book*, i. 263c, 268d, 269a-b. For details of the various changes of sovereignty see C.R. Williams, op. cit., pp. 74–87 and A.J. Roderick, 'The Four Cantreds: a Study in Administration' in *B.B.C.S.*, x (1939), p. 24.
4 Thomas Jones, ed., *Brut y Tywysogyon (Red Book of Hergest version)* (1955), pp. 268–69.
5 *FMA(2)*, pp. xi–xv.
6 CHES 30/10, mm.7, 8, 9, 10. The total perquisites of the sessions came to £37 (SC6 1186/21).
7 The first plea roll is printed by J.G. Edwards, ed., *Flint Pleas, 1283–1285* (1922), and the

Next to the sessions came another of Edward I's innovations, the county court, held monthly by the sheriff; in Flintshire it replaced a court held by the bailiff or *rhaglaw* of the cantref of Englefield.[8] In theory all the freeholders in the county owed suit to the court, but this was often regarded as a burden and the amercements imposed for non-suit may be seen as payments for licence to be absent.[9] In 1349–50 37 Welsh free tenants in Hopedale paid sixpence each to be excused suit to the county and in 1361–62 the sheriff accounted for fifteen pounds, an annual fine made by the tenants of Maelor Saesneg for the same purpose.[10] In his account for 1369–70 the sheriff answered for a payment called *arian sir*, a regular fine paid by the tenants of Englefield to be excused.[11] One of the charges against Cynwrig Sais, the *rhaglaw* of Englefield, in 1336 was that he had amerced men for non-suit although they had previously made fine.[12] The court usually met at Flint, although for a time in the fourteenth century it met at Flint and Hope alternately.[13]

The English criminal law introduced to Wales by the Statute brought with it the sheriff's tourn.[14] This was held twice a year, at Easter and Michaelmas, in each of the five commotes of the county, and each borough also had its own. A series of fourteenth-century tourn rolls from Flintshire has survived and these rolls show that the Coleshill tourn was usually held at Flint, the Rhuddlan one at Caerwys, the Prestatyn one at Diserth or Trelawnyd, the Hopedale one at Hope and the Maelor Saesneg one at Overton or at Hanmer.[15]

At the lowest level was the commote or hundred court.[16] This was not an innovation; the commote was the Welsh unit of local administration which had had its own court before 1284, and it corresponded in size to the English hundred. Consequently the commote court became the hundred court, and it dealt with much the same kind of business as the county court. As well as these courts, each borough had its own, held, like the hundred court, every three weeks. The townships of Coleshill, Ewloe, Faenol, Mostyn and Bachegraig had courts which

working of the courts in the county is discussed in the introduction. U.C.N.W. Bodrhyddan 2335 is a stray plea roll for 1316/17. In addition to the plea rolls, the Chester records include indictment rolls beginning in 1353 (CHES 25) and gaol files beginning in 1329/30 (CHES 24).
8 For the county court see *Statutes of Wales*, pp. 4–5 and *Flint Pleas*, pp. xlviii–liii and xxv. The working of the court in the northern principality is discussed by W.H. Waters, *The Edwardian Settlement of North Wales in its Administrative and Legal Aspects, 1284–1343* (1935), pp. 99–105.
9 Waters, op. cit., p. 100.
10 *FMA(2)*, p. 31; SC6 1186/21.
11 SC6 1187/12.
12 CHES 30/7, m.33d.
13 *B.P.R.*, iii. 322.
14 *Statutes of Wales*, pp. 5–7; *Flint Pleas*, pp. lviii–lx; Waters, op. cit., pp. 113–23.
15 CHES 19/8.
16 *Flint Pleas*, pp. liii–lvi; Waters, op. cit., pp. 105–13.

probably resembled manorial courts in England.[17] The bishop of St. Asaph had his own court within his lands and his own prison, and the abbot of Basingwerk had a court at Holywell, as did the community of lead-miners there.[18]

Like the courts, the county's officers were a mixture of old and new. The justiciar, the lieutenant-justiciar and the chamberlain served the whole earldom. The office of sheriff of Flintshire was established in 1284 and his duties were set out in the Statute; he was responsible for the whole county.[19] But by 1361–62 the sheriff also held a far older office; as well as farming the shrievalty he was farming the office of bailiff or *rhaglaw* of the cantref of Englefield. Under the Welsh princes the *rhaglaw* had been the royal representative in the commote or the cantref.[20] From 1340 the two offices were usually held together, and the same person sometimes held the office of escheator of Englefield as well.[21] The three commotes of Coleshill, Prestatyn and Rhuddlan which made up the cantref had lesser officials of their own, the bedells or *rhingylliaid*.[22] In the three counties of North Wales and elsewhere in the north-east each commote had a *rhaglaw* and a *rhingyll*, but in Englefield there were three *rhingylliaid* for each commote.[23] Hopedale had its own steward and *rhingyll*.[24] Maelor Saesneg, which remained a detached part of Flintshire until 1974, seems in some ways to have been in the county but not of it; there is no mention of the commote or of the borough of Overton in the 1361–62 account.[25] In 1309 it had been among the lands granted by Edward II to his wife Isabella, and after its resumption it was granted in 1331 to Ebulo Lestrange. It was held by the Lestranges throughout the fourteenth century and seems to have been regarded as a kind of lordship subject to the earldom of Chester, although the sheriff of Flintshire held his tourn within the commote. In 1367–68 Roger Lestrange, described as lord of Maelor Saesneg and of the manor of Overton, answered at the Flintshire sessions to a writ of *quo warranto*.[26]

These were not the only officials. Under the terms of the Statute there was a coroner of Englefield.[27] There was an escheator, first of Englefield and later of the county.[28] The *rhaglaw* of avowries was responsible for avowry tenants or

---

17 *Flint Pleas*, pp. lvi–lviii; when these townships were not farmed their bailiffs answered for the profits of justice (*FMA(1)*, pp. 7–8).
18 Williams, op. cit., p. 92; CHES 30/11, m.12. The dean and chapter made a similar response to a writ of *quo warranto* (ibid., m.16).
19 *Statutes of Wales*, pp. 4–5; *FMA(2)*, pp. xvii–xviii.
20 *FMA(1)*, pp. xii, xxxiii–xxxv; *FMA(2)*, p. xviii.
21 *FMA(2)*, p. xviii–xix.
22 Williams, op. cit., p. 91.
23 The ringildries are named in SC6 1189/8 and other accounts. For the office in North Wales see A.D. Carr, *Medieval Anglesey* (1982), pp. 64–65.
24 *FMA(2)*, pp. 29–31.
25 Ibid., pp. xix–xx; in 1385–86 it was described as the liberty of Maelor Saesneg (SC6 1189/1).
26 CHES 30/10, m.33; see also *B.P.R.*, iii. 167 (1354).
27 *Statutes of Wales*, pp. 8–9; *FMA(1)*, p. 12.
28 In 1361–62 the escheator of Englefield was Ithel ap Bleddyn ab Ithel Anwyl (SC6 1186/21); he was appointed during pleasure in 1357 (*B.P.R.*, iii. 288). Thomas Young had been escheator of both Cheshire and Flintshire since 1352.

outsiders who had come into the cantref; these had to place themselves under the earl's protection, for which they paid a small annual fine.[29] Each of the five boroughs of Flint, Rhuddlan, Caerwys, Hope and Overton had its bailiffs who were its executive officers, and the same office existed in the townships of Coleshill, Ewloe, Faenol and Bachegraig

The Statute of Wales really did little more than graft a new administrative tier on to an old stock. The Welsh of Englefield were not unfamiliar with English rule; they had been governed from Chester between 1241 and 1256. Under the terms of the Treaty of Gwern Eigron of 1241 Dafydd ap Llywelyn of Gwynedd was forced to cede the cantref to the Crown, and a year later Henry III granted a charter to the inhabitants.[30] This charter released them from various payments, renders and services which had been due to the prince of Gwynedd; their right to plead by Welsh law was confirmed and they were to pay an annual sum of fifty pounds for their lands and also to pay for the maintenance of 24 serjeants of the peace or *ceisiaid* to keep order in the cantref. A payment called *porthiant cais*, originally intended for the upkeep of the serjeants, was collected throughout the medieval period.[31] The bondmen of each unfree township owed the king three days mowing each autumn; this service was later commuted to an annual rent called *arian medi* or reapsilver, which was collected from the bond townships of each commote at threepence a head.[32] These liberties were jealously guarded and the community was to protest about infringements on several subsequent occasions. The charter was the authority under which courts were held in Flintshire, even after 1284, and it was enrolled at Chester as late as 1352.[33] In 1358 it was cited by the men of Englefield in their petition against the Black Prince's officials.[34]

But this charter had been granted to the Welsh community. Although Flintshire was in Wales there was a considerable English element in its population by the end of the thirteenth century. The 1292–93 subsidy roll for the county contains 2,181 Welsh names and 407 English ones, suggesting a proportion of Welsh to English taxpayers of rather more than four to one.[35] Most of the 270 Englishmen who contributed to the subsidy in the cantref of Englefield lived

---

29 *FMA(1)*, p. xxxi–xxxiii; in 1361–62 the office was being farmed by Clement le Welshman who was granted the farm of avowry fines during good behaviour, rendering nothing, in 1361 (*ChRR*, p. 513; *B.P.R*, iii. 417).
30 J.G. Edwards, ed., *Littere Wallie* (1940), pp. 9–10; *C. Chart. R.*, *1226–57*, pp. 274–75.
31 *FMA(1)*, pp. xxv–xxvii, 3–4; it amounted to a total of £26 12s. 6d. (*FMA(2)*, p. 67).
32 *FMA(1)*, p. xxviii; SC6 1189/1. The amount of *arian medi* varied from year to year. A similar payment was due from many of the unfree tenants of the bishop of Bangor in Anglesey and Caernarvonshire in 1306 (*Record of Caernarvon*, p. 100: Llangoed, Anglesey).
33 *ChRR*, p. 172; Stewart-Brown, *The Serjeants of the Peace in Medieval England and Wales*, pp. 33–34.
34 *B.P.R.*, iii. 318.
35 Williams, op. cit., pp. 92–93; this chapter is based on the unpublished work of Mr J.E. Messham who is preparing it for publication.

in the castle boroughs of Flint and Rhuddlan and in the townships of Ewloe, Mostyn, Prestatyn and Bachegraig, where lands were reserved for English settlement.[36] Of the other boroughs Hope and Overton were largely English communities, but Caerwys was a Welsh borough like Nefyn or Newborough in Gwynedd. Welshmen were not generally welcome in English boroughs; indeed, the Hope charter of 1351 specifically excluded them, and burgages previously held by Welshmen appear to have been confiscated, although there is a reference to a Welsh burgess of Hope in 1360.[37] Several actions were brought against Welshmen holding burgages in Flint in 1354 and 1355 and similar steps were taken over land in the English townships; an inquisition in 1365 found that a Welshman had acquired land from three Englishmen in Mostyn and it was confiscated.[38]

The creation of boroughs, especially castle boroughs, by Edward I had brought foreign bodies with their own charters and privileges into Flintshire. Now there were two communities, Welsh and English, both with liberties that might very well clash, and clash they did. In 1336 the men of Englefield petitioned for the revocation of the municipal privileges of Flint and Rhuddlan which were contrary to their liberties.[39] The burgesses of Rhuddlan complained in 1345 that the Welsh had been proceeding against them in the King's Bench for the past ten years to destroy their privileges, in addition to attacking them physically at St. Asaph fair the previous year.[40] In March 1351 the prince referred to a plea against the burgesses of Rhuddlan and ordered that no such plea should be sued outside his court on pain of imprisonment.[41] Money was being collected in the county in 1379 to pay for similar litigation, and a violent episode at Rhuddlan on 22 October 1369 may be a further symptom of the same tension, a tension not so much racial, perhaps, as a consequence of incompatible rights and privileges bestowed on different parties by different charters.[42]

The Chester officials were invariably English, but Welshmen were not excluded from office in the county. The raglotry of Englefield was usually held by a Welshman, although between 1340 and 1350 it was farmed, along with the shrievalty, by an Englishman, Richard del Hogh.[43] The fact that the *rhaglaw* was Welsh did not necessarily benefit that community; farming an office was an opportunity to make a profit. The most notorious *rhaglaw* in the fourteenth

---

36 Ibid. See also K. Williams-Jones, ed., *The Merioneth Lay Subsidy Roll, 1292–3* (1976), pp. lx, lxiii.
37 *FMA(2)*, p. xliv; *B.P.R.*, iii. 46; CHES 30/10 m.1d.
38 CHES 30/9, mm.8d, 21, 46; CHES 38/25/3, m.18; SC6 1187/7; CHES 30/11, m.32d.
39 C49/46/1.
40 J.G Edwards, ed., *Calendar of Ancient Correspondence Concerning Wales* (1935), p. 232; *FMA(2)*, pp. xlv–xlvi; CHES 19/8, m.5.
41 *B.P.R.*, iii. 4.
42 CHES 25/24, mm.17, 6d; see also R.R. Davies, *Lordship and Society in the March of Wales, 1282–1400* (1978), p. 17.
43 *FMA(2)*, p. xviii.

century was Cynwrig Sais, one of the sons of Ithel Fychan of Halkyn; he had been preceded in the office by his elder brother Ithel Person.[44] Cynwrig took up the farm of the raglotry and the escheatorship in 1336 at a total annual sum of £100, having previously farmed half the offices.[45] The first complaint against him was in December 1336, when he was accused of interfering with rights of pasture; there were also various charges relating to the holding of courts, but he was acquitted.[46] The charges of oppression and extortion brought against him and the sheriff, William de Praers, in 1341 were, however, far more serious.[47] He was amerced the large sum of £200 and five of his brothers and his son were also amerced for their complicity in his misdeeds.[48] As the late Sir David Evans suggested, his 'instincts and bearing were those of the lord of a commote, not of its bailiff'.[49]

But, despite the successful prosecution of Cynwrig Sais, things got no better. In 1350 Cynwrig's son Ithel and Rhys ap Roppert ap Gruffydd took up the farm of the shrievalty of Flintshire, the constableship of Flint castle (which carried with it the office of mayor of Flint) and the raglotry of Englefield at a total annual sum of £110 13s. 4d.[50] This was a new departure; Richard del Hogh had farmed the shrievalty and raglotry together but never before had the former office been entrusted to Welshmen. Nor were they trusted with the physical custody of the castle; their grant stipulated that they appoint an English deputy-constable 'because we will that the same castle be kept by none other than an Englishman.'[51] The joint shrievalty does not seem to have worked very well; although the original farm was for seven years, the office was granted in 1351 to Ithel alone for the remainder of the term, while Rhys farmed the raglotry and the escheatorship.[52] Rhys became sheriff in 1357; he held the office until 1360 when he was succeeded by Cynwrig ap Roppert ab Iorwerth who was still farming the office in 1361–62.[53] Thus Flintshire had three Welsh sheriffs in succession, but this made life no easier for the Welsh community; here Welshmen were oppressed by Welshmen, as was made clear in several petitions.[54] These culminated in a long petition submitted by the men of Englefield in September 1358; this was a catalogue of excessive amercements,

44   *FMA(1)*, p. 87; *FMA(2)*, p. 1; *ChRR*, p. 380.
45   *ChRR.*, p. 427.
46   CHES 30/7, m.33d.
47   CHES 30/8, m.2d; the case is discussed in detail in *FMA(2)*, pp. xxii–xxix.
48   *FMA(2)*, pp. 11–12. Cynwrig had also tried to cheat the prince over the marsh of Gronant (CHES 30/8, mm.2, 4, 5d; *FMA(2)*, pp. xxxv–xxxvi).
49   Ibid., p. xxviii.
50   Ibid., pp. 43, 46, 47–48.
51   Ibid., pp. 47–48. Welshmen were twice appointed as constables of castles in North Wales in the fourteenth century, one at Criccieth, *c* 1359 and one at Beaumaris in 1382.
52   *ChRR*, p. 427; *FMA(2)*, p. 85.
53   *B.P.R.*, iii. 137; *ChRR*, p. 409.
54   *B.P.R.*, iii. 89, 91–92, 307.

unjust accusations and extortion at the hands of Rhys ap Roppert and Ithel ap Cynwrig Sais.[55] It was followed in 1359 by a number of individual petitions against Rhys, again accusing him of ill-treatment and of lining his own pockets.[56]

Some slightly later evidence suggests that there was an ironic twist to Rhys ap Roppert's maltreatment of his fellow-countrymen. In 1372 and 1374 he was accused of communicating with the Welsh pretender Owain ap Thomas ap Rhodri or Owain Lawgoch on a number of occasions and of sending him money; his son Ieuan may have been Owain's principal lieutenant.[57] Thus the money extorted from the people of Flintshire in the name of the Black Prince may have been intended to help the last heir of the royal house of Gwynedd to recover his inheritance. And extortion and oppression were not restricted to the higher levels of local administration. Cynwrig Sais's subordinates had been involved with him in his disgrace, and in addition to the complaints about Ithel ap Cynwrig Sais and Rhys ap Roppert there were complaints about lesser officials, especially the *rhingylliaid* in each commote.[58] In the 1358 petition they were accused of extorting gifts and services and seed corn, along with wool and lambs for their wives, from the tenants, and similar presentments had been made at the sessions.[59]

Behind this misgovernment lay the practice of farming offices. The raglotry of Englefield had always been farmed, and the consequences may be seen in the career of Cynwrig Sais; indeed, in about 1322 the men of the cantref had asked that offices should not be farmed and that officials should be elected.[60] The fall of Cynwrig Sais should have been lesson enough for the authorities at Chester, but the practice continued unabated. It may be explained by the constant financial needs of the Black Prince's administration to help to pay for its master's campaigns in France as well as for its own upkeep. Matters were made worse by the Black Death, which hit Flintshire hard.[61] The county's taxable capacity was reduced and farming was one way in which the authorities could be guaranteed an assured income. The farmers paid over lump sums, but they had to do more than reimburse themselves; they had to make a profit, and the freedom of action which farming gave could all too easily lead to extortion. It seems, moreover, to have occurred to the authorities that Welshmen who were the natural leaders of the community could raise money far more efficiently.[62] In 1351 Rhys ap Roppert suggested that he could do this when he made a bid for the escheator-ship; he was granted it, along with one-sixth of any additional profit he might

55 Ibid., 318–23.
56 Ibid., 359–60.
57 A.D. Carr, 'Rhys ap Roppert' in *Trans. Denbs. Hist. Soc.*, 25 (1976), pp. 163–67.
58 CHES 30/8, m.2d.
59 CHES 25/24, mm.2d, 3d, 5d.
60 W. Rees, ed., *Calendar of Ancient Petitions Relating to Wales* (1975), pp. 176–77; they also asked for the confirmation of the 1242 charter.
61 For the Black Death in Flintshire see *FMA(2)*, pp. lxxii–lxxv, 29, 31, 41, 46, 47, 65, 68, 69, 87, 112; Williams, op. cit., pp. 100–3.
62 *FMA(2)*, p. xxxix; Williams, op. cit., p. 101.

make, and his subordinates were to be protected.[63] But he was unsuccessful and in 1354 the lieutenant-justiciar was ordered to investigate his activities; the great profits he had promised had not materialised and there were other complaints against him.[64] There seems to have been some rivalry between Ithel ap Cynwrig Sais and Rhys ap Roppert, a rivalry which may possibly reflect a struggle between two powerful kindreds for the control of the county. Ithel was a grandson of Ithel Fychan of Halkyn and thus a member of what had become the dominant kindred in Englefield, while Rhys was a descendant of Ednyfed Fychan; the line of Ednyfed also played an important part in the affairs of the northern and southern principalities in the fourteenth century and was to conquer new worlds in 1485.

Although Flintshire probably has the richest records of any part of medieval Wales, it lacks one source which, if it existed, would shed a great deal of light on the county's social and economic structure; no extent or survey of any part of medieval Flintshire has survived. Bromfield and Yale has two, made in 1315 and 1391, for Chirkland an extent was made between 1391 and 1393, Denbigh has the great survey of 1334, and for Anglesey and Caernarvonshire there is the extent made by John de Delves, the lieutenant-justiciar of North Wales, in 1352.[65] But Flintshire has nothing for Englefield, Hopedale or Maelor Saesneg. There is no primary record of the balance of free and bond in the population or of the services due to the earl of Chester from the Welsh communities.

As elsewhere, the fundamental social division in Flintshire was between free and bond.[66] The 1361–62 chamberlain's account does not say much about the unfree element; indeed, it says little or nothing about the social structure in the county. The only reference is in the entry relating to the large fine paid by the Welsh tenants of Englefield and Hopedale for acquiring lands in fee; this states that those resident in townships held by the unfree tenures of *tref welyog* and *tref gyfrif*, along with Englishmen and tenants of the bishop and chapter of St. Asaph, should not contribute.[67] *Tref gyfrif* was the more onerous of the two tenures since it involved a fixed burden of dues on the community, however few tenants there might be. In 1333 the townships of Picton, Axton, Trelawnyd, Hendrecaerwys, Kelston, Gwaunysgor, Rhyl and Carnychan were described as being of this tenure, which was actually defined.[68] There were also unfree

63 *B.P.R.*, iii. 46.
64 Ibid., 174.
65 T.P. Ellis, ed., *The First Extent of Bromfield and Yale, A.D. 1315* (1924); B.L. Add. MS. 10013; G.P. Jones, ed., *The Extent of Chirkland (1391–3)* (1933); P. Vinogradoff and F. Morgan, eds., *Survey of the Honour of Denbigh 1334* (1914); *Record of Caernarvon*, pp. 1–89.
66 For a comprehensive account of society in the march of Wales, parts of which were immediately adjacent to Flintshire, see R.R. Davies, *Lordship and Society*, pp. 354–91; the position in one of the North Wales counties is discussed by A.D. Carr, *Medieval Anglesey*, pp. 128–65.
67 These tenures are discussed in the notes to this account.
68 CHES 30/7, mm.22d, 23, where the tenure is defined.

tenants in Hiraddug, Gronant and Prestatyn, and it was they, along with those in the exclusively *tref gyfrif* townships, who paid *arian medi*; 42 did so in 1381–82.[69] Faenol was a mixed township with both free and bond tenants and Coleshill was entirely unfree; it was the only such township in the commote of that name.[70]

The free landed proprietors could vary greatly in wealth and status. The normal pattern of proprietorship in Wales was the free Welshman of free descent, and it was the leading free kindreds who dominated Flintshire society. But the free Welshman held his lands by Welsh law, and this meant that he had only what might be described as a life interest; if the lands belonged to anyone they belonged to the kindred and they could not be sold or otherwise alienated. The kindred group and the land which it held were known in some parts of North Wales as the *gwely* (resting-place) and in some as the *gafael* (holding).[71] The lack of an extent makes it difficult to know what the tenurial pattern was in most of Englefield, although the lands of the bishop of St. Asaph were organised in *gwelyau*.[72] The fact that the 1361–62 account refers to the exemption of *tref welyog* tenants from the common fine made by the community suggests that some bond tenants held their lands in *gwelyau*, although their rights would have been more circumscribed than those of the free; on the other hand an inquisition relating to lands in the township of Mostyn in 1308 refers to the 16 Welsh free tenants who held two *gafaelion* there.[73] The *gafael* also seems to have been the pattern in Hopedale; in 1349–50 the *rhingyll* answered for the rents of 'Welshmen holding by gavel'.[74] In Maelor Saesneg there were three *gwelyau*, those of Cuhelyn, Owain and Ionas; in the fourteenth and fifteenth centuries these were as much units of local administration and taxation as of tenure.[75]

The traditional pattern of free tenure in Englefield seems to have died out, even before the Black Death, which is usually seen as the great solvent of the traditional social structure. It is possible that the cantref's proximity to Chester and thus to new influences coming across the border may have contributed to this. Many fourteenth-century deeds have survived and they invariably refer, both in the descriptions of the property conveyed and in the details of abuttals,

69   SC6 1188/10; see also Williams, op. cit., p. 97.
70   *FMA(1)*, p. 28 et seq.
71   For the *gwely* see G.R.J. Jones, 'Post-Roman Wales' in H.P.R. Finberg, ed., *The Agrarian History of England and Wales*, i (2), *A.D. 43–1042* (1972), pp. 320–34, and T. Jones Pierce, 'Agrarian Aspects of the Tribal System in Medieval Wales' in his *Medieval Welsh Society* (1972), pp. 333–36; for the *gafael* see T. Jones Pierce, 'The Gafael in Bangor MS. 1939' in ibid., pp. 195–227, and Colin Thomas, 'Social Organisation and Rural Settlement in Medieval North Wales' in *Jnl. Mer. Hist. & Rec. Soc.*, vi (1970), pp. 121–31.
72   CHES 30/12, m.24; G.R.J. Jones, 'Nucleal Settlement and its Tenurial Relationships; some Morphological Implications' in B.K. Roberts and R.E. Glasscock, eds., *Villages, Fields and Frontiers: Studies in European Rural Settlement in the Medieval and Early Modern Periods* (1983), pp. 157–62.
73   N.L.W. Bettisfield 730 is a copy of this inquisition.
74   *FMA(2)*, p. 30.
75   Williams, op. cit., p. 98.

to the lands of individuals. They also show that there was a flourishing market in land in fourteenth-century Flintshire. The Mostyn papers, now at Bangor, are particularly rich in medieval deeds, and these show how one man in particular, Tudur ab Ithel Fychan, one of the brothers of the notorious Cynwrig Sais, was building up a substantial estate by purchase in and around Whitford.[76] Much of this land remains part of the Mostyn estate to this day. The Mostyn deeds, along with the Hopedale deeds among the Bodrhyddan papers at Bangor and the Maelor Saesneg ones among the Bettisfield papers at the National Library of Wales, show just how active the land market was. A great deal of land was being bought and sold, and the career of Tudur ab Ithel Fychan shows how a dynamic and ambitious Welsh proprietor could take advantage of a fluid situation.

These deeds also show how far the prohibition of alienation of hereditary Welsh land was being ignored. The prohibition was as unpopular in Englefield as it was in the three counties of Gwynedd, where the community had been given the right to alienate for a period of three years in 1316; the grant had been renewed for a further four years in 1321.[77] In their petition of 1358 the men of Englefield claimed to have enjoyed an unlimited right of free alienation, but the evidence does not support this; it seems clear that the prohibition applied to the cantref as well as the principality and lands could only be acquired without licence by the use of a Welsh legal transaction called conveyance in *tir prid*.[78] This was a kind of perpetual gage, usually for an initial term of four years and renewable indefinitely for further four-year periods until it was redeemed. It rarely seems to have been redeemed, and the money raised on the security of the land was therefore the purchase price. But the ban on alienation was more honoured in the breach than in the observance. In 1351 it was ordered that all Welsh lands purchased in fee without licence should be seized; three years later, however, the authorities decided to take fines from those who sought licence to alienate.[79] This may reflect an attempt to restore some kind of order while, at the same time, increasing the prince's revenue. *Tir prid* conveyances among the Mostyn deeds at this time are in the minority, and there are few licences to Tudur ab Ithel Fychan to acquire land on the plea rolls. In 1358 the men of Englefield and Hopedale were allowed to make fine of £800 for all their unlicensed acquisitions since the conquest.[80] This is the fine, payment of one

---

76   For the activities of Tudur ab Ithel Fychan see A.D. Carr, 'The Making of the Mostyns: the Genesis of a Landed Family' in *Trans. Hon. Soc. Cymmrodorion*, 1979, pp. 152–55.
77   Waters, op. cit., p. 159.
78   *B.P.R.*, iii. 318. For discussion of the *tir prid* conveyance, see L. Beverley Smith, 'The Gage and the Land Market in Late Medieval Wales' in *Econ. H.R.* New Series xxix (1976), pp. 537–41; idem, '*Tir Prid*: Deeds of Gage of Land in Late Medieval Wales' in *B.B.C.S.*, xxvii (1977), pp. 263–67; J. Beverley Smith, 'Crown and Community in the Principality of North Wales in the Reign of Henry Tudor' in *Welsh History Review*, iii (1966), pp. 149–51; R.R. Davies, op. cit., pp. 408–10.
79   *B.P.R.*, iii. 44, 167.
80   Ibid., 320; see also J. Beverley Smith, op. cit., 147–49.

instalment of which is accounted for in the 1361–62 account. It was probably a final settlement of the problem of unlicensed acquisitions, which now received retrospective sanction; it may also have been an attempt both to assert seigneurial control of the land market and to make some profit from it. Above all it reflects the break-up of the traditional social and tenurial pattern and the emergence of landed estates.

Men like Tudur ab Ithel Fychan and his brothers cannot in any way be regarded as unsophisticated tribal leaders. Although they were the inheritors of a different culture, language and tradition, they resembled their English neighbours in many ways. They were the natural leaders of the Welsh community and they knew it; they would also react very quickly to any threat to their leadership.[81] Nor did they have any exaggerated respect for the law and its officers. In 1391 Hywel ap Tudur ab Ithel Fychan led a band of armed men drawn from all over North Wales in an attack on his cousin Dafydd Whitmore, and three years later Hywel and Dafydd were joined by other leading Welshmen of Englefield in a violent outburst at the justiciar's sessions, an episode which led to their temporary imprisonment in the Tower of London.[82] In 1371 an inquisition found that Hywel and several others had been taking *commortha* or aids from tenants in various townships, which again suggests a certain arrogance.[83] These were the men on whom the authorities depended for effective administration at the local level; they had no choice. No English conqueror oppressed the Welsh community in fourteenth-century Flintshire; this was the prerogative of its own leaders. Like most medieval communities this one governed itself to all intents and purposes. As long as revenue was forthcoming and a reasonable level of order was maintained, the authorities at Chester were content to let well alone. It was only when the leading men or *uchelwyr* of the county overstepped the mark, as in 1394, that they reacted.

These were not poor men. A money economy was developing rapidly in North Wales during the thirteenth century, and the process gathered momentum as a result of the ever-increasing need of the princes of Gwynedd for money to pay for their attempt to create a Welsh state. There was certainly no lack of money in Flintshire. Cynwrig Sais of Northop (not the *rhaglaw*), who died in 1311, had £120 in cash as well as lands in many townships and a good deal of other property.[84] The amercements imposed on the sons of Ithel Fychan in 1341 came to a total of £431 13s. 4d., and the bids made for the farm of offices were often high. Tudur ab Ithel Fychan is recorded as having spent nearly £60 on land between 1330 and 1360; since less than half the deeds record any consideration

81 This class is discussed by R.R. Davies, 'Owain Glyn Dŵr and the Welsh Squirearchy' in *Trans. Hon. Soc. Cymmrodorion*, 1968, pp. 150–69.
82 A.D. Carr, 'The Making of the Mostyns', pp. 144–45.
83 CHES 25/24, m.7d.
84 CHES 30/5, m.13d; Williams, op. cit., pp. 99–100.

he may well have spent more than twice this sum.[85] There was poverty as well as wealth, of course. In 1301–2 the heirs of Dafydd ap Madog paid only 6s. 8d. relief on taking up their inheritance instead of the usual ten shillings 'because they are poor and only have half an acre of land hereditarily', and a similar concession was extended to others.[86] Some of Rhys ap Roppert's victims were poor men like William Colynessone of Bagillt, from whom the sheriff demanded eight marks (£5 6s. 8d.) for his release from prison although he had 'no lands or goods worth half a mark', or John le Salter of Flint who had 'no lands or goods worth half a mark, nor anything wherewith to support himself and his wife and children but carries salt on his back for sale.'[87]

This was not an economy based on barter; indeed, the economy of fourteenth-century Flintshire was rather more varied than that in other parts of North Wales. Its basis was, of course, agriculture; this was an area of mixed farming, growing wheat, barley and oats and raising sheep and cattle. Deeds show that most arable land was held in open fields and tenants enjoyed common of pasture on the uplands and wastes of the Clwydian range; one of the charges against Cynwrig Sais in 1336 was that he hindered the free tenants of Englefield in their enjoyment of rights to common of pasture in these lands.[88] But the accounts of the earl's officials make it clear that there was more to the economy of medieval Flintshire than this. The forests of Ewloe and of Llwydcoed and Estyn in Hopedale were important sources of building timber; timber from Ewloe was used for work on Chester castle in 1301–2 and for work at Flint in 1302–3.[89] These forests seem to have been carefully managed, and one of the earliest recorded forestry experiments in Britain was attempted in Hopedale in 1351 when the earl's officials were ordered to have part of the wood 'cut down to the ground and part not so low . . . so as to see which part grows best'.[90] Forests did not only yield timber; the pannage of pigs also added to the prince's income, while millstones were quarried in the two Hopedale forests.[91] Llwydcoed yielded honey from wild bees and at Ewloe underwood was used to make charcoal for the smelting of lead.[92]

Lead had been mined in north-east Wales since Roman times and the lead-miners formed self-contained communities. There is some evidence which suggests that lead was being bought in Englefield on behalf of Llywelyn ap Gruffydd early in 1282, and at Holywell the community of lead-miners was paying an annual sum of one pound for its liberties throughout the century.[93]

85 Carr, op. cit., p. 155.
86 *FMA(1)*, p. 10.
87 B.P.R., iii. 358–59.
88 CHES 30/7, m.33d.
89 *ChAcc*, p. 8; *FMA(1)*, p. 33.
90 B.P.R., iii. 4; W. Linnard, *Welsh Woods and Forests: History and Utilisation* (1982), p. 38.
91 *ChAcc*, p. 9; *FMA(2)*, p. 30–31.
92 Ibid., pp. 31, 35.
93 *Flint Pleas*, pp. 2–3; *FMA(1)*, p. 9; SC6 1189/9.

The issues of the Englefield mines had been granted by Edward I to the monks of Vale Royal, but during the fourteenth century they seem generally to have been let at farm; there were mines at Talar Goch near Diserth and at Faenol.[94] Mining activity fluctuated; even before the plague, in 1347–48, the sheriff answered for nothing from the Englefield mines 'because the miners there have for the most part died and the survivors refuse to work there'.[95] It is possible that this refusal may have been the result of an accident in what was always one of the most dangerous and unhealthy ways of earning a living. In 1350–51 the mines only yielded five shillings, and in 1352–53 there was again nothing because there had been no mining during the period of the account.[96] The miners of Holywell complained in 1352 about infringements of their liberties by local officials, and in the same year the miners of Hopedale offered to open up a new lead mine there; this may explain why the laws and customs of the mine were entered in the Chester register of the Black Prince in that year.[97] The prince was entitled to one-sixth of the lead smelted with wood from his forests, and in 1357 he ordered that his share at Faenol and at Halkyn should be smelted to find out if the finished lead was more profitable than the ore.[98] In 1383 the rector of Halkyn tried, without success, to tithe the product of the lead mines there, and in 1397 the bishop of St. Asaph claimed mining rights at Faenol.[99]

Lead was not the only metal mined in Flintshire. In 1303–4 iron was brought from the mine at Ewloe for work on the castles at Flint and Rhuddlan, and in the early 1350s some iron was mined in the forest of Estyn.[100] These workings were leased in 1379 to Hugh Sharp along with the right to mine anywhere he liked in the county.[101] And the county was already a centre of coal-mining. There were coal workings at Mostyn before the end of the thirteenth century, and the first reference to mining at Ewloe is in 1312; there was more than one mine there in 1361–62.[102] In the same year the coal mines in Hopedale were farmed at three pounds, and in 1346 a man called Bleddyn was crushed to death in an accident in a coal mine at Kelsterton; this must be one of the first recorded fatalities in an

---

94 W. Rees, *Industry before the Industrial Revolution* (1968), i. 42.
95 *FMA(2)*, p. 19; lead-mining in Flintshire is discussed in ibid., pp. lxiii–lxxi.
96 Ibid., pp. 68, 113.
97 *B.P.R.*, iii. 66–67, 80–81, 67–68, 71–73. In 1356 the miners at Faenol asked the earl for land near their mine on which they could build their houses (ibid., 232) and in the same year they built an aqueduct there and it was ruled that no outsider who had not contributed to the cost could have a stake without the consent of the earl and the other miners (*ChRR*, p. 484).
98 *FMA(2)*, p. lxxi; *B.P.R.*, iii. 272. In 1361–62 it was reported that the prince's council had forbidden the miners to sell his share, which was to be smelted on the spot for the use of his manors and castles in the earldom of Chester and the principality of Wales (SC6 1186/21).
99 CHES 25/24, m.20d; Rees, op. cit., p. 42.
100 *FMA(1)*, pp. 45, 47; *B.P.R.*, iii. 46; Rees, op. cit., p. 36.
101 *ChRR*, pp. 428–29.
102 N.L.W. Bettisfield 1489 (copy of original extent); *FMA(1)*, p. 63; SC6 1186/21. For coal-mining see also *FMA(2)*, pp. lxi–lxiii and K. Lloyd Gruffydd, 'Coal-mining in Flintshire during the Later Middle Ages' in *Jnl. Flints. Hist. Soc.*, 30 (1981–82), pp. 107–24.

ERRATA SLIP

The Record Society of Lancashire and Cheshire regrets that the
footnotes to page lxxix of Volume 125 were accidentally omitted
at the final stage of printing. The printer has now provided
the enclosed errata slip, which is adhesive-backed. Please
moisten the slip lightly and evenly and insert in the appropriate
position at the foot of page lxxix.

Peter McNiven
General Editor.

industry which has had more than its share over the centuries and it suggests that even then mines were fairly deep.[103]

The chamberlain's account summarises the money which came in from the various sources of the earl's income, but the accounts of local officials are far more detailed; they describe what was included in the different farms. The chamberlain, for example, recorded the receipt of the total issues of the town of Flint for the year; the bailiffs, however, answered for the rent of assize due from the burgesses, the rent of a piece of meadow, the farm of the pleas and perquisites of the courts and fairs, which were leased to Ithel de Birchover, and the farm of the town mills.[104] In the same way the chamberlain accounted for the total farm of the shrievalty and the issues of the office; in the sheriff's account the farm is described as including the profits of the county courts and the tourn, payments for suit of prison, strays and wrecks. Other moneys collected by the sheriff included *porthiant cais* and *twnc* or rent of assize from the three commotes of Englefield, the farm of the mills of Llinegr and Trelawnyd, the annual fine from the lead-miners of Holywell for their liberties, *tolcestr* (a fine paid annually by the abbot of Basingwerk for the privilege of brewing and selling ale in his manor of Holywell), the prince's share of the lead mined at Faenol and Halkyn, the farm of Gronant marsh, the profits of the justiciar's sessions and the money paid in commutation of the billeting rights of the justiciar and the chamberlain.[105] The farm of the raglotry comprised the profits of the commote courts, reliefs from heirs to take up their inheritance, and *arian medi*.[106] The accounts of divers ministers usually begin with those rendered for the borough of Hope and the lordship of Hopedale. In 1361–62 these were held, along with the town of Northwich, by Sir Richard de Stafford, a leading servant of the Black Prince, having been granted to him for life in 1358; they therefore rendered nothing and did not appear in the chamberlain's account.[107] This account provides an overall view of the prince's revenue from Flintshire, but any student of the history of the medieval county must also turn to the contemporary accounts of divers ministers.

---

103   SC6 1186/21; CHES 30/8, m.47d.
104   SC6 1186/21.
105   *FMA(2)*, p. 46; SC6 1186/21.
106   *FMA(2)*, p. 46.
107   SC6 1186/21; *B.P.R.*, iii. 323–24.

ACCOUNT OF THE CHAMBERLAIN OF CHESTER, 1361–62

⟨m 1⟩ {m 1}

1. *Compotus Magistri Johannis de* Brunham Junioris Camerarij Cestr' *de omnibus receptis misis et expensis per eum factis in officio predicto a* festo Sancti Michelis anno regni regis Edwardi tertij *post conquestum tricesimo quinto usque idem festum proxime sequens per unum* annum integrum.

2. *[AR]RERAGIA [COM]P[OTORUM] [DIVERSORUM] [MINISTRORUM] [COMITATUS] CESTR'*

2.1 *Idem respondet de xxxix s. ij d.* receptis de Alano de Whetelegh' Maiore *et Escaetore Civitatis Cestr' de arreragiis compoti [sui] terminati ad festum Sancti* Michelis anno regni regis Edwardi tertij post conquestum trice*simo quinto*.

2.2 *Et de ix li. ix s. vj* d. receptis de Ricardo Doune Forestario Foreste de *Mara in feodo de arreragiis compoti sui [terminati] ad idem festum Sancti Michelis.*

2.3 *Et de xij s. ij d. ob.* receptis de Willelmo Tappetrassh' Camerario et *Johanne le Fouler Cachepollo Ville de Medio Wyco de arreragiis compoti* termin*ati ad idem festum Sancti Michelis anno supradicto.*

2.4 *Et de xx s. receptis de* Roberto de Acton' Custode et Approviatore[a] terrarum que *fuerunt eiusdem Roberti* de [Acton'] de arreragiis *compoti sui terminati ad idem festu*m[b] anno supradicto.

2.5 *Et de lxx s. vj d. receptis* de Executoribus testamenti Willelmi de Diseworth'[c] nuper ballivi Manerij *de* Drakelowe de arreragiis compoti *ipsius Willelmi terminati ad idem* festum Sancti Michelis videlicet de heriettis placitis et perquisitionibus Curie more de [Overmerssh][d] *eodem anno.*[e]

2.6 *Et de xlj li. v s. vj d. ob. receptis* in[f] tribus particulis de diversis Bedellis[g] Hundredorum Comitatus Cestr' sub Thoma le Yong' nuper vicecomite eiusdem *Comitatus de parte arreragiorum compoti* ipsius Thome terminati ad idem festum Sancti Michelis anno supradicto.

2.7 *Et de lxxix li. ij s. vij d. qu.* receptis de diversis debitoribus liberatis super compotum Thome le Yong'[h] nuper Escaetoris Cestris' terminatum ad *idem festum Sancti Michelis pro toto* anno supradicto.

a   *approiatore* 772/4.
b   *Sancti Michelis* follows in 772/4.
c   *Dyseworth* 772/4.
d   *Overmersh'* followed by *de* 772/4.
e   *eodem anno* intl. 772/3.
f   *de* del., *in* intl. 772/3; *in tribus particulis* intl. 772/4.
g   intl. 772/3.
h   *Yonge* 772/4.

1.   Account of Master John de Brunham the younger, chamberlain of Chester, for all receipts, payments and expenses made by him in the aforesaid office from Michaelmas in the 35th year of King Edward III's reign (29 September 1361) to the same feast in the following year (29 September 1362), for one whole year.

2.   ARREARS OF THE ACCOUNTS OF VARIOUS OFFICIALS OF THE COUNTY OF CHESTER

2.1   He answers for 39s. 2d. received from Alan de Whetelegh, mayor and escheator of the city of Chester, for the arrears of his account which ended at Michaelmas in the 35th year of King Edward III's reign (1361).[1]

2.2   And for £9 9s. 6d. received from Richard Doune, forester-in-fee of the forest of Delamere, for the arrears of his account which ended at the same Michaelmas (1361).[2]

2.3   And for 12s. 2½d. received from William Tappetrassh, chamberlain, and John le Fouler, catchpoll of the town of Middlewich, for the arrears of their account which ended at the same Michaelmas in the aforesaid year (1361).[3]

2.4   And for 20s. 0d. received from Robert de Acton, keeper and manager of the lands which used to belong to the same Robert de Acton, for the arrears of his account which ended at the same feast in the aforesaid year (1361).[4]

2.5   And for 70s. 6d. received from the executors of the testament of William de Diseworth, who used to be bailiff of the manor of Drakelow, for the arrears of his account which ended at the same Michaelmas, namely for the heriots, pleas, and perquisites of the court of Kingsmarsh moor in the same year (1361).[5]

2.6   And for £41 5s. 6½d. received in three particulars from various Cheshire hundred-bedells under Thomas le Yong, who used to be sheriff of the same county, as part of the arrears of his account which ended at the same Michaelmas in the aforesaid year (1361).

2.7   And for £79 2s. 7¼d. received from various debtors, paid over upon the account of Thomas le Yong, who used to be escheator of Cheshire, which account ended at the same Michaelmas, for the whole of the aforesaid year (1361).[6]

1   Mayor and escheator of Chester's account, 1360–61 (SC6 785/8, m.4).
2   Forester of Delamere's account, 1360–61 (SC6 785/8, m.3).
3   Chamberlain and catchpoll of Middlewich's account, 1360–61 (SC6 785/8, m.3d).
4   Robert Acton's account, 1360–61 (SC6 785/8, m.4).
5   'William de Duisworth', bailiff of Drakelow, was indicted in the county court of 6 August 1359 of concealing in his account 20 bushels of wheat (at 10d. each), 40 bushels of barley (4d.), 80 bushels of oats (4d.) and the turbary and herbage of the wastes of Rudheath for the previous three years (30s. 0d.) (CHES 25/4, m.10). Despite this, and a previous accusation of concealment of revenue, he continued to account until Mich. 1361 when he was succeeded by John Peresson.
6   Yong's accounts as county sheriff, and escheator, for 1360–61, were audited in 1362, on 11 and 12 May respectively, by his clerk (SC6 785/8, mm. 5, 8). He served as escheator of Cheshire and Flintshire from 1352 to 1361, and sheriff from 1359 to 1361. He died in the summer or early autumn of 1361 (Sharp, *Contributions*, Appendix, 24).

⟨m 1⟩ {m 1}

2.8   *Et de liij li. xvij s. vj d. qu.* receptis de Henrico Torfot' Ballivo Manerij de Frodesham de arreragiis compoti sui terminati ad idem festum *Sancti Michelis anno xxxv.*

2.9   *Et de lxvij s. viij d.* receptis de Willelmo Jonet preposito Manerij de Shotewyk' de arreragiis compoti sui terminati ad idem festum *Sancti Michelis anno supradic*to.

2.10   *Et de xxviij li. ix s. ij d. qu.* receptis de Roberto de Hoghton' nuper Receptore exituum[a] terrarum et tenementorum que fuerunt Johannis de Sancto *Petro Militi (!) de arreragiis com*poti sui terminati ad idem festum Sancti Michelis anno supradicto.

2.11   *Et de xxij li. ij s. iiij d. qu.* receptis de Ricardo de Neuton' et Petro de Neuton' Executoribus testamenti Nicholai de Neuton' *subballivi et deputa*ti Ade de Mottreu' Ballivi foreste de Macclesfeld' in feodo de arreragiis compoti ipsius Nicholai *terminati ad idem festum Sancti* Michelis anno supradicto.

2.12   *Et de xiiij li.* viij s. x d. receptis de Willelmo le Poker Ballivo Hundredi de Macclesfeld' in feodo de arreragiis compoti *sui terminati ad idem* festum Sancti Michelis anno supradicto.[b]

2.13   *Et de* xxxv s. viij d. ob. qu. et di. receptis de Johanne le Tieu locum tenente Johannis de Chaundos Chivaler Senescalli[c] *dominij de* Logdendale[d] de arreragiis compoti ipsius Johannis le Tieu terminati in Crastino Annunciationis beate Marie anno supradicto.

2.14   *Et de lxix s. x d. qu. receptis* de Alano Pierresson' Cachepollo burgi de Maccli'[e] de arreragiis compoti sui *terminati ad idem festum Sancti* Michelis anno supradicto.[f]

Summa: CClxiiij li. x s. viij d. di. qu.
probatur[g]

3.   ARRERAGIA COMPOTORUM DIVERSORUM MINISTRORUM COMITATUS DE FLYNT'

3.1   Et de xxvj s. receptis de Reginaldo Balle Constabulario Castri de Hope et Maioris (!) eiusdem Ville de arreragiis compoti sui terminati ad idem festum Sancti Michelis anno supradicto per manus Executorum Nicholai de Eccleston'.

---

a   intl. 772/3.
b   772/3 has mistakenly called the subject of entry **2.12** *Alano Pierresson' Cachepollo Burgi de Maccli' in feodo*. The names in entry **2.12** are taken from 772/4, the rest from 772/3.
c   *Senescallo* 772/4.
d   *Longedenedale* 772/4.
e   *Macclesf'* 772/4.
f   772/4 places entry **2.14** before **2.13** (John le Tieu).
g   om. 772/3.

2.8   And for £53 17s. 6¼d. received from Henry Torfot, bailiff of the manor of Frodsham, for the arrears of his account which ended at the same Michaelmas in the 35th year (1361).[1]

2.9   And for 67s. 8d. received from William Jonet, reeve of the manor of Shotwick, for the arrears of his account which ended at the same Michaelmas in the aforesaid year (1361).[2]

2.10   And for £28 9s. 2¼d. received from Robert de Hoghton, who used to be receiver of the issues of the lands and tenements which belonged to John de Sancto Petro, knight, for the arrears of his account which ended at the same Michaelmas in the aforesaid year (1361).[3]

2.11   And for £22 2s. 4¼d. received from Richard de Neuton and Peter de Neuton, executors of the testament of Nicholas de Neuton, under-bailiff and deputy of Adam de Mottreum, bailiff-in-fee of the forest of Macclesfield, for the arrears of Nicholas's account which ended at the same Michaelmas in the aforesaid year (1361).[4]

2.12   And for £14 8s. 10d. received from William le Poker, bailiff-in-fee of the hundred of Macclesfield, for the arrears of his account which ended at the same Michaelmas in the aforesaid year (1361).[5]

2.13   And for 35s. 8¾d. and a half-farthing received from John le Tieu, lieutenant of John de Chaundos, knight, steward of the lordship of Longdendale, for the arrears of John le Tieu's account which ended on the morrow of Lady Day in the aforesaid year (26 March 1361).[6]

2.14   And for 69s. 10¼d. received from Alan Pierresson, catchpoll of the borough of Macclesfield, for the arrears of his account which ended at the same Michaelmas in the aforesaid year (1361).[7]

Sum: £264 10s. 8d. and a half-farthing. Approved.

3.   ARREARS OF THE ACCOUNTS OF VARIOUS OFFICIALS OF THE COUNTY OF FLINT

3.1   And for 26s. 0d. received from Reginald Balle, constable of Hope castle and mayor of the same town, for the arrears of his account which ended at the same Michaelmas in the aforesaid year (1361), by the hands of Nicholas de Eccleston's executors.[8]

1   Bailiff of Frodsham's account, 1360–61 (SC6 785/8, m.7).
2   Reeve of Shotwick's account, 1360–61 (SC6 785/8, m.6).
3   Receiver of the St Pierre lands' account, 1360–61, does not survive.
4   Bailiff of Macclesfield forest's account, 1360–61 (SC6 803/3, m.4).
5   Bailiff of Macclesfield hundred's account, 1360–61 (SC6 803/3, m.1).
6   Account of the steward and bailiff of Longdendale, Mich. 1360 to 26 March 1361. From the latter date, the lordship was leased by Sir William de Caryngton (SC6 803/3, m.5).
7   Reeves and catchpolls of Macclesfield borough's account, 1360–61 (SC6 803/3, m.1).
8   SC6 1186/20, m.1.

⟨*m 1*⟩ {*m 1*}

3.2   Et de Cix s. viij d. receptis de Willelmo Trussell' Avunculo Ballivo Manerij de Eulowe de arreragiis compoti sui terminati ad idem[a] festum Sancti Michelis per manus Executorum testamenti[b] predicti Nicholai.

3.3   Et de lxiij s. iiij d. receptis de Thoma de Wircestre[c] et Willelmo le Fisshere[d] Ballivis ville de Flynt' de arreragiis compoti sui terminati ad idem festum[e] anno supradicto.

3.4   Et de xiij s. ix d. ob. qu. receptis de[f] Thoma Sonky nuper Ballivo ville de Rothelan de arreragiis compoti sui terminati ad idem festum Sancti Michelis anno supradicto.[g]

3.5   Et de vj li. xj s. vj d. receptis de Ken' ap Bleth' ap Mad' Collectore reddituum terrarum escaetarum de Englefeld' de parte arreragiorum[h] compoti sui terminati ad idem festum Sancti Michelis[i] anno supradicto.

3.6   Et de Cxxviij li. xij s. ij d. ob.[j] receptis de Ken' ap Roppert' vicecomite de Flynt' de parte arreragiorum[k] compoti sui terminati ad idem festum Sancti Michelis[l] anno supradicto.

3.7   Et de ij s. x d. ob. receptis[m] de Ith' ap Bleth' ap Ith' Escaetore de Englefeld' de parte arreragiorum compoti sui terminati ad idem festum Sancti Michelis anno supradicto.

Summa: Cxlv li. xix s. iiij d. ob. qu.
probatur[n]

4.   EXITUS CIVITATIS CESTR'

4.1   De C li. de exitibus firme Civitatis Cestr' que solebant solvi singulis annis ad scaccarium Cestr' nichil redditur Camerario quia predicte C li. assignantur domino Ricardo Comiti Arundell' ad terminum vite ipsius domini[o] Ricardi per dominum Principem Aquitan' et Wall' in recompensationem feodi sui

---

a   *idem* om. 772/4, which substitutes *anno supradicto* after *Michelis*.
b   om. 772/4.
c   *Wyrcestre* 772/4.
d   *Fyssher* 772/4.
e   772/4 adds *Sancti Michelis*.
f   om. 772/3.
g   772/3 has *ad idem festum ut supra* for *ad idem . . . anno supradicto*.
h   772/3 has *de arreragiis compoti*.
i   *Sancti Michelis* om. 772/3.
j   *ob.* intl. 772/4.
k   772/3 has *de arreragiis compoti*.
l   *Sancti Michelis* om. 772/3.
m   om. 772/3.
n   om. 772/3.
o   om. 772/3.

3.2 And for 109s. 8d. received from William Trussell the uncle, bailiff of the manor of Ewloe, for the arrears of his account which ended at the same Michaelmas (1361), by the hands of the executors of the same Nicholas's testament.[1]

3.3 And for 63s. 4d. received from Thomas de Wircestre and William le Fisshere, bailiffs of the town of Flint, for the arrears of their account which ended at the same feast in the aforesaid year (1361).[2]

3.4 And for 13s. 9¾d. received from Thomas Sonky, who used to be bailiff of the town of Rhuddlan, for the arrears of his account which ended at the same Michaelmas in the aforesaid year (1361).[3]

3.5 And for £6 11s. 6d. received from Cynwrig ap Bleddyn ap Madog, collector of the rents of the Englefield escheated lands, as part of the arrears of his account which ended at the same Michaelmas in the aforesaid year (1361).[4]

3.6 And for £128 12s. 2½d. received from Cynwrig ap Roppert, sheriff of Flint, as part of the arrears of his account which ended at the same Michaelmas in the aforesaid year (1361).[5]

3.7 And for 2s. 10½d. from Ithel ap Bleddyn ab Ithel, escheator of Englefield, as part of the arrears of his account which ended at the same Michaelmas in the aforesaid year (1361).

Sum: £145 19s. 4¾d. Approved.

4. ISSUES OF THE CITY OF CHESTER

4.1 For £100, being the issues of the farm of the city of Chester which used to be paid every year at the exchequer of Chester, nothing is rendered to the chamberlain because the said £100 is assigned to Richard, earl of Arundel, for Richard's life, by the prince of Aquitaine and Wales, in recompense for the fee

---

1 Ibid.
2 Ibid.
3 Ibid., mm.1d., 2. The foot of this account has been badly damaged by damp.
4 Ibid., m.2.
5 Ibid., m.2d.

⟨*m 1*⟩ {*m 1*}

D marcarum per annum quas cepit in officio Justiciarij North'Wall' una cum C li. annuatim percipiendis de exitibus molendinorum de Dee per manus Camerarij Cestr' qui pro tempore fuerit prout patet per litteras ipsius domini Principis Justiciario et Camerario Cestr'[a] directas quarum datum est apud London' xj die Novembris anno regni regis nunc xxv irrotulatas in compoto vicecomitum Civitatis Cestr' de anno xxv.

4.2 Idem respondet de lv s. ij d. receptis de Henrico Doune et Hugone de Stretton' vicecomitibus Civitatis Cestr' de exitibus ballive sue in eadem Civitate per tempus huius compoti.

(*videatur compotum de anno xxxvj*[b])

4.3 Et de viij li. iij s. iij d. receptis de Alano de[c] Whetelegh' Maiore et Escaetore Civitatis Cestr' de exitibus ballive sue per tempus huius compoti.[d]

4.4 Et de Ciiij[xx] viij li. xiiij s. v d. receptis de Roberto de Bredon' et Simone de Asshewell'[e] clerico Firmariis molendinorum de Dee de[f] firma eorundem molendinorum de terminis Pasche et Sancti Michelis infra tempus huius compoti.

4.5 Et de vj s. receptis de Thoma de Warrewik'[g] Constabulario Castri Cestr' de exitibus ballive sue de hoc anno.

> Summa: Ciiij[xx] xix li. xviij s. x d.
> probatur

5. EXITUS MANERIORUM VILLARUM ET FORESTARUM

5.1 Idem respondet de xxiij li. iij s. receptis de Willelmo Jonet preposito Manerij de Shotewik'[h] de exitibus eiusdem Manerij infra[i] tempus huius compoti.[j]

5.2 Et de xxxv li. xiij s. iiij d. receptis de Nichola que fuit uxor Ranulphi le[k] Roter et Henrico Torfot' Firmariis Manerij de Frodesham de parte iiij[xx] li. de firma eiusdem Manerij de hoc anno.

---

a   om. 772/4.
b   note om. 772/3.
c   om. 772/3.
d   *per tempus huius compoti* intl. 772/3.
e   *Assewell'* 772/4.
f   *pro* 772/4.
g   *Warrewyk'* 772/4.
h   *Shotewyk'* 772/4.
i   *per* 772/4.
j   *huius* om. and *compoti* intl. 772/3.
k   *de* 772/3.

of 500 marks a year which the earl received as justiciar of North Wales. Also assigned to him for the same reason is £100 a year from the issues of the Dee mills, to be paid by the hands of the chamberlain of Chester for the time being, as appears from the prince's letters directed to the justiciar and chamberlain of Chester, dated at London 11 November in the 25th year of the reign of the present king (1351), which are enrolled in the account of the sheriffs of the city of Chester for the 25th year (1350–51).[1]

4.2   He answers for 55s. 2d. received from Henry Doune and Hugh de Stretton, sheriffs of the city of Chester, for the issues of their bailiwick in the same city during the time of this account.[2]

(*Examine the account for the 36th year*)

4.3   And for £8 3s. 3d. received from Alan de Whetelegh, mayor and escheator of the city of Chester, for the issues of his bailiwick during the time of this account.[3]

4.4   And for £188 14s. 5d. received from Robert de Bredon and Simon de Asshewell, clerk, farmers of the Dee mills, for the farm of the same mills for Easter and Michaelmas terms within the time of this account.[4]

4.5   And for 6s. 0d. received from Thomas de Warrewik, constable of Chester castle, for the issues of his bailiwick this year.[5]

Sum: £199 18s. 10d. Approved.

5.   ISSUES OF MANORS, TOWNSHIPS AND FORESTS

5.1   He answers for £23 3s. 0d. received from William Jonet, reeve of the manor of Shotwick, for the issues of the same manor within the time of this account.[6]

5.2   And for £35 13s. 4d. received from Nichola, widow of Ranulf le Roter,[7] and Henry Torfot, farmers of the manor of Frodsham, as part of £80, the farm of the same manor for this year.

1   The earl of Arundel had been appointed justiciar of North Wales for life in 1334 (*Complete Peerage*, i. 242–44). The grant of the farm of the city and £100 from the Dee mills in exchange for the justiciarship was made on 11 November 1351 (*B.P.R.*, iii. 52–53; *ChRR*, p. 8).
2   Sheriffs of the city of Chester's account, 1361–62 (SC6 785/9, m.1).
3   Mayor and escheator of Chester's account, 1361–62 (SC6 785/9, m.2).
4   Farmers of the Dee mills' account, 1361–62 (SC6 785/9, m.1d).
5   Constable of Chester castle's account, 1361–62 (SC6 785/9, m.2). Warwick was near the end of an unusually long period of office. He had been appointed constable by Earl Edward of Windsor (later King Edward III) in 1325, and survived two forfeitures of the office in the 1340s and 1359; he died in 1364 (SC6 786/3, m.3).
6   Reeve of Shotwick's account, 1361–62 (SC6 785/9, m.3).
7   According to the coroner of Eddisbury hundred, Roter was killed on 4 July 1362 at Kingsley (CHES 29/67, m.118d), during the financial year 1361–62. Nevertheless, Roter's account for that year was rendered in his name, without any reference to his death some nine months before the audit (SC6 785/9, m.5). The inclusion of Torfot as a joint-lessee is a mistake.

⟨*m 1*⟩ {*m 1*}

5.3   Et de vj li. viij s. receptis de Henrico Torfot' ballivo dicti Manerij in partem solutionis exituum eiusdem Manerij de[a] hoc anno.[b]

5.4   Et de lxviij s. receptis de Ricardo Doune Forestario Foreste de Mara in feodo per manus diversorum hominum diversarum villatarum Cestris' que dant xvij porcos de consuetudine sive fuerint glandes in eadem Foresta sive non per diversas tallias[c] penes predictas villatas remanentes.

5.5   Et de xvij li. xij s. iiij d. receptis de eodem Ricardo de exitibus ballive sue per manus diversorum hominum diversarum villatarum de Frithmote per diversas tallias penes easdem villatas remanentes.

5.6   Et de xxv li. xij d. receptis de eodem Ricardo pro corticis diversarum quercuum prostratarum in eadem foresta pro maeremio domini et croppis earundem quercuum et alia busca vento prostrata ibidem venditis[d] hoc anno.

5.7   Et de xvij li. iiij s. receptis de eodem Ricardo pro firma agistamenti et pannagij foreste de Mara per manus Henrici Torfot Petri de Northlegh[e] Nicholai del[f] Brugge Ade de Kyngeslegh' clerici et Johannis fratris eius et Ranulphi le Roter Firmariorum eorundem hoc anno.

5.8   Et de liij li. ij d. receptis de Hugone de Mulyngton[g] Camerario Henrico Soule et Willelmo le Flecch' Cachepollis ville de Medio Wico[h] de exitibus eiusdem ville hoc anno.

5.9   Et de xj li. xij d. receptis de Johanne filio Petri Ballivo More de Ruddeheth' in partem solutionis exituum eiusdem more per tempus huius compoti.

5.10   Et de xiiij li. ij s. iiij d. qu. receptis de eodem Johanne per manus Hugonis le Taillour ballivi More de Overmerssh'[i] de exitibus eiusdem more hoc anno.

5.11   De exitibus ville de Northwico[j] nichil redditur Camerario eo quod dominus Princeps concessit omnes exitus dicte ville Ricardo de Stafford' Militi ad terminum vite sue per litteras suas patentes dat' xxx die Septembris anno regni regis nunc xxxij[do].

a   om. *772/4.*
b   *Manerij hoc anno* intl. *772/4.*
c   intl. *772/4.*
d   *et croppis . . . ibidem venditis* intl. *772/4.*
e   *Norlegh'* *772/4.*
f   *le* *772/3.*
g   *Mulynton'* *772/4.*
h   *Wyco* *772/4.*
i   *Overmerch'* *772/4.*
j   *Northwyco* *772/4.*

5.3 And for £6 8s. 0d. received from Henry Torfot, bailiff of the said manor, in part payment of the same manor's issues for this year.[1]

5.4 And for 68s. 0d. received from Richard Doune, forester-in-fee of the forest of Delamere, by the hands of various men of various Cheshire townships which give seventeen customary pigs, whether there are nuts in the same forest or not, by various tallies remaining in the said townships' possession.

5.5 And for £17 12s. 4d. received from the same Richard for the issues of his bailiwick by the hands of various men of various townships for Frithmote, by various tallies remaining in the said townships' possession.

5.6 And for £25 12d. received from the same Richard for the bark of various oaks felled in the same forest for the lord's timber, and for the crops of the same oaks, and for other, wind-fallen, underwood sold there this year.

5.7 And for £17 4s. 0d. received from the same Richard for the farm of the agistment and pannage of Delamere forest, by the hands of Henry Torfot, Peter de Northlegh, Nicholas del Brugge, Adam de Kyngeslegh, clerk, and John, his brother, and Ranulf le Roter, farmers of the same this year.[2]

5.8 And for £53 0s. 2d. received from Hugh de Mulyngton, chamberlain, Henry Soule and William le Fleccher, catchpolls of the town of Middlewich, for the issues of the same town this year.[3]

5.9 And for £11 12d. received from John Peter's son, bailiff of the moor of Rudheath, in part payment of the issues of the same moor during the time of this account.[4]

5.10 And for £14 2s. 4¼d. received from the same John by the hands of Hugh le Taillour, bailiff of the moor of Kingsmarsh, for the issues of the same moor this year.[5]

5.11 For the issues of the town of Northwich nothing is rendered to the chamberlain, because the prince has granted all the issues of the said town to Richard de Stafford, knight, for the term of his life, by his letters patent dated 30 September in the 32nd year of the reign of the present king (1358).[6]

---

1 Torfot's account as bailiff of the manor comprised the sale of corn and stock still unsold at the beginning of Roter's lease, plus sale of moss and turves (SC6 785/9, m.6, 6d).
2 Forester of Delamere's account, 1361–62 (SC6 785/9, m.1, 1d). There are lists of the townships which paid Frithmote and owed custom pigs in *ChAcc*, p. 35. The lease of the herbage, agistment, escapes, fisheries and pannage of Delamere forest had been granted to Henry Torfot and four others (not including Ranulf Roter) from Xmas 1359, for £32 a year (SC6 785/6, m.2d).
3 Chamberlain and catchpolls of Middlewich's account, 1361–62 (SC6 785/9, m.1d).
4 'John Peresson', bailiff of Drakelow's account (including Rudheath and Kingsmarsh), 1361–62 (SC6 785/9, m.2d).
5 This bailiwick was split into two (Drakelow-Rudheath, and Kingsmarsh) from 1362–63 (SC6 786/1, m.3, 3d).
6 The Black Prince had granted Northwich town, together with other revenues, to Sir Richard Stafford on 1 October (!) 1358 (*B.P.R.*, iii. 323–24; *ChRR*, p. 441).

⟨*m 1*⟩ {*m 1*}
5.12   Et de xxvj s. viij d. receptis de Roberto de Acton' de parte firme terrarum
que fuerunt eiusdem Roberti sicut continetur {m 2} in pede compoti sui de hoc
anno.

Summa: CCvij li. xix s. x d. qu. probatur[a]

⟨m 2⟩

6.   EXITUS MANERII DE MACCLESFELD' CUM HUNDREDO

6.1   Idem respondet de iiij[xx] xj li. xx d. receptis de Roberto de Worth' de
Tyderynton'[b] subballivo et deputato Johannis de Somerford' gaolatoris gaole de
Macclesfeld' et Collectoris denariorum domini Principis infra Forestam ibidem
alternis annis in feodo de exitibus ballive sue per tempus huius compoti.
6.2   Et de iiij li. ij s. receptis de Thoma Oselcok' preposito Burgi de
Macclesfeld' de redditibus burgagiorum ibidem de terminis Sancti Hillarij et
Sancte Trinitatis infra[c] tempus huius compoti.
6.3   Et de xlj s. receptis de Ricardo de Kenworthay altero preposito eiusdem
burgi de redditibus burgagiorum ibidem de termino Sancti Michelis hoc anno.
6.4   Et de xxiiij li. iiij d. ob. receptis de Alano Pierresson' Cachepollo dicti burgi
de exitibus ballive sue de hoc anno.[d]
6.5   Et de xxxv li. xiiij s. viij d. receptis de Willelmo le Poker ballivo Hundredi
de Macclesf' in feodo et Collectore denariorum domini Principis ibidem de
exitibus ballive sue per tempus huius compoti.
6.6   Et de xxxiij li. receptis de Willelmo de Caryngton'[e] Chivaler Firmario
dominij de Longdendale[f] de parte xl li. per annum de firma eiusdem dominij hoc
anno.

a   om. 772/3.
b   *de Tyderynton'* om. 772/3.
c   *per* 772/4.
d   intl. 772/3.
e   *Carynton'* 772/4.
f   *Longedenedale* 772/4.

5.12   And for 26s. 8d. received from Robert de Acton, as part of the farm of the lands which used to belong to the same Robert, as is contained in the foot of his account for this year.[1]

Sum: £207 19s. 10¼d. Approved.

6.   ISSUES OF THE MANOR AND HUNDRED OF MACCLESFIELD

6.1   He answers for £91 20d. received from Robert de Worth of Tytherington, under-bailiff and deputy of John de Somerford, gaoler of Macclesfield gaol and collector of the prince's revenue within the forest there, in alternate years, in fee, for the issues of his bailiwick during the time of this account.[2]

6.2   And for £4 2s. 0d. received from Thomas Oselcok, reeve of the borough of Macclesfield, for the burgage-rents there for the terms of St. Hilary and Holy Trinity within the time of this account.

6.3   And for 41s. 0d. received from Richard de Kenworthay, the other reeve of the same borough, for the burgage-rents there for the term of Michaelmas this year.

6.4   And for £23 0s. 4½d. received from Alan Pierresson, catchpoll of the said borough, for the issues of his bailiwick this year.[3]

6.5   And for £35 14s. 8d. received from William le Poker, bailiff-in-fee of Macclesfield hundred and collector of the prince's revenue there, for the issues of his bailiwick during the time of this account.[4]

6.6   And for £33 0s. 0d. received from William de Caryngton, knight, farmer of the lordship of Longdendale, as part of the £40 annual farm of the same lordship this year.[5]

---

1   Acton lands account, 1361–62 (SC6 785/9, m.2). Robert son of Richard de Acton had forfeited his lands by 1353–54, and was allowed to lease them back on favourable terms, for eight marks a year, from 1 June 1355 (SC6 785/1, m.4d; *B.P.R.*, iii. 201). See **45.4**.
2   Robert de Worth's account, 1361–62 (SC6 803/5, m.1). The bailiwick, which had been held by Adam de Mottrum in right of his wife from 1347, was divided between him and his wife's brother-in-law, John de Somerford, from 1355 (SC6 1297/3; *B.P.R.*, iii. 199). Mottrum bought Somerford out in 1366 (*ChRR*, p. 355; SC6 786/6, m.5d).
3   The reeve and catchpoll of Macclesfield were chosen at the portmote after Michaelmas. Consequently, the reeve and catchpoll of the previous year were responsible for those revenues which were charged at the Michaelmas term following their election. The name of only one catchpoll appears because Alan Peter's son held the office continuously from 1358 to 1363 (SC6 803/5, m.2d).
4   Bailiff of Macclesfield hundred's account, 1361–62 (SC6 803/5, m.2, 2d).
5   Farmer of Longdendale's account, 1361–62 (SC6 803/5, mm.1d, 2).

⟨*m 2*⟩ {*m 2*}
6.7   Et de lx li. x s. iiij d. receptis de Johanne Alcok' Staurario domini Principis apud Macclesfeld' pro diversis animalibus de stauro domini per eum venditis hoc anno.

Summa: CCxlix li. x s. ob.

7.   REGARDUM FORESTE

De regardo foreste quod solebat fieri de tertio anno in tertium annum nichil redditur hoc anno quia nullum regardum fuit factum hoc anno.

Summa: Nichil

8.   FINES FACTE DIVERSORUM IN FORESTIS DIVERSIS

8.1   Et de Clxxv li. xj s. j d. receptis de Communitate Foreste de Wirhale[a] de parte CCCC li. aretro existentium de quodam fine M li. facto cum domino Principe Wall' coram Ricardo de Wiluhby[b] et sociis suis Justiciariis Itinerantibus ad placita foreste Cestris' pro frussuris et imbladationibus terrarum suarum vastatione et destructione bosci edificatione domorum et molendinorum ventriticorum factura marlerarum et pro transgressionibus viridis et venationis in eadem foresta a toto tempore quo Comitatus Cestr⸴ devenit in manus celebris memorie domini Henrici quondam Regis Anglie usque in festum Sancti Michelis anno regni regis nunc xxxij atterminato eidem Communitati ad solvendum infra v annos proxime sequentes ad festa Sancti Martini et Nativitatis Sancti Johannis Baptiste per equales portiones primo termino solutionis incipiente ad festum Sancti Martini anno regni regis nunc xxxij supradicto videlicet pro terminis Sancti Martini et Nativitatis Sancti Johannis Baptiste[c] infra hunc compotum[d] contingentibus hoc anno quarto. Et non plus eo quod dominus Princeps perdonavit Warino Trussell' Chivaler totam propartem ipsum contingentem de fine predicto pro tenementis suis in eadem foresta que quidem propars extendit se per annum ad xxiiij li. viij s. xj d. per litteras dicti domini Principis Camerario

---

a   *Wyrhale* 772/4.
b   *Wylughby* 772/4.
c   *per equales . . . Johannis Baptiste* intl. 772/3.
d   om. 772/3.

6.7 And for £60 10s. 4d. received from John Alcok, the prince's stock-keeper at Macclesfield, for various animals from the lord's stock sold by him this year.[1]

Sum: £249 10s. 0½d.

7. REGARD OF THE FOREST[2]

For the regard of the forest, which used to be made every third year, nothing is rendered this year because no regard was made this year.

Sum: Nothing.

8. FINES OF VARIOUS MEN MADE IN VARIOUS FORESTS

8.1 And for £175 11s. 1d. received from the community of the forest of Wirral, part of £400 in arrears of a fine of £1,000 made with the prince of Wales before Richard de Wiluhby and his fellows, justices in eyre for pleas of the Cheshire forest.[3] They inquired into lands which had been newly ploughed up and taken into cultivation, waste and destruction of woodland, erection of buildings and windmills, making of marl-pits, and also into trespasses of vert and venison in the same forest, during the whole time from when Cheshire came into the hands of Henry of famous memory, former king of England, up to Michaelmas in the 32nd year of the reign of the present king (1358). It was granted that the fine be paid by the same community within the five years following, at the feasts of Martinmas and the Nativity of St John Baptist, by equal payments, the first term of payment being Martinmas in the above mentioned 32nd year of the reign of the present king (1358). The above sum is, therefore, for the terms of Martinmas and the Nativity of St John Baptist falling within this account, being the fourth year of payment. It would be more, except that the prince has pardoned Warin Trussell, knight, his whole share of the said fine which relates to those tenements of his which are in the same forest, which share is valued at £24 8s. 11d. a year.

---

1 Stock-keeper of Macclesfield's account, 1361–62 (SC6 803/5, m.3).
2 The regards of Wirral and Delamere forests were accounted for in 1350–51, having been postponed from the previous year. In 1352–53, the regards of Delamere and Macclesfield were charged in the account. In the 1354–55 account it was stated that the regard of the three forests would be delayed until the forest eyre, which took place in 1357 (*ChAcc*, pp. 201, 207, 223–24; CHES 33/6). There appears to have been none held between 1357 and 1361.
3 Following the eyre of the Cheshire forests held in 1357 before Sir Richard Willoughby, Sir Richard Stafford, and John Delves, Wirral forest community agreed to a common fine of £1,000, payable by instalments over five years. Delamere forest likewise agreed a fine, of £2,000. In contrast, the community of Macclesfield forest, despite strong pressure from the Black Prince's government to follow suit, refused to agree to a common fine, which resistance was greatly to their financial advantage (Booth, *Financial Administration*, pp. 122–23; CHES 33/6).

⟨*m 2*⟩ {*m 2*}

directas quarum datum est apud London' xiiij die Julij anno regni regis nunc xxxiij et super compotum dicti Camerarij de eodem anno liberatas et[a] in fine eiusdem compoti irrotulatas per quas dominus Princeps mandavit dicto Camerario quod in casu quod dictus Warinus non possit se acquietare per cartas suas coram prefatis[b] Justiciariis de proparte dicti finis ipsum contingente quod faceret ipsum exonerari de summa super ipsum posita per Communitatem dicte Foreste de fine supradicto de dono ipsius domini et illam summam allocari eidem Communitati in solutione sua finis predicti.

8.2   Et de CCCiiij[xx] iij li. xvj s. ij d. receptis de communitate foreste[c] de Mara et Mondrem[d] de parte DCCC li. a retro existentium de quodam fine MM li. facto cum domino Principe coram eisdem Justiciariis pro transgressionibus supradictis assisam dictarum Forestarum tangentibus modo quo supra annotatur atterminato eidem Communitati ad solvendum infra v annos proxime sequentes ad festa Sancti Martini et Nativitatis Sancti Johannis Baptiste equaliter primo termino solutionis incipiente ad festum Sancti Martini anno regni regis nunc xxxij videlicet pro eisdem terminis infra hunc compotum contingentibus hoc anno quarto et non plus eo[e] quod dominus Princeps perdonavit domino Ricardo[f] Comiti Arundell' totam propartem ipsum contingentem de fine predicto pro tenementis suis in eadem foresta que quidem propars extendit se hoc anno ad xvj li. iij s. x d. per litteras domini Camerario directas quarum datum est apud London' xiiij die Julij anno regni regis nunc xxxiiij[to] super compotum dicti Camerarij de eodem anno liberatas per quas mandavit dicto Camerario quod non exigeret nec levari faceret de predicto Comite denarios ad quos assessus fuit in sessione Justiciariorum Itinerantium ad placita foreste infra Comitatum Cestr' pro transgressionibus per ipsum Comitem factis infra Forestam de Mara set ipsum Comitem de toto exonerari[g] faceret visis litteris domini supradictis.

8.3   Et de xj li. xj s. vij d. qu. receptis de Johanne de Stafford' de parte xxiij li. iij s. ij d. qu. a retro existentium de quodam[h] fine lvij li. xviij s. facto coram eisdem Justiciariis per predictum Johannem tam pro imbladationibus terrarum assartatarum dampno bosci edificatione domorum et aliis transgressionibus factis in Foresta de Macclesfeld' per eundem Johannem quam pro transgressionibus viridis et venationis ibidem atterminati (!) eidem Johanni ad solvendum infra quinque annos proxime sequentes ad festa Sancti Martini et Nativitatis Sancti Johannis Baptiste equaliter videlicet pro eisdem terminis infra hunc compotum contingentibus hoc anno quarto.

a   om. 772/3.
b   *predictis* 772/4.
c   *Forestarum* 772/4.
d   *Mondren* 772/3.
e   *et non plus* del., followed by *et non plus eo* intl. 772/3.
f   intl. 772/3.
g   *exoneri*, del. followed by *exonerari* 772/3.
h   intl. 772/3.

This pardon was granted by the prince's letters directed to the chamberlain, dated at London 14 July in the 33rd year of the reign of the present king (1359), and handed over upon the account of the said chamberlain for the same year (1358–59), and enrolled at the end of that same account. By these letters, the prince instructed the said chamberlain that, should Warin prove unable to acquit himself by his charters before the said justices of his share of the fine he, the chamberlain, should cause him to be exonerated by the prince's gift of the amount of the said fine imposed on him by the community of the said forest, and to allow that amount to the same community in their payment of the said fine.[1]

8.2   And for £383 16s. 2d. received from the community of the forest of Delamere and Mondrum, part of £800 in arrears of a fine of £2,000 made with the prince before the same justices for the aforesaid trespasses touching the assize of the said forests in the manner noted above. It was granted that the fine be paid by the same community within the five years following, at the feasts of Martinmas and the Nativity of St John Baptist, by equal payments, the first term of payment being Martinmas in the 32nd year of the reign of the present king (1358). The above sum is, therefore, for the same terms falling within this account, being the fourth year of payment. It would be more, except that the prince has pardoned Richard, earl of Arundel, his whole share of the said fine which relates to those tenements of his which are in the same forest, which share is worth £16 3s. 10d. this year. This pardon was granted by the lord's letters directed to the chamberlain, dated at London 14 July in the 34th year of the reign of the present king (1360), and handed over upon the account of the said chamberlain for the same year. By these letters the lord instructed the chamberlain not to exact or levy from the said earl the money which he was assessed to pay at the session of the justices in eyre for pleas of the forest within Cheshire for trespasses done by the same earl within the forest of Delamere, but to cause him to be wholly exonerated on sight of the lord's letters mentioned above.[2]

8.3   And for £11 11s. 7¼d. received from John de Stafford, part of £23 3s. 2¼d. in arrears of a fine of £57 18s. 0d. made by him before the same justices, for taking assarted lands into cultivation, damage to woodland, erection of buildings, and other trespasses committed by him in Macclesfield forest, both of vert and venison. It was granted that this fine be paid within the five years following, at the feasts of Martinmas and the Nativity of St John Baptist, by equal payments, namely for the same terms falling within this account, being the fourth year of payment.[3]

1   For the pardon to Sir Warin Trussell, in respect of his manor of Willaston see *B.P.R.*, iii. 348, 353–54. See also **45.3**, **45.6**, **45.8**, **45.15**.
2   For the pardon to the earl of Arundel, in respect of his manors of Dunham on the Hill and Mickle Trafford, see *B.P.R.*, iii. 347, 364, 389. See also **45.1**, **45.2**, **45.3**, **45.4**, **45.5**, **45.9**, **45.15**.
3   For Stafford's complaint that he was being fined for that part of Poynton manor in Macclesfield forest for offences committed when his wife's step-father was in possession of it, and for which he had had a pardon, see *B.P.R.*, iii. 325–26.

⟨m 2⟩ {m 2}

8.4 Et de xiij li. xv s. ij d. receptis de Roberto de Legh' de parte xxvij li. x s. ij d. ob. aretro existentium de quodam fine iiij^xx viij li. xv s. viij d. ob. qu. ultra xx li. perdonatas eidem Roberto ut patet in compoto dicti Camerarij de anno regni regis nunc xxxiij° facto coram eisdem Justiciariis per predictum Robertum pro consimilibus transgressionibus factis in eadem foresta per dictum Robertum sibi atterminato ad solvendum infra quinque annos proxime sequentes ad festa Sancti Martini et Nativitatis Sancti Johannis Baptiste equaliter primo termino^a solutionis incipiente ad festum Sancti Martini anno regni regis nunc xxxij videlicet pro terminis predictis^b infra hunc compotum contingentibus hoc anno iiij^to.

8.5 Et de xxxij li. x s. vj d. ob. receptis de Willelmo de Monte Acuto Comite Sar' de parte lxv li. xij d. ob. aretro existentium de quodam fine Clxij li. xij s. viij d. facto coram eisdem Justiciariis pro consimilibus transgressionibus factis in eadem foresta tam per predictum Comitem quam per antecessores suos atterminato eidem Comiti ad solvendum infra v annos proxime sequentes ad festa predicta equaliter modo quo supra videlicet pro eisdem terminis infra hunc compotum contingentibus hoc anno^c iiij°.^d

8.6 Et de vj s. iiij d. ob. receptis de Willelmo Pygot' de parte xij s. viij d. ob. a retro existentium de quodam fine xxxj s. x d. facto coram eisdem Justiciariis pro consimilibus transgressionibus factis in eadem foresta per predictum Willelmum sibi atterminato ad solvendum infra quinque annos proxime sequentes ad festa predicta equaliter modo quo supra videlicet pro eisdem terminis infra hunc compotum contingentibus hoc anno quarto.^e

8.7 Et^f de xx li. xix s. viij d. receptis de Isabella que fuit uxor Johannis de Legh' Chivaler de parte xlj li. xix s. iiij d. a retro existentium de quodam fine Cxxxviij li. v s. ultra l marcas perdonatas eidem Isabelle prout patet in compoto dicti Camerarij de anno regni regis nunc^g xxxiij facto coram eisdem Justiciariis per predictam Isabellam pro consimilibus transgressionibus factis in eadem Foresta tam per predictum Johannem de Legh' quam per predictam Isabellam Jacobum de Legh' et Robertum de Mascy de Sale atterminato eidem Isabelle ad solvendum infra v annos proxime sequentes ad festa predicta equaliter^h modo quo supra videlicet pro eisdem terminis infra hunc compotum contingentibus hoc anno quarto.

a   om. 772/3.
b   *predictis terminis* 772/4.
c   om. 772/3.
d   772/3 has placed entry **8.6** immediately after entry **8.10**, and then indicated the mistake by writing *b* and *a* next to the entries as instructions to change the order.
e   Because of the transposition of entries stated in the previous note, the last part of entry **8.6**, that is *proxime sequentes . . . hoc anno iiij^to*, is on m. 3 of 772/3.
f   772/3 has *Et*, del., followed by *Et*.
g   *regni regis nunc* om. 772/3.
h   *ad festa predicta equaliter* intl. 772/4; *predicta* rep., and del. the second time 772/3.

8.4 And for £13 15s. 2d. received from Robert de Legh, part of £27 10s. 2½d. in arrears of a fine of £88 15s. 8¾d., over and above £20 pardoned him, as appears in the said chamberlain's account for the 33rd year of the reign of the present king (1358–59). This fine was made by him before the same justices for the like trespasses committed by him in the same forest, and it was granted that it be paid within the five years following at the feasts of Martinmas and the Nativity of St John Baptist, by equal payments, the first term of payment being Martinmas in the 32nd year of the reign of the present king (1358), namely for the said terms falling within this account, being the fourth year of payment.[1]

8.5 And for £32 10s. 6½d. received from William de Monte Acuto, earl of Salisbury, part of £65 12½d. in arrears of a fine of £162 12s. 8d. made before the same justices for the like trespasses committed in the same forest, both by the earl himself and his predecessors. It was granted that this fine be paid within the five years following at the said feasts, by equal payments in the above manner, namely for the same terms falling within this account, being the fourth year of payment.[2]

8.6 And for 6s. 4½d. received from William Pygot, part of 12s. 8½d. in arrears of a fine of 31s. 10d. made before the same justices for the like trespasses committed by him in the same forest. It was granted that the fine be paid within the five years following at the said feasts, by equal payments in the above manner, namely for the same terms falling within this account, being the fourth year of payment.[3]

8.7 And for £20 19s. 8d. received from Isabel, widow of John de Legh, knight, part of £41 19s. 4d. in arrears of a fine of £138 5s. 0d., over and above 50 marks pardoned her as appears in the said chamberlain's account for the 33rd year of the reign of the present king (1358–59). The fine was made by her before the same justices for the like trespasses committed in the same forest, both by the said John de Legh and by Isabel, James de Legh and Robert de Mascy of Sale. It was granted that the fine be paid within the five years following at the said feasts, by equal payments in the above manner, namely for the same terms falling within this account, being the fourth year of payment.[4]

1 This fine was imposed on the elder Robert Legh of Adlington, as the pardon of £20 of it granted on 30 September 1359, enrolled on the 1358–59 chamberlain's account, makes clear (*ChAcc*, p. 257). A series of forest offences committed by 'Robert de Legh' at Adlington are recorded in the forest eyre roll (CHES 33/6, m.41). Some of them also mention Ellen de Legh, presumably the elder Robert's mother.
2 For the earl of Salisbury's petition concerning the forest offences of which he was accused in relation to Bosley manor see *B.P.R.*, iii. 312. In the Macclesfield forest eyre he was fined for assarting 240 acres of woodland, building 10 'houses', and constructing 12 marl-pits in Bosley (CHES 33/6, m.40d). See below, **42.1**.
3 This fine was for offences at Butley (CHES 33/6, m.40d).
4 Her pardon, enrolled in the chamberlain's account for 1358–59, was dated 5 December 1358 (*ChAcc*, p. 257). The offences were at Torkington, and included the building of a manor-house which is described in some detail. Robert de Mascy of Sale and James son of John de Legh acknowledged the fine together with Isabel (CHES 33/6, m.40).

⟨*m 2*⟩ {*m 2*}

8.8 Et de xx li. receptis de Thoma Fyton' de Gouseworth' de parte xl li. a retro existentium de quodam fine C li. coram eisdem Justiciariis facto[a] per predictum Thomam pro consimilibus transgressionibus factis in eadem Foresta tam per predictum Thomam quam per antecessores suos atterminato eidem Thome[b] ad solvendum infra v annos proxime sequentes ad festa predicta[c] equaliter modo quo supra videlicet pro eisdem terminis infra hunc compotum[d] contingentibus hoc anno quarto.

8.9 Et de xiiij li. ix s. ix d. qu. receptis de Willelmo de[e] Trussell' de Wermyngham[f] de parte xxviij li. xix s. vj d. qu. a retro existentium de quodam fine lxxij li. viij s. x d. facto coram eisdem Justiciariis pro consimilibus transgressionibus factis in eadem foresta tam per predictum Willelmum quam per antecessores suos atterminato eidem Willelmo ad solvendum infra v annos proxime sequentes ad festa predicta equaliter modo quo supra videlicet pro eisdem terminis infra hunc compotum contingentibus hoc anno quarto.

8.10 Et de lxvj s. iiij d. receptis de Thoma de Worth' de parte vj li. xij s. viij d. a retro existentium de quodam fine xvj li. xj s. viij d. facto coram eisdem Justiciariis per predictum Thomam pro consimilibus transgressionibus factis per ipsum in eadem foresta atterminato eidem Thome[g] ad solvendum infra v annos proxime sequentes ad festa predicta equaliter modo quo supra videlicet pro eisdem terminis infra hunc compotum[h] contingentibus hoc anno iiij^{to}.[i] ⟨*m 3*⟩

8.11 Et de vj li. xiij s. iiij d. receptis de burgensibus ville de Macclesfeld' de parte xx li. a retro existentium de quodam fine[j] xl li. facto coram eisdem Justiciariis per predictos Burgenses pro consimilibus transgressionibus per eos factis in eadem Foresta atterminato eisdem burgensibus ad solvendum infra sex annos proxime sequentes ad festa predicta equaliter primo termino solutionis incipiente ad festum Sancti Martini anno regni regis nunc xxxij videlicet pro eisdem terminis infra hunc compotum contingentibus hoc anno quarto.

8.12 Et de xx s. receptis de Isabella del Clyf' de parte lx s. aretro existentium de quodam fine vj li. facto coram[k] eisdem Justiciariis per predictam Isabellam pro consimilibus transgressionibus per eam et antecessores suos factis in eadem foresta sibi atterminato ad solvendum infra sex annos proxime sequentes ad festa predicta equaliter modo quo supra videlicet pro eisdem terminis infra hunc compotum contingentibus hoc anno quarto.

a   772/4 places *facto* after *C li.*
b   om. 772/3.
c   *predicta* rep., and del. the second time 772/3.
d   om. 772/3.
e   om. 772/4.
f   *Wermyncham* 772/4.
g   om. 772/3.
h   rep. 772/3.
i   *atterminato eidem . . . hoc anno iiij^{to}* intl. 772/3.
j   *de*, del., follows in 772/3.
k   intl. 772/3.

8.8 And for £20 received from Thomas Fyton of Gawsworth, part of £40 in arrears of a fine of £100 made before the same justices for the like trespasses committed in the same forest, both by the said Thomas and by his predecessors. It was granted that the fine be paid within the five years following at the said feasts, by equal payments in the above manner, namely for the same terms falling within this account, being the fourth year of payment.[1]

8.9 And for £14 9s. 9¼d. received from William de Trussell of Warmingham, part of £28 19s. 6¼d. in arrears of a fine of £72 8s. 10d. made before the same justices for the like trespasses committed in the same forest, both by the said William and by his predecessors. It was granted that the fine be paid within the five years following at the said feasts, by equal payments in the above manner, namely for the same terms falling within this account, being the fourth year of payment.[2]

8.10 And for 66s. 4d. received from Thomas de Worth, part of £6 12s. 8d. in arrears of a fine of £16 11s. 8d. made before the same justices for the like trespasses committed in the same forest. It was granted that the fine be paid within the five years following at the said feasts, by equal payments, in the above manner, namely for the same terms falling within this account, being the fourth year of payment.[3]

8.11 And for £6 13s. 4d. received from the burgesses of Macclesfield town, part of £20 in arrears of a fine of £40 made before the same justices for the like trespasses committed by them in the same forest. It was granted that the fine be paid within the six years following at the said feasts, by equal payments, the first term of payment being Martinmas in the 32nd year of the reign of the present king (1358), namely for the same terms falling within this account, being the fourth year of payment.[4]

8.12 And for 20s. 0d. received from Isabel del Clyf, part of 60s. 0d. in arrears of a fine of £6 made before the same justices for the like trespasses committed in the same forest, both by herself and her predecessors. It was granted that the fine be paid within the six years following at the said feasts, by equal payments in the above manner, namely for the same terms falling within this account, being the fourth year of payment.[5]

---

1 For his forest offences at Gawsworth, mostly of assarting, see CHES 33/6, m.40.
2 For offences of assarting, enclosure, building six granges, and constructing seven marl-pits at North Rode (CHES 33/6, m.40d). See below, **42.2**.
3 No reference to the offences for which this fine was imposed has been found so far.
4 In the pleas of vert side of the eyre, there appears a list of Macclesfield burgesses who seem to have cut down trees unlawfully (CHES 33/6, m.37d).
5 She had assarted land in Macclesfield (CHES 33/6, m.40).

⟨*m 3*⟩ {*m 2*}

8.13   Et de x s. receptis de Johanne Lymnour[a] de parte xxx s. a retro existentium de quodam fine lx s. facto coram eisdem Justiciariis per predictum Johannem pro consimilibus transgressionibus per eum factis in eadem Foresta sibi atterminato ad solvendum infra vj annos proxime sequentes ad festa predicta equaliter modo quo supra videlicet[b] pro eisdem terminis infra hunc compotum contingentibus hoc anno quarto.

8.14   Et de xiij li. vj s. viij d. receptis de hominibus Foreste de Macclesf' de parte xlvij li. a retro existentium de quodam fine iiij^{xx} vij li. facto coram eisdem Justiciariis pro consimilibus transgressionibus per eos factis in eadem foresta et expeditatione canum suorum atterminato eisdem hominibus ad solvendum iiij^{xx} li. infra vj annos proxime sequentes[c] ad festa predicta equaliter modo quo supra et vij li. infra septimum annum predictos vj annos proxime sequentem ad festa predicta equaliter videlicet pro eisdem terminis infra hunc compotum contingentibus hoc anno quarto.

8.15   Et de xxvj li. iiij s. iij d. receptis[d] de Johanne de Hyde Chivaler qui remanserunt super eum de quodam fine lxvj li. iiij s. iij d. facto coram eisdem Justiciariis pro diversis transgressionibus per ipsum Johannem factis in foresta de Macclesfeld' ultra xl li. sibi perdonatas per dominum Principem per litteras suas Camerario suo[e] Cestr' directas quarum datum est ultimo die Septembris anno regni regis nunc xxxiij prout patet in compoto eiusdem Camerarij de eodem anno.

---

a   772/3 starts to write *Lymnour*, del., and then writes it in full.
b   *proxime sequentes . . . supra videlicet* intl. 772/3.
c   *proxime sequentes* om. 772/3.
d   om. 772/3.
e   om. 772/3.

8.13   And for 10s. 0d. received from John Lymnour, part of 30s. 0d. in arrears of a fine of 60s. 0d. made before the same justices for the like trespasses committed by him in the same forest. It was granted that the fine be paid within the six years following at the said feasts, by equal payments in the above manner, namely for the same terms fallirg within this account, being the fourth year of payment.[1]

8.14   And for £13 6s. 8d. received from the men of Macclesfield forest, part of £47 in arrears of a fine of £87 made before the same justices for the like trespasses committed by them in the same forest, and also for the lawing of their dogs. It was granted that the fine be paid at the rate of £80 within the six years following at the said feasts, by equal payments in the above manner, and £7 in the seventh year at the said feasts, by equal payments, namely for the same terms falling within this account, being the fourth year of payment.[2]

8.15   And for £26 4s. 3d. received from John de Hyde, knight, which he is still liable to pay of a fine of £66 4s. 3d. made before the same justices for various trespasses committed by him in Macclesfield forest, over and above £40 pardoned him by the prince. This pardon was granted by the prince's letters directed to the chamberlain of Chester, dated 30 September in the 33rd year of the reign of the present king (1359), as appears in the chamberlain's account for the same year (1358–59).[3]

1   This fine may have been for cutting down oaks in Shrigley wood (CHES 33/6, m.38).
2   The community of Macclesfield forest as a whole had refused to negotiate a common fine with the prince's officials (see above, p. 15, n.3). On 13 April 1359, the 'poor tenants' of Macclesfield forest petitioned the prince saying that a fine of £60 was being required of them for trespasses in the forest eyre which, they claimed, they were too poor to pay in addition to their rents and services (*B.P.R.*, iii. 335). Other evidence suggests that the fine charged here represents part of a common fine, payable only by the tenants of the demesne townships within the forest (excluding Macclesfield borough and Shrigley), and not the forest community as a whole.
3   In October 1357, Hyde was excused from appearance at the forest eyre as he was in London on the prince's business, and the fate of any seized lands was to be referred to the prince and council for a decision (*B.P.R.*, iii. 280). On 11 July 1359 Hyde was in Princes Risborough to ask the prince in person for pardon of part of his fine, and a delay to the payment of the first instalment of the remainder, otherwise he would be prevented from setting out on the forthcoming military expedition to France (ibid., 352–53). His argument found favour, since he was pardoned £40 of his fine on 30 September 1359, while payment of the rest was postponed until further order. [The date given here is of the letters in the *Register* (ibid., 368–69); those enrolled on the 1358–59 chamberlain's account are dated 29 September (*ChAcc*, p. 256).] Forest offences by 'John de Hyde' are recorded at Norbury, including destruction of woodland, erecting of buildings, assarting, and digging of marl-pits. The pledges for Hyde's fine of £66 4s. 3d. were John Fitton, Hamo de Mascy, William de Dounes, Adam de Mottrum, John son of Henry de Honford, and John de Clyf (CHES 33/6, m.41d). See also **12.19**.

⟨m 3⟩ {m 2}

(*Respondeat anno futuro de pluribus quarteriis busce prostrate in foresta de Mondrem iuxta tenorem cuiusdam brevis forestario eiusdem foreste inde facti remanentis penes (Camerarium)*[a]

8.16 Et de xij li. receptis de David Cradok' et Ricardo de[b] Nortour Capellano pro xviij quarteriis busce que fuerunt Ricardi de Munshull' seisitis in manum domini et venditis eisdem David et Ricardo per Justiciarios pro eadem summa.

Summa: DCCxxxvj li. xj d. ob. probatur

{m 3}

9. PRISA VINORUM MAEREMII ET CORTICORUM CUM CARBONIBUS MARITIMIS

9.1 Idem[c] respondet de duobus doleis vini receptis in portu apud le Redebonk' de prisa domini hoc anno de Nave Walteri de Dertemouth'.

9.2 Et de vj s. viij d. receptis de Mad' le Sawer[d] del Oldecastell'[e] et David ap Jor' pro maeremio proveniente de prisa domini hoc anno sibi vendito.

9.3 Et de vj s. viij d. receptis de Ith' ap Mad' de Wylynton' et Jeuan Duy de Worthenbury pro maeremio proveniente de prisa domini hoc anno sibi vendito.

9.4 Et de vj s. viij d. receptis de Bleth' ap Eign' de Halton'[f] et Ith' With'[g] de Halton'[h] pro maeremio proveniente de prisa domini hoc anno sibi vendito.[i]

9.5 Et de xij s. vj d. receptis de Nicholao de Breghton'[j] et Ricardo Ketell'[k] pro corticis provenientibus de prisa domini hoc anno sibi[l] venditis per Camerarium.

9.6 Et de xxxiij s. iiij d. receptis de Johanne de Delves Chivaler et Magistro Johanne de Brunham' Juniore pro carbonibus maritimis provenientibus de consimili prisa domini hoc anno sibi[m] venditis.

9.7 Et de xx s. receptis de Johanne de Tranemol' de quodam pisse[n] regali domino pertinente ratione dominij sui vocato[o] *sturgen* invento apud Podynton' in Wirhale[p] mense Junij anno regni regis nunc xxxvj sibi vendito[q] per Camerarium pro eadem summa.

Summa: iiij li. v s. x d. probatur[r]

---

a	*iuxta tenorem . . . penes Camerarium* om. 772/3.		omitting *sibi vendito*.
b	*le* 772/4.	j	*Broghton'* 772/4.
c	preceded by *Et*, del., 772/3.	k	*Ketel'* 772/4.
d	*Sawyer* 772/4.	l	om. 772/3.
e	*Oldecastel* 772/4.	m	om. 772/3.
f	*Halghton'* 772/4.	n	For *de quodam pisse* 772/3 puts *de prisa*,
g	*Wyth'* 772/4.		then del. it, and intl. *de quodam pisse*.
h	*Halghton'* 772/4.	o	rep. and del., 772/3.
i	772/3 intl. paragraph **9.4**, and has *pro maer-*	p	*Wyrhale* 772/4.
	emio de prisa domini hoc anno proveniente,	q	intl. 772/3.
		r	om. 772/3.

(*Let him answer in a future year for the many quarters of wood blown down in the forest of Mondrum, in accordance with the tenor of a writ sent to the forester of that forest, which remains in the chamberlain's possession*).

8.16 And for £12 received from David Cradok and Richard de Nortour, chaplain, for 18 quarters of wood which belonged to Richard de Munshull seized into the lord's hand[1] and sold to the same David and Richard by the justices for the same sum.

Sum: £736 0s. 11½d. Approved.

9.   PRISE OF WINE, TIMBER, BARK AND SEA-COAL

9.1   He answers for two tuns of wine received in the port at *le Redebonk*,[2] of the lord's prise this year, from Walter de Dertemouth's ship.

9.2   And for 6s. 8d. received from Madcg le Sawer of Oldcastle and Dafydd ab Iorwerth for timber sold to them this year, which comes from the lord's prise.

9.3   And for 6s. 8d. received from Ithel ap Madog of Willington and Ieuan Ddu of Worthenbury for timber sold to them this year, which comes from the lord's prise.

9.4   And for 6s. 8d. received from Bleddyn ap Einion of Halghton and Ithel Chwith of Halghton for timber sold to them this year, which comes from the lord's prise.

9.5   And for 12s. 6d. received from Nicholas de Breghton and Richard Ketell for bark sold to them this year by the chamberlain, which comes from the lord's prise.

9.6   And for 33s. 4d. received from John de Delves, knight, and Master John de Brunham the younger, for sea-coal sold to them this year, which comes from the like prise.[3]

9.7   And for 20s. 0d. received from John de Tranemol for a certain royal fish called *sturgen*, which pertains to the lord by reason of his lordship, and which was found at Puddington in Wirral in June in the 36th year of the reign of the present king (1362), and was sold to him by the chamberlain for the above sum.[4]

Sum: £4 5s. 10d. Approved.

---

1   Munshull's lands – the manors of Aston juxta Mondrum and Church Minshull – were seized because of his inability to pay his share of the common fine of Delamere forest in July 1360; sufficient was set aside for the support of him and his family (*B.P.R.*, iii. 389).

2   The use of Red Bank, between Heswall and West Kirby, as an anchorage for ships using the port of Chester in the later Middle Ages is amply witnessed by the accounts published by K.P. Wilson, ed., *Chester Customs Accounts, 1301–1566*, R.S.L.C., cxi (1969), passim.

3   The collection of prise of wine at Chester first appears in 1274–75. It was payable by denizen merchants at the rate of 1 tun from 10 to 20 tuns, 2 tuns on 20 or more (Wilson, *ibid.*, p. 5). Surprisingly, Wilson does not mention the prises on timber, bark, or coal. 'Prisage of timber' appears in the chamberlain's account for June to Mich. 1315, which is mistakenly dated 1315–16 in *ChAcc*, p. 83, (SC6 771/8, m.1). The entries for wine and timber prise in this account relate them to Chester castle, suggesting that their original function was to provide materials and goods for the earl's household there. The prise of coal first appears in the account for 1331–32, mistakenly dated 1334–35 in *ChAcc*, p. 109 (SC6 771/13, m.1). See below, **33**, **48**.

4   For the expenses of catching and transporting this visible symbol of the earl of Chester's 'royal liberty', see **31.4** and **31.5**.

⟨m 3⟩ {m 3}
10.   CUSTUMA LANE ET CORIORUM

De custuma lane et coriorum nichil redditur Camerario quia nulle lane cariate fuerunt extra portum Cestr' hoc anno et licet et cetera dominus non habet sigillum coketti ibidem.

Summa: Nichil.

11.   EXITUS VICECOMITATUS CESTRIS' CUM ALIIS PROFICUIS

11.1   Idem respondet de CCxxj li. xj s. x d. receptis de Ricardo de[a] Whitelegh' vicecomite Cestris' et approviatore[b] eiusdem officij de extractionibus Comitatus et[c] Itineris hoc anno.

11.2   Et de lxiij li. xviij s. viij d. receptis[d] de eodem vicecomite de exitibus ballive sue de[e] hoc anno.[f]
(*fiat breve predicto firmario pro nominibus advocariorum liberandis citra proximum compotum*)[g]

11.3   Et de x li. receptis de eodem vicecomite per manus Ricardi de Mascy Custodis et Firmarij advocariarum Cestris' pro firma earundem advocariarum sic eidem Ricardo concessa per dominum Principem quamdiu idem Ricardus bene et fideliter se gesserit in eodem officio per litteras domini Justiciario et Camerario directas quarum datum est apud London' xiij die Julij anno regni regis nunc xxxj.

11.4   Et de xxxvj s. viij d. receptis de eodem vicecomite per manus Roberti le Hayward' Custodis et Firmarij passagij de Lauton˙ et Wicy Malbani de firma eiusdem passagij de hoc anno.[h]

---

a   om. 772/3.
b   *approiatore* 772/4.
c   intl. 772/3.
d   om. 772/3.
e   om. 772/4.
f   *sue de hoc anno* intl. 772/3.
g   note om. 772/3.
h   In 772/4 **11.4** is followed by a paragraph that has been del.: *De liij s. iiij d. de firma terrarum et tenementorum que fuerunt Johannis de Elton' existentium in manu domini ratione utlagarie eiusdem Johannis nichil redditur Camerario hoc anno eo quod idem Johannes obijt mense Septembris anno regni regis nunc xxxv et predicta tenementa descenderunt Thome de Elton' fratri et heredi predicti Johannis.*

10. CUSTOM OF WOOL AND HIDES

For the custom of wool and hides nothing is rendered to the chamberlain, because no wool was exported from the port of Chester this year and although, etc., the lord does not have a cocket-seal there.[1]

Sum: Nothing.

11. ISSUES OF THE SHERIFFDOM OF CHESHIRE WITH OTHER REVENUES

11.1 He answers for £221 11s. 10d. received from Richard de Whitelegh, sheriff of Cheshire and manager of that office, for the estreats of the county court and the eyre this year.[2]

11.2 And for £63 18s. 8d. received from the same sheriff for the issues of his bailiwick this year.

(*Send a writ to the aforesaid farmer to deliver the names of the avowrymen before the audit of the next account*).

11.3 And for £10 received from the same sheriff by the hands of Richard de Mascy, keeper and farmer of the Cheshire avowries, for the farm of the same avowries which was granted to him by the prince, during good behaviour, by his letters directed to the justiciar and chamberlain, dated at London 13 July in the 31st year of the reign of the present king (1357).[3]

11.4 And for 36s. 8d. received from the same sheriff by the hands of Robert le Hayward, keeper and farmer of the passage of Lawton and Nantwich, for the farm of the same passage this year.[4]

1   K.P. Wilson points out that at the time of the establishment of the 'new custom' on wool in 1303, the chamberlain, in his account for 1302–3, was charged for the custom on exported wool and hides. This remained the sole instance of the practice, and, despite royal orders concerning collection of customs being sent to Chester after that time, it is unlikely that wool exports were officially allowed there. In 1320, the account records that there was no yield from the custom of wool and hides because the liberty of the cocket is 'not yet' obtained from the King. In 1343 it was definitely established that the port of Chester was closed to wool exports, in a royal order which states that wool merchants had been evading customs and other dues by exporting wool through Wales, Cheshire and Cornwall (*Customs Accounts*, p. 4; *C.C.R., 1343–46*, p. 78). In the chamberlain's account for 1347–48 the standard entry concerning wool exports first appears, which shows that the 'etc.' in the present account stands for the words '(although) there is a seaport there'.

2   Sheriff of Cheshire's account, 1361–62 (SC6 785/9, m.4, 4d).

3   He was granted the keeping of the Cheshire avowries for good service at Poitiers, 13 July 1357 (*B.P.R.*, iii. 258; *ChRR*, p. 328). In June 1359 he complained that the farm of the avowries had been set at £1 above the office's yearly value (*B.P.R.*, iii. 357). For the history of this institution in the county see R. Stewart-Brown, 'The Avowries of Cheshire', *E.H.R.*, xxix (1914).

4   Although Hayward leased the passage of Lawton from 1349 to 1361, no record of the lease in being in 1361–62 has survived.

⟨*m 3*⟩ {*m 3*}

11.5   Et de liij s. iiij d. oneratis pro firma terrarum et tenementorum que fuerunt Johannis de Elton' existentium in manu domini ratione utlagarie eiusdem Johannis in Elton' utlagati anno regni regis nunc xxxj pro morte Willelmi Wasteneys sicut continetur in compoto precedenti.

Summa: CCC li. vj d. probatur

12.   ATTERMINATIONES ANTIQUE DIVERSORUM CESTR' ET CESTRIS'

12.1   Idem respondet de^a xl s. receptis^b de Willelmo de Basyngwerk' de atterminatione sua pro terminis Nativitatis Sancti Johannis Baptiste et Sancti Michelis infra tempus huius compoti equis portionibus.

12.2   Et de xl s. receptis de Willelmo de Chauldon' de parte Cvj s. viij d. a retro existentium de xx marcis de fine ipsius Willelmi facto coram Johanne de Delves locum tenente Justiciarij Cestr' sibi atterminato ad solvendum xl s. per annum ad festa Pasche et Sancti Michelis per equales portiones quousque predicte xx marce plenarie persolvantur per litteras domini Camerario directas penes ipsum Camerarium remanentes quarum datum est apud London' secundo die Novembris anno regni regis nunc xxxj videlicet pro terminis Pasche et Sancti Michelis infra hunc compotum contingentibus hoc anno quinto.

12.3   Et de xl s. receptis de Ricardo del Wodehouses in persolutionem x li. de fine ipsius Ricardi facto coram predicto locum tenente in Comitatu tento die Martis proxime ante festum Sancti Laurencij martiris anno regni regis nunc^c xxxj sibi atterminato ad solvendum infra v annos proxime sequentes ad festa Sancti Martini et Nativitatis Sancti Johannis Baptiste per equales portiones videlicet pro terminis Sancti Martini et Nativitatis Sancti Johannis Baptiste infra hunc compotum^d contingentibus hoc anno v et ultimo.^{e}

12.4   Et de xiij li. vj s. viij d. receptis de Stephano de Kelshale et sociis suis in persolutionem C marcarum de fine Johannis del Gre(n)e facto coram predictis locum tenente et Camerario sibi atterminato ad solvendum infra v annos

a   intl. 772/3.
b   om. 772/3.
c   *regni regis nunc* om. 772/3.
d   intl. 772/3.
e   *et ultimo* intl.

11.5   And for 53s. 4d. charged for the farm of the lands and tenements in Elton which used to belong to John de Elton, and which are in the lord's hand because John was outlawed in the 31st year of the reign of the present king (1357/58) for the death of William Wasteneys, as is contained in last year's account.[1]

Sum: £300 0s. 6d. Approved.

12.   PAYMENTS BY INSTALMENTS OF VARIOUS PEOPLE OF CHESTER AND CHESHIRE – FROM PREVIOUS YEARS

12.1   He answers for 40s. 0d. received from William de Basyngwerk for his instalment for the terms of the Nativity of St John Baptist and Michaelmas, by equal payments, within the period of this account.[2]

12.2   And for 40s. 0d. received from William de Chauldon as part of 106s. 8d. in arrears of a fine of 20 marks made before John de Delves, lieutenant – justiciar of Chester, which it was granted should be paid at the rate of 40s. 0d. a year at Easter and Michaelmas, by equal payments, until it be paid in full. This grant was made by the lord's letters directed to the chamberlain, dated at London 2 November in the 31st year of the reign of the present king (1357), which remain in the chamberlain's possession. The above sum is, therefore, for the terms of Easter and Michaelmas falling within this account, being the fifth year of payment.[3]

12.3   And for 40s. 0d. received from Richard del Wodehouses in full payment of a fine of £10 made by him before the said lieutenant in the county court held on Tuesday before the feast of St. Laurence, martyr, in the 31st year of the reign of the present king (8 August 1357). It was granted that the fine be paid within the five years following at the feasts of Martinmas and the Nativity of St John Baptist, by equal payments. The above sum is, therefore, for the terms of Martinmas and the Nativity of St John Baptist falling within this account, being the fifth and last year of payment.[4]

12.4   And for £13 6s. 8d. received from Stephen de Kelshale and his fellows in full payment of a fine of 100 marks made by John del Gre(n)e before the said lieutenant and chamberlain. It was granted that the fine be paid within the five

1   Both John son of John de Elton and Robert son of John de Elton petitioned the Black Prince in 1357 claiming that their father had granted them his lands in Elton before his indictment for Wasteneys' death, who was himself lord of Elton (*B.P.R.*, iii. 235–36). Richard le Marshall of Ince (**12.5**) leased the lands for 70s. 0d. in 1358 (*ChRR*, p. 325). See also **14.2**.
2   Although a man of that name was fined £200 in April 1329, payable by instalments, is it likely that the fine dates from such a long time previously? (*C.C.R., 1327–30*, p. 448). Yes, since the 40s. 0d. is charged in the 1342–43 account of John Burnham as receiver of fines in Cheshire and Flintshire as 'a certain old attermination of William de Basyngwerk' (*ChAcc*, p. 116).
3   A 'William de Chaweldon', fined 20 marks for a criminal trespass, was allowed to pay by instalments of 40s. 0d. a year, 2 December (!) 1357 (*B.P.R.*, iii. 284; *ChRR*, p. 89).
4   No record of this fine has been found in the county court plea roll for 1357 (CHES 29/66).

⟨m 3⟩ {m 3}

proxime sequentes ad festa Pasche et Sancti Michelis equis portionibus per recognitionem in Scaccario Cestr' factam x die Augusti anno regni regis nunc[a] xxxj videlicet pro eisdem terminis[b] infra hunc compotum contingentibus hoc anno quinto et ultimo.

12.5   Et de x s. receptis de Ricardo le Mareschall'[c] de Ins clerico de parte xxxv s. a retro existentium de lxx s. de quadam recognitione in Scaccario Cestr' ⟨m 4⟩ facta vj die Junij anno regni regis nunc xxxij sibi atterminatis ad solvendum x s. per annum ad festa Nativitatis Sancti Johannis Baptiste et Sancti Martini equaliter[d] quousque predicti lxx s. plenarie persolvantur unde pro terminis Sancti Martini et Nativitatis Sancti Johannis Baptiste infra hunc compotum contingentibus hoc anno quinto.

12.6   Et de iiij li. receptis de Adam Mottrum de parte xxj li. xv s. viij d. a retro existentium de xxxvij li. xv s. viij d. unde xxxj li. viij s. iiij d. de remanentia compoti ipsius Ade terminati ad festum Sancti Michelis anno regni regis nunc xxix° et vj li. vij s. iiij d. de remanentia x li. a retro existentium de xl li. de fine ipsius Ade facto[e] coram Willelmo de[f] Shareshull' et sociis suis Justiciariis et cetera qui quidem xxxvij li. xv s. viij d. atterminantur eidem Ade ad solvendum iiij li. per annum ad festa Pasche et Sancti Michelis equaliter[g] per litteras domini Camerario directas dat' xij die Julij anno regni regis nunc[h] xxxj videlicet pro dictis terminis[i] infra hunc compotum contingentibus hoc anno quinto.

12.7   Et de l s. receptis de Ricardo le Parker de parte C s. aretro existentium de xx li. de quodam fine facto coram predictis locum tenente et Camerario in Comitatu tento die Martis proxime ante festum Apostolorum Simonis et Jude

a   *regni regis nunc* om. 772/3.
b   *pro terminis Pasche et Sancti Michelis* 772/4.
c   *Mareschal'* 772/4.
d   *equis portionibus* 772/4.
e   *facti* 772/4.
f   om. 772/3.
g   *per equales portiones* 772/4.
h   *regni regis nunc* om. 772/3.
i   *pro terminis Pasche et Sancti Michelis* 772/4.

years following at the feasts of Easter and Michaelmas, by equal payments, by a recognizance in the exchequer of Chester which was made 10 August in the 31st year of the reign of the present king (1357). The above sum is, therefore, for the same terms falling within this account, being the fifth and last year of payment.[1]

12.5 And for 10s. 0d. received from Richard le Mareschall of Ince, clerk, as part of 35s. 0d. in arrears of a sum of 70s. 0d. for a certain recognizance made in the exchequer of Chester 6 June, in the 32nd year of the reign of the present king (1358), which it was granted be paid at the rate of 10s. 0d. a year at the feasts of the Nativity of St John Baptist and Martinmas, by equal payments, until it be paid in full. The above sum is, therefore, for the terms of Martinmas and the Nativity of St John Baptist falling within this account, being the fifth year of payment.[2]

12.6 And for £4 received from Adam de Mottrum as part of £21 15s. 8d. in arrears of a sum of £37 15s. 8d. Of this, £31 8s. 4d. is the remainder of his account which ended at Michaelmas in the 29th year of the reign of the present king (1354–55), and the rest, that is £6 7s. 4d., is part of £10 in arrears of a fine of £40 made by Adam before William de Shareshull and his fellows, justices et cetera. It was granted that this £37 15s. 8d. be paid at the rate of £4 a year, by equal payments, at the feasts of Easter and Michaelmas, by the lord's letters directed to the chamberlain dated 12 July in the 31st year of the reign of the present king (1357). The above sum is, therefore, for the said terms falling within this account, being the fifth year of payment.[3]

12.7 And for 50s. 0d. received from Richard le Parker as part of 100s. 0d. in arrears of a fine of £20 made before the said lieutenant and chamberlain in the county court held on Tuesday before the feast of the Apostles Simon and Jude in

1 Stephen de Kelshale was a merchant and ship owner who served as sheriff of the city of Chester 1351–52. It is not clear why he and his five associates should be paying John Grene's (or Greve's) fine. The recognizance referred to, which was made by Stephen together with Thomas de Hokenhull, Adam de Moldeworth, Richard de Prestlond, Thomas son of Adam de Kelshale, and William de Teverton on 10 August 1357, was for £40 only (*ChRR*, p. 267). Perhaps 'John Grene' was the same man as 'John, late cook to Stephen de Kelshale' who, with three others, had sought sanctuary for felony in St John's church, Chester, on 15 August 1356, and escaped the same day (*B.P.R.*, iii. 274). If he surrendered to justice, and was fined, Kelshale and the others may have acted as pledges for the fine, and, upon non-payment, have been left with the responsibility for paying it.

2 He made a recognizance for 70s. 0d. for having a lease of the lands which used to belong to John de Elton of Ince (**11.5**) on 6 June 1358 (*ChRR*, p. 325).

3 Mottrum's remainder on his 1354–55 account was £40 15s. 3½d, while the 'clear remainder', after the deduction of respited amounts from the above sum, was £[36] [0]s. 9½d. A note follows to the effect that since Adam had set out for Gascony in obedience to the prince, 'ideo fiat executio de terris suis' (SC6 802/11, m.2d). On 1 October 1356 the vicar of Sandbach was granted Adam's lands in Shideyord (Macclesfield manor) for three years, for the £10 due from his account for 1354–55 (*ChRR*, p. 470). For his fine of £40 as a result of crimes of which he was found guilty in the 1353 trailbaston sessions, see *Cheshire History*, 13 (1984), pp. 27–28. Letters granting him the right to pay his debts to the prince at £4 a year, 22 (!) July 1357 (*B.P.R*, iii. 269).

⟨*m 4*⟩ {*m 3*}

anno regni regis nunc[a] xxxj et non plus eo quod predictus locum tenens recordatur per rotulos suos Comitatus Cestr' super compotum dicti Camerarij ostensos de anno xxxiij quod de predicto fine xv li. erant atterminate ad solvendum infra sex annos proxime sequentes ad festum Natalis domini et Nativitatis Sancti Johannis Baptiste per equales portiones et C s. de eodem fine atterminantur[b] eidem Ricardo ad solvendum infra quatuor annos a predicto die Martis proxime ante festum Apostolorum Simonis et Jude ad festa predicta prout ostensum est per rotulos predictos.

12.8   Et de C s. receptis de Ranulpho filio Johannis de Wetenhale in persolutionem xx li. de quodam fine facto coram prefato locum tenente in Comitatu tento die Martis proxime ante festum Sancti Luce Evangeliste anno regni regis nunc xxxij atterminato[c] eidem Ranulpho ad solvendum infra iiij annos proxime sequentes ad festa Pasche et Sancti Michelis equaliter[d] videlicet pro eisdem terminis infra hunc compotum[e] contingentibus hoc anno iiij et ultimo.[f]

12.9   Et de lxvj s. viij d. receptis de Stephano de Merton' de parte xj li. xiij s. iiij d. aretro existentium de quodam fine xx li. facto coram predictis locum tenente et Camerario pro licencia talliandi certa tenementa sua atterminato eidem Stephano ad solvendum infra sex annos proxime sequentes ad festa Sancti Michelis et Pasche equis portionibus pro quibus quidem xx li. solvendis in forma predicta Willelmus de Stanlegh' senior[g] et alij fecerunt recognitionem in Scaccario[h] Cestr' xij die Augusti anno regni regis nunc xxxiij° videlicet pro eisdem terminis infra hunc compotum contingentibus hoc anno quarto.

12.10   Et de C s. receptis de Willelmo Gerard'[i] de parte x li. a retro existentium de quodam fine xx li. facto[j] coram predictis locum tenente et Camerario pro[k] licencia talliandi certa tenementa sua atterminato eidem Willelmo ad solvendum infra quatuor annos proxime sequentes ad festa Pasche et Sancti Michelis per equales portiones primo termino solutionis incipiente in festo Pasche anno regni regis nunc xxxiiij pro quibus quidem xx li. solvendis in forma predicta predictus Willelmus et alij fecerunt recognitionem in Scaccario Cestr' xiiij die Octobris anno regni regis nunc xxxiij videlicet pro terminis Pasche et Sancti Michelis infra hunc compotum contingentibus hoc anno tertio.

a   *regni regis nunc* om. 772/3.
b   intl. 772/3.
c   *terminato* 772/3.
d   *per equales portiones* 772/4.
e   om. 772/3.
f   intl. 772/4.
g   intl. 772/4.
h   772/3 has *Sca*, del., followed by *Scaccario*.
i   *Gerad* 772/3.
j   intl. 772/3.
k   *per* 772/3.

the 31st year of the reign of the present king (24 October 1357). It would be more except that the said lieutenant puts it on record, by his rolls of the county court of Chester which were shown at the audit of the said chamberlain's account for the 33rd year (1358–59), that it had been granted that £15 of the said fine be paid within the six years following at the feasts of Christmas and the Nativity of St John Baptist, by equal payments. The other 100s. 0d. of the fine is to be paid by Richard within the four years from the said Tuesday before the feast of the Apostles Simon and Jude, at the same feasts, as is revealed by the said rolls.[1]

12.8 And for 100s. 0d. received from Ranulf son of John de Wetenhale in full payment of a fine of £20 made before the said lieutenant at the county court held on Tuesday before the feast of St Luke. evangelist, in the 32nd year of the reign of the present king (16 October 1358) which it was granted should be paid within the four years following at the feasts of Easter and Michaelmas, by equal payments. The above sum is, therefore, for the same terms falling within this account, being the fourth and last year of payment.[2]

12.9 And for 66s. 8d. received from Stephen de Merton as part of £11 13s. 4d. in arrears of a fine of £20 made before the said lieutenant and chamberlain for licence to tallage certain of his tenements. It was granted that the fine be paid within the six years following at the feasts of Michaelmas and Easter, by equal payments. William de Stanlegh the elder and others made a recognizance in the exchequer of Chester on 12 August in the 33rd year of the reign of the present king (1359) for the payment of the same £20. The above sum is, therefore, for the same terms falling within this account, being the fourth year of payment.[3]

12.10 And for 100s. 0d. received from William Gerard as part of £10 in arrears of a fine of £20 made before the said lieutenant and chamberlain for licence to tallage certain of his tenements. It was granted that the fine be paid within the four years following at the feasts of Easter and Michaelmas, by equal payments, the first term of payment being Easter in the 34th year of the reign of the present king (1360). The said William and others made a recognizance in the exchequer of Chester on 14 October in the 33rd year of the reign of the present king (1359) for the payment of the same £20. The above sum is, therefore, for the terms of Easter and Michaelmas falling within this account, being the third year of payment.[4]

1 Neither the £20 fine of Richard le Parker, nor its attermination, have been found in the county court plea roll for 1357 (CHES 29/66).
2 This fine cannot be located in the plea roll for 1358, which is badly rubbed in places (CHES 29/67).
3 No record of the licence survives. Merton held the manors of Gayton, Lach and the island of Earl's Eye (CHES 3/23 Edw. III/8). The enrolment of the recognizance is in *ChRR*, p. 443. William Stanley was a fellow landowner in Wirral, and Stephen's son, John, who seems to have predeceased his father, was married to William's daughter, Ellen Stanley; on 6 August 1359 Stephen had acquired a licence to grant part of his property to his son and daughter-in-law, and entail the rest on them (ibid., p. 342; W. Fergusson Irvine, 'The Early Stanleys', *T.H.S.L.C.*, 105 (1953), pp. 45–68). Possibly Merton and Gerard were tallaging those of their properties which were the Cheshire equivalent of 'ancient demesne' – that is, land which had once belonged to the earls of Chester.
4 Gerard held half the manor of Kingsley, the manor of Bradley (as of Frodsham manor), and the manor of Cattenhall (CHES 3/26 Edw. III/5). No record of the licence or recognizance survives.

⟨*m 4*⟩ {*m 3*}

12.11   Et de vj li. xiij s. iiij d. receptis de Ricardo Aleyn de Vico[a] Malbano et Roberto de Wilaston[b] de parte x li. a retro existentium de quodam fine xx li. facto coram predictis locum tenente et Camerario in comitatu tento die Martis in Crastino Epiphanie domini anno regni regis nunc xxxiij atterminato ad solvendum infra tres annos proxime sequentes ad festa Nativitatis Sancti Johannis Baptiste et Natalis domini per equales portiones videlicet pro terminis Natalis domini et Nativitatis Sancti Johannis Baptiste infra hunc compotum contingentibus hoc anno tertio.

12.12   Et de ix li. xvj s. iiij d. receptis de Johanne de Bromlegh' nuper Bedello hundredi Wyci Malbani in persolutionem xix li. xij s. viij d. de parte[c] xxv li. quas[d] idem Johannes debuit de remanentia firme et exituum eiusdem hundredi de anno regni regis nunc xxxiij°.

12.13   Et de xxxiij li. vj s. viij d. receptis de Willelmo filio Willelmi de Bulkylegh'[e] de Alpraham de parte iiij[xx] iij li. vj s. viij d. aretro existentium de quodam fine C li. facto coram predictis locum tenente et Camerario pro certis transgressionibus per ipsum factis infra comitatum Cestr' per litteras domini dictis locum tenenti et Camerario directas dat' quinto die Maij anno regni regis nunc xxxv penes eundem Camerarium remanentes atterminato eidem Willelmo ad solvendum infra tres annos proxime sequentes ad festa Sancti Michelis et Nativitatis Sancti Johannis Baptiste per equales portiones primo termino solutionis incipiente in festo Sancti Michelis anno supradicto et[f] pro quibus quidem C li. solvendis in forma predicta predictus Willelmus et alij fecerunt recognitionem in Scaccario Cestr' xx die Septembris anno xxxv supradicto videlicet pro terminis Nativitatis Sancti Johannis Baptiste et Sancti Michelis infra hunc compotum contingentibus hoc anno secundo.[g]

12.14   Et de x s. receptis de Johanne Danyers Chivaler et Ricardo de Whitelegh' in persolutionem cuiusdam finis xx s. facti coram predicto locum tenente in comitatu tento die Martis in vigilia Sancti Hillarij anno regni regis nunc xxxiiij atterminati ad solvendum infra duos annos proxime sequentes ad festa Annunciationis beate Marie et Sancti Michelis per equales portiones

---

a   *Wyco* 772/4.
b   *Wylaston'* 772/4.
c   *xix li. xij s. viij d. de parte* intl. 772/4; 772/4 also has *aretro existentium* between *viij d.* and *de*, which was then del.
d   *quos* 772/3.
e   *Bilkylegh'* 772/3.
f   om. 772/4.
g   intl. 772/3.

12.11 And for £6 13s. 4d. received from Richard Aleyn of Nantwich and Robert de Wilaston as part of £10 in arrears of a fine of £20 made before the said lieutenant and chamberlain at the county court held on Tuesday the morrow of the Epiphany in the 33rd year of the reign of the present king (7 January 1360). It was granted that the fine be paid within the three years following at the feasts of the Nativity of St John Baptist and Christmas, by equal payments, namely for the terms of Christmas and the Nativity of St John Baptist falling within this account, being the third year of payment.[1]

12.12 And for £9 16s. 4d. received from John de Bromlegh, who used to be bedell of Nantwich hundred, in full payment of £19 12s. 8d. which was part of £25 which he owed of the remainder of the farm and issues of that same hundred for the 33rd year of the reign of the present king (1358–59).[2]

12.13 And for £33 6s. 8d. received from William son of William de Bulkylegh of Alpraham as part of £83 6s. 8d. in arrears of a fine of £100 made before the said lieutenant and chamberlain for certain trespasses committed by him within Cheshire. It was granted by the lord's letters directed to the said lieutenant and chamberlain, dated 5 May in the 35th year of the reign of the present king (1361), which remain in the chamberlain's possession, that the fine be paid within the three years following at the feasts of Michaelmas and the Nativity of St John Baptist, by equal payments, the first term of payment being Michaelmas in the aforesaid year (1361). The said William and others made a recognizance in the exchequer of Chester on 20 September in the 35th year aforesaid (1361) for the payment of the same £100. The above sum is, therefore, for the terms of the Nativity of St John Baptist and Michaelmas falling within this account, being the second year of payment.[3]

12.14 And for 10s. 0d. received from John Danyers, knight, and Richard de Whitelegh in full payment of a fine of 20s. 0d. made before the said lieutenant at the county court held on Tuesday the vigil of St Hilary in the 34th year of the reign of the present king (12 January 1361). It was granted that the fine be paid within the two years following at the feasts of Lady Day and Michaelmas, by

---

1 In the plea roll of the county court, session of 7 January 1360, their fine is marked 'vacated', because it is in the roll for the 38th year, 1363/64 (CHES 29/67, m.36d).

2 He acted as bailiff (bedell) and farmer of Nantwich hundred from 1349 to 1355 (*ChAcc*, pp. 134, 174, 214). Granted that he should pay £5 at each county court session of the £40 he owes as bailiff, 12 November 1359 (*B.P.R.*, iii. 377). On 22 November 1360 he asked to pay the £19 12s. 8d. of arrears still outstanding, by further instalments (ibid., 397–98).

3 William son of William de Bulkylegh of Alpraham, with six others, was indicted at the county court of 2 March 1361 of breaking into the manor-house of Nether Alderley by night on Saturday 23 January 1361, and forcibly abducting Christiana, widow of John Fitton, together with Richard, John's son and heir (CHES 25/4, m.12). On 10 February 1361 the council had ordered an inquiry and the arrest of the suspects, who were said to have taken the captives to Shropshire (*B.P.R.*, iii. 404). On 5 May 1361, as a prisoner in Chester castle, Bulkylegh petitioned to be admitted to a fine and released (ibid., 417).

⟨*m 4*⟩ {*m 3*}

videlicet pro eisdem terminis infra hunc compotum contingentibus hoc anno secundo et ultimo.

12.15   Et de xl s. receptis de Ricardo de Cholmundelegh' de parte lx s. a retro existentium de quodam fine vj li. facto coram predicto locum tenente in comitatu tento die Martis in crastino Sancti Bartholomei Apostoli anno regni regis nunc xxxiiij atterminato ad solvendum ad festum Natalis domini tunc proxime sequens xl s. et ad festum Nativitatis Sancti Johannis Baptiste tunc proxime sequens xx s. et ad festum Natalis domini tunc proxime sequens xx s. et ad festum Nativitatis Sancti Johannis Baptiste tunc proxime sequens xx s. et ad festum Natalis domini extunc proxime sequens xx s.[a] videlicet pro terminis Natalis domini et Nativitatis Sancti Johannis Baptiste infra hunc compotum contingentibus.

12.16   Et de vj li. xiij s. iiij d. receptis de Ranulpho filio Ricardi de Thornton' de parte x li. a retro existentium de quodam fine xx marcarum facto coram predicto locum tenente in comitatu tento die Martis in festo Sancti Mathei Apostoli anno regni regis nunc xxxv pro morte Willelmi de Frodesham atterminato ad solvendum infra ij annos proxime sequentes ad festa Nativitatis Sancti Johannis Baptiste et Sancti Michelis equaliter[b] videlicet pro eisdem terminis infra hunc compotum contingentibus hoc anno secundo et ultimo.[c]

12.17   Et de vj li. xiij s. iiij d. receptis[d] de[e] Henrico Chany et sociis suis de parte xxiij li. vj s. viij d. a retro existentium de quodam fine xl marcarum facto coram predicto locum tenente in comitatu tento die Martis proxime post clausum pasche anno regni regis nunc xxxv atterminato ad solvendum infra iiij annos proxime sequentes ad festa Nativitatis Sancti Johannis Baptiste et Sancti Martini per equales portiones videlicet pro terminis predictis infra hunc compotum contingentibus hoc anno secundo.

a   *ad festum Nativitatis Sancti Johannis tunc proxime sequens xx s. et ad festum Natalis domini extunc proxime sequens xx s.* intl., *Baptiste* om. 772/3.
b   772/4 has the two feasts in the reverse order to that given here, and has corrected the mistake by putting *b* and *a* over each. 772/3 has the same words, written over an erasure; *per equales portiones* 772/4.
c   *et ultimo* intl. 772/4. (This appears to be a mistake, as there was one further payment to be made.)
d   om. 772/3.
e   intl. 772/3.

equal payments. The above sum is, therefore, for the same terms falling within this account, being the second and last year of payment.[1]

12.15 And for 40s. 0d. received from Richard de Cholmundelegh as part of 60s. 0d. in arrears of a fine of £6 made before the said lieutenant at the county court held on Tuesday the morrow of St Bartholomew, apostle, in the 34th year of the reign of the present king (25 August 1360). It was granted that the fine be paid in the following instalments: 40s. 0d. at Christmas following, then 20s. 0d. at the Nativity of St John Baptist after that, 20s. 0d. at the next Christmas, 20s. 0d. at the next Nativity of St John Baptist, and 20s 0d. at the next Christmas. The above sum is, therefore, for the terms of Christmas and the Nativity of St John Baptist falling within this account.[2]

12.16 And for £6 13s. 4d. received from Ranulf son of Richard de Thornton as part of £10 in arrears of a fine of 20 marks made for the death of William de Frodesham before the said lieutenant at the county court held on Tuesday the feast of St Matthew, apostle, in the 35th year of the reign of the present king (21 September 1361). It was granted that the fine be paid within the two years following at the feasts of the Nativity of St John Baptist and Michaelmas, by equal payments. The above sum is, therefore, for the same terms falling within this account, being the second and last year of payment.[3]

12.17 And for £6 13s. 4d. received from Henry Chany and his fellows as part of £23 6s. 8d. in arrears of a fine of 40 marks made before the said lieutenant at the county court held on Tuesday after the close of Easter in the 35th year of the reign of the present king (6 April 1361). It was granted that the fine be paid within the four years following at the feasts of the Nativity of St John Baptist and Martinmas, by equal payments. The above sum is, therefore, for the said terms falling within this account, being the second year of payment.[4]

1   This fine cannot be traced in the county court plea roll for 1361 (CHES 29/67). Whitelegh, who was sheriff of Cheshire from 1361 to 1367, had acquired land in Antrobus in 1357 from the duke of Lancaster, not far from Danyers' estates at Latchford, Grappenhall and Lymm. Also, Danyers had been county sheriff in 1345, while in 1357 reference was made to Whitelegh's long service under the sheriffs of Cheshire (CHES 29/65, m.10d; *B.P.R.*, iii. 285, 292–93; *ChRR*, p. 522).

2   The recognizance in the county court plea roll for 25 August 1360 gives no indication of what the fine was imposed for (CHES 29/67, m.55d). Cholmondeley was dead by 28 May 1361 (*B.P.R.*, iii. 418).

3   At the county court of 12 January 1361, the coroner of Eddisbury hundred, and the townships of Elton, Hapsford, Dunham on the Hill, and Thornton le Moors presented that Ranulf son of Richard de Thornton of Elton feloniously killed William son of Richard de Frodesham at Elton on Sunday 3 January 1361 (CHES 29/67, m.60). Ranulf did not appear in court, and was exacted for a fourth time for homicide at the county court of 27 July 1361 (CHES 29/67, m.85d). After surrendering to justice, the recognizance for his 20 marks fine was made at the 21 September 1361 county court by Ranulf, with Richard de Thornton, Richard de Hugheley (!), William de Lachecote, David de Eddeslegh, Robert de Eddeslegh, and Robert le Cartewrught (CHES 29/67, m.88d).

4   Henry Chany made the recognizance for his 40 marks fine at the county court of 6 April 1361, together with William le Criour, Robert le Cartewrught de Ashton, Robert son of John de [. . . .], [. . . .] Kelshale, William de Teverton, Thomas de Yekheth (!), Ranulf de Ousecroft, Richard de Ousecroft, [. . . .] de Duddon, William son of Hugh de Huxlegh, and Hugh son of Hugh de Tatenhale; it is marked 'liberatur scaccario' (CHES 29/67, m.75d).

⟨*m 4*⟩ {*m 3*}

12.18   Et de l s. receptis de Philippo filio Ranulphi de Eggerton' de parte iiij li. vij s. vj d. a retro existentium de quodam fine C s. facto coram predictis locum tenente et Camerario pro Rogero de Careswall' indictato pro morte Johannis Hikoc[a] atterminato eidem Philippo ad solvendum infra duos annos proxime sequentes ad festa Sancti Michelis Natalis domini Pasche et Nativitatis Sancti Johannis Baptiste equis portionibus pro quibus quidem C s. solvendis in forma predicta predictus Philippus et alij fecerunt recognitionem in Scaccario Cestr' xxvj die Junij anno regni regis nunc xxxv videlicet pro terminis Sancti Michelis Natalis domini Pasche et Nativitatis Sancti Johannis Baptiste infra hunc compotum contingentibus.

{m 4}

(*Quietus hic*) (*pro littera*)[b]

12.19   De CC marcis de quodam fine facto coram consilio domini per Johannem de Hyde Chivaler pro Willelmo filio Johannis de Hyde Johanne filio Willelmi de Hyde et Hugone Frenshegh' indictatis de morte Galfridi filij Johannis de Honford' nichil redditur Camerario eo quod dominus Princeps mandavit litteras suas dicto Camerario dat' xvj die Junij anno regni regis nunc xxxvj penes eundem Camerarium remanentes per quas mandavit eidem Camerario quod pro eo quod dictus Johannes de Hyde Chivaler satisfecit dicto domino Principi de summa pro qua sibi[c] obligatus erat in Scaccario suo Cestr' de CC marcis per recognitionem ibi factam dictam recognitionem retrahere faceret et ipsum Johannem de Hyde Chivaler de predictis CC marcis faceret exonerari.

Summa: Cvij li. xvj s. iiij d. probatur.

13.   ATTERMINATIONES NOVE DIVERSORUM COMITATUS CESTR'

(*Memorandum dimidia marca de redditu de tannatoribus in compoto vicecomitum Civitatis Cestr'ex hac causa imperpetuum*)[d]

13.1   Et de xxxiij s. iiij d. receptis de Tannatoribus Cestr' de quodam fine xx marcarum per ipsos facto domino xxiiij die Maij hoc anno ad solvendum per iiij annos ad festa Sancti Michelis et Pasche equaliter videlicet pro termino Sancti

---

a   *Hycok'* 772/4.
b   notes om. 772/3.
c   intl. 772/4.
d   note om. 772/3.

12.18   And for 50s. 0d. received from Philip son of Ranulf de Eggerton as part of £4 7s. 6d. in arrears of a fine of 100s. 0d. made before the said lieutenant and chamberlain for Roger Careswall, who was indicted for John Hikoc's death. It was granted that the fine be paid within the two years following at the feasts of Michaelmas, Christmas, Easter and the Nativity of St John Baptist by equal payments. The said Philip and others made a recognizance in the exchequer of Chester for the payment of the same 100s. 0d. on the 26 June in the 35th year of the reign of the present king (1361). The above sum is, therefore, for the terms of Michaelmas, Christmas, Easter and the Nativity of St John Baptist falling within this account.[1]

(*Quit here*) (*For a letter*)

12.19   For 200 marks being the fine made before the lord's council by John de Hyde, knight, for William, his son, John son of William de Hyde, and Hugh Frenshegh, who were indicted for Geoffrey son of John de Honford's death, nothing is rendered to the chamberlain because the prince sent his letters to the said chamberlain, dated 16 June in the 36th year of the reign of the present king (1362), and which remain in the chamberlain's possession, whereby the prince instructed the chamberlain that, as the said John de Hyde, knight, had made satisfaction to him in the matter of the sum of 200 marks in which he was bound to the prince by a recognizance made in the exchequer of Chester, that recognizance should be withdrawn and John de Hyde, knight, exonerated of the said 200 marks.[2]

Sum: £107 16s. 4d. Approved.

13.   PAYMENTS BY INSTALMENTS OF VARIOUS CHESHIRE PEOPLE – FROM THIS YEAR

(*Remember that half a mark is to be charged for the tanners' rent in the account of the sheriffs of the city of Chester for this reason in perpetuity*).

13.1   And for 33s. 4d. received from the tanners of Chester for a fine of 20 marks made with the lord by them on 24 May this year (1362) payable within four years at the feasts of Michaelmas and Easter, by equal payments. The

1   Nothing has been found about Careswall, or his offence. Presumably he had failed to pay his instalments, and so the recognizance made by Philip son of Ranulf de Eggerton, David de Overton, and Kenard de Cholmundelegh became enforceable (*ChRR*, p. 168).

2   The prince had already pardoned Hyde the whole 200 marks fine, by letters of pardon under his privy seal of 12 December 1360 (*B.P.R.*, iii. 398–99), followed by a charter of pardon under the Chester exchequer seal dated 6 October 1361 (*ChRR*, p. 258). Neither the letters of 16 June 1362, nor the recognizance survive, and may not have been either registered or enrolled. Possibly the marginal note 'Quit here' refers to the pardon, while 'For a letter' refers to the note in the Register (*B.P.R.*, iii. 450) recording the withdrawal of the recognizance, presumably in response to the letters of 16 June. See also **8.15**.

⟨m 4⟩ {m 4}

Michelis infra tempus huius[a] compoti hoc termino primo videlicet ut Sutores Cestr' non se intromittant in officio tannarie predicto.

13.2 Et[b] de vj li. xiij s. iiij d. receptis de Ricardo de[c] Mascy Chivaler in partem solutionis cuiusdam finis xx li. facti coram predictis locum tenente et Camerario atterminati ad solvendum infra tres annos proxime sequentes ad festa Pasche et Sancti Michelis per equales[d] portiones pro quibus quidem xx li. in forma predicta solvendis predictus Ricardus et alij fecerunt recognitionem in Scaccario Cestr' xv die Decembris anno regni regis nunc xxxv videlicet pro eisdem terminis infra hunc compotum contingentibus hoc anno primo.[e]

13.3 Et de lxvj s. viij d. receptis de Roberto de Legh juniore in partem solutionis cuiusdam finis C marcarum facti coram predictis locum tenente et Camerario in Comitatu Cestr' tento die Martis in Crastino Sancti Petri Advincula anno regni regis nunc xxxvj sibi atterminato ad solvendum ad festum Sancti Michelis proxime sequens lxvj s. viij d. et ad festum Sancti Martini tunc proxime sequens lxvj s. viij d. et ad festum Nativitatis Sancti Johannis Baptiste tunc[f] proxime sequens lxvj s. viij d. et sic[g] de anno in annum ad predicta festa Sancti Martini et Nativitatis Sancti Johannis Baptiste quolibet festo lxvj s. viij d. quousque predicte C marce plenarie persolvantur videlicet pro termino Sancti Michelis infra hunc compotum contingente.

13.4 Et de C s. receptis de Johanne filio Ricardi de Coton' de Cestr' in partem solutionis cuiusdam finis xx li. facti coram predictis locum tenente et Camerario in Comitatu tento die Martis supradicto sibi atterminati ad solvendum ad festum Sancti Michelis proxime sequens C s. et ad festum Pasche tunc proxime sequens

a   om. 772/4.

b   *Idem respondet de 772/4.*

c   om. 772/3.

d   772/3 has *eqal*, del., followed by *equales*.

e   772/4 follows entry **13.2** with a del. entry, with an attached note. Note: *Cancellatur hic quia in onere Escaetoris.* Entry: *Et de xij li. xiij s. iiij d. receptis de Johanne Danyers Chivaler in partem solutionis cuiusdam finis xxxij li. xiij s. iiij d. facti coram predictis locum tenente et Camerario sibi atterminati ad solvendum ad festum Sancti Thome Apostoli infra hunc compotum vj li. et ad festum Pasche tunc proxime sequens lxv s. viij d. et ad festum Sancti Michelis tunc proxime sequens lxvj s. viij d. et sic de anno in annum ad dicta festa Pasche et Sancti Michelis quolibet termino lxvj s. viij d. quousque predicti xxxij li. xiij s. iiij d. plenarie persolvantur pro quibus quidem xxxij li. vj. s. viij d. (!) in forma predicta solvendis predictus Johannes Danyers et alij fecerunt recognitionem in Scaccario Cestr' xvj die Decembris anno xxxv supradicto.* The sum of this entry is not added into the sum total for section **13**.

f   *extunc* 772/4.

g   intl. 772/3.

above sum is, therefore, for Michaelmas term falling within this account, being the first term of payment. The fine was made so that the shoemakers of Chester be prevented from taking up the trade of tanning.[1]

13.2 And for £6 13s. 4d. received from Richard de Mascy, knight, as part payment of a fine of £20 made before the said lieutenant and chamberlain which it was granted should be paid within the three years following at the feasts of Easter and Michaelmas, by equal payments. The said Richard and others made a recognizance in the exchequer of Chester on 15 December in the 35th year of the reign of the present king (1361) for the payment of the·same £20. The above sum is, therefore, for the same terms falling within this account, being the first year of payment.[2]

13.3 And for 66s. 8d. received from Robert de Legh, the younger, as part payment of a fine of 100 marks made before the said lieutenant and chamberlain at the county court held on Tuesday the morrow of St Peter in Chains in the 36th year of the reign of the present king (2 August 1362). It was granted that it be paid at the rate of 66s. 8d. at the feast of Michaelmas following, and then at Martinmas after that 66s. 8d., and at the Nativity of St John Baptist after that 66s. 8d., and so on every year, paying 66s. 8d. at the said feasts of Martinmas and the Nativity of St John Baptist until the fine be paid in full. The above sum is, therefore, for Michaelmas term falling within this account.[3]

13.4 And for 100s. 0d. received from John son of Richard de Coton of Chester, as part payment of a fine of £20 made before the said lieutenant and chamberlain at the county court held on the Tuesday abovementioned (2 August 1362). It was granted that it be paid at the rate of 100s. 0d. at the feast of Michaelmas

1 On 4 December 1361, following a petition from the tanners of Chester, the prince ordered the lieutenant and chamberlain to have letters patent made out to forbid the shoemakers of Chester to 'meddle with the craft of tanning' (*B.P.R.*, iii. 428). A charter was issued under the Chester exchequer seal on 31 March 1362, following an inquiry in the county court (*ChRR*, p. 93). The mayor and sheriffs of the city were ordered to proclaim and enforce the charter in 1363 (ibid.). Some years later the shoemakers petitioned the prince asking to be allowed to tan leather, to which the tanners counter-petitioned; an inquiry was ordered on 31 October 1364 (ibid., p. 472). On 21 November 1365, following a further petition, the prince sent an order to the mayor and sheriffs of Chester which reinforced the 1361 charter and ordered an inquiry into those shoemakers who had infringed it (ibid., p. 486). The 6s. 8d. rent of the tanners, 'paid to exclude the shoemakers from the art of tanning', was first charged in the city sheriffs' account for 1362–63 (SC6 786/1, m.1). See **16.1**, below, for the fee for sealing the charter.

2 No direct evidence has so far been found for this fine. Mascy, described as a knight, together with his brother John, parson of Sefton (Lancashire), William de Maynwaring, and John de Leycestre made a recognizance to the prince for £20 on 15 December 1361 (*ChRR*, p. 328). A warrant to arrest the two brothers had been issued the previous 15 August, because of the violence they were accused of employing against Sir William de Carynton, in connection with the dispute that Sir William was waging against Jordan de Bowedon (**13.10**) and others over a forged charter relating to Ashton; this may have resulted in the fine (CHES 29/67, m.112d). See also **45.10**.

3 Robert de Legh the younger, Thomas de Wetenhale, Thomas de Mascy and Adam de Kyngeslegh, clerk, made a recognizance in the county court of 2 August 1362 for a fine of 100 marks, 'the reason for which appears in the roll of fines of that county' (CHES 29/67, m.118).

⟨*m 4*⟩ {*m 4*}

C s. et[a] ad festum Sancti Michelis tunc proxime sequens C s. et ad festum Pasche tunc[b] proxime sequens C s. videlicet pro termino Sancti Michelis infra hunc compotum contingente.

13.5   Et de l s. receptis de Roberto Goodmon in partem solutionis cuiusdam finis x li. facti coram predictis locum tenente et Camerario in Comitatu tento die Martis supradicto sibi atterminati ad solvendum ad festum Sancti Michelis proxime sequens l s. et ad festum Pasche tunc proxime sequens l s. et ad festum Sancti Michelis tunc proxime sequens l s. et ad festum Pasche tunc[c] proxime sequens l s. videlicet pro termino Sancti Michelis infra hunc compotum contingente.

13.6   Et de l s. receptis de Thoma de Clyve in partem solutionis cuiusdam finis x li. facti coram predictis locum tenente et Camerario in Comitatu tento die Martis supradicto sibi atterminati ad solvendum ad festum Sancti Michelis tunc proxime sequens l s. et ad festum Pasche tunc proxime sequens l s. et ad festum Sancti Michelis tunc proxime sequens l s. et ad festum Pasche tunc[d] proxime sequens l s. videlicet pro termino Sancti Michelis infra hunc compotum contingente.

13.7   Et de viij li. receptis de Ranulpho le Roter in partem solutionis cuiusdam finis Cx li. facti coram predictis locum tenente et Camerario die et anno supradictis videlicet pro fine suo proprio et iiij[or] hominum suorum pro vi et auxilio mortis Roberti de Frodesham atterminati eidem Ranulpho ad solvendum ad festa Sancti Michelis et Pasche proxime sequentia primo anno xxiiij marcas per equales portiones et quolibet anno vj annorum proxime sequentium ad eadem festa xxiij marcas et di. videlicet pro termino Sancti Michelis infra hunc compotum contingente.[e]

a   om. 772/3.
b   *extunc* 772/4.
c   *extunc* 772/4.
d   *extunc* 772/4.
e   intl. 772/4.

following, and then at Easter after that 100s. 0d., and then at Michaelmas after that 100s. 0d., and then at Easter after that 100s. 0d. The above sum is, therefore, for Michaelmas term falling within this account.[1]

13.5 And for 50s. 0d. received from Robert Goodmon, as part payment of a fine of £10 made before the said lieutenant and chamberlain at the county court held on the Tuesday abovementioned (2 August 1362). It was granted that it be paid at the rate of 50s. 0d. at the feast of Michaelmas following, and then at Easter after that 50s. 0d., and at the feast of Michaelmas after that 50s. 0d., and at Easter after that 50s. 0d. The above sum is, therefore, for Michaelmas term falling within this account.[2]

13.6 And for 50s. 0d. received from Thomas de Clyve, as part payment of a fine of £10 made before the said lieutenant and chamberlain at the county court held on the Tuesday abovementioned (2 August 1362). It was granted that it be paid at the rate of 50s. 0d. at the feast of Michaelmas following, and at Easter after that 50s. 0d., and at the feast of Michaelmas after that 50s. 0d., and at Easter after that 50s. 0d. The above sum is, therefore, for Michaelmas term falling within this account.[3]

13.7 And for £8 received from Ranulf le Roter, as part payment of a fine of £110, made before the said lieutenant and chamberlain on the day and year abovementioned (2 August 1362) namely for his own fine and for that of four of his men for giving forcible assistance with the killing of Robert de Frodesham. It was granted that these fines be paid by Ranulf at the feasts of Michaelmas and Easter following at the rate of 24 marks by equal payments in the first year, and then 23½ marks in each of the six years after that. The above sum is, therefore, for Michaelmas term falling within this account.[4]

1 John son of Richard de Coton of Chester, Ralph (parson of Plemstall), Thomas de Apelton of Chester, and John Adamesone of Chester made a recognizance in the county court of 2 August 1362 for a fine of £20, 'the reason for which appears in the roll of fines of that county' (CHES 29/67, m.118). A 'John Coton' served as one of the Chester city sheriffs, 1364–65 (SC6 786/4, m.1).

2 Robert Godmon, Edmund de Coton and Philip Filkyn made a recognizance for a fine of £10 on 2 August 1362 (CHES 29/67, m.118).

3 Thomas Clyve, Richard le Parker, John le Parker, Robert le Bailly de Eyton, John de Overton, David le Bailly, William son of Stephen le Parker, Thomas son of Nicholas de Wetenhale, William de Bulkylegh de Torperlegh, Thomas Water, Richard Filcok, Henry Doddok, Henry Pook, Robert Strech, Laurence de Kirkham, Richard de Pyrye and William le Sheremon made a recognizance for £10 in the county court of 2 August 1362 (CHES 29/67, m.118).

4 At the county court of 7 June 1362, the coroner of Eddisbury hundred and the townships of Kingsley, Norley, Alvanley and Helsby presented that William son of John de Bunbury, servant of David de Bostok, killed Robert de Frodesham at Newton on Friday 29 April 1362 and fled. Forcible help was given him by Ranulf le Roter the younger, David de Bostok, Thomas de Clyve, Robert Phelip of Kingeslegh, David le Sumpter of Munshull, Richard de Bostok, Henry Brokesmouth and Peter le Roter (CHES 29/67, m.115d). The recognizance for the fine was made by Ranulf le Roter, William de Bostok, Thomas de Whelok the elder, William le Roter (parson of Handley), Ughtred de Huxelegh, William de Caurthyn, Sir William de Brerton, Robert Foukesson de Haselwall, William de Larketon, Philip Fylkyn and Ken' del Lee (CHES 29/67, m.118).

⟨m 5⟩ {*m 4*}

13.8   Et de l s. receptis de David de Bostok' in partem solutionis cuiusdam finis xx li. facti coram[a] predictis locum tenente et Camerario predictis die et anno sibi[b] atterminati ad solvendum infra quatuor annos proxime sequentes ad festa Sancti Michelis et Pasche per equales portiones videlicet pro termino Sancti Michelis infra hunc compotum contingente.

13.9   Et de vj li. xiij s. iiij d. receptis de Johanne Godynogh' in partem solutionis cuiusdam finis xl li. facti coram predictis locum tenente et Camerario die et anno supradictis sibi atterminati ad solvendum infra tres annos proxime sequentes ad festa Sancti Michelis et Pasche per equales portiones videlicet pro dicto[c] termino Michelis infra hunc compotum contingente.

13.10   Et de xxxiij s. iiij d. receptis de Jordano de Boudon' in partem solutionis cuiusdam finis x li. facti coram predictis locum tenente et Camerario in Comitatu tento die Martis in septimana Pentecostes anno regni regis nunc xxxvj sibi atterminati ad solvendum infra duos annos proxime sequentes ad[d] festa Sancti Michelis et Pasche per equales portiones videlicet pro dicto termino Sancti Michelis[e] infra hunc compotum contingente.

13.11   Et de xxxiij s. iiij d. receptis de Johanne filio Johannis de Boudon' in partem solutionis cuiusdam finis x li. facti coram predictis locum tenente et Camerario dicto die Martis sibi atterminati ad solvendum infra duos annos proxime sequentes ad festa Sancti Michelis et Pasche per equales portiones videlicet pro eodem termino[f] Sancti[g] Michelis infra hunc compotum contingente.

13.12   Et de xvj s. viij d.[h] receptis de Hugone le Walker in partem solutionis cuiusdam finis C s. facti coram predictis locum tenente et Camerario predicto die Martis sibi atterminati ad solvendum infra tres annos proxime sequentes ad festa Sancti Michelis et Pasche per equales portiones videlicet pro eodem termino Michelis[i] infra hunc compotum contingente.

a   om. 772/3.
b   om. 772/3.
c   intl. 772/3.
d   *a* 772/3.
e   intl. 772/4.
f   772/4 has *eisdem terminis*, del., followed by *eodem termino*, intl.
g   om. 772/4.
h   *viij d.* intl. 772/3.
i   om. 772/3; 772/4 has *eisdem terminis*, del., followed by *eodem termino* intl.

13.8 And for 50s. 0d. received from David de Bostok, as part payment of a fine of £20 made before the said lieutenant and chamberlain on the day and year aforesaid. It was granted that it be paid within the four years following at the feasts of Michaelmas and Easter, by equal payments. The above sum is, therefore, for Michaelmas term falling within this account.[1]

13.9 And for £6 13s. 4d. received from John Godynogh, as part payment of a fine of £40 made before the said lieutenant and chamberlain on the day and year abovementioned. It was granted that it be paid within the three years following at the feasts of Michaelmas and Easter, by equal payments. The above sum is, therefore, for the said Michaelmas term falling within this account.[2]

13.10 And for 33s. 4d. received from Jordan de Boudon, as part payment of a fine of £10 made before the said lieutenant and chamberlain at the county court held on Tuesday in Whit week in the 36th year of the reign of the present king (7 June 1362). It was granted that it be paid within the two years following at the feasts of Michaelmas and Easter, by equal payments. The above sum is, therefore, for the said Michaelmas term falling within this account.[3]

13.11 And for 33s. 4d. received from John son of John de Boudon, as part payment of a fine of £10 made before the said lieutenant and chamberlain on the said Tuesday (7 June 1362). It was granted that it be paid within the two years following, at the feasts of Michaelmas and Easter, by equal payments. The above sum is, therefore, for the same Michaelmas term falling within this account.[4]

13.12 And for 16s. 8d. received from Hugh le Walker, as part payment of a fine of 100s. 0d. made before the said lieutenant and chamberlain on the aforesaid Tuesday (7 June 1362). It was granted that it be paid within the three years following at the feasts of Michaelmas and Easter, by equal payments. The above sum is, therefore, for the same Michaelmas term falling within this account.[5]

1 See above, p. 43 n.4. David de Bostok and William de Bostok made a recognizance for £20 for David's fine, indicted of Robert de Frodesham's death, at the county court of 29 March 1362 (CHES 29/67, m.121).
2 John Godynough and William de Bostok made a recognizance for £40, John's fine for the death of Robert de Frodesham, as in p. 43 n.4.
3 Jordan de Boudon, Richard de Hale and John son of John de Boudon made a recognizance for £10 in the county court of 7 June 1362 (CHES 29/67, m.115; see note 4, below).
4 John son of John de Boudon, Jordan de Boudon and Richard de Hale made a recognizance for £10 in the county court of 7 June 1362 (CHES 29/67, m.115). The fines of Jordan (**13.10**), John (**13.11**), and Hugh le Walker (**13.12**) were possibly the result of their being found guilty in the county court of 26 April 1362 of forging a title-deed in the name of Sir William de Caryngton's great-grandfather relating to land in Ashton on Wednesday 28 May 1354, and subsequently pleading the deed in an assize of *novel disseisin* (CHES 29/67, m.112d). For the consequent campaign of violence against Sir William, see **Sir Richard de Mascy of Tatton**, in the biographical Appendix. **13.10** and **13.11** appear to assume fines paid over *three* years, not two.
5 Hugh le Walker, John de Aldecroft, John le Walker, Robert le Walker, Richard le Criour de Modburlegh and Thomas le Baroun de Capesthorn made a recognizance for 100s. 0d. in the county court of 7 June 1362 (CHES 29/67, m.115). For Hugh's involvement in the forging of the Ashton deed, see note 4 above.

⟨*m 5*⟩ {*m 4*}

13.13   Et de^a vj li. xiij s. iiij d. receptis de Johanne Danyers Chivaler et sociis suis in partem solutionis cuiusdam finis xx marcarum facti coram predictis locum tenente et Camerario in Comitatu tento die Martis proxime post festum Epiphanie domini anno regni regis nunc xxxv^{to} pro Thoma de Merbury indictato de combustione molendini David Pynk' sibi atterminati ad solvendum infra duos annos proxime sequentes ad festa Nativitatis Sancti Johannis Baptiste et Sancti Michelis per equales portiones videlicet pro eisdem terminis hoc anno primo. (*Respondeat Camerario anno futuro de xxx li. de fine Willelmi de Lauton'*)^b

13.14   Et de C s. receptis de Jordano de Hethylegh' et sociis suis in partem solutionis cuiusdam finis x li. facti coram predictis locum tenente et Camerario in Comitatu tento die Martis in Crastino Sancte Lucie Virginis anno regni regis nunc xxxv^{to} pro^c Willelmo filio Jordani de Hethylegh' et Alexandro fratre eius indictatis de morte Ricardi de Pekton' sibi atterminati ad solvendum infra duos annos proxime sequentes ad festa Pasche et Sancti Michelis equis portionibus videlicet pro eisdem terminis hoc anno primo.

Summa: liiij li. xiij s. iiij d. probatur^d

14.   ATTERMINATIONES FINIUM PRO PACE FRACTA

14.1   Idem respondet de xxvj s. viij d. receptis de Roberto de Shryggelegh' uno quatuor manucaptorum Roberti de Foxwyst' de pace ferenda sub pena xl li. de parte liij s. iiij d. aretro existentium de x li. apportionatis ad solvendum per predictum Robertum de Shryggelegh' per quandam recognitionem coram Justiciario Cestr' factam in Itinere suo apud Macclesf' tento die lune proxime post festum^e Sancti Johannis ante Portam Latinam^f anno regni regis nunc xxx ad

---

a   om. 772/3.
b   note del. 772/4, om. 772/3.
c   *per* 772/3.
d   om. 772/3.
e   772/3 has *festum*, del., followed by *festum*.
f   772/3 follows *Latinam* with *anno*, rep.

13.13 And for £6 13s. 4d. received from John Danyers, knight, and his fellows, as part payment of a fine of 20 marks made before the said lieutenant and chamberlain at the county court held on Tuesday after the feast of the Epiphany in the 35th year of the reign of the present king (11 January 1362). This fine was made in respect of Thomas de Merbury who was indicted for the arson of David Pynk's mill, and it was granted that it be paid within the two years following at the feasts of the Nativity of St John Baptist and Michaelmas, by equal payments. The above sum is, therefore, for the same terms, this being the first year of payment.[1]

(*Let him answer to the chamberlain in a future year for the £30 of William de Lauton's fine*).

13.14 And for 100s. 0d. received from Jordan de Hethylegh and his fellows, as part payment of a fine of £10 made before the said lieutenant and chamberlain at the county court held on Tuesday the morrow of St Lucy, virgin, in the 35th year of the reign of the present king (14 December 1361). This fine was made in respect of William son of Jordan de Hethylegh and Alexander, his brother, who were indicted for killing Richard de Pekton, and it was granted that it be paid within the two years following at the feasts of Easter and Michaelmas by equal payments. The above sum is, therefore, for the same terms, this being the first year of payment.[2]

Sum: £54 13s. 4d. Approved.

14. INSTALMENTS OF FINES FOR BREACH OF THE PEACE

14.1 He answers for 26s. 8d. received from Robert de Shryggelegh, one of Robert de Foxwyst's four mainpernors to keep the peace on pain of £40, as part of 53s. 4d. in arrears of £10. Robert de Shryggelegh was to pay the £10 in instalments, as is contained in a recognizance made before the justiciar of Chester in his eyre at Macclesfield held on Monday after the feast of St John

---

1 David Pynk accused Thomas son of Ranulf de Marbury of arson of his windmill at Higher Walton at the county court of 14 December 1361; the accusation was repeated at the county court of 11 January 1362, when the fine was imposed (CHES 29/67, mm.92d, 96).

2 Jordan de Hethylegh, William son of Robert de Hulme and Henry son of Thomas de Torkington made a recognizance in the county court of 14 December 1361 for the £10 fine of William son of Jordan de Hethylegh and Alexander, his brother, indicted for the death of Richard de Pecton (CHES 29/67, m.95). The two accused had been exacted a fourth time at the county court of 26 October 1361 (CHES 29/67, m.91).

The note placed in the margin of entry **13.14**, cancelled in 772/4 and omitted from 772/3, does not appear to relate to it, or to any immediately adjacent entry. William de Lauton was pardoned 10 marks of his £30 fine for felony on 24 April 1363 (*B.P.R.*, iii. 455). This date was only a month after the audit of the 1361–62 account, when the clerks may well have been completing their work in Cheshire, and one of them added the note to the wrong document.

⟨*m 5*⟩ {*m 4*}

solvendum quolibet anno xxvj s. viij d. ad festa Nativitatis Sancti Johannis Baptiste et Sancti Martini equis portionibus[a] videlicet pro terminis Sancti Martini et Nativitatis Sancti Johannis Baptiste infra hunc compotum contingentibus hoc anno septimo.

14.2 Et de lxvj s. viij d. receptis de Thoma[b] de Elton' et Willelmo de Wystanesfeld' manucaptoribus Henrici del Shore de pace ferenda sub pena xx marcarum de parte C s. aretro existentium de predictis xx marcis et x marcis de catallis[c] Johannis de Elton' domino Comiti Forisfactis pro morte Willelmi Wasteneys que quidem xx marce atterminantur eisdem Thome et Willelmo per quandam recognitionem coram predicto Justiciario factam in Comitatu tento die Martis proxime post festum Sancte Trinitatis anno regni regis nunc xxxj ad solvendum infra sex annos proxime sequentes ad festa Nativitatis Sancti Johannis Baptiste et Sancti Martini equis portionibus videlicet pro eisdem terminis infra hunc compotum contingentibus hoc anno sexto.

(*pro fine[d] tannatorum*)[e]

Summa: iiij li. xiij s. iiij d.

15. ATTERMINATIONES FINIUM CORAM WILLELMO DE SHARESHULL'

Et de vj li. xiij s. iiij d. receptis de Johanne de Wetenhale plegio Alexandri Deneys de parte xx marcarum aretro existentium de iiij^xx xiij li. vj s. viij d. de fine ipsius Alexandri facto coram Willelmo de Shareshull' et sociis suis Justiciariis domini apud Cestr' ad diversas felonias et transgressiones ibidem audiendas et terminandas assignatis die lune proxime post festum Assumptionis beate Marie anno regni regis nunc xxvij atterminato eidem Johanni ad solvendum infra sex annos proxime sequentes ad festa Pasche et Sancti Michelis equaliter per litteras domini Camerario directas quarum datum est apud London' secundo die Novembris anno regni regis nunc[f] xxxj° supra compotum dicti Camerarij de

---

a   772/3 follows *portionibus* with *xxx ad solvendum quolibet xxvj s. viij d. ad festa Nativitatis Sancti Johannis Baptiste et Sancti Martini equis portionibus*, intl.
b   772/4 has *de Thoma*, del., followed by *de Thoma*.
c   *de catallis* intl. 772/3.
d   *finis* 772/3.
e   note del. 772/4. This note does not seem to relate to its adjacent paragraph.
f   intl. 772/4.

before the Latin Gate in the 30th year of the reign of the present king (9 May 1356), at the rate of 26s. 8d. a year at the feasts of the Nativity of St John Baptist and Martinmas, by equal payments. The above payment is, therefore, for the terms of Martinmas and the Nativity of St John Baptist falling within this account, being the seventh year of payment.[1]

14.2   And for 66s. 8d. received from Thomas de Elton and William de Wystanesfeld, mainpernors of Henry del Shore to keep the peace on pain of 20 marks, as part of 100s. 0d. in arrears of that sum and of 10 marks for the chattels of John de Elton which were forfeited to the earl for William Wasteneys' death. It was granted that the 20 marks be paid by Thomas and William by a recognizance made before the said justiciar at the county court held on Tuesday after the feast of the Holy Trinity in the 31st year of the reign of the present king (6 June 1357), within the six years following, at the feasts of the Nativity of St John Baptist and Martinmas, by equal payments. The above sum is, therefore, for the same terms falling within this account, being the sixth year of payment.[2]
(for the tanners' fine)[3]

Sum: £4 13s. 4d.

15.   INSTALMENTS OF FINES BEFORE WILLIAM DE SHARESHULL

And for £6 13s. 4d. received from John de Wetenhale, pledge of Alexander Deneys, as part of 20 marks in arrears of £93 6s. 8d., which was the fine Alexander made before William de Shareshull and his fellows, who were assigned as the lord's justices at Chester to hear and determine various felonies and trespasses on Monday after the feast of the Assumption in the 27th year of the reign of the present king (19 August 1353). It was granted that this fine be paid within the six years following at the feasts of Easter and Michaelmas, by equal payments, by the lord's letters directed to the chamberlain, dated at London 2 November in the 31st year of the reign of the present king (1357)

---

1   Foxwist's fine, together with the recognizance for £40, appears to have been for an unlicensed alienation which, so Foxwist claimed, was alleged through malice by his enemies. Only two pledges are named in the recognizance – Hugh de Foxwist and Robert de Worth – who, when they heard that Foxwist was planning to flee the county, arranged for him to be arrested. Foxwist responded by killing the arresting officer and taking to flight (*B.P.R.*, iii. 172–73).
2   The amount of money recorded in the recognizance made by Thomas de Elton and William de Whistansfeld in the county court session of 6 June 1357 has disappeared because of a defect in the roll (CHES 29/66, m.134). See p. 26 n.h, **11.5**.
3   This marginal note appears to have been another misplaced jotting. See p. 41 n.1, **16.1** for the charter of the tanners of Chester.

⟨m 5⟩ {m 4}
eodem anno liberatas videlicet pro eisdem terminis infra hunc compotum contingentibus hoc anno quinto.

Summa: vj li. xiij s. iiij d.

{m 5}

16.   EXITUS FEODI SIGILLI

(*Memorandum quod concessio in ista parte est libertas et non calumpniatur pro magno feodo sigilli domini et cetera. Respondeat*)
16.1   Et de xvj s. iiij d. receptis de Tannatoribus Civitatis Cestr' pro parvo feodo sigilli domini cuiusdam carte per quam dominus Princeps concessit eis quod nullus Sutorum in eadem Civitate nec per se nec per alium nec aliquis alius nisi eidem officio tannarie infra dictam Civitatem et nulli alteri officio ibidem intendere voluerit de cetero se[a] intromittat in officio tannarie predicte per finem xx marcarum unde Camerarius respondet superius[b] et per litteras domini Johanni de Delves locum tenenti Justiciarij Cestr' et Camerario directas dat' apud Berkhampsted'[c] iiij die Decembris anno regni regis nunc xxxv et penes eundem Camerarium remanentes.
(*videatur si escaetor fuit oneratus de exitibus et cetera et quo Warranto deliberavit tenementa*)[d]
16.2   Et de xvj s. iiij d. receptis de Thoma de Wetenhale de consimili feodo cuiusdam carte per quam dominus Princeps perdonavit Ranulpho de Becheton' persone ecclesie de Wodechirch' et Willelmo de Blaken capellanis transgres-

---

a   772/3 has *non*, del., followed by *se*, intl.
b   intl. 772/4.
c   *Berkhameford'* 772/4.
d   note om. 772/3.

which were handed over at the audit of the chamberlain's account for the same year (1356–57). The above sum is, therefore, for the same terms falling within this account, being the fifth year of payment.[1]

Sum: £6 13s. 4d.

16. ISSUES OF THE FEE OF THE SEAL[2]

(*Remember that the grant in this entry is a liberty, and that the great fee of the lord's seal is not claimed et cetera. Let him answer.*)[3]

16.1 And for 16s. 4d. received from the tanners of the city of Chester for the small fee of the lord's seal in respect of a charter by which the prince granted them that no shoemaker in that same city, neither by himself nor by another, or any other man, should in future intrude himself into the tanning trade, unless he be willing to apply himself to that same trade within the said city and to no other. For this charter they owe a fine of 20 marks, for which the chamberlain answers above, which was granted by the lord's letters sent to John de Delves, lieutenant-justiciar of Chester, and the chamberlain, dated at Berkhamsted 4 December in the 35th year of the reign of the present king (1361) and which remain in the chamberlain's possession.[4]

(*Let it be seen whether the escheator was charged for the issues et cetera, and by what warrant he has delivered the tenements*).

16.2 And for 16s. 4d. received from Thomas de Wetenhale for the same fee in respect of a charter by which the prince has pardoned Ranulf de Becheton, parson of Woodchurch, and William de Blaken, chaplains, the trespass which

1 Deneys withdrew from the trailbaston sessions held before Sir William Shareshull in 1353, for which he suffered a forfeiture of £40 and agreed a fine of £53 6s. 8d., for unspecified offences. John de Wetenhale, Robert Proudeglove of Congleton, Thomas de Becheton, William son of William del Yate of Congleton, John son of William de Morton, Roger son of Ranulf de Morton of Congleton, John de Knotesford of Chester and William de Wasteneys made a recognizance for the whole sum on 12 December 1353 (*ChRR*, ii. 144). Deneys was dead by 8 October 1354, and Robert Proudeglove, as one of the pledges for the fine, was having legal action taken against him for its recovery before 8 June 1357 (*B.P.R.*, iii. 178–79, 250). On 2 December 1357, John de Wetenhale was allowed to pay by instalments of 10 marks a year the £46 of Deneys' fine for which he had pledged (ibid., 284).
2 The practice of taking a fee from those receiving charters granted under the Chester exchequer seal was first established in 1348. The fee was, at first, 16s. 4d. for all charters. From 1354 a 'great fee' was taken for certain charters (*V.C.H.*, ii. 19).
3 Two 'great fees' were charged in the chamberlain's account for 1354–55. One was the charter to the city of Chester of 1354, the other a charter granting free warren to Sir Hugh de Venables, baron of Kinderton. In both cases, the fee was £7 11s. 8d., although the citizens of Chester had theirs reduced by half. Such fees were separate from the fines paid for the charters in question (*ChAcc*, pp. 210, 227). A further 'great fee' of £7 11s. 8d. was charged for the 'common charter of liberty' granted to the community of the county in 1353 – that is, the charter whereby the prince postponed the general eyre – in the 1356–57 account [mistakenly dated 1357–58 in *ChAcc*, p. 240] (SC6 771/21, m.5).
4 For the charter, and its associated fine, see **13.1** and p. 41 n.1.

⟨m 5⟩ {m 5}
sionem quam fecerunt in adquirendo sibi et heredibus suis de Johanne de
Wetenhale de Derfold' xviij^{am} partem Baronie Wici^a Malbani et alia tenementa
in eadem carta contenta sine aliquo fine inde solvendo per litteras domini
predictis^b locum tenenti et Camerario et Escaetori directas dat' apud
Kenyngton'^c xxj die Decembris anno regni regis nunc xxxv penes eundem
Camerarium remanentes.

16.3 Et de xvj s. iiij d. receptis de Willelmo de Hallu' de consimili feodo
cuiusdam carte per quam dominus Princeps perdonavit eidem^d transgressionem
quam fecit eidem domino Principi in adquirendo sibi ad terminum vite sue de
Henrico Duce Lanc' quandam annuitatem x marcarum exeuntem de Manerio de
Halton' sine licencia predicti domini Principis per finem xx marcarum unde
Adam de Kyngeslegh' Escaetor Cestres'^e respondet in compoto suo de hoc
anno.

Summa: xlix s.

17. EXITUS ESCAETORIE CESTRIS'

17.1 Et de xj li. xij s. j d. ob. receptis de Thoma de Swetenham Escaetore
Comitatuum Cestr' et Flynt' de exitibus ballive sue de^f hoc anno.

17.2 Et de Clxxiij li. xix s. iiij d. ob. receptis de Adam de Kyngeslegh'
Escaetore eorundem Comitatuum de exitibus ballive sue de^g hoc anno tam per
manus eiusdem Ade quam per manus diversorum.

17.3 Et de xv li. xix s. j d. receptis de pretio diversorum bonorum et catallorum
que fuerunt Thome le Yong' nuper Escaetoris Cestris'.

Summa: CCj li. x s. vij d. probatur

a   *Wyci* 772/4.
b   772/3 has *predictas*, del., followed by *predictis*, intl.
c   *Kenynton'* 772/4.
d   *ei* 772/4.
e   *Cestris'* 772/4.
f   om. 772/4.
g   om. 772/4.

they committed in acquiring to themselves and their heirs an eighteenth part of Nantwich barony and other tenements mentioned in that same charter from John de Wetenhale of Dorfold, without any fine having to be paid for it. This pardon was granted by the lord's letters directed to the said lieutenant and chamberlain and to the escheator, dated at Kennington 21 December in the 35th year of the reign of the present king (1361), which remain in the chamberlain's possession.[1]

16.3 And for 16s. 4d. received from William de Hallum for the same fee in respect of a charter by which the prince has pardoned him the trespass which he committed against the prince in acquiring to himself from Henry, duke of Lancaster, an annuity for the term of his life of 10 marks charged on the revenue of Halton manor, without the prince's licence. The pardon was granted in return for a fine of 20 marks for which Adam de Kyngeslegh, escheator of Cheshire, answers in his account for this year.[2]

Sum: 49s. 0d.

17. ISSUES OF THE ESCHEATRY OF CHESHIRE

17.1 And for £11 12s. 1½d. received from Thomas de Swetenham,[3] escheator of the counties of Chester and Flint, for the issues of his bailiwick for this year.
17.2 And for £173 19s. 4½d. received from Adam de Kyngeslegh, escheator of the same counties, for the issues of his bailiwick for this year both by his own hands and those of various other people.[4]
17.3 And for £15 19s. 1d. received as the price of various goods and chattels which used to belong to Thomas le Yong, former escheator of Cheshire.[5]

Sum: £201 10s. 7d. Approved.

1   On 21 December 1361 a writ to the lieutenant, chamberlain and escheator ordered an inquiry into whether John de Wetenhale of Dorfold (the father of Thomas) died seised of one-eighteenth part of the barony of Nantwich and other properties, whether he was of sound mind when he demised them to Randolf of Bechynton (parson of Woodchurch) and William de Blaken, chaplains, and whether this was done to deprive the prince of his rights of wardship and marriage – if so, charters of pardon were to be granted to the two feoffees. The inquiry was held at the county court of 29 March 1362, which found that Wetenhale did not die seised, that he was of sound mind when he delivered seisin, that the seisin was made in good faith and without collusion, and not to deprive the prince of his rights (CHES 29/67 m.105; *ChRR*, p. 518). The date given in the account is that of the writ ordering the inquiry, as the pardon was granted 2 April 1362 (*ChRR*, p. 519).
2   The pardon is enrolled in *ChRR*, p. 214.
3   Swettenham was deputy to Thomas Young, and took over as escheator following Young's death, from Mich. to 4 December 1361, when he was succeeded by Kyngeslegh. It was Swettenham who rendered Young's last account as escheator, that for 1360–61, on 12 May 1362, as 'clerk of the escheator' (SC6 785/8, m.8; 785/9, m.7).
4   Kyngeslegh's escheator's account, 4 December 1361 to Mich. 1362 (SC6 785/9, m.7).
5   The forfeiture of goods after the death of officials who died indebted to the prince indicates the full implementation of the doctrine of strict personal responsibility of accountants.

⟨m 5⟩ {m 5}

18. EXITUS TERRARUM QUE FUERUNT JOHANNIS DE SANCTO PETRO

Et de Clv li. xiij s. iiij d. receptis de Johanne le Clerc' de Brundelegh' Receptore exituum terrarum et tenementorum que fuerunt Johannis de Sancto Petro Militis infra Comitatum Cestr' in partem solutionis eorundem exituum tam per manus eiusdem Johannis quam per manus diversorum de^a hoc anno.

Summa: Clv li. xiij s. iiij d.

19. EXITUS VILLARUM ET MANERIORUM^b COMITATUS DE FLYNT'

19.1 Et de xiiij s.^c viij d. receptis de Reginaldo^d Balle Parcario Parci de Loytcoide^e pro bosco vento prostrato in eodem parco per eum vendito hoc anno.
19.2 Et de vij li. vj s. vij d. receptis de Willelmo Trussell' Chivaler de firma ville de Eulowe de hoc anno de terminis Pasche et Sancti Michelis infra hunc compotum contingentibus.
19.3 Et de vj li. xiij s. iiij d. receptis de eodem Willelmo per manus Ith' ap Bleth' ap Ith' de firma carbonum maritimorum hoc anno apud Eulowe dimissorum eidem Ith' pro x marcis per annum tam in terris dominicis domini Principis ibidem quam in terris que fuerunt Bleth' ap Ith' Anuell'^f nuper seisitis in manus dicti domini Principis.
19.4 Et de xlj li. xj s. vj d. receptis de Willelmo le^g Fissher et Ken' de Fakenhale ballivis ville de Flynt' de exitibus ballive sue de^h hoc anno.
19.5 Et de iiij li. v s. x d. receptis de Jeuan Bongam et Ith' ap Bleth' Ballivis ville de Colshull' de exitibus ballive sue deⁱ hoc anno.^j
19.6 Et de xvj li. receptis de Ken' ap Roppert' et Eden'^k ap Jeuan Ballivis ville de Cayrus de firma placitorum et perquisitionum Curie eiusdem ville cum molendin(o) ibidem hoc anno.
19.7 Et de Cj s. ix d. receptis de Willelmo de Heton' Ballivo ville de Baghegre de firma molendinorum ibidem hoc anno.

a   om. 772/3.
b   772/4 has *EXITUS MANERIORUM ET VILLARUM* . . .
c   *xiij s. viij d.* 772/3.
d   *Rign'* 772/3.
e   *Loytcoyd* 772/4.
f   *Annuel'* 772/4.
g   om. 772/3.
h   om. 772/4.
i   om. 772/4.
j   *de hoc anno* intl. 772/3.
k   *Edden'* 772/4.

18. ISSUES OF THE LANDS WHICH USED TO BELONG TO JOHN DE SANCTO PETRO

And for £155 13s. 4d. received from John le Clerc of Brindley, receiver of the issues of the lands and tenements within Cheshire which used to belong to John de Sancto Petro, knight, in part payment of the same issues by the hands of both the same John and those of various other people, for this year.[1]

Sum: £155 13s. 4d.

19. ISSUES OF THE TOWNS AND MANORS OF THE COUNTY OF FLINT

19.1 And for 14s. 8d. received from Reginald Balle, parker of Llwydcoed park, for wind-fallen wood sold by him this year.[2]

19.2 And for £7 6s. 7d. received from William Trussell, knight, for the farm of Ewloe township for this year, for the terms of Easter and Michaelmas falling within this account.[3]

19.3 And for £6 13s. 4d. received from the same William, by the hands of Ithel ap Bleddyn ab Ithel for the farm of sea-coal this year at Ewloe granted to the same Ithel for 10 marks a year. This farm applies both to the prince's demesne lands there and to the lands which used to belong to Bleddyn ab Ithel Anwyl and which were lately taken into the prince's hands.[4]

19.4 And for £41 11s. 6d. received from William le Fissher and Cynwrig de Fakenhale, bailiffs of the town of Flint, for the issues of their bailiwick this year.[5]

19.5 And for £4 5s. 10d. received from Ieuan Bongam and Ithel ap Bleddyn, bailiffs of the township of Coleshill, for the issues of their bailiwick this year.[6]

19.6 And for £16 received from Cynwrig ap Roppert and Ednyfed ab Ieuan, bailiffs of the town of Caerwys, for the farm of the pleas and perquisites of the court of that town and also of the mill there, this year.[7]

19.7 And for 101s. 9d. received from William de Heton, bailiff of the township of Bachegraig, for the farm of the mills there this year.[8]

---

1   This account does not survive. Sir John's lands were taken over by the prince in 1353, see Booth, *Financial Administration*, pp. 129–32.
2   Balle's account is SC6 1186/21, m.1.
3   SC6 1186/21, m.1 contains Trussell's account for Ewloe. He was granted it in 1350 (*F.M.A.(2)*, pp. 36–37) on relinquishing the grant for life of the Anglesey townships of Cleifiog and Llanllibio made to him in 1334 (*C.C.R., 1333–37*, p. 196).
4   SC6 1186/21, m.1. These grants had been made on 8 and 28 September 1358 (*ChRR*, p. 260).
5   SC6 1186/21, m.1. William le Fissher had been one of the bailiffs in the preceding year (**3.3**).
6   SC6 1186/21, m.1d. They had held the farm since 1350–51 (*F.M.A.(2)*, p. 50).
7   SC6 1186/21, m.1d. They had been granted the farm for six years on 10 August 1358 (*ChRR*, p. 409).
8   SC6 1186/21, m.1d. The farm was granted to Heton on 30 September 1356 for six years at £5 3s. 9d. annually (*ChRR*, p. 233). 2s. 0d. decay was allowed against the farm for one acre of land used for smelting lead at Faenol.

⟨m 5⟩ {m 5}

19.8   Et de x li. x s. receptis de David lloit'[a] ap Gruffry et Eign' ap Bleth' Firmariis ville de Vaynol' de firma eiusdem ville hoc anno.

19.9   Et de xxvij li. xj d. ob. receptis de Adam le Hert' et Thoma Sonky[b] Ballivis ville de Rothelan in partem solutionis exituum ballive sue hoc anno.

19.10   Et de xiiij li. xiij s. iiij d. receptis de Simone de Assewell' et Willelmo de Blorton' Ballivis et Firmariis ville de Moston' de firma eiusdem ville de[c] hoc anno.[d]

Summa: Cxxxiij li. xvij s. xj d. ob. probatur[e]

20.   EXITUS OFFICII VICECOMITIS DE FLYNT'

Et de iiij[xx] xvij li. xv s. vij d. receptis de Ken' ap Roppert' vicecomite de Flynt' et Firmario eiusdem vicecomitatus in partem solutionis firme dicti vicecomitatus et aliorum exituum ballive sue per tempus huius compoti.

Summa: iiij[xx] xvij li. xv s. vij d. probatur[f]

21.   EXITUS RAGLOTIE DE ENGLEFELD'

Et de xxxij li. receptis de Ken' ap Roppert' Ragloto de Englefeld' de firma Raglotie predicte de terminis Pasche et Sancti Michelis infra hunc compotum contingentibus.

Summa: xxxij li.

a   *loyt'* 772/4.
b   *Thoma le Sonky* 772/3.
c   om. 772/4.
d   intl. 772/3.
e   om. 772/3.
f   om. 772/3.

19.8 And for £10 10s. 0d. received from Dafydd Llwyd ap Gruffydd and Einion ap Bleddyn, farmers of the township of Faenol, for the farm of the same township this year.[1]

19.9 And for £27 0s. 11½d. received from Adam le Hert and Thomas Sonky, bailiffs of the town of Rhuddlan, in part payment of the issues of their bailiwick this year.[2]

19.10 And for £14 13s. 4d. received from Simon de Assewell and William de Blorton, bailiffs and farmers of the township of Mostyn, for the farm of the same township this year.[3]

Sum: £133 17s. 11½d. Approved.

20. ISSUES OF THE OFFICE OF THE SHERIFF OF FLINT

And for £97 15s. 7d. received from Cynwrig ap Roppert, sheriff of Flint and farmer of the same sheriffdom, in part payment of the farm of the said sheriffdom and of the other issues of his bailiwick during the time of this account.[4]

Sum: £97 15s. 7d. Approved.

21. ISSUES OF THE RAGLOTRY OF ENGLEFIELD

And for £32 received from Cynwrig ap Roppert, *rhaglaw* of Englefield, for the farm of the said raglotry for the terms of Easter and Michaelmas falling within this account.[5]

Sum: £32 0s. 0d.

1 SC6 1186/21, m.1d. They were granted the farm on 4 Jan. 1362 for three years at £12 annually (*ChRR*, p. 484).
2 SC6 1186/21, m.2. Much of the income from Rhuddlan and some from Caerwys and Bachegraig had been granted to Sir John de Byntre in 1353 (*ChRR*, p. 77); Byntre had been constable of Rhuddlan since 1350 (ibid.).
3 SC6 1186/21, m.2. They were granted the farm on 30 September 1360 for three years at 22 marks annually, (*ChRR*, p. 12).
4 SC6 1186/21, mm.2A, 2Ad. He was granted the farm of the sheriffdom on 30 September 1360 for three years at £46 13s. 4d. annually; the grant included the office of constable of Flint castle on condition that he appointed an Englishman as deputy-constable. On the same day, he was appointed to investigate infractions of the Statute of Labourers (*ChRR*, p. 409).
5 SC6 1186/21, m.2d. He was granted the farm for three years at £64 annually on 30 September 1360 (*ChRR*, p. 409). But according to his account, the farm of the office was £44, and it had been paid in full.

⟨m 6⟩ {m 5}

22.   EXITUS ESCAETORIE DE ENGLEFELD'

Et de l li. xij s. vj d. receptis de Ken' ap Bleth' ap Mad'ᵃ clerico Collectore reddituum terrarum escaetarum de Englefeld' de exitibus earundem terrarum per tempus huiusᵇ compoti.

Summa: l li. xij s. vj d. probaturᶜ

23.   ATTERMINATIONES FINIUM DIVERSORUM COMITATUS DE FLYNT'

23.1   Et de x li. receptis de Johanne de Stoke in persolutionem cuiusdam finis l li. pro terris et tenementis que fuerunt Johannis le Mercer in Cestr' sibi venditis solvendi infra v annos proxime sequentes ad festa Pasche et Sancti Michelis equaliterᵈ per litteras domini predictisᵉ locum tenenti et Camerario directas penes ipsum Camerarium remanentes dat' apud London' xiiij die Julij anno regni regis nunc xxxj. De quibus quidem l li. predictus Johannes de Stoke invenit securitatem per recognitionemᶠ in Scaccario Cestr' factam xviij die Augusti anno xxxj supradicto videlicet pro terminis Pasche et Sancti Michelis infra hunc compotum contingentibus hoc anno quinto et ultimo.

23.2   Et de xj li. xv s. receptis de Johanne de Stoke et sociis suis in persolutionem cuiusdam finis xlvij li. facti coram predictoᵍ locum tenente in sessione tenta die lune proxime ante festum Sancti Gregorij pape anno regni regis nuncʰ xxxiij atterminati ad solvendum infra quatuor annos proxime sequentes ad festa Pasche et Sancti Michelis equaliterⁱ videlicet pro eisdem terminis infra hunc compotum contingentibus hoc anno iiijᵗᵒ et ultimo.

23.3   Et de vj li. xiij s. iiij d. receptis de Burgensibus ville de Flynt' in persolutionem cuiusdam finis l marcarum facti coram predictis locum tenente et Camerario apud Flynt' die lune proxime ante festum Nativitatis Sancti Johannis Baptiste anno regni regis nuncʲ xxxjᵒ pro confirmatione carte sue et bundis dicte ville equitandis et in certo limitandis sibi atterminati ad solvendum infra v annos proxime sequentes ad festa Natalis domini et Nativitatis Sancti Johannis Baptiste

---

a   772/3 has *ap Roppert' ap Mad'*, del., followed by *ap Bleth' ap Mad'*.
b   *istius* 772/3.
c   om. 772/3.
d   *equis portionibus* 772/4.
e   om. 772/3.
f   *per recognitionem* intl. 772/4.
g   *predictis* 772/3.
h   *regni regis nunc* om. 772/3.
i   *per equales portiones* 772/4.
j   om. 772/3.

22. ISSUES OF THE ESCHEATRY OF ENGLEFIELD

And for £50 12s. 6d. received from Cynwrig ap Bleddyn ap Madog, clerk, collector of the rents of the escheated lands of Englefield, for the issues of the same lands during the time of this account.[1]

Sum: £50 12s. 6d. Approved.

23. INSTALMENTS OF FINES OF VARIOUS PEOPLE OF THE COUNTY OF FLINT

23.1 And for £10 received from John de Stoke in full payment of a fine of £50 for the sale to him of the lands and tenements in Chester which used to belong to John le Mercer, to be paid within the five years following, at the feasts of Easter and Michaelmas, by equal payments. This was granted by the lord's letters directed to the said lieutenant and chamberlain, dated at London 14 July in the 31st year of the reign of the present king (1357), which remain in the chamberlain's possession. The said John de Stoke found security for the £50 by a recognizance made in the exchequer of Chester on 18 August in the above-mentioned 31st year (1357). The above sum is, therefore, for the terms of Easter and Michaelmas falling within this account, being the fifth and last year of payment.[2]

23.2 And for £11 15s. 0d. received from John de Stoke and his fellows in full payment of a fine of £47 made before the said lieutenant at the session held on Monday before the feast of St Gregory, pope, in the 33rd year of the reign of the present king (11 March 1359). It was granted that the fine be paid within the four years following at the feasts of Easter and Michaelmas, by equal payments. The above sum is, therefore, for the same terms falling within this account, being the fourth and last year of payment.[3]

23.3 And for £6 13s. 4d. received from the burgesses of the town of Flint in full payment of a fine of 50 marks made before the said lieutenant and chamberlain at Flint on Monday before the Nativity of St John Baptist in the 31st year of the reign of the present king (19 June 1357), for confirmation of their charter and for having the bounds of the said town ridden and fixed for certain. It was granted that the fine be paid within the five years following at the feasts of Christmas and the Nativity of St John Baptist, by equal payments. The above sum is, therefore,

1 SC6 1186/21, mm.3, 3d., 4. This is not the account of the escheator of Englefield, Ithel ap Bleddyn ab Ithel Anwyl, granted the office during pleasure in 1357 (*B.P.R.*, iii. 288), but of the collector of rents of escheat lands in Englefield. Cynwrig was quit of suit to the county and hundred courts and the tourn while holding this office on 14 September 1358 (*B.P.R.*, iii. 317).

2 John de Stoke and his wife Alice petitioned for the lands of John le Mercer on 10 February 1355 (*B.P.R.*, iii. 189). They were granted to him on 14 July 1357 (*ChRR*, p. 452) and the lieutenant and chamberlain were ordered to deliver the lands to him on the same day (*B.P.R.*, iii. 270).

3 CHES 30/9, m.41d.

⟨m 6⟩ {m 5}

equaliter[a] videlicet pro eisdem terminis infra hunc compotum contingentibus hoc anno v^{to} et ultimo.

23.4 Et de lxvj s. viij d. receptis de Ith' ap ll' ap Ken' et sociis suis in persolutionem cuiusdam[b] finis x li. facti coram predictis locum tenente et Camerario in sessione tenta apud Flynt' die lune proxime post festum Sancti Gregorij pape anno regni regis nunc[c] xxxiiij^{to} atterminati eidem Ith'[d] ad solvendum infra tres annos proxime sequentes ad festa Pasche et Sancti[e] Michelis equis portionibus[f] videlicet pro eisdem terminis infra hunc compotum contingentibus hoc anno tertio et ultimo.[g]

23.5 Et de iiij li. receptis de Eign' ap Mad' ap Jeuan de parte ix li. vj s. viij d. aretro existentium de quodam fine xx marcarum facto coram predictis locum tenente et Camerario in sessione tenta apud Flynt' die lune in festo Sancti Mathei Apostoli anno regni regis nunc xxxiiij pro morte Gron' ap Eign' Taillour atterminato eidem Eign' ad solvendum ad festum Pasche proxime sequens xl s. et ad festum Sancti Michelis tunc proxime sequens xl s. et ad festum Pasche tunc proxime sequens[h] xl s. et ad festum Sancti Michelis tunc proxime sequens xl s. et ad festum Pasche tunc proxime sequens xl s. et ad festum Sancti Michelis tunc proxime sequens xl s. et ad festum Pasche tunc[i] proxime sequens ij marcas videlicet[j] pro terminis Pasche et Sancti Michelis infra hunc compotum[k] contingentibus hoc anno secundo.

23.6 Et de lxvj s. viij d. receptis de Eign' ap david ap Atha de parte vj li. xiij s. iiij d. a retro existentium de quodam fine x li. facto[l] coram predictis locum tenente et Camerario in sessione[m] tenta[n] apud Flynt'[o] die et anno predictis[p] pro licencia perquirendi totum ius tenementi quod fuit Ith' ap Eign' ap Lowarch'[q] in maeneva. Ita tamen quod si Wladus que fuit uxor Ith' ap Ririth' aliquod ius habeat in predictis tenementis que fuerunt predicti Ith' ap Eign' tunc predictus Eign' ap David de lx s. de predictis x li. omnino exoneretur atterminato eidem Eign' ap david ad solvendum infra tres annos proxime sequentes[r] ad festa Pasche et Sancti Michelis equaliter[s] videlicet pro eisdem terminis[t] infra hunc compotum contingentibus hoc anno secundo.

23.7 Et de x s. receptis de david ap Ith' Person' de parte xxx s. aretro existentium de quodam fine xl s. facto coram predictis locum tenente et Camerario in sessione predicta pro allocatione cuiusdam carte sibi atterminato

a *per equales portiones* 772/4.
c om. 772/3.
e intl. 772/3.
g *compotum contingentibus . . . et ultimo* intl. 772/3.
i *extunc* 772/4.
k rep. 772/3.
m *ad sessionem* 772/4.
o 772/3 follows with *tenta*, del.; 772/4 follows with *tenta*.
q *lowargh'* 772/4.
s *per equales portiones* 772/4.

b intl. 772/3.
d *Ith'* om. 772/3.
f *per equales portiones* 772/4.
h rep. 772/3.
j intl. 772/3.
l *facti* 772/3.
n om. 772/4; intl. 772/3.
p *predictis die et anno* 772/4.
r *proxime sequentes* om. 772/3.
t *pro terminis Pasche et Sancti Michelis* 772/4.

for the same terms falling within this account, being the fifth and last year of payment.[1]

23.4 And for 66s. 8d. received from Ithel ap Llywelyn ap Cynwrig and his fellows in full payment of a fine of £10 made before the said lieutenant and chamberlain at the session held at Flint on Monday after the feast of St Gregory, pope, in the 34th year of the reign of the present king (16 March 1360). It was granted that the fine be paid within the three years following at the feasts of Easter and Michaelmas, by equal payments. The above sum is, therefore, for the same terms falling within this account, being the third and last year of payment.[2]

23.5 And for £4 received from Einion ap Madog ab Ieuan as part of £9 6s. 8d. in arrears of a fine of 20 marks made before the said lieutenant and chamberlain at the session held at Flint on Monday the feast of St Matthew, apostle, in the 34th year of the reign of the present king (21 September 1360), for the death of Goronwy ab Einion Teiliwr. It was granted that the fine be paid at the rate of 40s. 0d. at Easter following, and then at Michaelmas after that 40s. 0d., and at Easter after that 40s. 0d., and at Michaelmas after that 40s. 0d., and at Easter after that 40s. 0d., and at Michaelmas after that 40s. 0d., and at Easter after that two marks. The above sum is, therefore, for the terms of Easter and Michaelmas falling within this account, being the second year of payment.[3]

23.6 And for 66s. 8d. received from Einion ap Dafydd ab Adda as part of £6 13s. 4d. in arrears of a fine of £10 made before the said lieutenant and chamberlain at the session held at Flint on the day and year aforesaid (21 September 1360) for licence to acquire the whole right to the tenement which belonged to Ithel ab Einion ap Llywarch in Maenefa, with the effect that if Gwladus, widow of Ithel ap Rhirid, should have any right in the said tenements which belonged to the said Ithel ab Einion then the said Einion ap Dafydd shall be entirely exonerated of 60s. 0d. of the said £10. It was granted that the fine be paid within the three years following at the feasts of Easter and Michaelmas, by equal payments. The above sum is, therefore, for the same terms falling within this account, being the second year of payment.[4]

23.7 And for 10s. 0d. received from Dafydd ab Ithel Person as part of 30s. 0d. in arrears of a fine of 40s. 0d. made before the said lieutenant and chamberlain at the aforesaid session, for having a charter allowed. It was granted that the fine

1 This confirmation was requested in 1353 and the justiciar and chamberlain were ordered to survey the boundaries and negotiate with the burgesses on 20 Sept. 1353 (*B.P.R.*, iii. 121). A new charter specifying the boundaries was granted on 20 September 1360 (*ChRR*, p. 184, printed in full in H. Taylor, *Historic Notes with Topographical and other Gleanings Descriptive of the Borough and County Town of Flint* (1883), pp. 40–42).
2 CHES 30/9, m.48d.
3 Ibid., m.50.
4 Ibid.

⟨m 6⟩ {m 5}

ad solvendum infra iiij annos proxime sequentes videlicet quolibet anno ad festum Sancti Martini x s.[a] unde pro eodem termino infra hunc compotum contingente hoc anno secundo.

23.8 Et de iiij li. viij s. xj d. receptis de Bleth' ap[b] Gwenliant fil' Bleth' ap Mad' de parte xvij li. xv s. vj d. ob. aretro existentium de[c] quodam fine xx li. facto coram predictis locum tenente et Camerario in sessione tenta apud Flynt' die lune proxime ante festum Sancti Michelis anno regni regis nunc xxxv pro licencia concessa David ap Ith' Vaghan quod ipse dare possit et concedere Jeuan ap Eign' Kest' Capellano manerium suum de North'hope[d] et alia tenementa sua ibidem prout patet per cartam eidem Jeuan inde factam atterminato eidem Bleth' ad solvendum infra quatuor annos et dimidium proxime sequentes ad festa Sancti Michelis et Pasche equaliter[e] videlicet pro eisdem terminis infra hunc compotum contingentibus hoc anno secundo.

{m 6}

23.9 Et de xliiij s. v d. receptis de david ap Ith' Vaghan de parte viij li. xvij s. ix d. ob. a retro existentium de quodam fine x li. facto coram predictis locum tenente et Camerario in sessione predicta pro licencia feoffandi Jeuan ap Eign' Kest' Capellanum de diversis tenementis suis infra Comitatum de Flynt' prout patet per cartam eidem Jeuan inde factam atterminato eidem david ad solvendum infra iiij annos et dimidium proxime sequentes ad festa Pasche et Sancti Michelis[f] equaliter[g] videlicet pro eisdem terminis infra hunc compotum contingentibus hoc anno secundo.

23.10 Et de lxvj s. viij d. receptis de Ith' de Byrchore de parte x li. aretro existentium de quodam fine xx marcarum facto[h] coram predictis locum tenente et Camerario in sessione tenta apud Flynt' die lune proxime post festum Sancti Barnabe Apostoli anno regni regis nunc xxxv pro uno burgagio et ij acris terre et dimidia cum pertinenciis in Flynt' que fuerunt Johannis Adynet et xx acris terre que quondam fuerunt Johannis Davyesson' Dokynesson' in Flynt' atterminato eidem Ith' ad solvendum lxvj s. viij d. ad festum Sancti Michelis infra compotum dicti Camerarij de anno ultimo preterito et xv marcas infra tres annos proxime sequentes ad festa Pasche et Sancti Michelis per equales portiones videlicet pro eisdem terminis infra hunc compotum contingentibus.

Summa: xlix li. xj s. viij d. probatur

a   intl. 772/3.
b   *filio* 772/4.
c   772/4 has *de*, del., followed by *de*.
d   *Northope* 772/4.
e   *per equales portiones* 772/4.
f   *ad festa Sancti Michelis et Pasche* 772/4.
g   *per equales portiones* 772/4.
h   *factis* 772/4.

be paid within the four years following, namely at the rate of 10s. 0d. at Martinmas each year. The above sum is, therefore, for the same term falling within this account, being the second year of payment.[1]

23.8 And for £4 8s. 11d. received from Bleddyn ap Gwenllian ferch Bleddyn ap Madog as part of £17 15s. 6½d. in arrears of a fine of £20 made before the said lieutenant and chamberlain at the session held at Flint on Monday next before the feast of Michaelmas in the 35th year of the reign of the present king (27 September 1361) for licence granted to Dafydd ab Ithel Fychan that he should be able to give and grant to Ieuan ab Einion *Kest*, chaplain, his manor of Northop and other tenements of his there, as appears by a charter made in favour of the same Ieuan. It was granted that the fine be paid within the four and a half years following at the feasts of Michaelmas and Easter, by equal payments. The above sum is, therefore, for the same terms falling within this account, being the second year of payment.[2]

23.9 And for 44s. 5d. received from Dafydd ab Ithel Fychan as part of £8 17s. 9½d. in arrears of a fine of £10 made before the said lieutenant and chamberlain at the same session for licence to enfeoff Ieuan ab Einion *Kest*, chaplain, with various tenements of his within the county of Flint, as appears by a charter made in favour of the same Ieuan. It was granted that the fine be paid within the four and a half years following at the feasts of Easter and Michaelmas, by equal payments. The above sum is, therefore, for the same terms falling within this account, being the second year of payment.

23.10 And for 66s. 8d. received from Ithel de Byrchore as part of £10 in arrears of a fine of 20 marks made before the said lieutenant and chamberlain at the session held at Flint on Monday after the feast of St Barnabas, apostle, in the 35th year of the reign of the present king (14 June 1361) for one burgage and two and a half acres of land, with appurtenances, in Flint, which used to belong to John Adynet, and 20 acres of land in Flint which used to belong to John Davyesson Dokynesson. It was granted that the fine be paid at the rate of 66s. 8d. at Michaelmas within the chamberlain's account of last year, and then 15 marks within the three years following at the feasts of Easter and Michaelmas, by equal payments. The above sum is, therefore, for the same terms falling within this account.[3]

Sum: £49 11s. 8d. Approved.

---

1 CHES 30/9, m.50d.
2 There is no record of these two fines (**23.8, 9**) on the plea roll for this session (CHES 30/10, mm.6, 6d).
3 CHES 30/10, m.5.

⟨*m 6*⟩ {*m 6*}
24.   ATTERMINATIONES NOVE COMITATUS DE FLYNT'

24.1   Et de x li. receptis de Thoma de Wircestre[a] de quodam fine facto coram predictis locum tenente et Camerario in sessione tenta apud Flynt' die lune in Crastino Sancte Lucie Virginis anno regni regis nunc xxxiiij pro viij acris terre et medietate unius mesuagij cum pertinenciis in Flynt' que fuerunt Ricardi de Bicton' Bastardi fratris ipsius Thome et etiam viij acris terre cum pertinenciis[b] in eadem villa quas Willelmus de Wircestre[c] pater predicti Thome perquisivit et pro medietate unius burgagij que fuit Mad' le Reve et medietate unius mesuagij que fuit Mad' le Cook' in eadem villa atterminato eidem Thome ad solvendum infra duos annos proxime sequentes ad festa Pasche et Sancti Michelis equaliter[d] videlicet pro eisdem terminis infra predictos ij annos contingentibus eo quod nichil responsum erat domino in compoto precedenti quia extracte ad levandum predictas x li. non fuerant liberate predicto Camerario infra idem tempus.
(*pro lxiij li. onerandis de fine eorundem a retro existente in North'Wall' unde litteras habuerunt et cetera*)[e]

24.2   Et de xxxiij li. vj s. viij d. receptis de Lewelino Episcopo Assavenense et Decano et Capitulo eiusdem loci in partem solutionis cuiusdam finis CC marcarum facti coram consilio domini pro CCCC ix acris terre cum pertinenciis in villis[f] de Dysserth' Dyncolyn Nannerch' Coytymyneth' et Relevenot'[g] in Comitatu de Flynt' quas predictus dominus coram Justiciario suo Cestr' in sessione sua apud[h] Flynt' anno regni regis nunc xxxv recuperavit versus predictos Episcopum Decanum et Capitulum per eorum defaltam rehabendis et tenendis sibi et successoribus suis in puram et perpetuam elemosinam atterminati eisdem ad solvendum infra iiij annos proxime sequentes ad festa Nativitatis Sancti Johannis Baptiste et Sancti Michelis equaliter[i] per litteras domini Camerario directas quarum[j] datum est apud Kenyngton'[k] xx die Maij anno regni regis nunc xxxvj penes eundem Camerarium remanentes videlicet pro predictis terminis infra hunc compotum contingentibus hoc anno primo.[l]

Summa: xliij li. vj s. viij d.

a   *Wyrcestre* 772/4.
b   *cum pertinenciis* intl. 772/3.
c   *Wyrcestre* 772/4.
d   *per equales portiones* 772/4.
e   note om. 772/3.
f   *villa* 772/3.
g   *Relevenenot* 772/3.
h   772/3 has *tenta apud*, del., followed by *apud* intl.
i   *per equales portiones* 772/4.
j   intl. 772/3.
k   772/3 has *London' Kex'*, del., followed by *Kenyngton'*.
l   *hoc anno primo* om. 772/3.

24. PAYMENTS BY INSTALMENTS OF THE COUNTY OF FLINT – FROM THIS YEAR

24.1 And for £10 received from Thomas de Wircestre for a fine made before the said lieutenant and chamberlain at the session held at Flint on Monday the morrow of St Lucy, virgin, in the 34th year of the reign of the present king (14 December 1360) for eight acres of land and half of one messuage, with appurtenances, in Flint which used to belong to Richard de Bicton, bastard, brother of the same Thomas, and also eight acres of land, with appurtenances, in the same town which William de Wircestre, the said Thomas's father, acquired, and for half of one burgage which used to belong to Madog le Reve, and half of one messuage which used to belong to Madog le Cook in the same town. It was granted that the fine be paid within the two years following at the feasts of Easter and Michaelmas, by equal payments. The above sum is, therefore, for the same terms falling within the said two years, because nothing was rendered to the lord in last year's account as the estreats for levying the said £10 had not been handed over to the said chamberlain within that time.[1]
(*For £63 to be charged for the fine of the same men being in arrears in North Wales for which they have letters, et cetera*).
24.2 And for £33 6s. 8d. received from Llewelyn, bishop of St Asaph, and from the dean and chapter of the same place, in part payment of a fine of 200 marks made before the lord's council for having back 409 acres of land, with appurtenances, in the townships of Diserth, Dincolyn, Nannerch, Coed-y-mynydd and Trelawnyd in the county of Flint, which land was acquired by the said lord by recovery in a session before his justiciar of Chester at Flint in the 35th year of the reign of the present king (1361/62) against the said bishop, dean and chapter, and by their default. This land is to be had back and held by them and their successors in pure and perpetual alms. It was granted that the fine be paid within the four years following at the feasts of the Nativity of St John Baptist and Michaelmas, by equal payments, by the lord's letters directed to the chamberlain dated at Kennington 20 May in the 36th year of the reign of the present king (1362), which remain in the chamberlain's possession. The above sum is, therefore, for the same terms falling within this account, being the first year of payment.[2]

Sum: £43 6s. 8d.

1 CHES 30/10, m.1.
2 Ibid., m.2; *B.P.R.*, iii. 445 is the record of the letters to the chamberlain. On 18 November 1277 at Rhuddlan the justiciar of Chester and Hywel ap Gruffydd, the bailiff of Englefield, were ordered to assign lands worth £10 p.a. to the bishop and lands of similar value to the dean and chapter (ibid.). On 13 September 1278 the justiciar and the bailiff were instructed that the grants should be in arable land, not in rents, homages, etc which they had assigned to the bishop and chapter (*C.C.R.*, *1272–79*, p. 476.). On 3 March 1279 the king ordered the justiciar to assign the lands at once as he had heard that this had not been done (*Cal. Chanc. R. Var.*, p. 180). Many episcopal lands in north Wales were held jointly by the bishop and the dean and chapter and the revenues were divided between them; this was a survival of an earlier pattern of ecclesiastical organisation (C.N. Johns, 'The Celtic Monasteries of North Wales' in *Trans. Caerns. Hist. Soc.* 21 (1960), pp. 15–16.)

⟨m 6⟩ {m 6}
25.   FINIS WALLENSIUM DE ENGLEFELD' ET HOPEDALE

Et de Clx li. receptis de hominibus Wallensibus de Englefeld' et Hopedale exceptis hominibus domini Comitis Cestr' manentibus in villis Wallice nuncupatis Trevewelyok' et Trevekevery et in villis tam^a burgis quam Anglicanis et exceptis tenentibus ipsius domini Comitis in Vaynol et exceptis tenentibus Episcopi et Capituli Assavenensis de parte CCCC li. a retro existente de DCCC li. pro quibus dicti Wallenses fecerunt finem cum dicto domino Comite in festo Nativitatis beate Marie anno regni regis nunc xxxij ad solvendum dictos denarios eidem domino ad scaccarium Cestr' per quinque annos proxime sequentes ad festa Nativitatis Sancti Johannis Baptiste et Sancti Martini per equales portiones primo termino solutionis incipiente in festo Nativitatis Sancti Johannis Baptiste anno regni regis nunc xxxiij videlicet pro perdonatione transgressionum habenda quas dicti Wallenses et eorum antecessores fecerunt in adquirendo sibi et heredibus suis terras et tenementa Wallensium^b licencia ipsius domini Comitis vel antecessorum suorum non inde^c obtenta. Et quod parvus Comitatus de Flynt' non teneatur in aliquo loco dicti Comitatus de Flynt' nisi apud Flynt' et hoc de mense in mensem. Item quod dicti Wallenses non debeant calumpniari pro aliquibus releviis vocatis Wallice Abedywes aliquorum Wallensium mortuorum ante festum Nativitatis beate Marie anno regni regis nunc xxxij. Item quod hundreda Commotorum de Colshull'^d Rothelan' et Prestaton' de Englefeld' debeant teneri de cetero per Raglotum ibidem de tribus septimanis in

a   772/3 follows with *in* del.
b   *Wallic'* 772/4.
c   772/4 has *inde non*; *inde* intl. 772/3.
d   *Closhull'* 772/3.

25. FINE OF THE WELSHMEN OF ENGLEFIELD AND HOPEDALE

And for £160 received from the Welshmen of Englefield and Hopedale, with the exception of the earl of Chester's men living in the townships called in the Welsh language *Tref welyog*[1] and *Tref gyfrif*,[2] and in the English towns and the boroughs, and also excepting the tenants of the earl in Faenol and the tenants of the bishop and chapter of St Asaph. It is part of £400 in arrears of £800, for which the said Welshmen made a fine with the said earl at the feast of the Nativity of Blessed Mary in the 32nd year of the reign of the present king (8 September 1358), which was to be paid at the exchequer of Chester during the five years following at the feasts of the Nativity of St John Baptist and Martinmas, by equal payments, the first term of payment being the Nativity of St John Baptist in the 33rd year of the reign of the present king (1359). The fine was made for having pardon for the trespasses committed by the said Welshmen and their predecessors in acquiring for themselves and their heirs lands and tenements of Welshmen without first obtaining the licence of the earl or his predecessors. The fine was also made so that the petty county court of Flint should not be held anywhere in the county of Flint except at Flint, and that it should be held there every month. Also, it was made so that the said Welshmen ought not to be liable to pay those reliefs called in the Welsh language *ebediw*[3] in respect of any Welshmen who died before the feast of the Nativity of the Blessed Mary in the 32nd year of the reign of the present king (8 September 1358), and also that the hundred courts of the commotes of Coleshill, Rhuddlan and Prestatyn in Englefield should be held every three weeks by the *rhaglaw* there in

1 Or *tir gwelyog*. Although the *gwely* or landholding kindred group was originally a free institution, many unfree townships came to be held by unfree *gwelyau*, which, held by *tir gwelyog* tenure, occupied an intermediate position between those which were free and those which were held by *tir cyfrif* tenure. Tenants were subject to the constraints of bond status, but they had a heritable interest in the *gwely* lands (Carr, *Medieval Anglesey*, pp. 142–43; T. Jones Pierce, 'Medieval Settlement in Anglesey' in *Medieval Welsh Society*, pp. 274–76; G.R.J. Jones, 'The Distribution of Medieval Settlement in Anglesey' in *Transactions of the Anglesey Antiquarian Society and Field Club*, 1955, pp. 56–57, 75–79).
2 *Tref gyfrif* or *tir cyfrif* was the most onerous form of Welsh unfree tenure. A township of this nature owed a fixed burden of rents and services which was shared equally among all the adult males; if there were only one in the township, he owed it all. The arable land was redistributed with every change in the adult male population. Such communities were generally nucleated ones or hamlets (Carr, *op. cit.*, pp. 30–31, 140–41; T. Jones Pierce, *op. cit.*, pp. 276–77; G.R.J. Jones, 'The Tribal System in Wales: a Reassessment in the Light of Settlement Studies' in *Welsh History Review*, i (1961), p. 119). The tenure is defined in CHES 30/7, m.22d and in Carr, 'The Extent of Anglesey, 1352' in *Transactions of the Anglesey Antiquarian Society*, 1971–72, pp. 175 and 247.
3 This was the relief paid by a direct heir to take up his inheritance. The free man's relief was usually ten shillings; bond tenants in Flintshire seem to have paid five shillings (*F.M.A.(1)*, pp. 10–11). The payment of this fine was the response of the prince and his council to some of the matters raised by the men of Englefield in their petition of 1358 (*B.P.R.*, iii. 318–23). See particularly pp. 320 (fine of 1,200 marks for pardon for all unlicensed acquisitions of land in the past), 322–23 (county court only to be held at Flint), and 319–20 (unjust reliefs).

⟨m 6⟩ {m 6}
tres septimanas in loco consueto videlicet pro terminis Sancti Martini et Nativitatis Sancti Johannis Baptiste infra hunc compotum contingentibus hoc anno iiij.

Summa: Clx li.

26. SUMMA TOTALIS RECEPTORUM: MMM CCviij li. xix s. viij d. ob. di. qu.

De quibus respondet in dorso

⟨m 1d⟩ {m 1d}

27. *[Compotus] Magistri* Johannis de Brunham Junioris *Camerarij de anno regni regis Edwardi* tertij post conquestum [. . . . .]

Duplic(amentum)ᵃ   DE ANNO XXXVI

p(ro) Chaundosᵇ

28. ELEMOSINE

28.1 Idem computat in denariis solutis Abbati Sancte Werburge Cestr' pro quod*am luminari inveniendo in Capella de Hildeburghegh'* de quadam elemosina ei constituta ex antiquo percipienda de exi*tibus Scaccarij Cestr' per annum ad festum Sancti Martini pro* toto anno per litteras acquietancie ipsius Abbatis super hunc compotum osten*sas et liberatas* – x s.
28.2 *Item Priori et Conventui* eiusdem loci percipientibus annuatim de decima exituum Civitatis Cestr' de ex*itibus predictis ad festa Pasche et Sancti* [. . . . .] per equales portiones per duasᶜ litteras acquietancie ipsius Prioris ostensas et super hunc compotum *liberatas* – x li.

a   om. 772/4.
b   *p(ro) Chaundos* om. 772/4.
c   om. 772/3; intl. 772/4.

the customary place. The above sum is, therefore, for the terms of Martinmas and the Nativity of St John Baptist falling within this account, being the fourth year of payment.

Sum: £160 0s. 0d.

26. SUM TOTAL OF RECEIPTS: £3,208 19s. 8½d. and a half-farthing.

For which he answers on the dorse.

(Dorse)

27. Account of Master John de Brunham the younger, chamberlain, for the year of the reign of King Edward the third after the conquest [. . . . .].

Duplicate   FOR THE 36TH YEAR

(for) Chaundos[1]

28. ALMS[2]

28.1 He accounts in money paid to the abbot of St Werburgh's, Chester, to provide a light in the chapel of Hilbre, as alms appointed to him from of old to be taken yearly from the issues of the exchequer of Chester at the feast of Martinmas, for the whole year; by the same abbot's letters of acquittance which have been shown and handed over upon this account – 10s. 0d.[3]

28.2 And to the prior and convent of the same place, who take yearly as the tithe of the issues of the city of Chester, for the same issues at the feasts of Easter and St [. . . . .] by equal payments; by the same prior's two letters of acquittance shown and handed over upon this account – £10.

1 It is not clear what, if anything, this note signifies. Possibly a copy of the account had been made for Sir John Chandos, the prince's companion in arms, who had been granted valuable offices in Cheshire by the prince; see **30.4, 30.5, 30.6** for example.
2 The *antique elemosine* comprised those annually payable charitable gifts established by the Anglo-Norman earls of Chester, together with some post-1237 additions. The reason for the payments in **28.2, 28.3, 28.4** being made to the prior and not the abbot of St Werburgh's, Chester, is that on 16 March 1362 the lieutenant, chamberlain and escheator were commissioned by the prince to take the abbey into his hands, together with its property, and not let the abbot, Richard Sainsbury, have any powers of administration (*B.P.R.*, iii. 440). The Hilbre chapel payment (**28.1**) had already been made on 11 November 1361, and so had gone to the abbot in the usual way.
3 Earl John of Scotland granted 10s. 0d. a year from the exchequer of Chester to the chapel of Hilbre for the light of St Mary, between 1232 and 1237 (G. Barraclough, ed., *Charters of the Anglo-Norman Earls of Chester*, R.S.L.C., cxxvi (1988), p. 438). Barraclough states that the light 'was presumably a lighthouse or navigational aid for mariners'. This seems to stretch the evidence somewhat, and it is more likely that the payment was for a light in the chapel, as the account suggests.

⟨*m 1d*⟩ {*m 1d*}

28.3   *Et eisdem Priori et* Conventui percipientibus annuatim de eisdem exitibus pro decima proveniente de exitibus pro*ficui novem partium piscarie pontis de* Dee et aliarum piscationum ibidem ad terminos predictos per equales portiones per litteras acquietancie dicti Pr*ioris super hunc compotum* liberatas – C s.

28.4   Et eisdem Priori et Conventui percipientibus annuatim de eisdem exitibus ad eosdem terminos de dono domini Edwardi quondam Regis Anglie Avi domini Regis nunc in *re*compensationem quarundam decimarum que fuerunt predicti Abbatis apud Frodesham quas resignavit ad opus Abbatis de Valle Regali ad rogatum eiusdem domini Regis per litteras acquietancie dicti Prioris et litteras domini Camerario directas tam pro istis elemosinis quam pro feodo in eisdem contento quarum datum est apud London' secundo die Julij anno xxj et remanent predicte littere inter Waranta compoti eiusdem anni xxj per litteras acquietancie ipsius Prioris super hunc compotum liberatas – iiij li.

28.5   Item Priorisse et Monialibus Civitatis Cestr' percipientibus annuatim de eisdem exitibus ad eosdem terminos Pasche et Sancti Michelis equis portionibus de antiqua elemosina eis constituta per litteras acquietancie ipsarum Priorisse et Monialium super hunc compotum ostensas et liberatas per litteras domini superius allegatas – xvj li.

28.6   Item eisdem Priorisse et Monialibus per assignationem domini Edwardi Regis Avi Regis nunc in recompensationem quarundam decimarum ad ecclesiam de Overe spectantium quas dimiserunt ad opus Abbatis de Valle Regali ad rogatum eiusdem Regis ad festa predicta per equales portiones per predictas litteras acquietancie ipsarum Priorisse et Monialium super hunc compotum liberatas – iiij li. xvij s.

28.7   Eisdem Priorisse et Monialibus per assignationem domini Edwardi Regis Avi domini nostri Regis nunc in recompensationem quatuor acrarum terre prope Godesbache quas in manus eiusdem Regis reddiderunt ad opus dicti Abbatis de Valle Regali ad eadem festa per equales portiones per predictas litteras acquietancie ipsarum Priorisse et Monialium super hunc compotum ostensas et liberatas – x s.

28.3   And to the same prior and convent, who take yearly from the same issues for tithe accruing from the issues of the profit of nine parts of the fishery of the Dee Bridge and of the other fisheries there at the said terms, by equal payments; by the said prior's letters of acquittance handed over upon this account – 100s. 0d.[1]

28.4   And to the same prior and convent, who take yearly from the same issues at the same terms, of the gift of Edward, former king of England, grandfather of the present king, in recompense for certain tithes at Frodsham which used to belong to the said abbot, and which he gave up for the abbot of Vale Royal's use at the same king's request; by the said prior's letters of acquittance and the lord's letters directed to the chamberlain which relate both to these alms as well as to the fee contained within them, dated at London 2 July in the 21st year of the reign of the present king (1347), which letters remain among the warrants of account for the same 21st year (1346–47); by the same prior's letters of acquittance handed over upon this account – £4.[2]

28.5   Item, to the prioress and nuns of the city of Chester, who take yearly from the same issues at the same terms of Easter and Michaelmas, by equal payments, of ancient alms given to them; by letters of acquittance of the same prioress and nuns shown and handed over upon this account, and by the lord's letters cited above – £16.[3]

28.6   Item, to the same prioress and nuns, by assignment of King Edward, the grandfather of the present king, in recompense for certain tithes belonging to the church of Over which they handed over for the abbot of Vale Royal's use at the same king's request, at the said feasts. by equal payments; by the aforesaid letters of acquittance of the prioress and nuns shown and handed over upon this account – £4 17s. 0d.[4]

28.7   To the same prioress and nuns, by assignment of King Edward, the grandfather of our present king, in recompense for four acres of land next to Godesbache which they rendered into the same king's hands for the said abbot of Vale Royal's use, at the same feasts, by equal payments; by the aforesaid letters of acquittance of the prioress and nuns shown and handed over upon this account – 10s. 0d.

1   Between 1141 and 1150 Earl Ranulf II granted to the abbey a tenth part of the rents from the city of Chester, and 'the tenth penny from the nine pennies received from the bridge and the other fisheries'. By Edward I's charter to the city, the city rents were consolidated to a fee-farm of £100 a year (Barraclough, *Charters*, pp. 36–38; *C.Cnart.R.*, *1257–1300*, pp. 486–87).

2   The grants of compensatory alms to the institutions that had been persuaded to endow Vale Royal Abbey recorded in **28.4**, **28.6**, and **28.7** are listed, without date, in *The Ledger-Book of Vale Royal Abbey*, ed. J. Brownbill, R.S.L.C., lxviii (1914), p. 124. They are also entered in the commission of Sir Robert Holland as justiciar of Chester, 1312 (ibid., pp. 42–43). For the endowment of the abbey, see *V.C.H.*, iii. 156–59).

3   There appears to be no surviving charter granting the alms mentioned in this entry. As Barraclough points out, there are other charters of grants to this house which have disappeared (*Charters*, p. 224).

4   Between 1190 and 1194 Earl Ranulf III confirmed the grant by his father, Hugh II, of the rectory of Over to the nuns (Barraclough, *Charters*, pp. 223–34).

⟨*m 1d*⟩ {*m 1d*}

28.8   Eisdem Priorisse et Monialibus in recompensationem quarundam decimarum provenientium de villis[a] de Bradford' Sutton' Litelovere[b] et Merton' in parochia de Overe que quidem ville assignabantur per dictum dominum Regem Abbati de Valle Regali ad festa Pasche et Sancti Michelis per predictas litteras acquietancie ipsarum Priorisse et Monialium per litteras domini superius allegatas – Cv s. ij d.

28.9   Item fratribus Predicatoribus Civitatis Cestr' percipientibus annuatim de eisdem exitibus de antiqua elemosina eis constituta ad festa Pasche et Sancti Michelis per equales portiones per litteras acquietancie ipsorum fratrum super hunc compotum liberatas et per litteras domini superius allegatas – viij li. xiij s. iiij d.

28.10   Item solut(i) Johanni de Brunham juniori Custodi Hospitalis Sancti Johannis extra portam borialem Civitatis Cestr' de quadam elemosina eidem hospitali constituta per litteras domini superius allegatas et recognitionem ipsius Johannis super hunc compotum presentatam – iiij li. xj s. et sic allocatur in compoto precedenti.[c]

28.11   Item leprosis Sancti Egidij de Boghton' percipientibus de eisdem exitibus de antiqua elemosina eis constituta per litteras acquietancie ipsorum leprosorum et litteras domini superius allegatas ad festum Sancti Michelis pro toto anno – xx s.

28.12   Item Abbati de Whallegh' quondam vocato Stanlowe percipienti annuatim de eisdem exitibus de antiqua elemosina ei[d] constituta per litteras acquietancie ipsius Abbatis et litteras domini superius allegatas ad festum Natalis domini pro toto anno - xx s.

Summa: lxj li. vj s. vj d. probatur[e]

29.   FEODA ET VADIA

29.1   Idem computat in denariis solutis domino Bartholomeo de Burgherssh' Justiciario Cestr'[f] percipienti C li. per annum[g] pro feodo suo in eodem officio Justiciarij predicti per litteras acquietancie ipsius Bartholomei et litteras domini

---

a   *villa* 772/3; *vill'* 772/4.
b   *Lytelovere* 772/4.
c   *et sic . . . compoto precedenti* intl. 772/4, om. 772/3.
d   *eis* 772/3.
e   om. 772/3.
f   *Cestris'* 772/3.
g   *percipienti per annum C li.* 772/4.

28.8 To the same prioress and nuns in recompense for certain tithes accruing from the townships of Bradford, Sutton, Little Over and Marton in Over parish, which were assigned by the said king to the abbot of Vale Royal, at the feasts of Easter and Michaelmas; by the aforesaid letters of acquittance of the same prioress and nuns, and by the lord's letters cited above – 105s. 2d.

28.9 Item, to the Friars Preachers of the city of Chester, who take yearly from the same issues, of ancient alms appointed to them, at the feasts of Easter and Michaelmas, by equal payments; by the friars' letters of acquittance handed over upon this account, and by the lord's letters cited above – £8 13s. 4d.[1]

28.10 Item, paid to John de Brunham the younger, warden of St John's Hospital outside the North Gate of the city of Chester, of alms given to the same hospital; by the lord's letters cited above, and the same John's acknowledgment presented upon this account – £4 11s. 0d., and thus allowed in last year's account.[2]

28.11 Item, to the lepers of St Giles of Boughton, who take from the same issues, of ancient alms appointed to them; by the same lepers' letters of acquittance and the lord's letters cited above; at the feast of Michaelmas, for the whole year – 20s. 0d.[3]

28.12 Item, to the abbot of Whalley, formerly called 'of Stanlow', who takes yearly from the same issues, of ancient alms appointed to him; by the same abbot's letters of acquittance and the lord's letters cited above; at the feast of Christmas, for the whole year – 20s. 0d.[4]

Sum: £61 6s. 6d. Approved.

29. FEES AND WAGES

29.1 He accounts in money paid to Bartholomew de Burgherssh, justiciar of Chester, who takes £100 a year for his fee as justiciar; by his letters of acquittance and the lord's letters directed to Master John de Brunham the

1 There appears to be no evidence for the payment of this sum until it was confirmed by Edward I in 1274 (*V.C.H.*, iii. 174).

2 In his grant of land to found the hospital in the early 1190s, Earl Ranulf III also gave £4 11s. 0d. a year 'to maintain three beds for the poor and infirm at the rate of 1d. a day in alms for each pauper' (*V.C.H.*, iii. 180).

3 During the minority of Ranulf III, before 1181, 20s. 0d. a year was paid to the 'infirm' of Chester, which may be the earliest evidence of alms to the Lepers of Boughton (*V.C.H.*, iii. 178). The two grants to the brethren by Earl Ranulf III, each of 20d. a year, which are recorded in the St Werburgh's Chartulary seem to have lapsed subsequently (Barraclough, *Charters*, pp. 235–36).

4 Earl Ranulf III granted an annual sum of 20s. 0d. to the monks of Stanlow abbey, who moved to Whalley in the thirteenth century. The gift was made between 1207 and 1211, in frankalmoign, and was to be taken from the 'vicecomitatu . . . de Cestria', cited by Barraclough as the earliest example of a separate shrievalty for the city. Although the gift was intended to be superseded by an endowment in land, it continued to be paid in cash, although by 1300 it was listed as one of the 'ancient alms' payable by the justiciar of Chester (Barraclough, *Charters*, pp. 213–14; *C.F.R*, *1272–1307*, p. 428).

⟨m 1d⟩ {m 1d}

Magistro Johanni de Brunham Juniori Camerario Cestr' directas quarum datum est apud London' xxvj die Octobris anno regni regis nunc xxvij penes ipsum Camerarium remanentes – lx li.

29.2 Item Johanni de Delves locum tenenti Justiciarij predicti in officio eiusdem Justiciarij percipienti per annum xl li. pro feodo suo de predictis C li. feodo Justiciarij predicti per litteras acquietancie ipsius Johannis de Delves et litteras predicti Bartholomei predicto Camerario[a] directas et super compotum dicti Camerarij de anno xxviij° ostensas – xl li.

29.3 Item Magistro Johanni de Brunham Juniori Camerario Cestr' percipienti per annum pro feodo et regardo suis in eodem officio – xxvj li. xiij s. iiij d. unde de regardo – x marce.

29.4 Item Johanni de Penbrugg' Equitatori Foreste de Wirhale[b] percipienti pro vadiis suis vj d. per diem in eodem officio a festo Sancti Michelis anno regni regis nunc[c] xxxv[to] usque idem festum proxime sequens per unum annum integrum per litteras acquietancie ipsius Johannis super hunc compotum liberatas et litteras domini Camerario directas penes ipsum Camerarium remanentes dat' apud London' xx die Decembris anno regni regis nunc xxxiij° – ix li. ij s. vj d.[d]

a   772/3 follows with *suo*, del.
b   *Wyrhale* 772/4.
c   *regni regis nunc* om. 772/3.
d   **29.4** is followed by a cancelled entry, with an explanatory note written over. Note: *Cancellatur quia heredes infra etatem et putatur tenementa debere esse* [intl. 772/3] *in manu domini ratione magne seriantie.* Entry: *Item heredibus Philippi de Raby Gardinarij Gardini* [intl. 772/3] *Castri Cestr' in feodo percipientibus pro vadiis suis iij d. per diem unde per tempus huius* [intl. and del. 772/3] *compoti et litteras acquietancie ipsorum heredum super hunc* [om. 772/3] *compotum liberatas – iiij li. xj s. iij d.* This entry's sum is not added into the sum for section **29**.

younger, chamberlain of Chester, dated at London 26 October in the 27th year of the reign of the present king (1353), which remain in the chamberlain's possession – £60.[1]

29.2 Item, to John de Delves, lieutenant of the aforesaid justiciar, who takes £40 a year for his fee out of the same justiciar's fee of £100; by John de Delves's letters of acquittance and the said Bartholomew's letters directed to the aforesaid chamberlain and shown upon the said chamberlain's account for the 28th year of the reign of the present king (1353–54) – £40.[2]

29.3 Item, to Master John de Brunham the younger, chamberlain of Chester, who takes each year for his fee and supplementary fee in the same office – £26 13s. 4d., of which 10 marks is for the supplementary fee.[3]

29.4 Item, to John de Penbrugg, rider of Wirral forest, who takes 6d. a day for his wages as rider, from Michaelmas in the 35th year of the reign of the present king (1361) to the same feast next following (1362) for one whole year; by his letters of acquittance handed over upon this account and the lord's letters directed to the chamberlain, in whose possession they remain, dated at London 20 December in the 33rd year of the reign of the present king (1359) – £9 2s. 6d.[4]

1 Burgherssh's letters of appointment of 26 October 1353 at the accustomed fee of £100 a year empowered him to act by deputy (*B.P.R.*, iii. 128; *ChAcc*, p. 219). This appointment, despite appearances, marks a substantial curtailment of the authority that previous justiciars had exercised, and the centralisation of decision-making in London. Although the most formal records, such as the plea rolls of the county court, assumed that Burgherssh was actively involved in administration, part three of the *Black Prince's Register* makes it clear that he treated the office as a sinecure, and his nominal deputy, John Delves – called 'the lieutenant' for short – performed all the official duties. Delves (see note 2) was appointed by the prince, and not by Burgherssh. It became usual for orders from London to be addressed to Delves directly, and only occasionally to 'Burgherssh or his lieutenant'. Consequently Burgherssh can be regarded as being in receipt of an annuity of £60, assigned on the revenues of the earldom of Chester.

2 John Delves was already lieutenant-justiciar of North Wales at the time of his appointment to the Chester post on 4 October 1353 (*B.P.R.*, iii. 125). Burgherssh, while he had no part in the appointment as he did not become justiciar until more than three weeks later, must have had to give his consent to part of his fee being assigned to the lieutenant. It is likely that previous justiciars had chosen their own deputies, as no appointments by kings or earls of Chester have survived, and that the remuneration was agreed between the two parties.

3 Master John Burnham (also spelt Brunham) the younger first appeared in the Chester administration as receiver of fines 1342–43 [*ChAcc*, p. 114, omits the fact that the accountant was called 'John de Brunham' *the younger*] (SC6 771/14, m.1). He replaced William Lynford as chamberlain in the autumn of 1346, and held the office continuously until his death *c.* 1371 (SC6 1268/3/5; SC6 772/5). He received his supplementary fee (*regardum*) of 10 marks in connection with his responsibility for the revenue of the manor-hundred of Macclesfield, the administration of which had been returned to the county officials in 1347 after several long periods when it was in the hands of successive royal consorts (Booth, *Financial Administration*, pp. 86–87).

4 Penbrugg was appointed rider, at the prince's pleasure, at 6d. a day wages, on 20 December 1359 (*B.P.R.*, iii. 379; *ChRR*, p. 377). Neither version of his letters of appointment either mentions a residence requirement or empowers him to act by deputy, but it is unlikely that he acted in person since he is described as 'yeoman of the prince's chamber', and the grant was made for past and future service. This is, therefore, another example of an office which can be regarded as the effectual assignment of an annuity.

⟨*m 1d*⟩ {*m 1d*}

(*set sequatur pro meliori littera erga proximum*)[a]

29.5   Item Ricardo de Ercal Carpentario domini in Comitatibus Cestr' et Flynt' percipienti pro vadiis suis vj d. per diem in officio predicto a quarto die Decembris anno regni regis nunc xxxv^{to} usque festum Sancti Michelis[b] proxime sequens per CCiiij^{xx} xix dies ultimo die et non primo computatis per litteras acquietancie ipsius Ricardi super hunc compotum liberatas et litteras domini Camerario directas quarum datum est quarto die Decembris anno regni regis nunc xxxv^{to} – vij li. ix s. vj d. et qui allocantur ad presens eo quod Justiciarius recordatur conventionem talem esse factam cum eo.[c]

29.6   Item eidem Ricardo pro Roba sua percipienti annuatim de dicto domino Principe ad festum Natalis domini per litteras acquietancie predictas – x s. et qui allocantur ad presens causa predicta.[d]

29.7   Item Willelmo de Heton' Forestario[e] Foreste de Baghegre percipienti pro vadiis suis in eodem officio j d. per diem unde per tempus compoti per litteras domini superius allegatas – xxx s. v d. et qui sic allocantur in compoto precedenti.[f]

29.8   Item Willelmo[g] de Apelton' Custodi et Venditori catallorum felonum et[h] fugitivorum et deodandorum in Comitatu Cestr' percipienti per annum pro feodo suo in eodem officio – xl s. per litteras domini Camerario directas penes ipsum Camerarium remanentes quarum datum est apud London' viij die Maij anno regni regis nunc xxxj et litteras acquietancie ipsius Willelmi super hunc compotum liberatas – xl s. et qui sic allocantur in compoto precedenti.[i]

29.9   Item Willelmo de Hulpeston' Cementario domini percipienti pro vadiis suis vj d. per diem in officio predicto a quarto die[j] Decembris anno regni regis nunc xxxv^{to} usque festum Sancti Michelis proxime sequens per CC iiij^{xx} xix dies[k] ultimo die et non primo computatis per litteras acquietancie ipsius Willelmi super hunc compotum liberatas et litteras domini predictas dat' iiij^{to} die Decembris anno regni regis nunc xxxv^{to} – vij li. ix s. vj d.

Summa: Cliiij li. xv s. iij d.

---

a   note om. 772/3.
b   om. 772/3 (defect in MS).
c   *et qui . . . cum eo* om. 772/3, intl. 772/4.
d   *et qui . . . causa predicta* om. 772/3, intl. 772/4.
e   intl. 772/3.
f   *et qui . . . compoto precedenti* intl.
g   om. 772/3 (defect in MS).
h   om. 772/3.
i   *et qui . . . compoto precedenti* intl.
j   om. 772/3 (defect in MS).
k   intl. 772/3.

(*But let him sue for a better letter before next time*).

29.5 Item, to Richard de Ercal, the lord's carpenter in the counties of Chester and Flint, who takes 6d. a day for his wages as carpenter, from 4 December in the 35th year of the reign of the present king (1361), until the feast of Michaelmas following (1362), that is 299 days counting the last and not the first; by his letters of acquittance handed over upon this account and the lord's letters directed to the chamberlain dated 4 December in the 35th year of the reign of the present king (1361) – £7 9s. 6d., and which are allowed at present because the justiciar records that an agreement of this type has been made with him.[1]

29.6 Item, to the same Richard for his robe, which he takes yearly from the said prince at Christmas, by the aforesaid letters of acquittance – 10s. 0d., and which are allowed at present, for the aforesaid reason.

29.7 Item, to William de Heton, forester of Bachegraig forest, who takes 1d. a day for his wages as forester during the time of this account; by the lord's letters cited above – 30s. 5d., and which are so allowed in last year's account.

29.8 Item, to William de Apelton, keeper and seller of the chattels of felons and fugitives and of deodands in Cheshire, who takes 40s. 0d. yearly for his fee in the same office; by the lord's letters directed to the chamberlain, in whose possession they remain, dated at London 8 May in the 31st year of the reign of the present king (1357) and William's letters of acquittance handed over upon this account – 40s. 0d., and which are thus allowed in last year's account.[2]

29.9 Item, to William de Hulpeston, the lord's mason, who takes 6d. a day for his wages as mason, from 4 December in the 35th year of the reign of the present king (1361) to the feast of Michaelmas following (1362), that is 299 days counting the last and not the first; by his letters of acquittance handed over upon this account and the lord's letters aforesaid dated 4 December in the 35th year of the reign of the present king (1361) – £7 9s. 6d.[3]

Sum: £154 15s. 3d.

1 Only the warrant ordering the issuing of letters of appointment for Ercal and three other officials survives, dated 4 December 1361 (*B.P.R.*, iii. 428; *ChRR*, p. 173). Consequently, there is no way of knowing why Ercal's actual letters of appointment were insufficient; it may have been because they did not give the full details of his contract of employment. For the organisation of works within the earldom and principality see R.A. Brown, H.M. Colvin and A.J. Taylor, *The History of the King's Works*, i. 465–70, ii. 1056–57. See also **34.13**.

2 The grant of this office to Apelton, during good behaviour, on 8 May 1357 was for good service at Poitiers (*B.P.R.*, iii. 238; *ChRR*, p. 192).

3 At the time of his appointment, 4 December 1361 (*B.P.R.*, iii. 428; *ChRR*, p. 230), Hulpeston was already in charge of the over-ambitious plans to build the chevet – the 'chapel of twelve altars' – at the east end of the unfinished church of Vale Royal Abbey, the nave of which had been blown down in 1360. This task dominated his tenure of the office of master mason of the earldom and North Wales, although this, and the routine work on castles and other buildings, did not prevent him from having the usual responsibility for the walls of Chester. His wages were increased to 8d. a day in 1369–70 (SC6 772/5 m.1d; *The History of the King's Works* (1963), i. 248–57 and J. Harvey, *English Mediaeval Architects: a Biographical Dictionary*, Revised Edition (1984), p. 134). See also **34.13**.

⟨*m 1d*⟩ {m 2d}

30.   FEODA ET VADIA DE NOVO CONSTITUTA CUM ANNUITATIBUS

30.1   Idem computat in denariis solutis Willelmo de Stretton' Chivaler nuper Cissori Camere domini pro quadam annuitate sibi[a] concessa per dominum Comitem ad terminum vite sue percipienda de exitibus molendinorum de Dee ad terminos Natalis domini et Nativitatis Sancti Johannis Baptiste equis portionibus per litteras acquietancie ipsius Willelmi super hunc compotum[b] liberatas – x li.

30.2   Item Ricardo Comiti Arundell' de quadam annuitate C li. per annum sibi concessa per dominum Principem ad terminum vite ipsius Comitis percipienda de exitibus molendinorum de Dee per manus Camerarij Cestr' una cum C li. percipiendis de exitibus Civitatis Cestr' in recompensationem D marcarum quas solebat percipere de predicto Principe pro feodo suo in officio Justiciarij North'Wall' et quas quidem D marcas annuatim percipiendas idem Ricardus remisit dicto domino Principi pro predictis CC li. modo quo superius percipiendis per litteras acquietancie ipsius Ricardi super hunc compotum liberatas et litteras domini Justiciario et Camerario directas quarum datum est apud London' xj die Novembris anno regni regis nunc xxv[to] – C li.

⟨m 2d⟩

30.3   Item Reginaldo Balle Custodi Parci de Loytcoyt[c] percipienti pro vadiis suis j d. per diem in eodem officio per certam conventionem secum factam per locum tenentem Justiciarij et Camerarium a festo Sancti Michelis anno regni regis nunc xxxv[to] usque idem festum proxime sequens per unum annum integrum per litteras acquietancie ipsius Reginaldi super hunc compotum liberatas – xxx s. v d.

30.4   Item Johanni Chaundos Chivaler Seneschallo de Macclesfeld' percipienti per annum pro feodo suo in eodem officio per litteras acquietancie Roberti de Morton' generalis attornati ipsius Johannis super hunc compotum liberatas et litteras domini Camerario directas penes eundem Camerarium remanentes quarum datum est apud Cestr' xx die Septembris anno regni regis nunc xxvij – x li.

30.5   Item eidem Johanni Custodi et Magistro Forestario Foreste de Macclesfeld' et Supervisori eiusdem Foreste et omnium aliarum Forestarum domini Principis infra Comitatum Cestr' percipienti per annum pro uno equitatore inveniendo in foresta de Macclesfeld' per predictas litteras acquietancie ipsius Roberti et litteras domini predictas – lx s.

---

a   om. 772/3 (?defect in MS).
b   om. 772/3.
c   *Loytcoyd* 772/4.

30. NEWLY-ESTABLISHED FEES AND WAGES, AND ANNUITIES

30.1 He accounts in money paid to William de Stretton, knight, who used to be tailor of the lord's chamber, for an annuity granted him by the earl for the term of his life to be taken from the issues of the Dee mills at the terms of Christmas and the Nativity of St John Baptist, by equal payments; by William's letters of acquittance handed over upon this account – £10.[1]

30.2 Item, to Richard, earl of Arundel, for an annuity of £100 a year granted him by the prince for the term of Arundel's life to be taken from the issues of the Dee mills by the hands of the chamberlain of Chester, together with £100 to be taken from the issues of the city of Chester, in recompense for 500 marks which he used to receive from the prince as his fee when he was justiciar of North Wales, and which annual fee he remitted to the prince in return for the £200 to be taken as above; by Arundel's letters of acquittance handed over upon this account and the lord's letters directed to the justiciar and chamberlain, dated at London 11 November in the 25th year of the reign of the present king (1351) – £100.[2]

30.3 Item, to Reginald Balle, keeper of Llwydcoed park, who takes 1d. a day for his wages as parker by agreement made between him and the lieutenant-justiciar and chamberlain, from Michaelmas in the 35th year of the reign of the present king (1361) to the same feast following (1362) for one whole year; by his letters of acquittance handed over upon this account – 30s. 5d.

30.4 Item, to John Chaundos, knight, steward of Macclesfield, who takes the following sum yearly for his fee as steward; by letters of acquittance of Robert de Morton, his general attorney, handed over upon this account and the lord's letters directed to the chamberlain, in whose possession they remain, dated at Chester 20 September in the 27th year of the reign of the present king (1353) – £10.

30.5 Item, to the same John, keeper and master forester of Macclesfield forest, and surveyor of that forest and of all the prince's other forests within Cheshire, who takes the following sum yearly for providing a rider in Macclesfield forest; by Robert's aforesaid letters of acquittance and the lord's aforesaid letters – 60s. 0d.[3]

---

1 Stretton's £10 annuity was being paid as early as 1347–48 (*ChAcc*, p. 123).
2 *B.P.R.*, iii. 52–53; *ChRR*, p. 8. Arundel was still receiving the two annuities in 1373–74, the last surviving chamberlain's account before the prince's death (SC6 772/9, m.1; 772/10, m.1).
3 Chandos's endowment with these largely sinecure offices occurred in the aftermath of the 1353 state visit of the prince to Cheshire in which Sir John took part. The letters appointing him to the stewardship of Macclesfield and the keeping of the three forests do not survive on the 1353 recognizance roll, which is in a poor state, but the register contains the grant of £53 13s. 4d. annual expenses, dated 19 September 1353, 'which he must needs incur in managing the said forests and the game there' (*B.P.R.*, iii. 122–23). For the letters of 22 January 1361, see *B.P.R.*, iii. 404.

⟨*m 2d*⟩ {*m 2d*}
(*per acquietanciam de xxviij li. vj s. viij d. deficientibus de termino Sancti Michelis*)[a]

30.6   Et pro diversis custibus et expensis per predictum Johannem circa officia predicta[b] annuatim faciendis per litteras acquietancie eiusdem Roberti predictas et litteras domini superius allegatas - xliij li. xiij s. iiij d. Et non plus eo quod dominus Princeps mandavit litteras suas de privato sigillo suo Magistro Johanni de Brunham Juniori Camerario suo Cestr' dat' apud London' xxij die Januarij anno regni regis nunc xxxiiij[to] per quas mandavit eidem Camerario quod retineat in manu dicti domini Principis decem libras per annum de denariis quos dictus dominus Johannes Chaundos percipit de eodem domino Principe annuatim per manus Camerarij Cestr' qui pro tempore fuerit pro eo quod idem dominus Princeps ad rogatum dicti domini Johannis concessit cuidam Wilym[c] ap ll' Scutifero ipsius Johannis Ballivas Ragloti de Malthayn et de Maynaurdylaw in Comitatu de Kermerdyn ad terminum vite ipsius Wilym[c] per litteras predictas.

30.7   Item Willelmo de Wakebrugg' Narratori domini Principis in Comitatibus Cestr' et Flynt' percipienti per annum pro feodo suo in eodem officio per litteras acquietancie ipsius Willelmi super hunc compotum liberatas et litteras domini Camerario directas penes eundem Camerarium remanentes quarum datum est apud London' xiij die Novembris anno regni regis nunc xxviij° – C s.

30.8   Item Johanni de Davenport' Narratori pro placitis domini Principis in Comitatibus Cestr' et Flynt' et Wall' percipienti per annum pro feodo suo in eodem officio per litteras acquietancie ipsius Johannis super hunc compotum liberatas et litteras domini Camerario directas quarum datum est apud London' xvj die Februarij anno regni regis nunc xxxv[to] penes ipsum Camerarium remanentes – C s.

30.9   Item Johanni le Porter janitori Castri Cestr' percipienti per annum in subsidium sustentationis sue quamdiu custodiam[d] porte dicti Castri habuerit per litteras acquietancie ipsius Johannis super hunc compotum liberatas et litteras domini Camerario directas penes eundem Camerarium remanentes quarum datum est apud Cestr' xiij die Septembris anno regni regis nunc xxvij – xxx s.

30.10   Item Margarete de Tranemol' percipienti quolibet die per annum unum obolum ad terminum vite sue in subsidium sustentationis sue per litteras acquietancie ipsius Margarete super hunc compotum liberatas et litteras domini Camerario directas penes eundem Camerarium remanentes quarum datum est apud[e] Cestr' xx die Septembris anno regni regis nunc xxvij – xv s. ij d. ob.

a   note om. 772/3.
b   *predicta officia* 772/4.
c   *Willym* 772/4.
d   772/3 follows with *dicte*, del.
e   om. 772/3.

(For the acquittance of £28 6s. 8d. lacking for Michaelmas term).

30.6 And for various costs and expenses incurred each year by the said John, in connection with the said offices; by Robert's aforesaid letters of acquittance and the lord's letters cited above - £43 13s. 4d. It would be more except that the prince sent letters of his privy seal to Master John de Brunham the younger, his chamberlain of Chester, dated at London 22 January in the 34th year of the reign of the present king (1361), by which he instructed the chamberlain to retain in the prince's hand the £10 a year which the said John Chaundos took from the prince by the hands of the chamberlain of Chester for the time being, because the prince has granted, at John's request, the bailiwicks of the *rhaglaw* of Mallaen and Maenordeilo in the county of Carmarthen to Gwilym ap Llywelyn, John's esquire, for the term of Gwilym's life, by the said letters.

30.7 Item, to William de Wakebrugg, the prince's pleader in the counties of Chester and Flint, who takes the following sum yearly for his fee as pleader; by his letters of acquittance handed over upon this account and the lord's letters directed to the chamberlain, in whose possession they remain, dated at London 13 November in the 28th year of the reign of the present king (1354) – 100s. 0d.[1]

30.8 Item, to John de Davenport, the prince's pleader in the counties of Chester and Flint, and in Wales, who takes the following sum for his fee as pleader; by his letters of acquittance handed over upon this account and the lord's letters directed to the chamberlain, in whose possession they remain, dated at London 16 February in the 35th year of the reign of the present king (1361) – 100s. 0d.[2]

30.9 Item, to John le Porter, gate-keeper of Chester castle, who takes yearly in aid of his sustenance as long as he should retain the keeping of the castle gate the following sum; by his letters of acquittance handed over upon this account and the lord's letters directed to the chamberlain, in whose possession they remain, dated at Chester 13 September in the 27th year of the reign of the present king (1353) – 30s. 0d.[3]

30.10 Item, to Margaret de Tranemol, who takes ½d. a day each year for the term of her life in aid of her sustenance; by her letters of acquittance handed over upon this account and the lord's letters directed to the chamberlain, in whose possession they remain, dated at Chester 20 September in the 27th year of the reign of the present king (1353) – 15s. 2½d.[4]

---

1 He was retained as serjeant pleader 'in the counties of Chester, Flint and elsewhere' from Michaelmas 1353 (*B.P.R.*, iii. 180).
2 A reference to Davenport as 'serjeant in court' occurs in September 1352. He was retained as serjeant pleader 'in the parts of Cheshire, Flintshire, Wales and elsewhere', 16 February 1361 (*B.P.R.*, iii. 78, 406).
3 For the order to pay him his porter's wages, 13 September 1353, see *B.P.R.*, iii. 117. The order was made 'as a gift and act of charity from the prince' at the time that Edward was dispensing 'acts of grace' with the proceeds of the trailbaston sessions, towards the end of his 1353 visit to Cheshire.
4 *B.P.R.*, iii. 122. Why the prince chose this particular 'poor woman' as an example on whom to demonstrate the more positive side of his royal lordship in Cheshire is not known.

⟨*m 2d*⟩ {*m 2d*}

30.11   Item Thome de Warrewyk' Constabulario Castri Cestr' percipienti pro vadiis suis xij d. per diem in officio predicto unde per tempus huius compoti per litteras acquietancie ipsius Thome super hunc compotum liberatas et litteras domini Johanni de Delves locum tenenti Justiciarij Cestr' et Camerario directas et penes ipsum Camerarium remanentes dat' xxvj die Octobris anno regni regis nunc xxxiij° – xviij li. v s.

30.12   Item Alano de Cheyne Chivaler de quadam annuitate C marcarum sibi concessa per dictum dominum Principem ad terminum vite sue percipienti per manus Camerarij Cestr' qui pro tempore fuerit ad festa Pasche et Sancti Michelis equis portionibus per litteras domini Camerario directas et penes ipsum Camerarium remanentes quarum datum est apud Byflet' vij die Julij anno regni regis nunc xxxv^{to} per litteras acquietancie ipsius Alani super hunc compotum liberatas – lxvj li. xiij s. iiij d.

30.13   Item Ricardo de Dokesey pistori domini pro quadam annuitate x marcarum sibi concessa per dominum Principem ad terminum vite sue percipienti de exitibus molendinorum et furni de Macclesfeld' ad festa Pasche et Sancti Michelis equis portionibus per litteras domini Camerario directas quarum datum est primo die Februarij anno regni regis nunc xxxj° et per litteras acquietancie ipsius Ricardi super hunc compotum liberatas – vj li. xiij s. iiij d.

30.14   Item Roberto de Nevill' Chivaler pro quadam annuitate C marcarum sibi concessa per dominum Principem ad terminum vite sue percipienti per manus Camerarij Cestr' qui pro tempore fuerit ad festa Pasche et Sancti Michelis equis portionibus quousque idem dominus^a Princeps sibi providerit aliunde de terris et tenementis ad valorem annualem predictarum C marcarum per litteras domini Camerario directas dat' viij die Augusti anno regni regis nunc xxxij° et litteras acquietancie ipsius Roberti super hunc compotum liberatas – lxvj li. xiij s. iiij d.

a   intl. 772/3.

30.11   Item, to Thomas de Warrewyk, constable of Chester castle, who takes 12d. a day for his wages as constable during the time of this account; by his letters of acquittance handed over upon this account and the lord's letters directed to John de Delves, lieutenant-justiciar of Chester, and the chamberlain, in whose possession they remain, dated 26 October in the 33rd year of the reign of the present king (1359) – £18 5s. 0d.[1]

30.12   Item, to Alan de Cheyne, knight, for an annuity of 100 marks granted him by the prince for the term of his life, to be taken by the hands of the chamberlain of Chester, for the time being, at the feasts of Easter and Michaelmas, by equal payments; by the lord's letters directed to the chamberlain, in whose possession they remain, dated at Byfleet 7 July in the 35th year of the reign of the present king (1361), and by Alan's letters of acquittance handed over upon this account – £66 13s. 4d.[2]

30.13   Item, to Richard de Dokesey, the lord's baker, for an annuity of 10 marks granted him by the prince for the term of his life, to be taken from the issues of Macclesfield mills and oven at the feasts of Easter and Michaelmas, by equal payments; by the lord's letters directed to the chamberlain dated 1 February in the 31st year of the reign of the present king (1357), and by Richard's letters of acquittance handed over upon this account – £6 13s. 4d.[3]

30.14   Item, to Robert de Nevill, knight, for an annuity of 100 marks granted him by the prince for the term of his life, to be taken by the hands of the chamberlain of Chester for the time being, at the feasts of Easter and Michaelmas, by equal payments, until the prince should be able to provide him with lands and tenements elsewhere to the value of the annuity; by the lord's letters directed to the chamberlain dated 8 August in the 32nd year of the reign of the present king (1358), and by Robert's letters of acquittance handed over upon this account – £66 13s. 4d.[4]

1   Warwick had originally been appointed constable on 10 May 1325, nominally by Earl Edward of Windsor. After he became king, as Edward III, he continued the appointment, and made it a life grant in 1344. Some time afterwards Warwick was dismissed, to be reinstated at the king's insistence in 1355 following the dismissal and disgrace of Richard Done of Utkinton two years earlier. Warwick lost the office a second time as a punishment for not preventing Master Benet ab Iorwerth's escape from custody, to be restored yet again on 26 October 1359 to hold at pleasure (*B.P.R.*, iii. 374–75). He died in March 1366, nearly 40 years after his first appointment as constable of Chester castle (SC6 786/3, m.3).

2   He was granted a life-annuity of £40 on 1 February 1357 as a reward for his personal attendance on the prince at the battle of Poitiers. It was raised to 100 marks on 7 July 1361, for further good service (*B.P.R.*, iii. 237, 419; *ChRR*, p. 105). Cheyne's wife, Joan, had property in south Cheshire, and it may have been for that reason that the annuity was assigned on the chamberlain's account (*B.P.R.*, iii. 468–69). The annuity was confirmed by Richard II in 1381 (*C.P.R.*, *1377–81*, p. 613).

3   The grant of this life-annuity to Dokesey states that it is only to be until he can be provided with land and rents to that value. [The enrolment of the warrant and grant in the published calendar of recognizance rolls gives the figure, probably mistakenly, as £10 a year.] (*B.P.R.*, iii. 234; *ChRR*, p. 148; *ChAcc*, p. 243). Despite the intention expressed in the original grant, Dokesey was still being paid the annuity in the last surviving account, 1374, of the Black Prince's time (SC6 772/10, m.2).

4   The grant of 8 August 1358 specifies that it was for good service at Poitiers (*B.P.R.*, iii. 306; *ChRR*, p. 360).

⟨*m 2d*⟩ {*m 2d*}

30.15   Item Willelmo Braas Attornato domini Principis[a] in Comitatibus Cestr' et Flynt' percipienti per annum in eodem officio[b] xx s. per litteras domini Camerario directas dat' xv die Februarij anno regni regis nunc xxxij et litteras acquietancie ipsius Willelmi super hunc compotum liberatas – xx s. et sic allocatur in compoto preterito.[c]

30.16   Item Thome le Parker de Dynbiegh'[d] Attillatori domini Principis in partibus Cestris' et North'Wall' percipienti pro vadiis suis iij d. per diem in eodem officio a festo Sancti Michelis anno regni regis nunc xxxv[to] usque idem festum proxime sequens per litteras domini Camerario directas et penes ipsum remanentes quarum datum est apud London' primo die Decembris anno regni regis nunc xxxiiij[to] et litteras acquietancie ipsius Thome super hunc compotum liberatas – iiij li. xj s. iij d.

30.17   Item Johanni de Creye Equitatori foreste de Mara et Mondrem percipienti pro vadiis suis iij d. per diem in eodem officio a festo Sancti Michelis anno regni regis nunc xxxv[to] usque xxix diem[e] Aprilis proxime sequentem per CCxij dies ultimo die et non primo computatis per litteras domini Camerario directas quarum datum est apud Kenyngton'[f] viij die Julij anno regni regis nunc xxxvj[to] et super hunc compotum liberatas per quas mandavit eidem Camerario quod solvere faceret predicto Johanni de Creye[g] vadletto Camere sue nuper equitatori foreste predicte vadia sua iij d. per diem a dato Commissionis sue usque illud tempus quo[h] alius per Commissionem eiusdem domini ad dictam ballivam fuerit ordinatus Non obstante quod dictus Johannes in propria persona sua dictam ballivam non occupavit[i] per litteras acquietancie Johannis de Scolehalgh' attornati predicti Johannis de Creye[j] super hunc compotum liberatas – liiij s.[k]

30.18   Item Hugoni de Wyrlegh' Equitatori eiusdem Foreste percipienti pro vadiis suis iij d. per diem in eodem officio a predicto xxix die Aprilis usque festum Sancti Michelis proxime sequens per Cliij dies per litteras domini Camerario directas quarum datum est apud Busshegh' xiiij die Maij anno regni regis nunc xxxvj[to] et litteras acquietancie ipsius Hugonis super hunc compotum liberatas – xxxvij s. iij d.

30.19   Item Hugoni de Pyrye Ballivo Itineranti in Comitatibus Cestr' et Flynt' percipienti pro feodo suo xl s. per annum in eodem officio videlicet ab xj die Marcij anno regni regis nunc xxxvj[to] usque festum Sancti Michelis proxime

---

a   intl. 772/4.
b   *officio predicto* 772/4.
c   *et sic allocatur in compoto preterito* om. 772/3, intl. 772/4.
d   *Dynbegh'* 772/4.
e   intl. 772/3.
f   *Kenynton'* 772/4.
g   *Crey'* 772/4.
h   772/4 has *quo*, which another hand later extended to *quousque*.
i   *ocupavit* 772/3.
j   *Crey'* 772/4.
k   772/4 has a del. note: *pro acq' sigill'*.

30.15 Item, to William Braas, the prince's attorney in the counties of Chester and Flint, who takes 20s. 0d. a year as attorney; by the lord's letters directed to the chamberlain dated 15 February in the 32nd year of the reign of the present king (1358), and by William's letters of acquittance handed over upon this account – 20s. 0d., and it is thus allowed in the last account.[1]

30.16 Item, to Thomas le Parker of Denbigh, the prince's artiller in Cheshire and North Wales, who takes 3d. a day for his wages as artiller, from Michaelmas in the 35th year of the reign of the present king (1361) to the same feast next following (1362); by the lord's letters directed to the chamberlain, in whose possession they remain, dated at London 1 December in the 34th year of the reign of the present king (1360), and by Thomas's letters of acquittance handed over upon this account – £4 11s. 3d.[2]

30.17 Item, to John de Creye, rider of the forest of Delamere and Mondrum, who takes 3d. a day for his wages as rider, from Michaelmas in the 35th year of the reign of the present king (1361) until 29 April following, for 212 days counting the last and not the first; by the lord's letters directed to the chamberlain dated at Kennington 8 July in the 36th year of the reign of the present king (1362), and handed over upon this account, whereby he instructed him to pay John de Creye, valet of his chamber and late rider of the said forest, his wages of 3d. a day from the date of his commission until another was appointed to that bailiwick by the lord's commission, notwithstanding the fact that the said John did not fill the said office in person, and by letters of acquittance of John de Scolehalgh, John de Creye's attorney, handed over upon this account – 54s. 0d.[3]

30.18 Item, to Hugh de Wyrlegh, rider of the same forest, who takes 3d. a day for his wages as rider, from the said 29 April until Michaelmas following (1362), for 153 days; by the lord's letters directed to the chamberlain, dated at Bushey 14 May in the 36th year of the reign of the present king (1362), and by Hugh's letters of acquittance handed over upon this account – 37s. 3d.[4]

30.19 Item, to Hugh de Pyrye, bailiff-itinerant in the counties of Chester and Flint, who takes 40s. 0d. a year for his fee as bailiff, namely from 11 March in the 36th year of the reign of the present king (1362), until the feast of Michaelmas

---

1 The letters of 15 February 1358 ordered the chamberlain to pay Braas 40s. 0d. for his past labours, and 20s. 0d. a year in future (*B.P.R.*, iii. 292). A 'William Brace' had been active in the administration in 1342 (*C.P.R.*, *1340–43*, p. 408).
2 Parker had been a member of the garrison of Caernarfon castle in 1354, when he was first appointed to make and repair the prince's artillery (*B.P.R.*, iii. 489). The letters of 1 December 1360 are the warrant for the payment of his wages (ibid., 402).
3 Creye was appointed rider, during good behaviour, by letters dated 22 June 1361, and on 8 July 1362 the order to pay him his wages, as 'late rider', until a replacement was appointed, was issued (*B.P.R.*, iii. 419, 447).
4 Wirley's letters of appointment, confirming the actual decision to appoint by the lieutenant and chamberlain, are dated 14 May 1362 (*B.P.R.*, iii. 443).

⟨m 2d⟩ {m 2d}
sequens per CCj dies ultimo die et non primo computatis iuxta ratam predictorum xl s. per annum per certam conventionem secum factam per Auditores et
Camerarium per litteras acquietancie ipsius Hugonis super hunc compotum
liberatas – xxj s. ix d.[a]

Summa: CCC xlix li. xviij s. ij d. ob.
probatur[b]

⟨m 3d⟩

31.   CUSTUS PERGAMENI ET ALIORUM NECESSARIORUM

31.1   Idem computat in denariis solutis pro pergameno empto pro brevibus
rotulis compotorum et placitorum et aliis memorandis tam coram Justiciario
Cestr’ in communibus placitis quam coram Camerario Cestr’ in Scaccario ibidem
per tempus huius compoti – lj s. viij d.
(*respondeat de veteri cathena*)
31.2   Item in una cathena argenti empta pro sigillo domini – x s.
31.3   Item in denariis solutis pro diversis rebus emptis per Thomam le Parker
Attillatorem domini et aliis expensis per eum factis officium suum[c] concernentibus infra tempus huius compoti ut patet per particulas super hunc compotum
examinatas et liberatas – xvj s. vj d. ob.[d]
31.4   Item in denariis solutis Willelmo filio Johannis piscatori de quodam
regardo sibi facto pro inventione cuiusdam pissis Regalis vocati *Sturgen* apud
Podynton’ in Wirhale[e] mense Junij anno regni regis nunc xxxvj[to] de consuetudine – xij d.
31.5   Item in cariagio eiusdem pissis de Podynton’ usque Castrum Cestr’ – xij d.
31.6   Et in denariis solutis Abbati et Conventui Sancte Werburge Cestr’
persone ecclesie de Shotewyk’ in cuius parochia dictus pissis inveniebatur pro
decima sua dicti pissis – xxj d. ob.

---

a   intl. 772/3. **30.19** is followed by a cancelled entry, with an explanatory note written over. The entry’s
    sum is not included in the sum total for section **30**. Note: *cancellatur pro defectu in Warranto*. Entry:
    *Item Willelmo de Stanlegh [Stanle 772/4] Forestario Foreste de Wirhale [Whirale 772/4] pro custodia
    parci de Shotewyk’ [Shotewhik’ 772/4] pro quodam regardo xxx s. annuatim sibi [sibi annuatim 772/4]
    concesso ad terminum vite sue per dominum Principem pro custodia predicti Parci [Parci predicti
    772/4] per litteras domini Johanni de Delves [Johanni de Delves om. 772/4] locum tenenti et Camerario
    directas quarum datum est apud Berghamested’ [quarum . . . Berghamested’ om. 772/4, which has
    simply dat’] quinto die Decembris anno regni regis nunc [regni regis nunc om. 772/4] xxxv[to] et [om.
    772/4] penes eundem Camerarium remanentes et litteras acquietancie ipsius Willelmi super hunc
    compotum liberatas – xxx s.*
b   om. 772/4.
c   intl. 772/3.
d   *vj d. ob.* intl. 772/3.
e   *Wyrhale* 772/4.

following, for 201 days counting the last and not the first, as a proportion of the fee, by an agreement made with him by the auditors and the chamberlain; by Hugh's letters of acquittance handed over upon this account – 21s. 9d.[1]

Sum: £349 18s. 2½d. Approved.

31.   COST OF PARCHMENT AND OTHER NECESSARIES

31.1   He accounts in money paid for parchment bought for writs, account rolls, plea rolls and other memoranda, concerned with both common pleas before the justiciar of Chester and with business before the chamberlain of Chester in the exchequer there, during the time of this account – 51s. 8d.
(*Let him answer for the old chain*).
31.2   Item, for one silver chain bought for the lord's seal – 10s. 0d.
31.3   Item, in money paid for various things bought by Thomas le Parker, the lord's artiller, and other expenses incurred by him in connection with his official position during the time of this account; as appears by the particulars examined and handed over upon this account – 16s. 6½d.[2]
31.4   Item, in money paid to William John's son, fisherman, for the customary reward paid for finding a certain royal fish called *sturgen* at Puddington in Wirral in June in the 36th year of the reign of the present king (1362) – 12d.
31.5   Item, for carriage of the same fish from Puddington to Chester castle – 12d.
31.6   And in money paid to the abbot and convent of St Werburgh's, Chester, as parson of Shotwick church, in which parish the said fish was found, for their tithe of the same – 21½d.[3]

1   In a comprehensive set of instructions to the lieutenant and chamberlain on 6 July 1355, the prince's council told them to use their own initiative about the continuance of the two year old office of 'bailiff errant', with the responsibility 'to levy the prince's moneys in default of other ministers' (*B.P.R.*, iii. 209). With the exploitation of various types of judicial revenue to increase the yield of the earldom to the prince, this should be regarded as a supplement to the official establishment responsible for this type of revenue, rather than an indication that it had failed. For Pyrye's appointment [the calendar gives only the year, 1361] see *ChRR*, p. 383.
2   As the particulars do not survive, it is not possible to know what is referred to here. The purchase of arrows and heads is recorded in **37.1**, as well as in the dead stock account, **52** and **53**.
3   See **9.7** for the yield of the sturgeon. If the fish were found at Puddington, as the account suggests, then it is difficult to see why the abbot, as parson of Shotwick, should receive the tithe, since Puddington was in Burton ancient parish.

⟨*m 3d*⟩ {*m 2d*}

31.7   Item in[a] denariis solutis Executoribus testamenti Stephani de Merton' pro quadam placea pasture super quam tentores domini molendinorum Fullonicorum Cestr' consistunt pro hoc anno et anno proxime precedenti utroque anno ij s. per conventionem secum factam per Camerarium – iiij s.

31.8   Item in iiij bagis de corio albo emptis pro rotulis compotorum ministrorum Comitatuum Cestr' Flynt' et Macclesfeld' et Johannis de Sancto Petro pro hoc anno imponendis – xvj d.

31.9   Item in[b] duabus duodenis et[c] dimidia pergameni emptis et expensis pro rotulis compotorum[d] et aliis memorandis istos compotos tangentibus – vij s. vj d.[e]

31.10   Et in stipendiis et expensis clericorum scribentium et duplicantium hunc compotum et predictorum ministrorum et terrarum Johannis de Sancto Petro – xl s. per ordinationem Auditorum et litteras domini allocatas in compoto Camerarij de anno xxxij.

Summa: vj li. xiiij s. x d.

{m 3d}

32.   CUSTUS NUNCIORUM

Idem computat in denariis solutis diversis nunciis portantibus diversa brevia domini Principis vicecomitibus Comitatuum[f] Cestr' et Flynt' Coronatoribus et aliis ministris domini in Comitatibus predictis per diversas vices per tempus huius compoti – iiij s. ij d. ob.

Summa: iiij s. ij d. ob.

33.   CUSTUS PRISE VINORUM

Idem computat in denariis solutis pro uno dolio[g] vini recepto in portu apud le Redebonk' de nave Walteri de Dertesmouthe de prisa domini Principis Wall' videlicet pro j dolio[g] xl s. ultra unum dolium[h] captum quietum de eadem nave – xl s.

Summa: xl s.

a   intl. 772/3.
b   intl. 772/3.
c   om. 772/3.
d   om. 772/4; rep. and repetition del. 772/3.
e   *vij s. vj d.* intl. 772/4.
f   om. 772/3; intl. 772/4.
g   *doleo* 772/4.
h   *doleum* 772/4.

31.7 Item, in money paid to the executors of Stephen de Merton's testament for a piece of pasture occupied by the fullers of the lord's fulling mills of Chester, for this year and last year, 2s. 0d. each, by agreement between him and the chamberlain – 4s. 0d.[1]

31.8 Item, for four bags of white leather bought as containers for the account rolls of the officials of the counties of Chester and Flint, of Macclesfield, and of the lands of John de Sancto Petro this year – 16d.

31.9 Item, for two and a half dozens of parchment bought and used for the account rolls and other memoranda touching the accounts – 7s. 6d.[2]

31.10 And for the stipends and expenses of the clerks writing and duplicating this account and those of the aforesaid officials, and of the lands of John de Sancto Petro – 40s. 0d., by order of the auditors and by the lord's letters allowed in the chamberlain's account for the 32nd year (1357–58).[3]

Sum: £6 14s. 10d.

32. COST OF MESSENGERS

He accounts in money paid to various messengers carrying various of the prince's writs to the sheriffs of the counties of Chester and Flint, and to the coroners and others of the lord's officials in the aforesaid counties, on various occasions during the time of this account – 4s. 2½d.

Sum: 4s. 2½d.

33. COST OF THE PRISE OF WINES

He accounts in money paid for one tun of wine received in the port at *le Redebonk* from Walter de Dertesmouthe's ship, of the prince of Wales's prise, namely 40s. 0d. for one tun over and above one tun which is taken quit from the same ship – 40s. 0d.

Sum: 40s. 0d.[4]

1 For the fulling mills attached to the mills of Dee, see SC6 785/9, m.1d. Merton had been lord of Earl's Eye, which included the bank of the River Dee opposite the city.
2 Why has parchment for account rolls been bought here, as well as in entry **31.1**? If it is assumed that entry **31.9** refers to parchment used by the auditors' clerks to write the extant accounts of the earldom, presumably that mentioned in **31.1** could have been used for drawing up draft accounts, which have not survived, or for the 'originals' of the accounts which were pre-written before the audit team's arrival. 772/4 calls them simply 'rotulis'.
3 The account published in *ChAcc*, pp. 237–43, as the chamberlain's account for 1357–58 is, in fact, for 1356–57 (that is, the 31st year of Edward III, or 30–31 Edward III). The order to pay the auditor's clerks was issued 23 October 1352 (*E.P.R.*, iii. 79), and in the account for 1353–54 payment was made for three clerks doing this work [omitted from *ChAcc*, pp. 206–19] (SC6 771/18, m.2d).
4 See above, **9.1**; below, **48**.

⟨*m 3d*⟩ {*m 3d*}
34.   OPERA DIVERSA

34.1   Idem computat in denariis solutis diversis Carpentariis Sarratoribus et aliis operariis operantibus in Castro Cestr' circa reparationem domorum ibidem et molendinorum de Dee et in lucratione maeremij in[a] Foresta de Mara pro eisdem operibus et in cariagio eiusdem maeremij de dicta Foresta usque Castrum Cestr' per tempus huius compoti ut patet per unum rotulum indentatum particularum contra Ricardum de Ercal Carpentarium domini contrarotulatorem super hunc compotum liberatum – xxij li. ij s. j d. ob.

34.2   Item in denariis solutis diversis Cementariis quarrariis et aliis operariis operantibus circa reparationem fundamenti molendinorum ultra Aquam de Dee et calceti eorundem molendinorum infra tempus huius compoti ut patet per unum rotulum indentatum particularum contra Willelmum de Hulpeston' Cementarium domini contrarotulatorem super hunc Compotum liberatum – xiiij li. iij d. ob.

34.3   Item in denariis solutis diversis Cementariis quarrariis et aliis operariis operantibus circa facturam unius hostij infra cameram domini in eodem Castro et reparationem defectuum eiusdem Castri infra tempus huius[b] compoti ut patet per unum rotulum indentatum particularum contra predictum Willelmum Cementarium domini contrarotulatorem super hunc compotum liberatum – liij s. vij d.

34.4   Item in denariis solutis diversis Cementariis quarrariis et aliis operariis operantibus circa reparationem Castri de Beston' in parte per tempus huius compoti et in Cemento Ferro et Assere emptis pro eisdem operibus infra idem tempus ut patet per unum rotulum indentatum particularum contra predictum Willelmum contrarotulatorem super hunc compotum liberatum – xj li. xiiij s. vij d.

34.5   Item in denariis solutis Ade de Kyngeslegh' Clerico super cariagio duorum magnorum *Throwes* de *lyme* usque Macclesfeld' pro molendino fullonatico ibidem et pro factura j loge[c] in parco de novo pro salva[d] custodia ferarum domini in[e] eodem parco per litteras domini Camerario directas quarum datum est[f] xviij die Februarij anno regni regis nunc[g] xxxv penes eundem Camerarium remanentes[h] et reparationem diversorum defectuum Manerij et Stagni apud Macclesfeld' infra tempus huius compoti ut patet per particulas super hunc compotum examinatas et liberatas – vj li. vij s. viij d.

a   intl. 772/4.
b   intl. 772/3.
c   *logg'* 772/4.
d   *salvo* 772/3.
e   772/3 has *de*, del., followed by *in* written over.
f   om. 772/3.
g   *regni regis nunc* om. 772/3.
h   *et pro factura . . . Camerarium remanentes* intl.; 772/4 has mistakenly put the caret before *ibidem.*

34. VARIOUS WORKS

34.1 He accounts in money paid to various carpenters, sawyers and other workers working in Chester castle on the repair of the buildings there, and of the Dee mills, and for cutting timber in Delamere forest for the same works, and for carrying the timber from that forest to Chester castle, during the time of this account; as appears by an indented roll of particulars handed over upon this account counter to Richard de Ercal, the lord's carpenter, as controller – £22 2s. 1½d.

34.2 Item, in money paid to various masons, quarrymen and other workers working on the repair of the foundations of the mills beyond the river Dee, and of the causeway of the same mills, within the time of this account; as appears by an indented roll of particulars handed over upon this account, counter to William de Hulpeston, the lord's mason, as controller – £14 0s. 3½d.

34.3 Item, in money paid to various masons, quarrymen and other workers for their work in making a door within the Lord's Chamber in the same castle,[1] and on the repair of the same castle's faults within the time of this account; as appears by an indented roll of particulars handed over upon this account, counter to the aforesaid William, the lord's mason, as controller – 53s. 7d.

34.4 Item, in money paid to various masons, quarrymen and other workers working on the repair of Beeston castle, in part during the time of this account, and in mortar, iron and board bought for the same works within the same time; as appears by an indented roll of particulars handed over upon this account, counter to the aforesaid William as controller – £11 14s. 7d.

34.5 Item, in money paid to Adam de Kyngeslegh, clerk, for the carriage of two great *throwes* of *lyme* to Macclesfield for the fulling mill there,[2] and for making a new lodge in the park for the safe keeping of the lord's wild beasts in the same park; by the lord's letters directed to the chamberlain, in whose possession they remain, dated 18 February in the 35th year of the reign of the present king (1361); and for the repair of various faults in the manor house and mill-pond at Macclesfield within the time of this account; as appears by the particulars examined and handed over upon this account – £6 7s. 8d.

1 The 'Lord's Chamber' in Chester castle does not seem to have been identified.
2 The fulling mill at Macclesfield was constructed by Robert le Walker on the manorial mill-pond around 1356, but was not a financial success (*B.P.R.*, iii. 389; Booth, *Financial Administration*, p. 98).

⟨*m 3d*⟩ {*m 3d*}

34.6   Item in denariis solutis Alano de Maurdyn plumbatori domini existente[a] apud Flynt' pro coopertura diversorum turrium ibidem et reparatione diversorum defectuum eiusdem Castri in opere plumbi a quartodecimo die Octobris anno regni regis nunc xxxv[to] usque xij diem mensis Marcij proxime sequentem per Cl dies utroque die computato ipso capiente per diem pro vadiis suis in officio predicto vij d. ad terminum vite sue ex concessione domini Principis per litteras suas Camerario Cestr' directas quarum datum est apud London' xxviij die[b] Augusti anno regni regis nunc xxxiij penes ipsum Camerarium remanentes et in fine compoti eiusdem Camerarij de anno regni regis nunc xxxiiij[to] irrotulatas et per unam indenturam sub sigillo dicti Alani super hunc compotum liberatam – iiij li. vij s. vj d.

34.7   Item Johanni de Flynt' servienti predicti Alani per xxj septimanas et duos dies infra tempus predictum ipso capiente per septimanam xvj d. ex concessione dicti domini Principis per litteras domini supradictas et per indenturam predictam – xxviij s. iiij d. ob.

34.8   Item in denariis solutis diversis operariis operantibus cum predicto Alano in officio predicto[c] infra tempus predictum et in clavis emptis pro operibus domini ibidem officium dicti Alani concernentibus ut patet per unam[d] indenturam particularum contra predictum Alanum contrarotulatorem super hunc compotum liberatam – viij s. iij d.

34.9   Item in denariis solutis Johanni ap Meiller Carpentario pro factura paliciorum pro clausura parci de Loytcot[e] et positione eorundem paliciorum circa eundem parcum infra tempus huius compoti ipso capiente pro factura C paliciorum vj d. et pro positione unius perticate cum paliciis ij d. – xliiij s. viij d. per defectum Reginaldi Parkar'.[f]

⟨*m 4d*⟩

(*loq' ad consilium*)[g]

34.10   Item in denariis solutis diversis Cementariis quarrariis et aliis operariis operantibus super opere petroso[h] cuiusdam Aule et aliarum domorum de novo in interiori ballia Castri Cestr' pro locum tenente Justiciarij et in Cemento ferro et Assere emptis pro eodem opere infra tempus huius compoti ut patet per particulas super hunc compotum examinatas et[i] liberatas ultra xxx li. assignatas ad idem opus per Johannem de Delves locum tenentem Justiciarij – vij li. ij s. viij d. ob.

a   om. 772/3.
b   om. 772/3.
c   *predicto officio* 772/4.
d   om. 772/3.
e   *Loytcoyd* 772/4.
f   *per defectum Reginaldi Parkar'* om. 772/3, intl. 772/4.
g   note om. 772/3.
h   intl. 772/3.
i   *examinatas et* intl. 772/3.

34.6   Item, in money paid to Alan de Maurdyn, the lord's plumber resident at Flint, for roofing various towers there and for the repair of various faults in the same castle, in lead work from 14 October in the 35th year of the reign of the present king (1361) until 12 March following, for 150 days counting both days, taking 7d. a day for his wages as plumber for the term of his life by grant of the prince; by the prince's letters directed to the chamberlain, in whose possession they remain, dated at London 28 August in the 33rd year of the reign of the present king (1359), and which were enrolled at the end of the same chamberlain's account for the 34th year of the reign of the present king (1359–60); and by an indenture under the seal of the said Alan handed over upon this account – £4 7s. 6d.[1]

34.7   Item, to John de Flynt, the aforesaid Alan's servant, for 21 weeks and two days within the time aforesaid, taking 16d. a week by grant of the said prince; by the lord's letters abovesaid and by the aforesaid indenture – 28s. 4½d.

34.8   Item, in money paid to various workers working with the aforesaid Alan on the aforesaid job within the time aforesaid, and for nails bought for the lord's works there which relate to the said Alan's job; as appears by an indenture of particulars handed over upon this account, counter to the aforesaid Alan as controller – 8s. 3d.

34.9   Item, in money paid to John ap Meilir, carpenter, for making palings for the enclosure of Llwydcoed park, and for putting the same palings in position around the same park within the time of this account, taking 6d. himself for making 100 palings, and 2d. for positioning one perch of palings – 44s. 8d., by the default of Reginald Parkar.

(Speak to the council).

34.10   Item, in money paid to various masons, quarrymen and other workers working on the renewal of the stone-work of a hall and of other buildings in the inner bailey of Chester castle for the lieutenant-justiciar, and in mortar, iron and board bought for the same job within the time of this account; as appears by the particulars examined and handed over upon this account, over and above the £30 assigned to the same job by John de Delves, lieutenant-justiciar – £7 2s. 8½d.

---

1   Maurdyn was appointed master plumber of Cheshire, Flintshire and the principality of Wales on 14 September 1353 (*B.P.R.*, iii. 119). The letters of 28 August 1359, of which there is no copy enrolled on the 1359–60 chamberlain's account (SC6 771/23), presumably extended the appointment for life.

⟨m 4d⟩ {m 3d}

34.11　Et in denariis solutis diversis Carpentariis Sarratoribus et aliis operariis operantibus super opere ligneo tecti dicte Aule infra tempus huius compoti ut patet per j rotulum indentatum particularum contra predictum Magistrum Ricardum Carpentarium contrarotulatorem super hunc compotum liberatum – lxxvij s.

34.12　Item in denariis solutis diversis Carpentariis Sarratoribus et aliis operariis operantibus circa reparationem grangie manerij de Frodesham et molendin(i) ibidem in parte et in factura j *gote* de novo ibidem infra tempus huius[a] compoti ut patet per unum rotulum indentatum particularum contra predictum Magistrum Ricardum Contrarotulatorem super hunc compotum liberatum – ix li. xviij s. iiij d. ob.

34.13　Et[b] in denariis solutis Magistro Willelmo de Helpeston'[c] Cementario domini et Magistro Ricardo de Ercall'[d] Carpentario pro vadiis suis pro utroque eorum vj d. per diem per conventionem secum factam per Justiciarium et Camerarium ab xj die Novembris anno xxxv usque iiij diem[e] Decembris ultimo die et non primo computatis per xxiij dies – xxiij s.

Summa: iiij[xx] vij li. viij s. j d. ob.

35.　DONA ET REGARDA

(*fiat venire facias Abbat' ad computandum de receptis et liberationibus*)[f]

Idem computat in denariis solutis Abbati et Conventui de Valle Regali in auxilium perficiendi opera Cementaria duodecim capellarum circumeuntium chorum ecclesie sue versus orientem de parte Dxxvj li. xiij s. iiij d. aretro existentium de DCCClx li. concessis eisdem[g] Abbati et Conventui per dominum Principem Wall' ex causa predicta solvendis eisdem[h] Abbati et Conventui per sex annos et dimidium ad festa Pasche et Sancti Michelis[i] per equales portiones videlicet quolibet anno predictorum sex annorum CC marcis ad festa predicta per litteras domini Camerario directas et penes ipsum remanentes quarum datum est apud London' xxiiij die Augusti anno regni regis nunc xxxiij° videlicet pro terminis Pasche et Sancti Michelis infra hunc compotum contingentibus per litteras acquietancie ipsius Abbatis super hunc compotum liberatas – Cxxxiij li. vj s. viij d.

Summa: Cxxxiij li. vj s. viij d. probatur

a　*istius* 772/3.
b　*Item* 772/4.
c　*Helpuston'* 772/4.
d　772/4 has *Ercal'* and om. *de*.
e　*die* 772/3.
f　note om. 772/3.
g　772/3 has *eidem*, del., followed by *eisdem* written over.
h　*eidem* 772/3.
i　772/3 has carets between *festa* and *Pasche*, and before *Sancti Michelis*. 772/4 has *ad festa Sancti Michelis et Pasche*. The clerk of 772/3 apparently had the intention of reversing the order of the feasts, but did not implement it.

34.11 And in money paid to various carpenters, sawyers and other workers working on the woodwork of the roof of the said hall within the time of this account; as appears by an indented roll of particulars handed over upon this account, counter to Master Richard the carpenter as controller – 77s. 0d.[1]

34.12 Item, in money paid to various carpenters, sawyers and other workers working on the repair of the grange of Frodsham manor and of the mill there in part, and on renewing one *gote* there within the time of this account; as appears by an indented roll of particulars handed over upon this account, counter to Master Richard as controller – £9 18s. 4½d.

34.13 And in money paid to Master William de Helpeston, the lord's mason, and to Master Richard de Ercall, carpenter, for the wages of both of them at 6d. a day, by agreement made with them by the justiciar and chamberlain, from 11 November in the 35th year (1361) up to 4 December for 23 days, counting the last day and not the first – 23s. 0d.[2]

Sum: £87 8s. 1½d.

35. GIFTS AND REWARDS

(*Cause the abbot to come to account for the receipts and liveries*).

He accounts in money paid to the abbot and convent of Vale Royal as assistance towards the completion of the masonry work of the twelve chapels which go round the choir of their church at the east end, as part of £526 13s. 4d. in arrears of £860 granted by the prince of Wales to the same abbot and convent for the same purpose, payable within six and a half years at Easter and Michaelmas, by equal payments, namely in each of the aforesaid six years 200 marks at the aforesaid feasts; by the lord's letters directed to the chamberlain, which remain in his possession, dated at London 24 August in the 33rd year of the reign of the present king (1359); namely for the terms of Easter and Michaelmas falling within this account, by the same abbot's letters of acquittance handed over upon this account – £133 6s. 8d.[3]

Sum: £133 6s. 8d. Approved.

---

1 On 14 April 1364, letters warranted by Sir Richard de Stafford and John Delves ordered the chamberlain to complete the works 'begun in the inner ward' of Chester castle, presumably in response to the marginal note to this entry (*B.P.R.*, iii. 465).

2 The orders to admit Ercal and Helpeston to their respective offices are dated 4 December 1361 (*B.P.R.*, iii. 428; *ChRR*, p. 173). It is presumably because the warrant was dated after the beginning of the financial year that their wages from November to 4 December 1361 appear here, and not in **29.5** or **29.9**.

3 *B.P.R.*, iii. 361–62.

⟨*m 4d*⟩ {*m 3d*}
36. CUSTUS PLUMBI

(*respondeat de plumbo*)[a]
36.1 Idem computat in denariis solutis Minerariis pro combustione iij fodrorum x pedum et dimidij xiiij librarum plumbi combusti apud Baghegre de parte[b] minere dominum concernente et ponderati ibidem quarto die Maij anno regni regis nunc xxxvj[to] et pro cariagio dicte minere ad idem plumbum et succisione busce et cariagio eiusdem et omnibus aliis expensis circa dictum plumbum appositis ipsis capientibus pro quolibet fodro xiiij s. per certam conventionem secum factam per Camerarium Cestr' – xlvij s. xj d.
36.2 Idem computat in expensis Camerarij et aliorum secum existentium apud Baghegre quarto die Maij anno supradicto[c] circa ponderationem plumbi combusti ibidem cum busca domini – vj s. viij d.

Summa: liiij s. vij d. probatur[d]
{m 4d}

37. EMPTIO SAGITTARUM CUM CAPITIBUS[e]

(*respondeat de sagittis et capitibus*)[f]
37.1 Idem computat in denariis solutis pro lxx garbis sagittarum sine capitibus emptis apud Dynbiegh'[g] per Thomam le Parker attillatorem domini pro garnistura Castri Cestr' infra tempus huius compoti – lxx s.
37.2 Item in cariagio earundem sagittarum de Dynbiegh'[h] usque Cestr' – xvj d.
37.3 Item in MMDC xxiiij[i] capitibus sagittarum emptis per predictum Thomam in Comitatu Lancastr' tam pro predictis sagittis quam pro sagittis remanentibus in Castro Cestr'[j] de anno precedenti ad diversa precia[k] – xxx s. vj d. ob.
37.4 Item in M capitibus sagittarum emptis per eundem Thomam ibidem pro predictis sagittis – xij s. vj d.
37.5 Item in uno equo conducto ad cariandum predicta capita de Comitatu Lancastr' usque Cestr' – vj d.

Summa: Cxiiij s.[l] x d. ob. probatur[m]

---

a   note om. 772/3.
c   *xxxvj* 772/4.
e   772/4 has *r(espondeat)* after *CAPITIBUS*.
g   *Dynbegh'* 772/4.
i   *xxiiij* intl. 772/3.
k   *ad diversa precia* om. 772/3.
m   om. 772/3.

b   *proparte* 772/4.
d   om. 772/3.
f   Note om. 772/3.
h   *Dynbegh'* 772/4.
j   intl. 772/3.
l   772/3 has *Cx* del., followed by *Cxiiij*.

36.   COST OF LEAD

(*Let him answer for the lead*)
36.1   He accounts in money paid to miners for smelting three fothers 10½ feet fourteen pounds of lead smelted at Bachegraig, for the part of the ore which relates to the lord, weighed there 4 May in the 36th year of the reign of the present king (1362). And for carriage of the said ore for the same lead, and for cutting and carriage of wood, and all other expenses which have been paid for the said lead. Those miners take 14s. 0d. a fother, by an agreement with them by the chamberlain of Chester – 47s. 11d.
36.2   He accounts in the expenses of the chamberlain and others staying with him at Bachegraig on 4 May in the abovesaid year, in connection with the weighing of the lead which was smelted there with the lord's wood – 6s. 8d.

Sum: 54s. 7d. Approved.

37.   PURCHASE OF ARROWS AND HEADS

(*Let him answer for the arrows and heads*).
37.1   He accounts in money paid for 70 sheaves of arrows without heads, bought at Denbigh by Thomas le Parker, the lord's artiller, for stocking Chester castle, within the time of this account – 70s. 0d.
37.2   Item, for the carriage of the same arrows from Denbigh to Chester – 16d.
37.3   Item, for 2,624 arrow-heads bought by the aforesaid Thomas in Lancashire, both for the aforesaid arrows and for the arrows remaining in Chester castle from the previous year, at various prices – 30s. 6½d.
37.4   Item, for 1,000 arrow-heads bought by the same Thomas there, for the aforesaid arrows – 12s. 6d.
37.5   Item, for a horse which was hired to carry the aforesaid heads from Lancashire to Chester – 6d.

Sum: 114s. 10½d. Approved.

⟨*m 4d*⟩ {*m 4d*}
38. LIBERATIO DENARIORUM

(*respondeat Parcarius*)
Idem computat in denariis solutis Willelmo de Chorlegh' Parcario Parci de Macclesfeld' de prestito super vadiis suis per tempus huius compoti per unam indenturam – lx s. De quibus idem Willelmus debet respondere.

Summa: lx s.

39. SUMMA TOTALIS EXPENSARUM: DCCCvij li. iij s. iij d.

Et debet MM CCCCj li.
xvj s. v d. ob di. qu.
40. Et DCC viij li. xvij s. iij d. de
remanentia compoti sui
de anno ultimo
preterito. Summa debiti
Coniuncta MMM Cx li.
xiij s. viij d. ob. di. qu.
41. De quibus liberavit domino
Petro de Lacy generali Receptori
domini Principis Aquit' et
Wall' apud London' M lxxvj li.
xij s. ix d. per Octo indenturas
sigillo dicti Petri signatis et
super hunc compotum liberatas

Respondeat Lacy[a] Quarum prima continet Dlxvj li.
xiij s. iiij d. dat' xiiij die

Respondeat Lacy[a] Maij anno xxxvj Secunda continet
xxvj li. vij s. ij d. dat' xxvj die

Respondeat Lacy[a] Maij eodem anno Tertia continet
xxxiij li. ij s. iij d. dat'

Respondeat Lacy[a] xxvj die Junij eodem anno Quarta
continet lxxiij li. dat' tertio

Respondeat Lacy[a] die[b] Julij eodem anno Quinta
continet xvij li. x s. dat' xix

Respondeat Lacy[a] die Julij eodem anno Sexta continet
xl li. dat' xxiiij die Julij eodem

Respondeat Lacy[a] anno Septima continet CC li. dat'
xxiij die Augusti eodem anno et

Respondeat Lacy[a] viij[va] continet Cxx li. dat' xx die
Augusti eodem anno.

a   *Respondeat Lacy* om. 772/4.
b   intl. 772/3.

38. DELIVERY OF MONEY

(*Let the parker answer*)

He accounts in money paid to William de Chorlegh, parker of Macclesfield park, as a prest upon his wages during the time of this account, by an indenture – 60s. 0d. for which the same William ought to answer.[1]

Sum: 60s. 0d.

39. SUM TOTAL OF EXPENSES: £807 3s. 3d.
And he owes £2,401 16s. 5½d. and a half-farthing;

40. and £708 17s. 3d. from
the remainder of his account for the year
last past. JOINT SUM OF INDEBTEDNESS:
£3,110 13s. 8½d. and a half-farthing.

41. Of which he has delivered to Peter de Lacy, receiver
general of the prince of Aquitaine and Wales
at London £1,076 12s. 9d. by eight indentures
sealed with the said Peter's seal and handed over
Let Lacy answer   upon this account. The first, dated 14 May in the 36th
Let Lacy answer   year (1362), contains £566 13s. 4d; the second, dated
Let Lacy answer   26 May in the same year, contains £26 7s. 2d.; the third
dated 26 June in the same year, contains £33 2s. 3d;
Let Lacy answer   the fourth, dated 3 July in the same year, contains
Let Lacy answer   £73 0s. 0d.; the fifth, dated 19 July in the same
Let Lacy answer   year, contains £17 10s. 0d.; the sixth, dated 24 July
Let Lacy answer   in the same year, contains £40; the seventh dated 23
Let Lacy answer   August in the same year, contains £200; the eighth,
dated 20 August in the same year, contains £120 0s. 0d.
And to the same Peter, the receiver, £9 13d. by an

---

1   This advance is charged in Chorlegh's account as parker of Macclesfield, 1361–62, as 'receipt of money' from the chamberlain (SC6 803/5, m.2).

⟨*m 4d*⟩ {*m 4d*}

Respondeat Lacy[a]   Et eidem domino Petro Receptori ix li. xiij d.
per j acquietanciam sigillo ipsius Petri
signatam et super hunc compotum liberatam
dat'[b] secundo die Junij anno xxxvj supradicto.
Et eidem Receptori DCCC lxvj li. xiiij s.
per tres acquietancias sigillo ipsius
Receptoris[c] signatas et super hunc compotum
Respondeat Lacy[a]   liberatas Quarum prima continet DCC lxiiij li.
xij s. viij d. dat' xviij die Octobris anno
Respondeat Lacy[a]   xxxvj Secunda continet lxviij li. xj s.
iiij d. dat' die et anno predictis et
Respondeat Lacy[a]   tertia continet xxxiij li. x s. dat'
xxviij die Novembris anno xxxvj predicto.[d]

42.1   Et allocantur ei x li. qu. in persolutionem xlij li. x s. vj d. ob. qu. Comiti
Sar' debitorum in pede compoti sui de exitibus ij partium dominij de Dynbiegh'
a vigilia Sancti Michelis anno xviij° [e] Regis huius usque xx diem Decembris anno
xxj° eiusdem Regis de fine eiusdem Comitis Sar' unde idem Camerarius oneratur
inter regardum foreste sicut continetur in pede compoti ipsius Camerarij de
anno ultimo preterito per litteras domini Camerario directas et super compotum
suum de anno ultimo preterito liberatas[f] dat' xiiij die Julij anno xxxiiij per quas
dominus mandavit eidem Camerario quod de summa quam (!) idem Comes
tenetur de fine suo pro transgressione per ipsum in foresta de Macclesfeld' facto
deduci et allocari faciet predictos xlij li. x s. vj d. ob. qu. et per acquietanciam
Thome de Thressk[g] Receptoris dicti Comitis super hunc compotum liberatam de
deductione et allocatione predictarum x li. qu. in persolutionem predictorum
xlij li. x s. vj d. ob. qu.[h]

42.2   Et exoneratur de xxvj li. xiij s. iiij d. unde oneratur pro Willelmo Trussell'
de Wermyngeam[i] infra xlij li. xiij s. iiij d. accidentes super Clx acras per ipsum
Willelmum et predecessores suos assartas infra forestam de Macclesfeld' de
maiore summa imbladationis earundem imposita coram Ricardo de Wilughby et
sociis suis nuper Justiciariis Itinerantibus in foresta ibidem anno regni regis nunc
xxxj° pro eo quod continuato processu de alleg(atione) per ipsum Willelmum in
eodem Itinere de assartatione terre predicte usque diem Martis proxime post

a   *Respondeat Lacy* om. 772/4.
b   *cuius acquietancie datum est* 772/4.
c   *Petri* 772/4.
d   *supradictis* 772/3.
e   intl. 772/3.
f   772/4 puts *liberatas* before *de anno*.
g   *Thresk* 772/4.
h   *predictorum* rep. after the sum. A note follows, which does not seem to relate to its adjacent
entry: *Memorandum de onere Camerarij de CC li. quos* (!) *dominus mut' de episcopo Cestr'*.
i   intl. 772/4.

Let Lacy answer   acquittance sealed with his seal and handed
over upon this account, dated 2 June in the aforesaid 36th year.
And to the same receiver £866 14s. 0d. by three acquittances
sealed with the seal of the same receiver and handed over
Let Lacy answer   upon this account. The first, dated 18 October in the 36th year
Let Lacy answer   (1362), contains £764 12s. 8d.; the second, dated the same day
Let Lacy answer   and year, contains £68 11s. 4d; the third, dated 28 November in
the aforesaid 36th year (1362), contains £33 10s. 0d.

42.1 And there are allowed to him £10 0s. 0¼d. in full payment of £42 10s. 6¾d. owed by the earl of Salisbury in the foot of his account for the issues of two parts of the lordship of Denbigh from the vigil of Michaelmas in the 18th year of this king (28 September 1344) until 20 December in the 21st year of the same king (1347),[1] for the fine of the same earl of Salisbury for which the same chamberlain is charged within the Regard of the Forest, as is contained in the foot of the same chamberlain's account for the year last past; by the lord's letters directed to the chamberlain and handed over upon his account for the year last past, dated 14 July in the 34th year (1360) by which the lord instructed the same chamberlain to deduct and allow the aforesaid £42 10s. 6¾d. of the sum for which the same earl is bound for his fine for the trespass committed by him in Macclesfield forest,[2] and by the acquittance of Thomas de Thressk, the said earl's receiver, handed over upon this account for the deduction and allowance of the aforesaid £10 0s. 0¼d. in full payment of the £42 10s. 6¾d. aforesaid.

42.2 And he is exonerated of £26 13s. 4d. for which he is charged in respect of William Trussell of Warmingham, forming part of £42 13s. 4d. for 160 acres which had been assarted by the same William and his predecessors within Macclesfield forest, the larger sum having been imposed for the new ploughing of the same before Richard de Wilughby and his fellows, who used to be justices-in-eyre in the forest there in the 31st year of the reign of the present king (1356/57). This was because, following the adjournment of the law-suit concerning the allegation made by the same William in the same eyre about the assarting of the aforesaid land until the Tuesday after the feast of St. Chad, bishop, in the

---

1   In the prince's letters of 14 July 1360, warranted by the council, the earl of Salisbury is said to have paid £42 10s. 6¾d. more than was due from when he was farmer of two-thirds of the lordship of Denbigh, which was in the prince's hands because of Salisbury's nonage, from Mich. 1344 to 20 October (!) 1347. Consequently, that sum was allowed to him out of his fine for trespass in Macclesfield forest (*B.P.R.*, iii. 389–90).

2   For the earl of Salisbury's offences in Macclesfield forest, see above, **8.5**.

⟨m 4d⟩ {m 4d}
festum Sancti Cedde Episcopi anno predicti Regis xxxvij° consideratum erat per eosdem Justiciarios quod predictus Willelmus quo ad assartationem Centum acrarum terre post confirmationem cuiusdam carte sue ibidem placitatam assarte omnino exoneretur et de sexaginta acris terre ante confirmationem eiusdem[a] carte respondeat et cetera sicut constat Auditoribus per inspectionem rotulorum Itineris predicti et pro quibus lx acris terre[b] idem Camerarius remanet oneratus inter fines[c] foreste predicte.[d]

42.3　Et allocantur ei iiij li. solute Johanni de Davenport' et Ade de Kyngeslegh' Justiciariis laborariorum in Hundredo de Macclesfeld' anno xxxv nomine regardi pro laboribus suis in eadem sessione ex assensu Justiciarij Camerarij et Auditorum et de qua sessione responsum erat domino de xl marcis ut patet in compotis diversorum[e] ministrorum de Macclesfeld' de eodem anno.

43.　Et debet M Cxvij li. xij s. vj d. qu. di qu.[f]

44.　De quibus respondet in pede compoti sui de anno proxime sequenti.[g]

⟨m 5d⟩ {m 5d}

45.　RESPECTUS[h]

45.1　Respectuantur[i] eidem Cx li. xiiij d. ob. qu. unde oneratur pro Thoma de Swynerton' et heredibus suis pro manerio suo de Barrewe infra finem Communitatis foreste de Mara[j] et Mundrem pro hoc anno et tribus annis proxime precedentibus unde pro anno xxxiij° xx li. xviij d. ob. anno xxxiiij xlvj li. xij s. j d. et pro termino Sancti Martini tunc[k] proxime sequenti xxj li. xj s. v d. qu. per litteras domini Camerario directas dat' xiij die Octobris anno xxxiiij de predictis[l] denariis respectuandis usque xv^{nam} Sancti Hillarij proxime sequentem et xxj li. xvj s. ij d. pro termino[m] Nativitatis[n] Sancti Johannis Baptiste anno xxxv et terminis Sancti Martini et Nativitatis Sancti Johannis Baptiste[o] hoc anno xxxvj ultra xlv li. viij s. v d. ob. qu. quos levavit de exitibus dicti manerij pro eisdem terminis post dictam quindenam Sancti Hillarij.

---

a	intl. 772/3.	b	om. 772/4.
c	772/4 has *perquis'*, del., followed by *fines* written over.	d	772/4 adds *et cetera*.
e	om. 772/4.	f	772/4 om. second *qu.*
g	*De quibus . . . proxime sequenti* om. 772/3.	h	*Respectuantur* 772/4.
i	*De quibus respectuantur* 772/4.	j	*Mare* 772/4.
k	intl. 772/4.		
l	*predictos* 772/3.		
m	*terminis* 772/4.		
n	intl. 772/3, om. 772/4.		
o	om. 772/4.		

37th year of the aforesaid king (7 March 1363), it had been considered by the same justices that the aforesaid William should be entirely exonerated of the assarting of the 100 acres of land assarted after the confirmation of a charter of his which was impleaded there, and that he should answer for the 60 acres of land assarted before the confirmation of the same charter et cetera, as is agreed by the auditors on inspection of the rolls of the aforesaid eyre. The chamberlain is still charged for the 60 acres of land among the fines of the aforesaid forest.[1]

42.3 And there are allowed to him £4 paid to John de Davenport and Adam de Kyngeslegh, justices of labourers in the hundred of Macclesfield in the 35th year (1360–61), as a reward for their labours in the same session, by agreement of the justiciar, chamberlain and auditors, and for which session 40 marks ought to have been answered for to the lord as appears in the accounts of various officials of Macclesfield for the same year.[2]

43. And he owes: £1,117 12s. 6¼d. and a half-farthing.

44. For which he answers in the foot of his account for the year following.

45. RESPITES

45.1 There are respited to the same, £110 14¾d. for which he is charged in respect of Thomas de Swynerton and his heirs for their manor of Barrow, within the fine of the community of the forest of Delamere and Mondrum, for this year and the three years preceding it, of which £20 18½d. is for the 33rd year (1358–59), £46 12s. 1d. for the 34th year (1359–60) and £21 11s. 5¼d. for the term of Martinmas following (1360); by the lord's letters directed to the chamberlain dated 13 October in the 34th year (1360), which effect the respite of the aforesaid money until the quindene of Hilary following (27 January 1361); and £21 16s. 2d. for the term of the Nativity of St John Baptist in the 35th year (1361), and the terms of Martinmas and the Nativity of St John Baptist this 36th year (1361–62) over and above £45 8s. 5¾d. which he has levied from the issues of the said manor for the same terms after the said quindene of St Hilary.[3]

---

1 See above **8.9**.
2 'Fines of divers workmen and servants' were charged in the following Macclesfield accounts for 1360–61: Hundred bailiff (£14 11s. 8d.), Borough (£1 4s. 4d.), Forest collector (£4 19s. 4d.) (SC6 803/3, mm. 1, 4).
3 For the letters of respite, see *B.P.R.*, iii. 394

⟨*m 5d*⟩ {*m 5d*}
(*pro littera videnda*)ᵃ

45.2   Et eidem xxiiij li. xix s. iij d. qu. unde oneratur infra summam regardi foreste de Mara pro terris nuper Willelmi Wasteneys in villa de Elton' infra dictam forestam videlicet pro anno xxxiij° vj li. vj s. viij d. ob. anno xxiiijᵗᵒ vj li. xiij s. j d. qu. anno xxxv Cxvj s. iiij d. et pro hoc anno xxxvjᵗᵒ vj li. iij s. j d. ob. et respectuati usque adᵇ legitimam etatem heredis predicti Willelmi per litteras domini Camerario directas dat' v die Septembris anno xxxijᵈᵒ.

45.3   Et eidem xiij li. xj s. ix d. unde oneratur infra summam regardi foreste pro Petro de Dutton' et Matheo de Weverham duobus heredibus Petri de Thorneton' in manu domini existentibus ratione minoris etatis eorundem heredum videlicet xlj s. viij d. pro diversis villis in foresta de Mara pro anno xxxiij° et x s. viij d. de diversis villis infra Forestamᶜ de Wirhall'ᵈ pro eodem anno lxiij s. xj d. ob. pro diversis villis in foresta de Mara pro anno xxxiiijᵗᵒ x s. viij d. pro diversis villis infra forestamᵉ de Wirhale pro eodem anno xxxiiijᵗᵒ lix s. x d. pro diversis villis in foresta de Mara pro anno xxxv et x s. viij d. pro diversisᶠ villis infra forestamᵍ de Wirhale proʰ eodem anno et lxxiiij s. iij d. ob. pro hoc anno xxxvjᵗᵒ unde x s. viij d. pro tenementis infra forestam de Wirhale et respectuati ex hac causa usque ad legitimam etatem dictorum heredum.

45.4   Et eidem vij li. v s. iiij d. qu. unde oneraturⁱ supraʲ infra summam regardi foreste pro terris que fuerunt Roberti filij Ricardi de Acton' in Acton' existentibus in manu domini ratione utlagarie ipsius Roberti unde pro anno xxxiiijᵗᵒ xlix s. vj d. ob. qu. anno xxxv xlvj s. vj d. et pro hocᵏ anno xxxvj xlix s. iij d. ob.

45.5   Et eidem xxv li. xv s. vij d. ob. qu. unde oneratur pro Ricardo Munchull' infra summam regardi foreste de Mare et Moundremˡ unde xiiij li. xv s. ob. qu. de anno xxxv proxime preterito de parte xxvij li. xvij s. vij d. super ipsum existentium de dicto regardo de eodem anno et xj li. vij d. de parte xxxj li. vij d. pro hoc anno xxxvjᵗᵒ per litteras domini dat' xiiij die Julij anno xxxiiijᵗᵒ per quas dominus mandavit locum tenenti Justiciarij et Camerario quod superviderent omnia terras et tenementa bona et catalla ipsius Ricardiᵐ et rationabilem

---

a   note om. 772/3.
b   om. 772/3.
c   *in foresta* 772/4.
d   *Wirhale* 772/4.
e   *in foresta* 772/4.
f   om. 772/4.
g   *in foresta* 772/4.
h   om. 772/4.
i   intl. 772/3.
j   om. 772/4.
k   om. 772/3.
l   *Mundrem* 772/4.
m   772/4 has *Willelmi*, del., followed by *Ricardi*.

(*For the letter to be seen*).

45.2   And to the same, £24 19s. 3¼d. for which he is charged within the sum of the Regard of the Forest of Delamere for the lands which used to belong to William Wasteneys in the township of Elton within the said forest, namely £6 6s. 8½d. for the 33rd year (1358–59), £6 13s. 1¼d. for the 34th year (1359–60), 116s. 4d. for the 35th year (1360–61), and £6 3s. 1½d. for this 36th year (1361–62), respited until the lawful age cf the said William's heir; by the lord's letters directed to the chamberlain dated 5 September in the 32nd year (1358).[1]

45.3   And to the same, £13 11s. 9d. for which he is charged within the sum of the Regard of the Forest in respect of Peter de Dutton and Matthew de Weverham, two of Peter de Thorneton's heirs, who are in the lord's hand by reason of their minority, namely 41s. 8d. for various townships in Delamere forest for the 33rd year (1358–59), and 10s. 8d. for various townships within Wirral forest for the same year, 63s. 11½d. for various townships in Delamere forest for the 34th year (1359–60), 10s. 8d. for various townships within Wirral forest for the same 34th year (1359–60), 59s. 10d. for various townships in Delamere forest for the 35th year (1360–61) and 10s. 8d. for various townships within Wirral forest for the same year, and 74s. 3½d. for this 36th year (1361–62), of which 10s. 8d. is for tenements within Wirral forest, respited for this reason until the lawful age of the said heirs.

45.4   And to the same, £7 5s. 4¼d. for which he is charged above within the sum of the Regard of the Forest for the lands which used to belong to Robert son of Richard de Acton, in Acton, which are in the lord's hand by reason of the same Robert's outlawry, of which 49s. 6¾d. is for the 34th year (1359–60), 46s. 6d. for the 35th year (1360–61), and 49s. 3½d. for this 36th year (1361–62).[2]

45.5   And to the same, £25 15s. 7¾d. for which he is charged in respect of Richard Munchull within the sum of the Regard of the Forest of Delamere and Mondrum, of which £14 15s. 0¾d. is for the 35th year, last past, (1360–61), part of £27 17s. 7d. still due from him in the said Regard of the same year, and £11 0s. 7d. as part of £31 0s. 7d. for this 36th year (1361–62); by the lord's letters dated 14 July in the 34th year (1360), by which the lord instructed the lieutenant-justiciar and chamberlain to survey all the same Richard's lands and tenements,

1   *B.P.R.*, iii. 307; *ChRR*, p. 459. (Presumably this refers to the Regard held prior to the 1357 Forest Eyre, **8.2**.)
2   See **5.12**.

⟨*m 5d*⟩ {*m 5d*}

sustentationem[a] pro dicto Ricardo uxore sua et pueris suis ordinare facerent et residuum terrarum suarum facerent assidere pro comodo domini quousque predictus Ricardus totam propartem ipsum contingentem de proparte finis MM li. facti cum domino per communitatem foreste de Mare et Mondrem[b] plenarie persolverit[c] et unde ex assidentia et ordinatione predictorum locum tenentis et Camerarij satis erit domino de xx li. per annum pro predicto Ricardo ultra sustentationem suam predictam quousque satis et cetera.

(*respondeat Escaetor*)

45.6   Et eidem vj li. xv s. vj d. unde oneratur infra regardum foreste de Wirhale pro terris et tenementis que fuerunt Johannis de Warrewik' in Upton' et Fraunkeby pro hoc anno et anno proxime preterito eo quod tenementa predicta sunt in manu domini de quorum exitibus Escaetor Cestris' respondeat in compoto suo de hoc anno.

45.7   Et eidem xxxviij s. iiij d. ob. unde oneratur infra fines foreste de Wirhale pro terris et tenementis Willelmi de Bechedon' in Kirkeby Walley et Storton' eo quod eadem terre et tenementa sunt in manu domini pro hoc anno de quorum exitibus Escaetor Cestris' respondeat in compoto suo predicto.

45.8   Et eidem xxxv s. v d. qu. pro Roberto de Foulleshurst' Chivaler unde oneratur pro ipso Roberto pro hoc anno xxxvj inter fines foreste de Wirhale eo quod dominus Princeps per litteras suas manu sua scriptas dat' apud Kenyngton' in Crastino Sancti Luce Evangeliste sub secreto sigillo suo mandavit Camerario quod de denariis qui sunt in demando versus ipsum Robertum in foresta sua de Wirhale nichil levare faceret sine expresso precepto domini de secretis litteris suis et que littere remanent penes dictum[d] Camerarium.

45.9   Et eidem lxj s. vij d. unde oneratur hoc anno pro terris et tenementis que fuerunt Philippi de Eggerton' in Crouton' et Wordull' inter fines foreste[e] de Mare et Moundrem[f] eo quod tenementa predicta sunt in manu domini pro[g] hoc anno de[h] quorum exitibus Escaetor Cestris' respondeat in compoto suo de hoc anno.[i]

45.10   Et eidem usque alias vj li. xiij s. iiij d. unde oneratur pro Ricardo Mascy Chivaler pro[j] quodam fine xx li. per ipsum facto sicut continetur supra in titulo de novis atterminationibus per consilium Johannis de Delves locum tenentis eo quod idem locum tenens testatus est Auditoribus quod idem Ricardus habiturus

a   772/3 has *sustentationem* written over a del. word, possibly *sumpt'*.
b   *Mundrem* 772/4.
c   *persolvitur* 772/3.
d   om. 772/3.
e   772/4 has *videlicet* (del.) after *foreste.*
f   *Mundrem* 772/4.
g   om. 772/3.
h   intl. 772/3.
i   *de hoc anno* om. 772/4.
j   *de* 772/4.

goods and chattels, and make an order for his reasonable sustenance, and that of his wife and children, and then assess the rest of his lands for the lord's profit until the aforesaid Richard should have paid in full his entire share of the part of the fine of £2,000 made with the lord by the community of the forest of Delamere and Mondrum, and for which, by the assessment and ordinance of the aforesaid lieutenant and chamberlain, £20 a year will be sufficient to the lord on Richard's behalf, over and above his aforesaid sustenance, until sufficient et cetera.[1]

(*Let the escheator answer*).

45.6   And to the same, £6 15s. 6d. for which he is charged within the Regard of Wirral forest for the lands and tenements which used to belong to John de Warrewik in Upton and Frankby, for this year and last year, because the aforesaid tenements are in the lord's hand, for the issues of which the escheator of Cheshire should answer in his account for this year.[2]

45.7   And to the same, 38s. 4½d. for which he is charged among the fines of Wirral forest for William de Bechedon's lands and tenements in Wallasey and Storeton, because the same lands and tenements are in the lord's hand for this year, for the issues of which the escheator of Cheshire should answer in his aforesaid account.

45.8   And to the same, 35s. 5¼d. in respect of Robert de Foulleshurst, knight, for which he is charged for the same Robert for this 36th year (1361–62) among the fines of Wirral forest, because the prince, by letters written with his own hand dated at Kennington the morrow of St Luke, evangelist, (19 October) under his secret seal, and which remain in the said chamberlain's possession, has instructed the chamberlain to levy nothing of the money which was demanded against the same Robert in his forest of Wirral without the lord's express order by his secret letters.[3]

45.9   And to the same, 61s. 7d. for which he is charged this year for the lands and tenements which used to belong to Philip de Eggerton in Crowton and Wardle, among the fines of the forest of Delamere and Mondrum, because the aforesaid tenements are in the lord's hands for this year,[4] for the issues of which the escheator of Cheshire should answer in his account for this year.

45.10   And to the same, until another time, £6 13s. 4d. for which he is charged in respect of Richard Mascy, knight, for a certain fine of £20 made by him, as is contained above under the heading New Instalments, by advice of John de Delves, lieutenant, because the same lieutenant has witnessed to the auditors that Richard will have from the lord a larger sum in recompense for the horses

1   *B.P.R.*, iii. 389. See **8.16**.
2   Warrewik's lands in Upton and Frankby had been seized by the escheator before 7 July 1359, as being held in chief. He was dead by 9 May 1360 (*B.P.R.*, iii. 351–52, 438).
3   Order to respite the collection of his share of the common fine of Wirral forest, 20 June 1359 (*B.P.R.*, iii. 339).
4   Following his death. His I.P.M. was held 4 Jan. 1363 (CHES 3/5/36 Edw. III/4).

⟨*m 5d*⟩ {*m 5d*}
est de domino maiorem summam in restaurationem equorum suorum nuper perditorum in servicio domini[a] unde computandum est cum[b] Thesaurario domini apud London'.

45.11   Et eidem lxxiij s. iiij d. unde oneratur pro Johanne de[c] Stokes inter fines atterminatos Comitatus de Flynt'[d] usque festum Assumptionis beate Marie virginis proxime futurum per considerationem Auditorum[e] et Camerarij certis de causis coram ipsis super compotum ostensis.

45.12   Et eidem xl li. quas liberavit Magistro Johanni[f] de Assheton'[g] ad se parandum pro viagio suo ituro in obsequium domini versus partes Vascon' per litteras domini de secreto sigillo suo dat' apud Kyrketon'[h] xiij die Septembris penes Camerarium remanentes per quas dominus mandavit eidem quod visis dictis litteris dictas xl li. sibi solveret ita quod citra[i] proximum compotum sequatur pro sufficienti Warranto de[j] dictis denariis allocandis si sibi viderit expedire.

45.13   Et eidem xx li. solute domino Willelmo de Spridlyngton' uni Auditori compotorum ministrorum domini Principis ad deferendum domino Petro de Lacy pro ipso Camerario London' et eas ibidem ad opus domini liberandum per indenturam ipsius domini[k] Willelmi.

45.14   Et eidem lxxij li. xx d. ob. qu. unde oneratur in titulo de regardo foreste pro Rogero le Strangee[l] pro terris et tenementis que nuper fuerunt Henrici Ducis Lancastr' infra forestas de Wirhale et Mara[m] tam per litteras domini dat' xxj die Marcij anno xxxvj per quas dominus mandavit dicto Camerario quod habere faceret eidem Rogero atterminationem de eo quod tunc foret aretro super eum pro dictis terris et tenementis ad solvendum infra duos annos[n] tunc[o] proxime sequentes ad festa Sancti Michelis et Pasche per equales portiones[p] primo termino incipiente[q] ad festum Sancti Michelis anno xxxvj[to] et unde tunc aretro fuerunt pro ij terminis[r] xlviij li. v s. x d. quam per alias litteras domini dat'

a   *suorum nuper . . . servicio domini* intl. 772/4.
b   om. 772/3.
c   om. 772/4.
d   *de Comitatu Flynt'* 772/4.
e   intl. 772/3.
f   intl. 772/3.
g   *Asshton'* 772/4.
h   *Kirton'* 772/4.
i   *in proximo compoto* 772/3.
j   *pro* 772/4.
k   intl. 772/3.
l   *Lestraunge* 772/4.
m   *Mare* 772/4.
n   intl. 772/3.
o   om. 772/3.
p   *equaliter* 772/4.
q   *incipiente primo termino* 772/4.
r   *terminos* 772/4.

which he lately lost in the lord's service, for which he has accounted with the lord's treasurer in London.[1]

45.11 And to the same, 73s. 4d. for which he is charged in respect of John de Stokes among the fines by instalments of the county of Flint, until the feast of the Assumption next, by consideration of the auditors and chamberlain for certain reasons put forward before them upon the account.[2]

45.12 And to the same, £40 which he delivered to Master John de Assheton so that he could prepare himself to set out on his voyage to Gascony in obedience to the lord; by the lord's letters of his secret seal dated at Kirton 13 September, which remain in the chamberlain's possession, by which the lord instructed the same to pay him the said £40 on the sight of the said letters, providing that he should seek a sufficient warrant before the next account for the allowance of the said money if it should seem expedient to him.[3]

45.13 And to the same £20, paid to William de Spridlyngton, one of the auditors of the accounts of the prince's officials, to be conveyed to Peter de Lacy in London on the chamberlain's behalf, and handed over there for the lord's use, by indenture of the same William.

45.14 And to the same, £72 20¾d. for which he is charged under the heading of Regard of the Forest in respect of Roger le Strangee for the lands and tenements which used to belong to Henry, duke of Lancaster, within the forests of Wirral and Delamere. This was granted, first, by the lord's letters dated 21 March in the 36th year (1362), by which the lord instructed the said chamberlain to cause the same Roger to be allowed to pay by instalments the sum for which he was in arrears for the said lands and tenements within the two years following at the feasts of Michaelmas and Easter, by equal payments, the first term of payment beginning at Michaelmas in the 36th year (1362), and of which there were then in arrears for two terms £48 5s. 10d. It was further signified to the

1   See **13.2**
2   See **23.1** and **23.2**.
3   Assheton was a clerk of the prince. He was granted six oaks from Delamere forest, 20 November 1362, and presented by the prince to a prebend in St John's, Chester, 11 April 1363 (*B.P.R.*, iii. 453, 455).

⟨m 5d⟩ {m 5d}

xxv die Marcij anno xxxvj predicto per quas dominus significavit eidem Camerario quod ipse de gracia sua perdonavit et relaxavit eidem Rogero quaterviginti libras de summa ipsum currente et quod domino aretro est de communi fine[a] forestarum de Mare et Wirhale pro terris et tenementis que nuper fuerunt predicti Ducis et que iiij[xx] li. restant allocari in proximo compoto ipsius Camerarij virtute litterarum predictarum.

45.15 Et eidem xxx s. quos solvit Willelmo de Stanlegh'[b] Forestario Foreste[c] de Wirhale de quodam regardo xxx s. sibi concesso per dominum ad terminum vite sue pro custodia parci de Shotewik[d] et qui[e] disallocati supra pro defectu sufficientis Warranti ita quod prosequeret de Warranto emendando citra proximum.

46. SUMMA RESPECTUS: CCCxxxix li. ij s. vj d. ob. examinatur[f]

47. Et remanent DCClxxviij li. ix s. xj d. ob. qu. di. qu. probatur[g]

⟨m 6d⟩ {m 6d}

48. PRISA VINORUM

48.1 Idem respondet de ij doleis vini rubei Vascon'[h] receptis de prisa domini proveniente de navi[i] Walteri de Dertemouth'[j] in portu apud le Redebonk' hoc anno.

Summa: ij dolea[k]

48.2 Idem computat liberasse Abbati de Valle Regali de antiqua elemosina ei ab antiquo constituta per dominum Edwardum Regem Avum[l] Regis nunc pro divinis celebrandis pro anima ipsius domini Edwardi[m] Regis avi[n] predicti et

---

a *finis* 772/3.
b 772/3 has *Stanle*, del., followed by *Stanlegh'*; 772/4 has *Stanle*.
c om. 772/4.
d *Shotewyk'* 772/4.
e *que* 772/3.
f om. 772/4.
g second *qu.* and *probatur* om. 772/4.
h *rubei Vascon'* intl. 772/4.
i *nave* 772/4.
j *Dertesmouth'* 772/4.
k om. 772/4.
l *Avi* 772/3.
m intl. 772/3.
n om. 772/3.

chamberlain by the lord's other letters, dated 25 March in the 36th year (1362), that he has, of his grace, pardoned and released to the same Roger £80 of the sum for which he is responsible, and for which he is in arrears to the lord, of the common fine of the forests of Delamere and Wirral for the lands and tenements which used to belong to the aforesaid duke, and which £80 is to be allowed in the chamberlain's next account by virtue of the aforesaid letters.[1]

45.15   And to the same, 30s. 0d. which he has paid to William de Stanlegh, forester of Wirral forest, for a certain supplementary fee of 30s. 0d. granted him by the lord for the term of his life for the keeping of Shotwick park, which is disallowed above for the lack of a sufficient warrant. He should, however, sue for the warrant to be emended before the next account.[2]

46.   SUM OF RESPITE: £339 2s. 6½d. Examined.

47.   And there remain: £778 9s. 11¾d. and a half-farthing. Approved.

48.   PRISE OF WINE

48.1   He answers for two tuns of red Gascon wine of the lord's prise received from Walter de Dertemouth's ship this year in the port at *le Redebonk*.

Sum: two tuns.

48.2   He accounts in delivery made to the abbot of Vale Royal, of ancient alms appointed to him of old by King Edward, the present king's grandfather, for celebration of divine service in the same abbey for the soul of the same King

---

1   Letters of attermination, 21 March 1362, and letters of pardon, 25 March 1362, granted to Sir Roger Lestrange of Knockin (*B.P.R.*, iii. 441).
2   This refers to the cancelled entry, which follows **30.19** (see p. 86 n.a). Warrant to make out letters patent for a life grant of the keeping of Shotwick park, with a fee of 30s. 0d. a year, and to pay him that fee from the time of his father's death, 5 December 1361 (*B.P.R.*, iii. 429, 435). The chamberlain was again ordered to pay him his wages, 29 May 1363 (ibid., 456).

⟨*m 6d*⟩ {*m 6d*}
animabus antecessorum suorum in eadem Abbathia per litteras acquietancie ipsius Abbatis super hunc compotum liberatas unum doleum vini.

48.3 Item eidem Abbati de nova elemosina domini ei et Conventui suo constituta per litteras patentes eiusdem domini Principis dat' Mense Septembris anno regni regis nunc xxvij in presencia ipsius domini tunc existentis apud Cestr' per litteras acquietancie ipsius Abbatis supradictas unum doleum vini.

Summa: ij. Et nichil remanet.

49. MINERA PLUMBI

49.1 Et de xviij lodis vj discis minere plumbi mensurati apud Vaynol' viij die Maij anno xxxvj^to.[a]

Summa: xviij lode vj disci.
Quos computat in combustione apud Baghegre pro plumbo inde habendo pro garnistura Castrorum et Maneriorum domini.
(*respondeat anno futuro*)
49.2 De plumbo inde proveniente respondeat in[b] anno proxime[c] futuro.

Summa: ut supra. Et Eque.[d]

50. PLUMBUM

50.1 Idem respondet de j fodro xj pedibus iiij libris receptis de remanentia fodro continente xxv pedes et quolibet pede continente lxxij libras.

50.2 Et de iij fodris x pedibus et dimidio xiiij libris plumbi recepti de minera plumbi[e] domini tam de minera lucrata apud Vaynol hoc anno quam de minera de remanentia[f] apud Baghegre ad bolam ibidem ad comburendum de diversis annis preteritis ponderata apud Baghegre iiij die Maij anno regni regis nunc xxxvj^to.

50.3 Et de iiij fodris dimidio pede j libra plumbi recepti de Rogero Maudyt Nicholao le Dryver et sociis suis minerariis provenientis de combustione minere plumbi lucrati apud Vaynol et combusti apud Baghegre cum busca domini capta

a　*anno regni regis nunc xxxvj* 772/4.
b　om. 772/3.
c　intl. 772/3.
d　*Et nichil remanet* 772/4.
e　om. 772/3.
f　*remanente* 772/4.

Edward, the grandfather aforesaid, and the souls of his predecessors; by the same abbot's letters of acquittance handed over upon this account – one tun of wine.

48.3   Item, to the same abbot of the lord's new alms appointed to him and his convent, by letters patent of the same prince dated in the month of September in the 27th year of the reign of the present king (1353) in the presence of the lord, who was then staying at Chester; by the same abbot's aforesaid letters of acquittance – one tun of wine.[1]

Sum: two. And none remains.

49. LEAD-ORE

49.1   And for 18 loads 6 dishes of lead-ore measured at Faenol 8 May in the 36th year (1362).

Sum: 18 loads 6 dishes, which he accounts as having been smelted for lead at Bachegraig for use in the lord's castles and manor-houses.
(*Let him answer next year*).
49.2   From the lead issuing thence he answers next year.

Sum: as above. And equal.

50. LEAD

50.1   He answers for one fother 11 feet 4 pounds received from the remainder, the fother containing 25 feet, and each foot containing 72 pounds.
50.2   And for 3 fothers 10½ feet 14 pounds of lead received from the lord's lead-ore, both from the ore mined at Faenol this year and from ore remaining at the furnace at Bachegraig for smelting from various past years, weighed at Bachegraig 4 May in the 36th year of the reign of the present king (1362).
50.3   And for 4 fothers half a foot 1 pound of lead received from Roger Maudyt, Nicholas le Dryver and their fellow-miners, issuing from the smelting of lead-ore mined at Faenol and smelted at Bachegraig with the lord's underwood

1   The grant of a tun of wine each year to Vale Royal Abbey for the celebration of Mass was made by Edward I on 28 May 1276 (*V.C.H.*, iii. 158–59). On 11 September 1353, the Black Prince granted a charter to Vale Royal Abbey, which comprised an *inspeximus* of the 1276 charter together with a grant of an additional tun of wine each year. This charter was defective, and it was exemplified with an interlineation on 16 July 1354. The original of this exemplification survives as E41/144. See above, **9.1, 33**.

⟨*m 6d*⟩ {*m 6d*}
in bosco domini[a] ibidem domino capiente sextam partem plumbi sic combusti
pro busca sua.

Summa: viij fodri xxij pedes xix libre. De quibus

50.4   Idem[b] computat liberasse Johanni de Wodhull' Camerario Suth'Wall' pro
garnistura Castrorum domini Principis in eisdem partibus per ordinationem
Johannis de Delves Chivaler et domini Willelmi de Spridlyngton'[c] unius
auditorum dicti domini Principis et per indenturam inter Magistrum Johannem
de Brunham[d] Juniorem Camerarium Cestr' et Gilbertum de Wodhull' attor-
natum predicti Johannis de Wodhull' inde factam vij fodros xj pedes xv libras.

Summa: vij fodri xj pedes xv libre. Et remanent j fodrus xj pedes iiij libre.

51.   ARCUS PRO GARNISTURA CASTRORUM DOMINI[e]

Et de vij duodenis arcuum et iiij arcubus receptis de remanentia.

Summa patet. Et remanent.

52.   SAGITTE SINE CAPITIBUS

Et de[f] CCCvij garbis sagittarum receptis de remanentia.
Et de lxx garbis sagittarum receptis de emptione hoc anno ut supra.

Summa: CCClxxvij garbe. Et remanent.

53.   CAPITA SAGITTARUM

Et de[f] MM DCCC xlviij capitibus sagittarum per maius Centum receptis de
remanentia.
Et de MMM DC xxiiij capitibus sagittarum[g] receptis de emptione ut supra[h] hoc
anno.

Summa: M^{vj} CCCC lxxij. Et remanent.

a   om. 772/4.
b   om. 772/4.
c   *Sprydlynton'* 772/4.
d   *de Brunham'* intl. 772/3.
e   *CASTRORUM DOMINI* om. 772/3.
f   *Idem respondet de* 772/4.
g   intl. 772/3.
h   *superius* 772/4.

taken in the lord's wood there, the lord taking a sixth part of the lead thus smelted for his underwood.

Sum: 8 fothers 22 feet 19 pounds. Of which:

50.4 He accounts in delivery to John de Wodhull, chamberlain of South Wales, for use in the prince's castles in the same parts, by ordinance of John de Delves, knight, and William de Spridlyngton, one of the said prince's auditors, by indenture made between Master John de Brunham the younger, chamberlain of Chester, and Gilbert de Wodhull, the aforesaid John de Wodhull's attorney – 7 fothers 11 feet 15 pounds.

Sum: 7 fothers 11 feet 15 pounds. And 1 fother 11 feet 4 pounds remain.

51. BOWS FOR THE STOCK OF THE LORD'S CASTLES

And for 12 dozen bows, and 4 bows received from the remainder.

Sum: appears. And they remain.

52. HEADLESS ARROWS

And for 307 sheaves of arrows received from the remainder. And for 70 sheaves of arrows bought this year, as above.

Sum: 377 sheaves. And they remain.

53. ARROW-HEADS

And for 2,848 arrow-heads, by the greater hundred, received from the remainder.
And for 3,624 arrow-heads purchased, as above, this year.

Sum: 6,472. And they remain.

⟨*m 6d*⟩ {*m 6d*}
54. CORDE PRO ARCUBUS

Et de[a] M^v Dxxviij cordibus pro arcubus per minus Centum receptis de remanentia.

Summa patet. Et remanent.

55. CANABUM

Et de[a] xj petris canabi receptis de remanentia.

Summa patet. Et remanent.

56. CAPITA PRO LANCIIS[b]

Et de[a] xxiiij capitibus pro lanciis[c] receptis de remanentia.

Summa: xxiiij.[d] Et remanent.

Examinatur[e]

a   *Idem respondet de* 772/4.
b   *CAPITA LANCIARUM* 772/4.
c   *capitibus lanciarum* 772/4.
d   *Summa xxiiij* om. 772/4.
e   om. 772/4.

54. STRING FOR BOWS

And for 5,528 bow-strings, by the lesser hundred, received from the remainder.

Sum: appears. And they remain.

55. HEMP

And for 11 stones of hemp received from the remainder.

Sum: appears. And they remain.

56. LANCE-HEADS

And for 24 lance-heads received from the remainder.

Sum: 24. And they remain.

Examined.

BIOGRAPHICAL NOTES

CHESHIRE

Acton, Robert son of Richard de

His father, Ric. de Acton, appears to have married twice: Alan was his son by his first wife, Alice. By his second wife, name unknown, he had Robt. On 1 Mar. 1342 Thos de Venables and 'Robt de Acton' made a fine of £80 for crimes of which they had been indicted in Berwick's sessions (*ChAcc*, p. 116). He was subsequently outlawed, and his lands forfeited to B.P. by 1353–54 (SC6 785/1, m.4d). He petitioned that the outlawry had been by his enemies' procurement, and it was agreed that he should have his lands back for life, either for an annual rent or a lump sum, 17 May 1354 (*B.P.R.*, iii, 166). Order to grant one-third manor of Acton to him for 8 marks a year, although it was extended at £8, 2 marks having been pardoned by B.P., 1 June 1355 (ibid., 201). Letters of protection granted him to go to Gascony in B.P.'s company on the king's business, 30 July 1355. At that time he had the keeping of Margaret, daughter and heiress of Owen de Shokelache (ibid., 212). Petitioned B.P. for aid to prevent Thos de Dutton, county sheriff, helping Alan de Acton to recover Acton manor to the B.P.'s loss; order to deal with them for B.P.'s profit. Also complained that the sheriff would not compel Robt son of Thos. de Acton to pay arrears of rent; order to escheator or coroner to execute, 3 July 1357 (ibid., 252–53). Order to let him have livery of the one-third of Acton recently granted him by B.P. for life at £4 a year, 11 July 1357 (ibid., 255). Alan, son of Ric. de Acton petitioned that Robt son of Ric., his half-brother, had seized one-third of Acton manor, whereupon Alan sued by *formedon*, and won, except that the writ was abated because part of the land was in B.P.'s hand by forfeiture; he asked for further trial, claiming to be so impoverished he could not sue further; forest eyre justices ordered to consider the petition, 18 Feb. 1358 (ibid., 294). Received pardon, for good service in Gascony, for alienating lands held in chief to Thos, vicar of Weaverham, 10 Sept. 1358 (ibid., 310–11). Order to deliver his lands in Delamere forest to his children, following the pardon, so they could pay their part of the common fine. Same date (ibid.)

Alcock, John de

Accounted as keeper of the manor (house), park, stock and stud of Macclesfield, 1356–57 (SC6 802/13, m.4). He then lost the stud (which was transferred to Denbigh) and the park (which was given to a separate keeper, **Wm de Chorlegh**). He continued to account as keeper of the stock in Macclesfield forest until May 1373 (SC6 802/15, m.3 to 804/4, m.4B). In 1366–67, he used hay and straw of his own for the stock (SC6 803/13, m.15).

For the identification of John de Macclesfield (keeper of the king's privy seal, and of the great wardrobe, d. 1422) with the son of John Alcock, the stock-keeper, see Bennett, *Community, Class*, p. 150).

Apelton, William de

Granted office of seller of felons' goods in Cheshire, at pleasure, for service at Poitiers, usual wages, 8 May 1357 (*B.P.R.*, iii., 238; *ChRR*, p. 192). He had been replaced by 1372–73 (SC6 772/8, m.4).

Arundel, Richard Fitz Alan, earl of *c.* 1313 to 1376

An exceedingly wealthy landowner, with considerable interests in the northern March of Wales. Justiciar of North Wales for life from 1334. He was a great lender of money to both the King and Black Prince (*D.N.B.* vii., 95–98; *Complete Peerage.*, i. 242–44).

Agreed with B.P. to exchange justiciarship of North Wales, and annual fee of 500 marks, for £200 a year from city of Chester and Dee mills, for life, 11 Nov. 1351 (*B.P.R.*, iii. 52–53; *ChRR*, p. 9). Grant, at his request, to his tenants of Dunham (on the Hill) in Delamere, of housebote and haybote in the forest on their own soil, without view of foresters, 2 Sept. 1352 (*B.P.R.*, iii. 76). Acting as lord of Bromfield and Yale 1353, 1367 (*C.C.R., 1349–54*, p. 562; *C.C.R., 1364–68*, p. 371). At his request, everything demanded against **Sir Roger Lestrange**, lord of Maelor Saesneg, to be respited until B.P.'s return to England, 28 July 1355 (*B.P.R.*, iii. 212). Order to return his bondmen, who had escaped from Bromfield and Yale and were living as avowrymen in Cheshire, 7 May 1358 (ibid., 300). Order to certify B.P. of sums assessed on him, his termors and tenants, in Dunham (on the Hill) and (Mickle) Trafford, for common fine of Delamere, 5 June 1359 (ibid., 347). He lent £1,000 to B.P., 25 July 1359 (ibid., 354, 364). On 30 Aug. 1359 he complained that his portions of the common fines of Wirral, Delamere and Macclesfield forests had been unreasonably assessed (ibid., 364). Order to chamberlain to pay Arundel's debt, 20 May 1360 (ibid., 381). He was pardoned the sums due from him in the Delamere forest eyre, 14 July 1360 (ibid., 389). Mention of £1,000 loan by him to B.P., 25 July 1362 (ibid., 449). Order not to distrain his tenants of (Mickle) Trafford to appear at Broxton hundred court until following Mich., 24 Oct. 1363 (ibid., 460). Granted £400 in perpetuity out of the demesnes of Cheshire, 1 June 1365 (ibid., 480). Grant confirmed by the king, 12 July 1365 (*C.P.R., 1364–67*, p. 155). Purchased the marriage of Thomas Holland, son of the princess of Wales, for 4,000 marks 1 July 1365 (*B.P.R.*, iv. 558). Received annuity through the chamberlain of £50 (reduced from £100), 1369–70 (SC6 772/5, m.2d). Still receiving fee-farm of Chester (£100) and £100 from Dee mills in 1373–74 (SC6 772/9, m.1).

Assheton, Master John de (clerk)

B.P. gave him 6 oaks in Delamere forest, 20 Nov. 1362 (*B.P.R.*, iii. 453). On 11

Apr. 1363, B.P. presented him to Master John de Cravene's prebend in St John's Church, Chester (ibid., 455). The receiver-general was acquitted of the £40 paid by Burnham to Assheton, and ordered to acquit Burnham in turn, 22 May 1363 (*B.P.R.*, iv. 495).

Asshewell, Simon de (clerk of the chamberlain)

Granted 1½ burgages in Hope, 1351 (*ChRR*, p. 11). As clerk of Chester exchequer he received a gift (40s. 0d.) from the proceeds of the 1353 trailbaston sessions, as a reward for his long labours, 10 Sept. 1353 (*B.P.R.*, iii. 115). Ref. to 'Simon, clerk of chamberlain of Chester', 1353–54, (SC6 809/2, m.4). Joint receiver of St. Pierre lands, with **Robt de Hoghton**, 1353–54; with Adam de Praers, 1354–55 (SC6 783/1; 783/2). Joint lessee of Dee mills, with **Robt Bredon** et al., 1355–58; with Robt Bredon alone, 1358–69. Appointed with **Thos le Yong** (escheator) and Ralph de Brunham to arrest Benet ab Iorwerth, who had procured the deanery of St Asaph by provision, and bring him to Chester castle, 24 Nov. 1357 (*B.P.R.*, iii. 282). Granted £5 reward for great labours in B.P.'s service, 13 Sept. 1358 (ibid., 313). Order that letters about the seizure of Denbigh lordship be opened in his presence, 9 May 1360 (ibid., 381). With Wm Blorton, leased Mostyn from B.P. for 3 years, for 22 marks a year, 30 Sept. 1360; again from 1 Oct. 1364; again for 4 years from Mich. 1367, for 23 marks a year (*ChRR*, p. 12; **19.10**). He had a rental of Kingsmarsh in his keeping, 1361–62 (SC6 785/9, m.2d). B.P. granted him an oak from Delamere forest, 2 Nov. 1363 (*B.P.R.*, iv. 515). He made a recog. for £10, for part of the £80 fine of John de Seynesbury, chaplain, for the death of Robt Cliderow, chaplain, 6 Dec. 1364 (ibid.) He agisted his horse(s) in Shotwick park, 1365–66 (SC6 786/7, m.9). One of the feoffees to grant land to St John's Hospital, Chester, 24 Nov. 1365 (*B.P.R.*, iii. 486–87).

Basyngwerk, William de

Possibly connected with a man of same name, who was alive in the 1320s; he was granted attermination of a fine of £200, made before Roger Amory, justiciar, for 'certain trespasses', on grounds of poverty, Apr. 1329 (*C.C.R.*, *1327–30*, p. 448). 40s. 0d., being a certain old attermination of Wm de Basyngwerk, was charged in the receiver's account, 1342–43 (*ChAcc*, p. 116).

Bechedon, William de

He held land in Wallasey and Storeton (**45.7**). Matthew de Wallasey was found not guilty of assaulting 'Wm de Bechyngton' at Wallasey in 1349 (CHES 29/65, m.3d). 'Wm de Bechynton' complained that a porpoise taken on his, and Ric. Sampson's, land at Wallasey was being held to be a grampus, and thus pertaining to B.P.; order to do right to him, because of service at Poitiers, 21 June 1357 (*B.P.R.*, iii. 250–51). 'Wm son of Philip de Bechinton' was heir to Ric. de

Bechynton, and was present at the battle of Poitiers, 3 July 1357 (ibid., 252, 256).

Becheton, Ranulf de (chaplain, parson of Woodchurch)

Order to inquire whether **John de Wetenhale** of Dorfold had enfeoffed him and Wm de Blaken with part of the barony cf Nantwich without licence. If so, the alienation was to be pardoned at the instance of Thos de Wetenhale, B.P.'s yeoman, and they were be permitted to grant the property to Agnes, John's widow, and Thos, his son, 4 May 1361 (*B.P.R.*, iii. 416–17). Similar order, 21 Dec. 1361 (ibid., 437; *ChRR*, p. 518). Result of the inquiry found that John de Wetenhale was of sound mind when he made the enfeoffment, and it was not done by collusion to deprive B.P. of wardship, 24 Aug. 1362 (*B.P.R*, iii. 451; *ChRR*, p. 519).

Blaken, William de (chaplain)

Jt.-feoffee with **Ranulf de Becheton**.

Bostok, David de

With Wm de Bostok and Ric. le Bret of Davenham, made recog. to B.P. for 20 marks, part of Ranulf le Roter's fine of £40, 15 Sept. 1363 (*ChRR*, p. 44).

Boudon, John son of John de

With 13 others made recog. to B.P. for £1,066 13s. 4d., payable at £100 a year, which replaced an earlier recog., 25 April 1363 (*B.P.R.*, iii. 455). See **Jordan de Boudon**.

Boudon, Jordan de

Sir Wm de Caryngton recovered land against him, whereupon Boudon's supporters, led by John de Mascy (parson of Sefton, Lancs.) and **Sir Ric. de Mascy**, began a campaign of violence against Sir Wm., 21 Aug. 1361 (*B.P.R.*, iii. 421). At the county court of 26 Apr. 1363, Jordan and **John son of John de Boudon**, and Hugh, brother of Robt le Walker, were found guilty of forging a charter of Sir Wm de Caryngton's great-grandfather, which was the title to part of Ashton manor, on 28 May 1354, and then pleading it in an assize of *novel disseisin* (CHES 29/67, m.112d). With 13 others, including the two Mascys, he made a recog. to B.P. for £1,066 13s. 4d., payable at £100 a year, which replaced an earlier recog., 25 April 1363 (*B.P.R.*, iii. 455).

Braas, William (Prince's attorney in the counties of Chester and Flint)

Appointment of 'Wm Brace' as keeper of the smaller part of the seal for recog. for debts, 10 April 1342 (*C.P.R.*, *1340–43*, p. 408). As farmer of Hopedale lordship, petitioned B.P. and council about Hopedale mine, and an unnamed bondman, 12 June 1353 (B.P.R., iii. 107). Order to pay him 26s. 8d. a year as steward and keeper of Hopedale and Ewloe, which had been withheld from him, 13 June 1353 (ibid.) 'Wm Braas' sheriff of Chester city with Adam Ingram, 1353–54 (SC6 784/3, m.1). Order to allow 'Wm Brace' to have Ric. de Burton's two tenements 8 July 1354 (*B.P.R.*, iii. 174). Sheriff of Chester city with Roger Ledsham, 1354–55 (SC6 784/5, m.1). Order to pay him 40s. 0d. for his past labours, and 20s. 0d. a year in future, as B.P.'s attorney in the counties of Chester and Flint, 15 Feb. 1358 (*B.P.R.*, iii. 292). Revenue from his farm of Hopedale granted to **Sir Ric. de Stafford**, with other revenues, 1 Oct. 1358 (ibid., 324).

Bredon, Robert de

Farmer of Dee mills, with Richard Coten (1351–53), with **Simon Asshewell**, John Neuwerk (clerk), Nich. de Eccleston (carpenter) (1355–60), with **Simon de Assewell** (1361–69), alone (1370–74), (SC6 783/17, m.1; 784/2, m.1; 784/10, m.1d; 785/1, m.1; 785/5, m.1d; 785/9, m.1d; 786/1, m.10d; 786/3, m.2d; 786/5, m.1d; 786/6, m.1d; 786/7, m.1d; 786/8, m.1d; 786/10, m.1d; 787/2, m.1; 787/4, m.1; 787/5, m.1; 787/7, m.1). Reference to a felony committed by John, former cook to Robt de Bredon, 15 Aug. 1357 (*B.P.R.*, iii. 274). There is a reference to his grant, as 'parson of St Peter's Church, Chester', of a messuage and 13 shops in Foregate Street to the chantry of Holy Trinity, the Assumption, and St Anne, in St John's, Chester, 22 Feb. 1361 (ibid., 409, 450). As 'chaplain', reference to him acting as one of the feoffees to grant land in the city to St John's Hospital, Chester, 24 Nov. 1365 (ibid., 486).

Bromlegh, John de

Acting as bailiff (bedell) and farmer of Nantwich hundred, 1349–55 (*ChAcc*, pp. 134, 174, 214). Grant that he should pay the £40 he owed B.P. as bailiff, charged in Thos de Dutton's county sheriff's account, by instalments of £5 at each county court session, 12 Nov. 1359 (*B.P.R.*, iii. 377). Still bound to pay £19 12s. 8d. of his arrears, which were due to losses he suffered during his time as bailiff, 'whereby he is much impoverished', he asked to pay by further instalments, 22 Nov. 1360 (ibid., 397–98).

Bulkylegh, William son of William de (of Alpraham)

'Wm de Bulkylegh of Alpram the younger' received letters of protection to go to Gascony in Hugh de Calvylegh's company, on the king's service, 8 July 1354 (*B.P.R.*, iii. 173). With 3 others made a recog. to Margaret, widow of John son of Hugh Fyton, for £21 6s. 8d., 7 April 1359 (*ChRR*, p. 71). 'Wm de Bulkelegh' was accused, with others, of abducting the wife and the heir of Sir John Fitton from Alderley manor-house, and taking them to Salop, 10 Feb. 1361 (*B.P.R*, iii.

404). Imprisoned in Chester castle for 'certain trespasses', he petitioned to pay a fine and go free, 5 May 1361 (ibid., 417). With **Sir Ric. de Mascy** and 10 others made a recog. for £1,000 to B.P. and to Thos de Warrewyk, constable of Chester castle, guaranteeing that John de Leycestre and 4 others should not escape from the castle, 1362 (*ChRR*, p. 328). 'Wm de Bulkylegh of Alpraham' made a recog. with 2 others to B.P. for 25 marks for the wardship and marriage of Wm son of Wm de Hadelegh, 7 March 1363 (ibid., p. 71).

Burgherssh, Bartholomew de (the younger; Knight of the Garter) d. 1369

The younger Bartholomew succeeded to his father's estates in southern England in September 1355 (*C.F.R., 1347–56*, p. 434). He served the prince as a banneret, and was appointed justiciar of Chester 26 October 1353 (*B.P.R.*, iii. 128). It has been argued elsewhere that he treated the office as a sinecure (Booth, *Financial Administration*, p. 65). From 7 November 1353 to 6 March 1354, letters from the prince's central administration are addressed to 'Sir Bartholomew de Burgherssh the younger, justiciar of Chester, or his lieutenant'. His lieutenant was **John Delves**, who had been appointed to the office by the prince on 4 October 1353 (*B.P.R.*, iii. 125). From 6 March 1354 to 22 February 1357, letters are normally addressed only to the lieutenant, and following that date there are only five letters addressed to 'the justiciar, or his lieutenant' (ibid., 129, 151, 235, 281, 294, 311, 365, 464). The very considerable amount of evidence in the accounts and Registers confirms that Burgherssh never acted as justiciar of Chester, despite his name appearing as the addressee of official letters at some times, and the invariable practice of putting his name as president of the county court, and hundred eyres. So, although Adam de Cokirham of Rhuddlan petitioned Burgherssh as justiciar of Chester seeking redress for the armed attack he alleged Sir John de Byntre, the constable of Rhuddlan castle, had inflicted upon him, the resultant order of the prince's council was sent to Delves and Burnham (ibid., 164).

However, Burgherssh's connection with Cheshire was not completely nominal, and he looked after the interests of his clients there. On 9 September 1353, he acquired a pardon from the prince for the arrears of the deceased Hugh Hamsone, as bailiff of Northwich (ibid., 128). The following year, he asked the prince to pardon five marks of Robert de Prenton's 20-mark fine in the 1353 trailbaston sessions (ibid., 154). In 1358 he assured the prince that John and Thomas de Twenebrok had been wrongly accused of fraudulently concealing half the ransom of a prisoner they had taken at the battle of Poitiers (ibid., 294–95). Subsequent direct interventions with the prince involved the free chapel of Flint (1358), the right of John Blount of Chester to hunt the hare and fox at his new estate at Little Neston (1359), the pardon of part of **Sir Warin de Trussell's** contribution to the Wirral forest fine of 1357 (1359), and the grant of the avowries of Englefield (1361) (ibid., 324, 351, 354, 417). His principal connection with the county was through William Soty, described as his 'yeoman', to whom the prince granted the township and mill of Bollington for life, at Burgherssh's request, in 1354 (ibid., 167). The negative side of this exercise of patronage appears in the factional activities in Macclesfield hundred that Soty's right-hand man, **Adam de Mottrum**, involved himself and his partner in, in the years that followed (Booth, *Financial Administration*, pp. 102–3; see above, pp. lxiii–lxiv).

Burgherssh's principal offices held of the prince, apart from the justiciarship, were in the southern part of the appanage: he was warden of the Devon stannary, and steward of Wallingford castle, and keeper of the honours of Wallingford and St Valery (*B.P.R.*, ii. 84, 159, 189; iv. 26, 32, 105).

Burnham (Brunham), Master John de (the younger) died *c.* 1371

Chamberlain of Chester, 1346/71, receiver of the lordship of Denbigh, 1360/65.

There were two men with the name 'Master John de Burnham' who held office in the administration of kings of England and their sons in the fourteenth century, and it is not always possible to distinguish them. The elder Burnham appeared as a clerk of the royal wardrobe in 1326, and transferred to the infant Lord Edward's service, becoming keeper (treasurer) of his wardrobe from 1332 to 1335 (*C.C.R., 1323–27*, p. 621; *C.C.R., 1330–33*, p. 517; *C.C.R., 1333–37*, pp. 45, 523; Tout, v. 433; E368/103, rot. 176). It appears that he had returned to the king's government by 1336, and was sent to head the Irish financial administration in 1343, (*C.C.R., 1343–46*, p. 9; *C.F.R., 1337–47*, p. 319; *C.C.R., 1343–46*, p. 412). He last appears when he was presented to the rectory of a moiety of Malpas in 1362 (*B.P.R.*, iii. 443).

The younger Burnham's first recorded appointment in the administration of the earldom of Chester was as receiver of the judicial revenues arising out of Hugh de Berwick's sessions of 1341, for which he accounted in 1342–43 (SC6 771/14; *ChAcc*, pp. 114–18). Although he was clearly exercising some office in Cheshire in 1345, and was keeper of the temporalities of the bishopric of St Asaph the following year (SC1 54/43; *B.P.R.*, i. 19), it was not until Michaelmas 1346 that he was appointed chamberlain of Chester, and 'receiver of all monies arising from the issues of the county of Chester and Flint' (*B.P.R.*, i. 20). He held this office for the unprecedentedly long period of a quarter-century, and made his last financial livery on 22 February 1371 (on the account for 1369–70). Presumably he died between then and the time of the 1371 audit, the date of which is not recorded but was probably in that spring (SC6 772/5).

He undertook other financial tasks for the prince during his period of office. On the death of the last earl of Warenne, he and the lieutenant were ordered to take possession of Holt castle and the lordship of Bromfield and Yale in July 1347, which remained in the prince's hands until it was restored to the widowed countess in the following month (*B.P.R.*, i. 93, 114). From 24 March 1351, he was given the responsibility for receiving the issues of Macclesfield manor-hundred, for which he was granted an annual supplementary fee of ten marks (**29.3**; *B.P.R.*, iii. 7, 11). Another commitment came when the prince ordered the seizure of the lordship of Denbigh in 1360, and Burnham acted as receiver of the lordship until May 1365, for which he received an annual fee of ten marks (ibid., 382, 418, 480).

Although there is no evidence for the younger Burnham's university career, he consistently used the title 'master', and presumably claimed a Master of Arts degree. His main ecclesiastical preferment was his wardenship of the Hospital outside the North Gate of Chester, which was probably his home in the city, since, unlike the lieutenant, there is no reference to any rooms being reserved for him at the castle. Although a clerk, he clearly had considerable legal expertise, since he served as one of the justices of the 1357 forest eyre in Cheshire, and a commissioner to hear appeals from the lordship of Denbigh in 1364 (*B.P.R.*, iii. 294, 462–63). His main responsibilities, in addition to the collection of revenue, comprised the surveying (measuring and valuing) and leasing of land and other properties, the supervision of subordinate officials, and arranging to pay and equip military forces going from Cheshire to France. In addition, as chamberlain he was keeper of the seal of the earldom, and head of its official secretariat.

From 1353 he worked at Chester as the junior colleague of **John Delves**, lieutenant of Chester and North Wales. As Delves came to be given wider administrative responsibilities by Sir John Wingfield for the government of the whole principality of Wales from 1359, and then succeeded Wingfield as the prince's business manager in 1361, he was more and more away from Chester. John Pole began acting as lieutenant-justiciar of Chester, together with Delves, from 1364 onwards, but the balance of power between chamberlain and lieutenant appears to have changed. From the mid-1360s, administrative orders in the *Black Prince's Register* addressed to the lieutenant and chamberlain jointly, which had been the usual form hitherto, became comparatively rare. This may indicate the beginnings of specialisation of the two offices: the chamberlain becoming the financial and administrative head of the earldom's government, the justiciar (or lieutenant) the judicial head.

During his term of office, Burnham was the recipient of some rewards from the prince. In 1360, a book called *Concordante*, which had belonged to the bishop of St Asaph, was given to him; in 1357 he received two oaks from Llywdcoed park, and, in 1363, he was given another six from the prince's estates in Nottinghamshire, probably for the Chester hospital (*B.P.R.*, iv. 515; iii. 259, 400). In

1365–66 he was allowed to agist some horses in Shotwick park (SC6 786/7, m.9). As the key figure in the earldom's financial administration, he was well placed to acquire some landed property from the prince. In 1355 he bought a small amount of escheated land in Englefield (Flints.), and followed this with the much more substantial acquisition of Henry Dunfoul's property in Chester and district, another escheat, for 80 marks in July 1358 (SC6 784/7, m.6; *B.P.R.*, iii. 305). During the prince's visit to Macclesfield in the following September, he applied for, and was granted, property in the borough of Hope and near Llwydcoed park (ibid., 316). In 1367, he was granted land in Overton on Dee (Flints.) that had belonged to John son of Jordan de Macclesfield (*D.K.R. 28*, p. 65). Some of these acquisitions were used to add to the endowment of St John's Hospital, Chester (*B.P.R.*, iii. 487; *Cheshire Sheaf*, 3rd series, 1934, [6444]).

Careswall, Roger

Phil. son of Ranulf de Egerton, David de Overton, and Kenard de Cholmundel-egh made a recog. to B.P. of 100s. 0d. for the fine of Roger Careswell, indicted for John Hycok's death, 26 June 1361 (*ChRR*, p. 168).

Caryngton, William de (knight)

A Cheshire retainer of the prince, who served on the Poitiers campaign, Caryngton leased Longdendale lordship from 1361 to 1374.

'Wm de Carington', with Hamo de Ashley and 11 others, found guilty in 1353 of attempting to kill Wm Motlowe (CHES 29/65, m.3). 'Wm de Carenton' was an indentured retainer of B.P. in May 1355 (*B.P.R.*, iii. 200). 'Wm de Caryngton' was paid £6 13s. 4d. by the chamberlain in 1354–55, retained by B.P. for war, this being part (possibly half) of his annual fee (SC6 771/19, m.4d). Ordered, as 'prince's bachelor', to receive the £5 which he lost for a horse spoiled in the last Gascon war, 7 March 1359 (*B.P.R.*, iii. 332). Retained by B.P. for 1359/60 expedition, with 3 esquires, at £20 a year, 16 Aug. 1359 (ibid., 356). He was granted letters of protection to go overseas with B.P. for the war, 9 Oct. 1359 (ibid., 371). Took the farm of lordship of Longdendale, 10 year lease, March 1361 (SC6 803/3, m.5). Acted as farmer of Longdendale from Lady Day 1361 to Lady Day 1366, when the B.P.'s council seized the property for his slowness of payment (SC6 772/2, m.1; 803/7, m.4; 803/9, m.3d; 803/10, m.3; 803/12, m.3). Bought 2 messuages 30 acres of land from Ric. Wolegh in Wooley, 1367/68 (SC6 786/9). Petitioned B.P. alleging that armed outrages had been committed by **John de Mascy** (parson of Sefton, Lancs.), **Sir Ric. de Mascy** et al. in aid of **Jordan de Boudon** against him, because he had recovered land from Jordan in a lawsuit, 21 Aug. 1361 (*B.P.R.*, iii. 421). B.P. granted him a life-annuity of 20 marks, 28 Jan. 1364, payable retrospectively from Easter 1363 (ibid., 473; *ChRR*, p. 85). Appointed one of the commissioners to arrest the boats operating an illegal ferry service across the Mersey at Warrington, the bridge having been destroyed, 12 Oct. 1365 (*B.P.R.*, iii. 483; *ChRR*, p. 522). Retained by B.P. for life, in peace and war – with 1 esquire in wartime – for which he already received a life-annuity of 20 marks from Longdendale, with the addition of an extra 20 marks from April 1368 (SC6 803/15, m.2d). Witness (first of 5) to gift by John de Oldham, chaplain, of Ralph de Wolegh's lands in Broadbottom to Ralph's children, 1369 (*EC*, ii. 154). The farm of Longdendale was restored to him on 11 April 1368, and he continued to hold it until 28 Nov. 1374, when the lordship was delivered to Sir John and Maud Lovel (SC6 804/1, m.3d; 804/2, m.2d; 804/4, m.4Ad; 804/5, m.4d; 804/6, m.4d; 804/7, m.3d). Ric., prince of Wales, confirmed his life-annuity of 40 marks to be received from the exchequer of Chester, 10 Feb. 1377 (*ChRR*, p. 85). Granted wardship and marriage of Thos son and heir of Ric. de Wevere, 29 Aug. 1378 (ibid.)

Chandos, John (knight of the Garter) died 2 Jan. 1370

Chandos, who came from a Derbyshire family, was the prince's devoted friend, and the most famous of his companions in arms. He visited Chester during the state visit of 1353 (and witnessed the charter granted to the community of the county, C53/162, m.11), and again in 1354 (*B.P.R.*, iv. 136). His main connection with the county came through the newly-created, well-fee'd, but largely sinecure offices that he was given in the aftermath of the 1353 visit. He was appointed steward of the manor of Macclesfield, with **Robert de Legh of Adlington**, the elder, as his deputy, and also keeper and surveyor of the three forests of Cheshire (the letters for which do not survive, but see the grant of his expenses on 19 Sept. 1353 in *B.P.R.*, iii. 122–23). As far as the forest office was concerned, it meant that the riding foresters of the three forests were regarded as his deputies, but there is no evidence that his post was anything more than a sinecure.

He was granted the demesnes of Drakelow manor, plus £40 annual rent from Rudheath, in 1357 (ibid., 231, 267). On 13 September 1358, during the prince's second visit to Cheshire, he was appointed steward of the lordship, and keeper of the chase of Longdendale, keeper of the forest of Estyn in Hopedale, and keeper of the parks of Peckforton and Llwydcoed, all for life, with an annual fee of 100 marks and 2d. a day for the office in Longdendale (ibid., 314). As with the 1353 offices, he acted through deputies. Early in 1363, he granted £20 a year for life out of the issues of Drakelow to his esquire, Richard de Hampton, probably a Cheshire man (ibid., 473).

He died, unmarried, on 2 January 1370 (SC6 772/5, m.4d, although J.G. Bellamy in 'Sir John de Annesley and the Chandos inheritance', *Nott. Med. Studs*, x (1966), p. 94, suggests that he died on 31 Dec. 1369).

Chauldon, William de

'Wm de Chaweldon', indicted of trespass, was allowed to pay his fine of 20 marks in instalments of 40s. 0d. a year, 2 Dec. 1357 (*B.P.R.*, iii. 284; *ChRR*, p. 89).

Cheyne, Alan de (knight)

Retainer of the prince, who fought at Poitiers. He was married to a Cheshire heiress. Constable of Beeston castle, 1363/85. Constable of Rhuddlan castle from 1366.

Granted wardship and marriage of Elizabeth, daughter and heiress of Thos de Praers of Barthomley, 6 Oct. 1349 (*ChRR*, p. 105). As 'prince's yeoman' granted a sum out of Sir Jas Audley's arrears as sheriff, of which sum £61 was outstanding, 20 Dec. 1351 (*B.P.R.*, iii. 54). With his wife, Joan, petitioned B.P. against Wm Praers, to whom Joan's (step-) father had granted Ruddynges manor, in Willaston by Nantwich, although it was of Joan's mother's inheritance, 24 Oct. 1352 (ibid., 74). Received order to proceed in lawsuit Wm Hamelyn *v*. Eliz. Praers and others, over land in Crewe by Haslington, 24 Oct. 1352 (loc. cit). He and Joan received licence to convert their one-sixteenth of Nantwich barony to fee tail, 18 June 1353 (ibid., 109–10, 139) – fine of £4 for final concord recording same transaction pardoned, 7 Jan. 1354 (ibid., 140). Pardoned £15 relief due from him for land in Cheshire, same date (ibid., 148). He acted as surety for a bond of Thos and John Starky; when it was forfeited, his liability to pay £100 was pardoned by B.P., 21 Sept. 1353 (ibid., 148). Letters of general attorney and protection granted him, as he was going with B.P. overseas, 20 Aug. 1355 (ibid., 213). Received wages from B.P. in Gascony during December 1355 (Duchy of Cornwall Office, *Jornale* of John de Henxteworth, fo. 7). As 'prince's bachelor' granted £40 life-annuity from Easter 1357, because of his personal attendance on B.P. at the battle of Poitiers, 1 Feb. 1357 (ibid., 237; *ChRR*, p. 105). Complained he was in great debt because of the forthcoming expedition; order follows for his annuity to be paid promptly, 22 Oct. 1359 (*B.P.R.*, iii. 373–74). Granted life-annuity of 100 marks, in place of that for £40, for good service, 7 July 1361 (ibid., 419). Appointed constable of Beeston castle for life, together with 2d. a day for the porter's wages, 24 April 1363 (ibid., 455). His 100 marks annuity also granted to his wife, Joan, jointly, 24 May 1364 (ibid., 468–69). Appointed keeper or constable of Rhuddlan castle, at £40 a year, 13 Dec. 1366 (*ChRR*, p. 105). Ric., prince of Wales, confirmed his father's grants to him, 26 March 1377, and confirmed them again, as king (*ChRR*, p. 105; *C.P.R., 1377–81*, p. 613). He granted the office of constable of Beeston castle to John Cartlege, 24 Nov. 1385 (*ChRR*, p. 106).

Cholmundelegh, Richard de

Helsby's pedigree in Ormerod, ii, 637 is difficult to relate to the evidence in the Cholmondeley deeds published in *Cheshire Sheaf*, 3rd ser., 54, (1960). This Ric.

could be either Ric., lord of Cholmondeley, who died in 1361, or another Ric. A 'Ric. lord of Chelmundelegh' was bound over to keep the peace, with Sir John St Pierre and 7 others, for menacing Wm le Maistresson, 28 July 1352 (*B.P.R.*, iii. 61, 69). He sued for the peace, following his indictment, with 8 others, for trespass, 5 Dec. 1352 (ibid., 84). With Roger Forthewynd, he owed 70s. 0d. to John de Cravene, 20 Oct. 1353 (ibid., 127). With 13 others acted as surety for Robt de Houghton, constable of Beeston castle, 9 Nov. 1358 (*ChRR*, p. 107). The wardship of his heir granted to Thos de Aldrington, B.P.'s pantler, 28 May 1361 (*B.P.R.*, iii. 418).

Chorlegh, William de

He was to be shown favour in the repayment of a debt he owed B.P., since he was about to go overseas as an archer with the prince, 14 Aug. 1355 (*B.P.R.*, iii. 213). Granted keeping of Macclesfield park by B.P., during pleasure and good behaviour, for good service in Gascony, 12 May 1357 (ibid., 238). Granted by B.P. keeping of manor (house), park and stud of Macclesfield, during pleasure, for wages of £4 10s. 0d. a year, same reason, (ibid., 318). Granted same by B.P., for life, for wages of 3d. a day, 22 Aug. 1359 (ibid., 358). Ordered, as keeper, to pay tithe of foals to the abbot of Chester, 24 Aug. 1359 (ibid., 363). The stud was removed to Denbigh lordship in 1361 (SC6 803/3, m.2). Sold hay and straw to the stock-keeper of Macclesfield, 1366–67 (SC6 803/13, m.5). He continued to account as keeper of the park until Mich. 1369 (SC6 804/1, m.1d). a 'Wm de Chorlegh' was deputy steward of the duchy of Lancaster manor of Penwortham, before 14 Aug. 1378 (*D.K.R. 32*, p. 350).

Clerc, John le (of Brindley)

Servant of the abbot of Combermere, he was excused from serving B.P. as an archer in the war, as he feared being killed by one of his enemies among the other archers, 11 July 1359 (*B.P.R.*, iii. 353). Acted as receiver of the lands of **Sir John St Pierre**, 1361–62 (SC6 772/3, m.5). With others, 'John le Clerc' farmed the herbage, agistment and pannage of Delamere, from 1372 (SC6 787/5, m.2).

Clyf, Isabel del

Granted 2 dry, leafless oaks in Fence wood, Macclesfield forest, gift of B.P., 13 September 1358 (*B.P.R.*, iii. 315). Leased the common oven of Macclesfield from July 1359 to 1364 (SC6 802/15, m.2d; 802/17, m.2d; 803/5, m.2d; 803/7, m.2d; 803/9, m.3). Charged 20s. 0d., part of £6 fine for trespasses in Macclesfield forest, 1358–59 (*ChAcc*, p. 249). Another instalment charged, 1359–60 (ibid., p. 263).

Clyve, Thomas de

Leased office of rider of Delamere and Mondrum, for 26s. 8d. a year, 1351–53, (SC6 783/17, m.1d; 784/2, m.2d). His guarantors were Ric. Done of Utkinton,

John de Frodesham, and John Fogg (*ChRR*, p. 112). 'Thos Clyve who lives in Stanthorne, and Ellen (his wife)' had 10s. 0d. extorted from them by John Craven, Official of the archdeacon of Chester, before 1353 (CHES 29/65, m.4). Leased the pannage, herbage, escapes, agistment and fisheries of Delamere for £25 6s. 8d. a year 1354–57 (SC6 784/5, m.1; 784/7, m.1; 784/10, m.1). His guarantors for the lease of the above revenues for 1356–57 were Roger Russell of Norley, and Thos son of Wm de Venables (*ChRR*, p. 112). Allowed to pay his 20 marks arrears for the lease of the agistment of Delamere by instalments, 17 July 1357 (*B.P.R.*, iii. 260). Appointed keeper of Delamere forest, 1 Oct. 1357 (*ChRR*, p. 112). Responsible for attaching the escapes of Delamere forest, 1358–59 (SC6 785/3, m.1). Ordered to pay the 10 marks owed for the agistment of the forest at Easter and Michaelmas following, 13 Sept. 1358 (*B.P.R.*, iii. 313). 'Thos de Clive' was one of the abbot of Chester's men who threatened **Wm Stanley**, forester of Wirral, at the instigation of **Ranulf Roter**, 28 Nov. 1360 (ibid., 401).

Coton, John son of Richard de (of Chester)

There are several references to men of this name. A 'John Coten', who flourished at the end of the 13th century, was keeper of the avowries, and leased Middlewich town (CHES 29/11, m.3d). Another 'John Cotton', king's yeoman, was escheator of Cheshire *c.* 1331 (*C.F.R., 1327–37,* p. 278). Yet another was one of the keepers of the stock of Frodsham manor in 1355–56 (SC6 784/7, m.9d), and it may have been he who served in the Poitiers campaign, and, as a result, was pardoned on 13 July 1357 his involvement in an affray, and then appointed keeper of Peckforton park on 29 June 1360 (*B.P.R.*, iii. 161, 173, 386). There is also a reference to a 'John de Coton' who served as one of the Chester city sheriffs in 1364–65 (SC6 786/4, m.1). It is only this last reference that is likely to refer to the John Coton mentioned in this account.

Cradok, David

A man of this name served as lieutenant-seneschal of the Rouergue under Sir Thos Wettenhall in the 1360s, and later became justiciar of North Wales, and then, briefly, justiciar of South Wales also. He was mayor of Bordeaux in the 1380s. He was the father of Sir Ric. Cradok, and the family had land near Nantwich (Morgan, *War and Society*, pp. 160, 168, 170).

Cranewell, William de

'William de Cranewell' referred to as clerk of the chamberlain of North Wales in 1359; it does not seem likely that it was he who acted as one of the auditors of the accounts of the prince's officials, from 1361 to 1369 (SC6 785/9, m.4; 786/1, m.1; 786/3, m.1; 786/5, m.1; 786/6, m.1; 786/7, m.1; 786/8, m.1; 786/10, m.1). It is not possible to know which Cranewell received, with Thos de Nesse, a grant by B.P.

of the mills of Beaumaris, for £4 13s. 4d. a year, 28 June 1355 (*B.P.R.*, iii. 492). It was most likely Wm Cranewell, the chamberlain's clerk, who acted as an intermediary in 1363 between **Master John Burnham**, and **Sir John St Pierre** following the law-suit of **John Delves** and his wife for part of the St Pierre inheritance (ibid., 487).

Cranewell, 'one of the auditors of the accounts of the prince's officials' was appointed with Robert de Parys, chamberlain of North Wales, to deliver seisin to Delves of the land granted him by the prince to maintain his estate of knighthood, 4 Nov. 1362 (ibid., 453). With Delves and Peter de Lacy, made an allowance to Burnham on his account, 8 July 1365 (ibid., 482). Acting as steward and sheriff of Cornwall, Dec. 1371 (*C.C.R.*, *1369–74*, pp. 264, 270).

Creye, John de (yeoman of prince's chamber)

Appointed riding forester of Delamere and Mondrum, for good service, during good behaviour, at 3d. a day, 22 June 1361 (*B.P.R.*, iii. 419). Paid his wages until 29 April 1362, and referred to as 'late rider' 27 May 1362, when the order to pay him his wages was referred to as having had effect, despite the fact that he did not perform the office in person, until another was appointed in his place (ibid., 447). He was replaced by **Hugh de Wyrlegh** 29 April 1362.

Danyers, John (knight) d. 1372

Cheshire landowner, and military retainer of the Black Prince, who fought at Poitiers. He was the eldest surviving son of Sir Thomas Danyers, who had served at Crécy. There were two men called John Danyers active in the 1350s. In the chamberlain's account for 1354–55, sums of money paid to 'John Danyers, knight' and 'John Danyers, retained for war' are both mentioned (SC6 771/19, m.4d).

Eliz., widow of Ralph Boydel, arraigned an assize of *novel disseisin* against him, 3 Feb. 1351 (*B.P.R.*, iii. 1, 20, 33). With Joan (his wife) he petitioned B.P. that part of their manor of Dodleston had been seized by the justiciar and chamberlain, and that the escheator had seized part of the manor of Latchford, whereas the property should have gone to them after Ralph Boydel's death and to Howel, a ward whose guardianship had been bought by him; order to inquire, 28 July 1351 (ibid., 39–40). Complaint that he was wasting the lands of his ward, Howel ap Howel (!) in Latchford; order to inquire, 10 Jan. 1352 (ibid., 85). He was severely rebuked by B.P.'s administration, and ordered to cease harassing Roger de Chester, parson of Grappenhall, 12 Feb. 1352 (ibid., 58–59). With Thos Danyers, he pledged the fine of Wm de Goldburne, for poaching at Saighton, 1 Oct. 1352 (*Cheshire History*, 11 (1983), p. 41). Howel ap Oweyn Voil petitioned concerning the above waste, stating that Sir John had compelled him to grant his (the ward's) lands to him (Sir John); the consequent order to inquire stipulates that executions are not to be made by the sheriff, who is Sir John's father, 17 Feb. 1353 (*B.P.R.*, iii. 93–94). The escheator was ordered to seize the lands of Howel ap Oweyn (one of the heirs of Wm Boydell), and then also seized those of Joan, Sir John's wife (the other heir), as well as the wardship of Roger de Twenbrokes; an order followed to give Joan and Sir John their part back. They also complained that they had been deprived of the manor of Sale, which Joan claimed as widow of Thos de Sale, on the grounds that Thos's heir was a minor, although the lands were not held in chief; a list of the jury to inquire into the waste in Howel's lands follows, 10 June 1353 (ibid., 106–7). Escheator ordered to inquire into what lands held in chief he and Joan had acquired without licence, 2 Feb. 1354 (ibid., 143). Paid 20-mark fine for grant of pardon for himself and Joan, who had acquired without licence, from Howel ap Oweyn Voil, half of 17 messuages 160 acres of land, 100 acres of wood, 6 acres of meadow, and 14s. 0d. of rent in Grappenhall, held of B.P. in chief; he had also agreed a 50-mark fine for the marriage of Robt son of Robt de Assheton, which pertained to B.P. because of Howel's minority; order to escheator to deliver above property and marriage to him, 10 May 1354 (ibid., 159–60; *ChRR*, pp. 135–36). In the escheator's account for 1354–55 he is charged for a fine, payable for the relief for half of Wm Boydell's lands ($2\frac{1}{2}$ fees), for acquiring land in Grappenhall, and acquiring the wardship and marriage of Robt de Assheton; also paid a fine for the wardship of Thos Danyers' daughter and lands – 1 mess. 2 carucates of land in Appleton (held of Geoff. de Warburton), 2 messuages, 1 cottage in Thelwall (held of the duke of Lancaster), 4 cottages in Lymm (held of same Geoff.), 1 messuage in Oughtrington (held of the same duke), two thirds of one quarter of the township of Over Tabley (held of Sir Hugh de Venables), 2 acres of land in Hale (which Thos Danyers acquired from Sir Hamo de Mascy without licence, held of the earl of Chester in chief, by military service), (SC6 784/5, mm.6, 7). With Adam de Tabbelegh, Hugh de Foxwist, and Hen. le Vernon he made a recog. to B.P. for £46 13s. 4d., 10 June 1354 (*ChRR*, p. 136). Escheator ordered to certify why he has seized the manor of Bradley, and lands in Thelwall, Lymm, and Tabley, which belong to him, the prince's bachelor, 15 Feb. 1355 (*B.P.R.*, iii. 192). On the same date Sir John complained that, following a dispute between him and Sir Geoff. de Warburton the younger, he had agreed to be bound over; his opponent, refusing to do the same, was threatening his life (ibid., 192–93). He made a recog. of £10 to John de Burnham the younger, 28 March 1355 (*ChRR*, p. 136). Margaret, daughter and heiress of Sir Thos Danyers, arraigned a *novel disseisin* against him, and others, for tenements in Hale; he claimed to be seised as next friend, by socage tenure, but had arranged for the lands to be seized by the escheator, alleging that part were held by knight service. Order to the escheator to inquire, 18 May 1355 (*B.P.R.*, iii. 196–97). In London with Sir Ralph de Mobberley advising B.P. about conscripting archers from Cheshire, 21 May 1355 (ibid., 199–200). On the same date B.P. retained him in war for an annual fee of £11 13s. 4d., half to be paid immediately; he was granted letters of protection (ibid., 200). Order to postpone the assize of *novel disseisin* (Robt Boydell *v*. Ellen, widow of Peter de Legh) over tenements in Handley, since he and Joan, his wife, claimed the reversion after Ellen, and he was about to set out with B.P. to Gascony, 21 Aug. 1355 (ibid., 214). Letters of protection granted him in 29 Edw. III (*DKR.28*, p. 57). With Adam de Tabbelegh he owed £30 to John de Cravene, which debt had been taken over by B.P., 3 July 1356 (*B.P.R.*, iii. 228). B.P. granted him a general pardon, for offences up to 3 April 1357, for good service at Poitiers, 13 July 1357 (ibid., p. 257). Granted an oak for a mill-post by B.P. from Peckforton park, 21 July 1357 (ibid., p. 268). Pardoned 20 marks out of the £26 13s. 4d. he owed B.P., for good service at Poitiers, 1 July 1358 (ibid., pp. 302–3). With Sir Wm de Caryngton, Hamo de Mascy of Puddington, and Adam de Tabley, he made a recog. to Ric. de Wolveston, parson of Rostherne, for £106 13s. 4d., 18 July 1358 (*ChRR*, p. 136). Alice, widow of John Danyers of Lymm, sued him for the custody of the lands and heir of John son of Hen. Danyers, and property in Lymm, 32 Edw. III (*DKR.28*, p. 59). Granted wardship and marriage of Wm, son and heir of Wm de Tranemol, for the sum he paid Sir Robt de Holand, 3 June 1359 (*B.P.R.*, iii. 344). B.P. retained him in war for an annual fee of £23 6s. 8d., for himself and four esquires, for one year from previous 1 Aug., 16 Aug. 1359 (ibid., p. 356). Letters of protection granted to Wm Janny the younger, who was to go with B.P. overseas in J.D.'s company, 30 Sept. 1359 (ibid., p. 369). Similar letters for John de Drokenfeld and John de Holyngworth, going in the company of him and of Sir John de Hyde, 8 Oct. 1359 (ibid., 370). Roger de Mottresheved and 11 other archers given leave to remain home, at the request of Sir John and others, their leaders, 14 Oct. 1359 (ibid., 371). With John de Dokenfeld and Wm Danyel he made a recog. for 40 marks to Master John de Burnham the younger and four others, 27 July 1361 (*ChRR*, p. 136). Licence to him, and his wife Joan, to convert Grappenhall manor to fee tail, so that half would go to John's heirs and half to Joan's; fine, £32 13s. 4d., 8 Dec. 1361 (*B.P.R.*, iii. 437). Letters of protection granted him, on his going to Gascony in B.P.'s retinue, 13 Dec. 1362 (*ChRR*, p. 136; *DKR.28*, p. 62). Granted life-annuity of 20 marks, for good service, payable at Chester exchequer, 20 Nov. 1362 (*B.P.R.*, iii. 453). Granted a pension for good service, Nov. 1363 (*ChRR*, p. 134). Letters of protection granted him, as he was about to set out with B.P. to Aquitaine; a plea of *quo warranto* against him was to be adjourned, 1 Aug. 1364 (*B.P.R.*, iii. 471; *DKR.28*, p. 63). With Thos de Stathum he stood pledge for Roger de Holford's performance in the office of seller of felons' goods in Cheshire, the office having been granted him for good service as one of B.P.'s archers, 11 May 1365 (*B.P.R.*, iv. 478). Before 1366 he paid a fine of £106 13s. 4d. for wardship and marriage of Peter, son and heir of Hamo and Eliz. Fitton – she being a daughter of Peter de Thornton, (SC6 787/7, m.5d). He accounted as under-constable of Chester castle, under Thos Chaundeler, Xmas 1366 to Michaelmas 1368 (SC6 786/7, m.3d; 786/8, m.3d). Grant to him and Joan, his wife, of the right to hold a market and fairs at Latchford, 3 March 1367 (*ChRR*, p. 134). He was granted the ferry boat at Warrington, and the stone given by Sir Geoff. de Werberton to Matt. de Rixton for the building of a bridge there, 20 Oct. 1367 (*ChRR*, p. 136).

Died on or shortly before 10 March 1372, holding Grappenhall manor in chief of B.P. by knight service, and was succeeded by Margaret and Nichola. He also held lands in Latchford and Handley, which were delivered to his second wife, Alice, by then his widow. (SC6 787/4, m.6; Ormerod, i.473).

Davenport, John de

As serjeant in court (with Hen. Motlowe) ordered to assist Robt de Foxwist, who had important business to undertake in the court of Chester for the B.P.'s profit, 8 Sept. 1352 (*B.P.R.*, iii. 78). On a panel from which a jury was to be chosen to inquire into waste committed by **Sir John Danyers** in Howel ap Oweyn Voil's lands, 10 June 1353 (ibid., 107). With Wm Maynwaryng acted as general attorney of **Sir Alan Cheyne** during his absence abroad, 20 Aug. 1355 (ibid., 213). Granted 40s. 0d. for his work as pleader in the last Flint sessions, 29 Nov. 1355 (ibid., 219–20). Obtained writ of *diem clausit extremum* upon death of Robt del Heth, 14 May 1358 (ibid., 301). Retained by B.P. as serjeant pleader in Cheshire, Flintshire, Wales and elsewhere, for £5 a year, 16 Feb. 1361 (ibid., 406). With Robt Legh, 'John de Davenport of Wheltrough' took fines of workmen and servants, 1360–61 (SC6 803/3, m.1). Acting as justice of labourers in Macclesfield hundred in 1360–61 (with **Adam de Kyngeslegh**), and in 1364–65 (with same, and **Robert de Legh**) (ibid., 486). B.P. gave him 4 oaks in Lyme wood, 23 Nov. 1363, and 3 oaks in same for his building work, 19 May 1365 (ibid., 460, 486). A 'John Daunport' served as second justice at Lancaster, during pleasure, in 1383 (Somerville, *Duchy of Lancaster*, i. 472).

(Not to be confused with Sir John de Davenport, serjeant of the peace of Macclesfield hundred, d. 1358, or his son of the same name, d. 1370).

Delves, John de (knight) d. 1369

He came from a minor landed family, who lived near Uttoxeter (Staffs.), and despite his membership of the Black Prince's council by the mid-1350s, he was called 'yeoman' (or 'valet') and was not knighted until 1362, when the prince gave him land worth 100 marks a year to maintain his new status (D.L. Broughton, *Records of an Old Cheshire Family* (1908); *B.P.R.*, iii. 452–53). Delves' was the most striking example of the rise to power of a man from a relatively humble background through the prince's service, and, if fate had been kinder, he could have ended his career as steward of the king's household, or as treasurer of the kingdom. Despite the view of Philip Morgan that he was a 'soldier/administrator', Delves made his career through the law, and in this respect he can be contrasted with Sir John Wingfield, to whom that description can properly be applied.

'John de Delves' first appears as the attorney of Sir Edmund Hacluyt, a prisoner of war, in Nov. 1347 (*B.P.R.*, i. 139). He had joined the service of the **earl of Arundel**, under whom he was acting as under-sheriff of Shropshire, by 1348 (Public Record Office, *List of Sheriffs*, p. 118). Doubtless it was Arundel who brought him to the prince's attention, and he was acting as the B.P.'s attorney in the *quo warranto* pleas in North Wales in 1348 (*Record of Caernarvon*, p. 151). Arundel's life-appointment, as justiciar of North Wales, may have facilitated Delves' next promotion, to the office of lieutenant-justiciar of North Wales in 1348 (Tout, vi. 60). In 1352 he made an extent of Anglesey and Caernarvonshire (see above, p. lxxiii). He retained the Welsh post when he was appointed lieutenant-justiciar of Chester on 4 October 1353 (*B.P.R.*, iii. 125). Although **Sir Bartholomew de Burgherssh the younger** was appointed justiciar of Chester on 26 October 1353, it is clear that the office was a sinecure (ibid., 128). The remainder of Delves' career consisted of promotion to ever-wider administrative responsibilities in the prince's service, while retaining, at least for some time, his regional offices. In 1360, it is said that he was dividing his time between his 'bailiwicks' (i.e. at Chester and Caernarfon) and his responsibilities at the centre, in London and Westminster (*B.P.R.*, iv. 501).

Delves was brought forward in the prince's central administration by **Sir John Wingfield**, the prince's first business-manager, and seems to have been functioning as a *de facto* member of the prince's council by the mid 1350s, although he is not definitely referred to as such until 1357 (*B.P.R.*, iv. 211). During Wingfield's absences on the Poitiers campaign, from Oct. 1355 to the spring of 1357, and again on the Rheims expedition of 1359, Delves acted as his deputy in England. For example, on 26 Feb. 1357, the decision on the future of the temporalities of the bishopric of St Asaph was taken by a group of men meeting in the bishop of Winchester's Inn, in Southwark. They were the bishop of Winchester, chancellor of England, the bishop of Rochester, treasurer of England, the keeper of the king's privy seal, Sir David de Wollore, Peter de Lacy (the prince's receiver-general), and John Delves. Delves was also given the job of supervising the sale of the late bishop's personal property (*B.P.R.*, iii. 236). On 26 Sept. 1359, on the eve of his departure with the prince on the expedition to Rheims, Wingfield formally assigned to Delves the control of the administration of the earldom of Chester and the principality of Wales (ibid., 368).

He was knighted on 4 November 1362, and the prince granted him property in Wales worth 100 marks a year 'to maintain his estate' (*B.P.R.*, iii. 452–53). Sir John Wingfield had died the previous year, and Delves clearly succeeded him as the prince's business manager, albeit without the power of independent decision-taking that his predecessor had wielded (Booth, *Financial Administration*, pp. 74–75; Morgan, *War and Society*, p. 122). On 3 Feb. 1364, 'John Delves' was appointed a royal justice of the court of Common Pleas at Westminster, and acted as such up to the Easter term 1365 (*C.P.R., 1361–64*, p. 461; G.O. Sayles, ed., *Select Cases in the Court of King's Bench*, Selden Soc., 82 (1965), p. lxxi). It is difficult to know whether this is the same John Delves or not. On the one hand, it could have been a counter-example to the seconding of royal justices to the prince's service (Shareshull and Hillary, for example). However, although he did remain in England when the prince went to Aquitaine to take up his lordship there in 1363, Delves is known to have followed him there in late 1364, returning in March 1365 (*B.P.R.*, iv. 540, 543). This does not seem consonant with him sitting in the court of Common Pleas at Hilary term, 1365.

In July 1364 his status was further enhanced when the prince granted him a licence to crenellate his manor-house at Doddington, on the estate in south Cheshire that he had bought from John Brescy in 1351/52 (*B.P.R.*, iii. 469; Ormerod, iii. 523). It was in 1364 that he and his second wife, Isabel, were given the custody of Joan, the widowed duchess of Brittany. This unfortunate Flemish lady, who lived in England from 1343, was probably insane (*Complete Peerage*, x. 820–21). Delves died in 1369, and was buried at Audley, in Staffordshire (Morgan, *War and Society*, p. 176).

As an expert in law and finance, Delves held other offices on the prince's estates. In 1357, he was one of the justices of the Cheshire forest eyre held under the presidency of **Sir Richard Willoughby** (CHES 33/6). With the death of the bishop of Coventry and Lichfield in 1358, he was appointed joint-keeper of the temporalities of the see, but was excused in 1360 from rendering account at the royal exchequer because he 'is so occupied about the business of Edward prince of Wales that he can in nowise attend to that duty' (*C.C.R., 1360–64*, p. 28). He was appointed constable and steward of the lordship of Denbigh in 1360, and he and **Burnham** administered the lordship until 1364, when his general responsibilities led to him shedding some of his local ones (*B.P.R.*, iii. 381). After the dismissal of Abbot Sainsbury in 1362, he became joint-keeper, with a monk, of the abbey of St Werburgh, Chester (*B.P.R.*, iii. 444). In April and May 1364, he served as assessor and arrentor of the duchy of Cornwall, at the periodic session held to value the property of the duchy tenants and renew their leases (*B.P.R.*, ii. 205).

As someone who rose to an office well above his social station, one aim of his career was to increase his landed property. This proved to be surprisingly difficult. He married twice: first Elizabeth, the widow of Walter Baskerville, and then, after her death in 1363, Isabel Egerton, who brought him a tenuous claim to a portion of the St Pierre part of the barony of Malpas (Ormerod, iii. 522; *D.K.R.28*, p. 71; *V.C.H. Staffs.*, viii. 75). In June 1358 he bought for ten marks the land in Chester which had belonged to one of Sir Peter Thornton's co-heiresses (*B.P.R.*, iii. 306). Such small purchases, and leases, were made possible through his employment by the prince, and influence of the prince's associates. In 1361–62 he secured the lease of land at Handbridge (where he established a chantry in his will) which had belonged to the Grey family, and in 1366, the earl of Salisbury gave him the small manor of Bosley, in east Cheshire, for life (SC6 785/9, m.1. The grant was voided, presumably because of the lack of a licence to alienate, SC6 786/9.) He leased a wardship in the Midlands from the prince for £50 a year from 1362 (*B.P.R.*, iv. 421). The following year, he leased part of Nantwich barony from Sir John Lovel of Titchmarsh, for £50 a year (*C.C.R., 1364–68*, p. 378). The only substantial grant of heritable property that the prince conferred on him was that of 1362, intended to support his new estate of knighthood, which consisted of scattered rents and properties in North Wales worth 100 marks a year (*B.P.R.*, iii. 452–53).

The early 1360s were not an easy time to acquire permanent gifts of land from the Black Prince. The land-revenue base was beginning to shrink, and the requirements of the expensive foreign policy had to be made up by new, unpopular sources of revenue which proved difficult to collect. Doubtless this was the reason why Delves decided to use his official position, with the prince's encouragement, to prosecute his wife's claim to the Malpas lands (one-eighth part of the barony) in 1363, (Booth, *Financial Administration*, pp. 130–32). The property in question was in the prince's hands for the life of Sir John St Pierre, formerly of Peckforton, who had exchanged them with the prince in 1353. Delves used this position of strategic weakness against St Pierre, who complained that both illegality and trickery had been used against him. This incident made the point as cogently as possible that the only way to prosper in the 1360s and 1370s was through the prince's service.

Deneys, Alexander

With **John de Wetenhale** of Dorfold, Wm de Wetenhale of Alpraham, and **Wm Wasteneys** he made a recog. to Sir John de Chorleton, junior, for £10, 26 Sept. 1352 (*ChRR*, p. 144). After withdrawing from Shareshull's sessions (1353), he was exacted, and subsequently agreed a fine of £53 6s. 8d. and suffered a forfeiture of £40. Allowed to pay by instalments over 5 years, and offered charter of pardon, he was also bound over to keep the peace, as were his enemies (Ric. de Deryngton and 8 others), 20 Nov. 1353 (*B.P.R.*, iii. 130–31; *ChRR*, p. 144). With John de Wetenhale, Robt Proudeglove of Congleton, Thos de Becheton, Wm son of Wm del Yate of Congleton, John son of Wm de Morton, Roger son of Ranulf de Morton of Congleton, John de Knotesford of Chester, and Wm de Wasteneys, he made a recog. to B.P. for £93 6s. 8d., 12 Dec. 1353 (ibid.) He and his ward, Joan (daughter and heiress of John Biroun) granted letters of protection until his fine was paid, 9 May 1354 (*B.P.R.*, iii. 157). His widow, Isabel, claimed that Joan Biroun, who lived with her in Salop, had been abducted by Robt Proudglove and John de Morton and others; her husband was bound to B.P. in a large sum at his death. Order to seize Joan, 8 Oct. 1354 (ibid., pp. 178–79). Order to supersede the action against Robt Proudglove in connection with Alex. Deneys' fine, for which Robt stood pledge, 8 June 1357 (ibid., p. 250). John de Wetenhale allowed to pay £46 by instalments, being that part of Alex.'s fine for which he stood pledge, at 10 marks a year, 2 Dec. 1357 (ibid., p. 284). Wetenhale paid one instalment in 1359–60 (*ChAcc*, p. 267).

Diseworth, William de

Bailiff of the manor of Drakelow, 1353–61 (SC6 784/4, m.1; 784/5, m.12; 784/6, m.8; 784/10, m.7; 785/1, m.9; 785/3, m.3; 785/6, m.5; 785/8, m.4d). Granted 10-year lease of manor-house and demesnes of Drakelow, 1355–56 (SC6 784/7, m.8). Ordered to provide the auditors with a list of those who had bought turves from the manor, presumably because of suspicion of concealment of revenue, 1355–56 (SC6 784/7, m.8). His grant of the demesnes of Drakelow was superseded by the grant of the same to **Sir John Chandos** for life, Oct. 1357 (*B.P.R.*, iii. 231, 267). At the county court of 6 Aug. 1359, 'Wm de Duisworth', bailiff of Drakelow, was indicted of concealing in his accounts for the previous three years 20 bushels of wheat (10d. each), 40 bushels of barley (4d. each), 80 bushels of oats (4d. each), and the turbary and herbage of the wastes of Rudheath (30s. 0d.) (CHES 25/4, m.10). He leased the turbary and pasture of Rudheath (in Drakelow manor) for £2 a year, 1360–61 (SC6 785/8, m.4d). He had died by 1361–62, as in that year the turbary of 'flaghtes' and pasture of Rudheath had been granted to his widow, for £2 a year (SC6 785/9, m.2d).

Dokesey, Richard de

As B.P.'s baker, granted 10 marks life-annuity, for good service in England and Gascony, to be taken from the mills and common oven of Macclesfield until he could be provided with land and rent to that value, 1 Feb. 1357 (*B.P.R.*, iii. 234). (The enrolment of the warrant for this grant, and of the grant itself, both calendared in *ChRR*, p. 148, give its value as £10 a year; there is a further enrolment of the grant in *ChAcc*, p. 243, which confirms the value as 10 marks.) The annuity was paid in 1358–59 (*ChAcc*, p. 253), and 1359–60 (ibid., p. 270).

Doune, Henry

He made a recog. for £8 to Sir John de Byntre, 8 June 1351 (*ChRR*, p. 152). Appointed constable of Chester castle 6 April 1359 on the dismissal of **Thomas de Warrewyk** (SC6 785/3, m.2d). Held the office until 20 December 1359, when Warrewyk was restored (SC6 785/5, m.2). Upon Warrewyk's death, 7 March 1364, Doune held the constableship again for a short period (until 8 April 1365, when he was succeeded by Thos Chaundeler) (SC6 786/5, m.2d).

Doune, Richard (Done) *c.* 1311 to 1369

Hereditary master forester of Delamere and Mondrum. He leased the office of constable of Chester castle between 1349 and 1353, from which he was dismissed as the result of oppressive behaviour.

His father, also called Ric., had done homage to Prince Edward in Chester for his forestership, 13 April 1301 (*C.P.R., 1343–45*, p. 227). He was born 1311/12, and as forester in fee of Delamere was a royal ward in 1332 (*C.C.R.*,

1330–33, p. 437). Leased the constableship of Chester castle for £30 a year 1349–50, **not** 1350–51 (*ChAcc*, p. 142) and again from Michaelmas 1351 to 20 Aug. 1353, for £33 6s. 8d. a year, when he was dismissed by the B.P. 'with his own mouth', and replaced by Thos Bradegate (SC6 784/2, m.1). Accounted as forester in fee of Delamere, 1350–68 (*ChAcc*, pp. 201–2; SC6 783/17, m.1d; 784/2, m.1d; 784/3, m.1d; 784/5, m.1; 784/7, m.1; 784/10, m.1; 785/1, m.1; 785/3, m.1; 785/6, m.2d; 785/8, m.2; 785/9, m.1; 786/1, m.4; 786/3, m.4d; 786/5, m.2d; 786/6, m.3; 786/7, m.3; 786/8, m.3). Letter to him, as master forester of Delamere and Mondrum, enclosing ordinances for the forest, 24 March 1351 (*B.P.R.*, iii. 16). He and his under-foresters pardoned for killing Robt Cousyn, caught red-handed with venison, 29 Oct. 1351 (ibid., 45; *ChRR*, p. 152). In the trailbaston sessions of 1353, he was accused of several crimes of oppression and extortion while acting as constable of Chester castle (*Cheshire History*, 12 (1983), pp. 26–27; 13 (1984), pp. 26–27). For these he was fined 100 marks, (*B.P.R.*, iii. 260). Damages of £20 were also awarded against him in favour of Ric. de Deryngton, for which he was ordered to prison, although he managed to remain at large; order to imprison him should he not pay, 18 Feb. 1354 (ibid., 144–45). Further damages awarded against him of £5 (to Ric. son of Alan), £10 (to Ric. son of Thos), and 8 marks (to Alan Webbe of Nantwich) were reduced by half on condition he pay by Xmas 1353. On his failure to comply, an order was issued to compel him to give satisfaction 28 Feb. 1354 (ibid., 150). Order to inquire into threats allegedly made by him to Peter de Gildesburgh's commissaries, who were holding a chapter in the prebend of Tarvin. Also involved were Adam son of Adam, and at least 15 others, who came armed, 31 Dec. 1354 (ibid., 187). Order by B.P. to let him have allowance for part of his 50-mark lease of the constableship of Chester castle, as it had been taken from him on 16 Aug. 1353, 2 March 1355 (ibid., 194). Order to let him have respite of the 16 marks arrears of the 100 mark fine he made in the trailbaston sessions, 17 July 1357 (ibid., 260). He was tenant of Wm de Cholmondele for lands in Clotton, 28 Feb. 1358 (ibid., 297). With John de Bromlegh and 6 others, he made a recog. for £50 to B.P. on behalf of Wm de Praers of Baddiley, 20 Dec. 1358 (*ChRR*, p. 152). He owed homage and service to the late **John de Wetenhale** of Dorfold, for unspecified properties, 21 Dec. 1361 (*B.P.R.*, iii. 437; *ChRR*, p. 518). With Wm de Cholmundelegh and 5 others he made a recog. to B.P. for 110 marks, for the wardship and marriage of Wm son of Hugh de Cholmundelegh, and the keeping of his inheritance, 7 March 1363 (*ChRR*, p. 152). He made a recog. to B.P. for 16s. 0d., for acquiring a life interest in a piece of land called Cleycroft in Anderton from Sir John de St Pierre, 11 March 1363 (ibid.) Order to respite the sum in which he was bound to the B.P. until **John Delves's** return to England, 2 June 1364 (*B.P.R.*, iii. 469). He died 10 Sept. 1369, and his I.P.M. gives his son, John, as his heir, who was 14 years of age. It states also that he held the manor of Utkinton of Hugh de Venables of Kinderton, by knight service, which was worth £8 13s. 4d. a year, as well as other lands. He held the bailiwick of the forest of Delamere of the earl of Chester in chief, by grand serjeanty, worth £6 a year

(*D.K.R. 28*, pp. 67–68). Katherine, his widow, rendered the account for her late husband, 1368–69 (SC6 786/10, m.2d). The account for 1370–71 (1369–70 is missing) was rendered by Hugh Venables, acting as forester by reason of his wardship of Doune's son (SC6 787/2, m.2).

Dutton, Peter de

Order, at his request, to take his proof of age, 4 May 1358 (*B.P.R.*, iii. 299). In 1364–65 it was stated that his inheritance from Sir Peter de Thorneton comprised a pourparty shared with Matt. de Weverham (SC6 786/5, m.1d). With John del Hall of Chester, made a recog. for 40s. 0d. to Ric. Dunfull of Chester, 6 Feb. 1390 (*ChRR*, p. 160).

Eggerton, Philip de died *c.* 1362

With David de Eggerton and 17 others made a recog. for £100 to B.P., 10 Dec. 1341, for a fine imposed in the sessions of oyer and terminer held before Hugh de Berwyk and his fellow justices in the autumn of that year (*ChRR*, p. 167; *ChAcc*, p. 115). With John de Warenna and 5 others made a recog. for £10 to B.P., 15 March 1342 (*ChRR*, p. 167). He witnessed several Cholmondeley family title deeds between 1348 and 1355 (*Cheshire Sheaf*, 3rd ser., 54 (1960). With John Blount of Chester, and 6 others, made a recog. for £106 13s. 4d. to B.P., 1 Dec. 1350 (*ChRR*, p. 167). Inquiry into whether the manor of Duckington, half the manor of Crowton, and the manors of Eaton and Duddon, which are held by him in chief, have been alienated without licence, 15 July 1351 (*B.P.R.*, iii. 36). Petitioned for licence to buy land worth £20 to grant in mortmain to chantry of Our Lady of Egerton; order to hold inqu. *ad quod dampnum*, 4 Feb. 1352 (ibid., 56). He was ordered by B.P. not to hinder Wm Trusthorp's attempt to execute a decree of the court of Canterbury ordering Wm to receive a share of the revenues of St John's, Chester, 16 May 1352 (ibid., 64). B.P. ordered him to give security for the payment of the revenues of St John's, Chester, which church had been seized because of a dispute between the dean and canons, 24 Aug. 1352 (ibid., 74–75). He was to be on the panel from which the jurors were to be chosen to try the action of waste sought by Howel ap Oweyn Voil, 10 June 1353 (ibid., 106). With his wife, Maud, he held the manor of Bradwall for life, the reversion belonging to Sir Hugh Venables of Kinderton, 20 Nov. 1353 (ibid., 130). He claimed a right in the lands of Sir John de Sutton, 22 March 1354 (ibid., 155). With David, his brother, Ranulf le Bruyn and Thos de Capenhurst he made a recog. for £40 to Hugh de Thrigyngham, dean of St John's, Chester, 14 Feb. 1355 (*ChRR*, p. 167). Inquiry into the amount of land in Rudheath that was recovered against him, its rent before 1349, its present value, and how much it could be let for, 28 June 1355 (*B.P.R.*, iii. 205). As former proctor of Master John de Marisco, sometime dean of St John's, he owed John de Cravene a year's commons, 3 July 1356 (ibid., 228). With Hamo de Mascy of Puddington and 11 others made a recog. to B.P. for £366 13s. 4d. for the wood of

Bickley, 1 July 1357 (*ChRR*, p. 167). B.P. granted him land in Rudheath, at an annual rent of 26s. 8d. and suit of court of Drakelow, 19 July 1357 (*B.P.R.*, iii. 266–68; *ChRR*, p. 167; *ChAcc*, p. 240). With David de Egerton, Thos de Capenhurst, and Ken. Pecok made a recog. to B.P. for 116s. 8d., 30 Jan. 1358 (*ChRR*, p. 167). He and 12 others were ordered to put Wm de Walsingham in possession of Bunbury church, which the B.P. had given him, and also the £60 granted by inquiry for repairs to the chancel and rectory buildings which they have hindered him from receiving, 16 Feb. 1361 (*B.P.R.*, iii. 406). Isabel, his daughter, was entitled to part of the lands left by her father, after the death of her brother, David, 1 Dec. 1361 (ibid., 426). His I.P.M. was held 4 Jan. 1363, when he was stated to have held the manors of Egerton and Wychough, together with other properties (CHES 3/5/36 Ed. III/4).

Eggerton, Philip son of Ranulf de

He may have been a cousin of the previous **Philip de Eggerton**. A Ranulf de Eggerton, who was in wardship to the B.P. in 1354–55 for lands in Caldecott and Newton by Malpas, was surely too young to be this Philip's father (SC6 784/5, m.6). With David de Overton and Kenard de Cholmundelegh he made a recog. to B.P. for the 100s. 0d. fine charged in this account, 26 June 1361 (*ChRR*, p. 168). With Urian de Egerton, Thos de Shokelache, and David de Wovere made a recog. for £48 to **Sir John de Delves** and Thos de Budenhale, 28 June 1368 (ibid.)

Elton, John de d. Sept. 1361

With Wm de Lynford made a recog. to Thos de Ferrers for 20s. 0d., 15 Apr. 1345 (*ChRR*, p. 171). 'John de Elton' found guilty, in the 1353 trailbaston sessions, of housebreaking in Offerton (1347), Ince (1342), and Plemstall (1343); also of receiving Wm Swan, who had killed Wm Doukele at Elton (*Cheshire History*, 13 (1984), p. 22). 'John son of John de Elton' petitioned on 22 Feb. 1357 concerning three and a half bovates of land in Stone Dunham, and half the manor of Hapsford, with which he claimed his father had enfeoffed him in 27 Edward III. The land had been seized as a result of his father's indictment for the death of **Wm Wasteneys**, who died in 30 Edward III, and for which he had been exacted (*B.P.R.*, iii. 235–36). (There is a similar petition from Robt son of John Elton, concerning land in Elton). Order to inquire into above allegations, 18 Oct. 1357 (ibid., 281). Ric. le Mareschall of Ince made a recog. to B.P. for 70s. 0d. for a lease of the lands which had belonged to 'John de Elton of Ins', 6 June 1358 (*ChRR*, p. 325). A further petition from the two brothers followed, and an order to inquire 5 July 1358 (*B P.R.*, iii. 303).

The deleted entry, which follows **11.4** in the account, states that John de Elton, who was outlawed, had died in Sept. 1361, whereupon his tenement descended to Thos de Elton, his brother.

Elton, Thomas de (clerk of the prince's exchequer)

In or before 1354–55 he acquired rent in Picton and Shipbrook from Sir Ralph de Vernon, without B.P.'s licence (SC6 784/5, m.7d). Margaret, sister and heiress of Sir Ralph de Vernoun, denied that her brother had granted him an annuity; order to inquire 26 Oct. 1357 (*B.P.R.*, iii. 281). In 34 Edward III he enfeoffed Thos son of Ralph de Congelton and John Passelegh, chaplains, with all his lands and tenements in Elton, to be regranted to himself and his wife, Agnes (*D.K.R. 28*, p. 60).

Ercal, Richard de

Master carpenter and surveyor of the earldom of Chester, 1361 to 1374.

Order to admit him to the office of master carpenter and surveyor of carpentry works in Cheshire and Flintshire, with the usual wages and fees, 4 Dec. 1361 (*B.P.R.*, iii. 428; *ChRR*, p. 173). Accused of fraudulently concealing timber sold from Delamere forest, 1362–63 (SC6 786/1, m.4). Under his direction, carpenters spent two weeks in 1364–65 repairing the Dee mills (SC6 786/5, m.1d). He was last paid his wages as carpenter in the chamberlain's account for Michaelmas 1373 to July 1374 (SC6 772/9, m.3). From July 1374, Wm Neuhall was receiving wages as carpenter (SC6 772/10, m.2).

Fleccher, William le

Acted as catchpoll of Middlewich, 1358–63 (SC6 785/3, m.2; 785/5, m.1d; 785/9, m.1d; 786/1, m.1d). With John le Bowere, he was granted licence by B.P. to trade freely in Middlewich, for the usual payment, in return for good service at the battle of Poitiers, 16 July 1357 (*B.P.R.*, iii. 261). This grant, which appears to have been opposed by the burgesses of the town, was repeated on 4 Oct. following (ibid., 280).

> (A 'Wm Flecchere of Bikerton' was granted lands in Bickley and Astwood for good service in Gascony, 7 June 1357 (*B.P.R.*, iii. 248–49). 'William le Fleccher of Crue' arraigned a *novel disseisin* over tenements in Crewe by Haslington, 24 Oct. 1352 (ibid., 79). It is not possible to identify either of them as William the catchpoll.)

Fouler, John le

Catchpoll of Middlewich, with **Wm de Tappetrassh**, 1360–61 (SC6 785/8, m.3d).

Foulleshurst, Robert de (knight) d. 1389

> The third son of Richard de Fouleshurst of Edleston, according to Ormerod he was living in 1325/26 (Ormerod, iii. 385). He had a nephew of the same name, who was born *c.* 1339. Sir Robert was first in the service of Queen Philippa, and then transferred to that of the Prince.

'Robt de Foulleshurst, yeoman of Queen Philippa' married Eliz., daughter and heiress of Thos de Praers of Barthomley; a grant of livery of her lands followed, despite her not being of full age, because of B.P.'s love for Robt, 4 Nov. 1352 (*B.P.R.*, iii. 79). B.P. granted 'Robt son of Ric. de Foulleshurst' free warren in demesnes of Barthomley and Crewe, out of respect for Queen Philippa, 6 Feb. 1355 (ibid., 193). He was granted letters of protection, as he was going overseas on the king's service, 28 June 1355 (ibid., 207). B.P. ordered that the demands on 'Robt de Foulleshurst, the prince's yeoman' for his share of the common fine of Wirral forest be stayed, in respect of the lands he held there in his wife's right, 20 June 1359 (ibid., 339). Order reissued, 16 June 1359 (ibid., 349). As 'prince's bachelor' he claimed that the abbot of Combermere had organised armed threats against him while he was on the king's service at Winchelsea, despite the B.P.'s prohibition. The abbot then led a group of armed men into Salop. Order to inquire, 13 June 1360 (ibid., 383). Grant of defeasance of an £80 bond, owed to B.P., on condition that he pay £40 of it to the prince at Martinmas and Easter following, 24 Mar. 1361 (ibid., 413). As a Wirral landowner he was summoned with all the other free tenants of the forest to an assembly to discuss the puture payable to Wm de Stanley, 1 Dec. 1361 (ibid., 434). Order, at the request of the king and queen, to cancel a demand for repayment by him of money owed to B.P., 22 March 1365 (ibid., 476). The sum of £80, in which he was bound to B.P., was respited, 1366–67 (SC6 786/7, m.10). He was exempted from serving on juries, 1372–73 (SC6 772/8, m.2; *D.K.R. 28*, p. 69). He was dead by 17 Nov. 1389 (*ChRR*, p. 187); the resultant I.P.M. showed that he held the manors of Crewe, Barthomley, and Landican, with the advowsons of Barthomley and Woodchurch, with other properties, in right of his late wife.

Foxwyst, Robert de

A forester in fee of Macclesfield until 1354, he appears to have fallen victim to the hostility provoked by the prince's revenue-raising campaign of the early 1350s.

Ordered, as one of the foresters of Macclesfield, to observe a detailed forest ordinance, 24 March 1351 (*B.P.R.*, iii. 15). With other Macclesfield foresters, he performed homage and fealty to B.P. in London, 25 Oct. 1351 (ibid., 43). Order to postpone all lawsuits, including indictments, pending against him and his son, Edmund, 4 Feb. 1352 (ibid., 56). Order to give him the record of an action for 2 carucates of land in Sutton that he lost to **Adam de Mottram**; he complained that he cannot obtain the 100s. 0d. awarded him for crops growing on that land, 8 Feb. 1352 (ibid., 57). He was taken into B.P.'s protection until Whitsun 1352, so that he could travel from London to Cheshire, and back, 12 Feb. 1352 (ibid., 58). Order to Sir John and **Robt de Legh** to ensure that he was kept safe from his 'hardened ill-wishers', who have prevented him from acting as forester. If he had been attacked, the B.P. informed them that he would know who was behind it, and punish them severely, 20 April 1352. This order was to be proclaimed in the county court. **Sir Wm Trussell** was also ordered to assist Foxwyst, whose letters of protection were extended to Michaelmas 1352, (ibid., 62). These letters were further renewed to the Octave of Hilary, 1353; Hen. de Motlowe, serjeant in court, was ordered to help him, as Foxwyst had important business to prosecute in the court of Chester, and many matters in hand for B.P.'s profit; a similar letter was sent to 'John de Deynport' (see **John de Davenport**). Both orders were issued at Foxwyst's request, 8 Sept. 1352 (ibid., 78). He was fined £10 in the 1353 trailbaston sessions; the offence is not mentioned in the trailbaston roll, but the fine is recorded in the poker of Macclesfield's account, 1353–54 (SC6 802/9, m.3). He complained that when B.P. was in Chester (1353), the steward of Macclesfield failed to inquire into an offence that Thos de Boseden was alleged to have committed in Macclesfield forest, despite having been ordered to do so. Further, he complained that Adam de Mottram had assaulted Ric. Janny, Foxwyst's deputy-forester, at Macclesfield. Order to inquire, 18 Feb. 1354 (*B.P.R.*, iii. 145). He complained that his lands and bailiwick had been seized by the prince's officials, at the instigation of his enemies, on the pretext of his having made an unlicensed alienation; he claimed to have made a fine for that alienation, and vouched the rolls of the court of Chester to warranty. Order to have the rolls searched, and if a fine be found, to let him have his property back; if not, impose a reasonable fine, and levy it from his lands as quickly as possible, without creating excessive hardship, 18 Feb. 1354 (ibid., 145). Order to levy the 100s. 0d. which Foxwyst owed the prince from his debtor, **John de Coton**, 11 May 1354 (ibid., 161). He was fined £40, and bound over on pain of another £40 to keep the peace (pledges Hugh de Foxwist and Robt de Worth); his pledges, suspecting that he was planning to flee the country, sued to have his lands, but the escheator refused because of the seizure complained of on 18 Feb.; consequently, they sued for Robt to be arrested, but when Wm Asthull was coming to take him into custody, Foxwyst killed him and fled; his property was, therefore, forfeit to the B.P. Order to levy the debts due to Robt, viz. £40, 40 marks, £10 and 40 marks (owed by Wm de Mottelowe and John de Craumache, Thos Fitoun, John de Cotton, and Adam Nikke's son), as the pledges had been promised half of these debts; if Robt should surrender to the peace, the pledges were to have all this property, 7 July 1354 (ibid., 172–73). Foxwyst's forfeited lands leased to Roger Wodecock, for 12 years from 1354–55 (SC6 802/11, m.1). Foxwyst's lands and bailiwick were granted to John de Cresswell for life, except for the buildings, which had been disposed of elsewhere, 14 Sept. 1358 (*B.P.R.*, iii. 316–17). The burgesses of Macclesfield complained that they had been indicted for using wood growing on a place which was their common land, by the false suggestion of Robt de Foxwyst and others, 18 April 1359 (ibid., 336–37).

Frenshegh, Hugh

'Hugh Frenshie', together with Wm son of John de Hide and John son of Wm de Hide, was indicted of the death of **Geoff. de Honford**, whereupon **Sir John de Hyde** agreed a fine of 200 marks for their pardon, 24 Nov. 1360 (*B.P.R.*, iii. 398–99; *ChRR*, p. 258).

Frodesham, Robert son of Richard de (bastard) oc. 1362

With Wm Praers, **Ric. Doun of Utkinton, Wm le Wasteneys**, and Nic. de Manlegh, 'Robt son of Ric. de F.' made a recog. for £61 6s. 8d. to B.P., 15 Nov. 1347 (*ChRR*, p. 191). Leased 57-odd acres of the demesnes of Frodsham, at 1s. 3d. an acre, with his brother, **William**, 1349–50 (SC6 801/14, m.1). Served on jury to inquire into encroachments on Frodsham haven made by the abbot of Chester, the prior of Birkenhead, and the lords of Wallasey, 27 Jan. 1351 (*B.P.R.*, iii. 7). 'Robt son of Ric. de F.' made a recog. for £4 13s. 0d. to B.P., 4 July 1351, (*ChRR*, p. 191). He held villein-land in Frodsham, with Hen. Stile and John Pykemere, which was *in decasu* by 1351–52 (SC6 801/14, m.1). With **Henry Torfot**, 'Robt son of Ric. de F.' leased part of the manor of Frodsham, on a seven-year lease, from 1352, at £55 a year (SC6 784/2, m.11; *ChRR*, p. 192). In Jan. 1353, the two lessees, with Wm son of Ric. de Frodesham, Thos son of John [. . . . .]de Litleheth, made a recog. to B.P. for £385, for the seven-year lease (*ChRR*, p. 191). He leased, by himself, the herbage of two acres in Frodsham manor, 1353–54 (SC6 784/4, m.2). Wm son of John de Bunbury (servant of David de Bostok) was indicted in the county court of 7 June 1362 (CHES 29/67, m.115d) for killing 'Robt de Frodesham' in self-defence on 29 April 1362. On his death his lands escheated to the earl of Chester on account of his bastardy (SC6 786/1, m.10). They yielded £5 19s. 6½d., including the properties of Robt Netherton, Maud Spark and Wm Netherton which he held in pledge, 1362–63 (SC6 786/1, m.10). In the account for 1364–65 it was reported that he held Mulnefeld in Frodsham manor, freely, for an annual rent of 20s. 0d. (SC6 786/5, m.3). His lands were sold for £20 to John de Frodsham in 1365–66, by command of B.P.'s council (SC6 786/6, m.2d).

Frodesham, William son of Richard de

'Wm son of Ric. de F.' leased, with others, the mills of Frodsham, Dec. 1346 to Michaelmas 1347 (SC6 801/13, m.1). 'Wm son of Ric. de F.' was brother of **Robt de Frodesham**, with whom he leased part of the demesne land of Frodsham manor, 1349–50 (SC6 801/14, m.1). Acted as one of the guarantors of the seven-year lease of Frodsham manor to Robt de Frodesham and **Hen. de Torfot**, 11 Jan. 1353 (*ChRR*, p. 191). Reference 18 June 1353 to a gift by him to Hugh de Dutton, and Joan, his wife, of lands in Weston by Runcorn, Bartington and Little Leigh, (*B.P.R.*, iii. 109). With Nich. de Manley and David de Prestlond made a recog. for 51s. 8d. to Thos. and Simon de Bradgate, 15 Oct. 1354 (*ChRR*, p. 192). Acted as bedell of Eddisbury hundred, with David Prestlond (1354–55), alone (1355–56), (SC6 784/5, m.4; 784/7, m.3). Sir Hugh de Dutton, **Ric. de Whitelegh**, and Thos Tochet made a recog. for £36 13s. 4d. to B.P., being the fine for alienation of the manor of Ness by Hugh de Dutton to Wm de Frodsham, 20 Jan. 1368 (*ChRR*, p. 160).

Fyton, Thomas (of Gawsworth) died *c*. 1397

Ordered, as one of the foresters of Macclesfield, to observe a detailed forest ordinance, 24 March 1351 (*B.P.R.*, iii. 14). **Adam de Mottram** complained that 'Thos son of Thos F. of G.' was demanding land from him on the basis of a seisin made outside court; order to maintain Adam in the ancient custom, 11 May 1354 (ibid., 160). He owed a debt to **Robt de Foxwist**, fugitive, which was to be paid to Robt's mainpernors, 7 July 1354 (ibid., 172–73). Order to postpone the proceedings in Macclesfield halmote by *novel disseisin*, arraigned by 'Thos son of Thos F. de G.' against **Adam de Mottron** and John, his son, over lands in Sutton, as B.P. had been informed that the assize tends to his manifest disherison, 20 March 1355 (ibid., 198–99). Order not to take an inquisition in the lawsuit over land between him and Adam de Mottram, 13 July 1357 (ibid., 259). A further order to the same effect, B.P. having heard that **Sir John Chaundos**, or his deputy (as steward of Macclesfield) had detained Adam de Mottram in that plea; the plea might turn to B.P.'s disherison, 16 Dec. 1357 (ibid., 289). He was a member of the panel chosen to try the case between Wm Soty and the tenants of Bollington; Wm Dounes, Soty's steward, and Adam de Mottrum interrupted the trial, as the composition of the jury was not to their liking, 24 May 1359 (ibid., 338). With John Pygot, acted as attorney to deliver the offices of steward and bailiff of Macclesfield hundred, forester, and keeper of Macclesfield park, to the earl of Stafford, 9 Aug. 1386 (*ChRR*, p. 442). Appointed one of the justices of the three hundreds after the eyre of Macclesfield, 12 Aug. 1386; 14 Aug. 1387; 31 Aug. 1389; 18 Aug. 1390; 13 Sept. 1391 (ibid., pp. 310, 311, 181). Appointed one of the justices of labourers for Macclesfield hundred, 15 Dec. 1390 (ibid., 181). One of the commissioners appointed to levy the subsidy of 3,000 marks granted to the King by the community of the county of Chester in return for a confirmation of their charters; the commissioners were also appointed to arrest those who had hindered the collection of the subsidy, 8 Dec. 1391 (*ChRR*, p. 96). Died not long before 2 April 1397 (ibid., p. 180).

Gerard, William son of William

He succeeded his father, at the age of 30 or above, not long before 21 March 1352; this is the date of the inquisition post mortem, which shows that his father held half the manor of Kingsley, the manor of Bradley (as of the manor of Frodsham), and the manor of Cattenhall of the abbot of Chester (CHES 3/26 Ed. III/5). He paid 13s. 4d. for having the sheriff's aid, 1351–52 (SC6 783/17, m.3). In the same year he paid £2 10s. 0d. as relief for (half) the manor of Kingsley, rated at half a knight's fee (SC6 783/17, m.5); the same year he also paid a relief for land in Nether Bradley, (SC6 783/17, m.8). A postponement of the distress for 8 marks which was being levied from him was ordered, which fine had been imposed because his father, Wm Gerard, had acquired lands held in chief of the earl of Chester, without licence, 27 April 1353 (*B.P.R.*, iii. 102). (In 1349–50, and 1350–51, a piece of land and waste in Kingsley was in B.P.'s hand because Wm the father of Wm Gerard had acquired it from Wm Lancelin, who had held it in chief, *ChAcc*, pp. 151, 205). On 4 Aug. 1353, after having complained that the 8-mark fine had been imposed wrongfully, because Earl Ranulf of Chester's charter had granted his ancestors and their heirs permission to acquire lands throughout the whole of his lordship without licence, it was ordered that the fine should be discharged as the charter had been inspected by B.P. and his council, 4 Aug. 1353 (*B.P.R.*, iii. 112). With Peter, his son, and **Ranulf le Roter**, he made a recog. for £10 to B.P., 22 Aug. 1358 (*ChRR*, p. 195).

Hallum, William de

The duke of Lancaster's receiver of the honour of Halton, he was living as a corrodian in Norton Priory by early 1360.

With Adam de Hallum, and 15 others made recog. to earl of Chester for 40 marks, 1 Aug. 1325 (*ChRR*, p. 214). Reference to 'Goditha, daughter of Wm de Hallum' in 23 Edward III (*D.K.R. 28*, p. 51). He was a member of the panel from which a jury was to be selected to inquire into alleged waste in Howel ap Oweyn Voil's lands, 10 June 1353 (*B.P.R.*, iii. 106–7). He was acting as receiver of the Cheshire lands of **Hen.** de Grosmont, late **duke of Lancaster**, 1360–61 (SC6 772/1, m.2d). On 7 Jan. 1360, he sued the prior of Norton in the county court, by *novel disseisin*, for a corrody which he claimed to have bought (CHES 29/67, m.36). B.P. pardoned him a fine of 20 marks imposed for acquiring a life-annuity from Henry, earl of Lancaster, payable out of the manor of Halton, 10 April 1361 (*ChRR*, p. 214). Safeconduct granted to 'Wm de Hallum of Weryngton' and 6 others, to enable them to come to Cheshire on business, 11 May 1365 (*B.P.R.*, iii. 478).

Hayward, Robert le

Farmer of the passage of Lawton, alone, 1349–56 (SC6 783/17, m.3; 784/2, m.3; 784/3, m.3; 784/5, m.4; 784/7, m.3); with Wm Strider, first half of 1356–57 (SC6 784/10, m.2). The bailiwick of the passage of Lawton and Nantwich leased to 'Robt le Hayward of Lawton' for 3 years at 25s. 0d. a year, 25 March 1350 (*ChRR*, p. 227). With Ad. de Morton, made a recog. to B.P. for 50s. 0d., 29 March 1350 (ibid.) The passage of Lawton and Nantwich, from 'Arthull to Huggebrugge' leased to him and Wm de Lawton 'Mareschall', for 4 years, at 36s. 8d. a year, 10 March 1357 (ibid., 282).

Hikoc, John

Roger Careswell was indicted for J.H.'s death, 26 June 1361 (*ChRR*, p. 168).

Hoghton, Robert de

A general lay official of the earldom, he served, *inter alia*, as receiver of the St Pierre lands, and as acting constable of both Beeston and Chester castles. In the early 1360s he was seconded to the office of escheator of the lordship of Denbigh.

Paid 20s. 0d. out of the revenue of the 1353 trailbaston sessions for his work in Cheshire, 10 Sept. 1353 (*B.P.R.*, iii. 116). With **Simon Assewell** accounted as receiver of the lands which used to belong to Sir John de St Pierre, 1353–54 (SC6 783/1). Granted 12 acres of land in Prestatyn (Flints.), escheated for failure of Wm Adynet's issue, for as much as others would give (by petition endorsed), 15 Nov. 1354 (*B.P.R.*, iii. 182). Bedell of Broxton hundred, with Ken del Lee, 1356–57 (SC6 784/10, m.2d). Allowed to pay the £7 17s. 0d. in which he was bound to B.P. by two instalments, 14 Sept. 1358 (*B.P.R.*, iii. 317). Appointed resident constable of Beeston castle, receiver of the St Pierre lands, and keeper of Peckforton park, 23 Nov. 1358. If the present keeper of the park, Roger de Bosedon, should agree to reside, then Hoghton would be paid only £4 a year – otherwise £5 (*B.P.R.*, iii. 325; *ChRR*, p. 252). Accounted as receiver of the St Pierre lands 1358–59; 1359–60; 1360–61 (SC6 783/7; 783/8; 772/1, m.5). Appointed escheator of the lordship of Denbigh by B.P. at the customary fee, 13 July 1360 (*B.P.R.*, iii. 387). He had been indicted and outlawed for making off with the muniments of the lordship of Denbigh when the earl of March was lord; B.P. pardoned him, the lordship now being in his hands because of the minority of Edmund, the earl's son, 13 July 1360 (loc. cit.). Order by B.P. to pay his expenses on going with **John de Delves** on business to Montgomery, Ceri and Cydewain, 13 July 1360 (ibid., 388). Acted as escheator of Denbigh 12 Nov. 1360; 3 July 1361; 1 Sept. 1361; 4 Dec. 1361; 4 Feb. 1364 (ibid., 395–96, 420, 422–23, 429, 463). Ordered, with 12 others, to put Wm de Walsingham in possession of Bunbury church, and give him the £60 for repairs to the chancel and rectory buildings, which he and the others had been withholding from him, 16 Feb. 1361 (ibid., 406). With Philip de Raby and three others made a recog. to B.P. for 50 marks, 5 March 1361 (*ChRR*, p. 252). With his wife, Joan, he petitioned B.P., complaining that land of theirs in Denbigh lordship had been seized by the **earl of Salisbury**, while he was lord, and granted to Rhys ap Roppert; order to inquire, 10 Jan. 1362 (*B.P.R.*, iii. 439). Reginald de Swynemore complained that Robt. the 'late escheator of Denbigh', had seized property of his on the grounds that John de Swynemore had conveyed it to him collusively, 18 April 1364 (ibid., 468). B.P. ordered that he be allowed to pay his arrears as escheator of Denbigh (£13 19s. 0d.) by instalments within four years, 1 Aug. 1364 (ibid., 471). Ordered to deliver to Thos de Holond the muniments of the escheatry of Denbigh, 27 Oct. 1364 (ibid., 472). Acting and accounting as deputy constable of Chester castle, (under Thos Chaundeller), 1365–66 (SC6 786/6, m.3). Made a recog. for 40s. 0d. to John de Brundelegh of Wistaston, 11 Oct. 1385 (*ChRR*, p. 252). Made a recog. for £4 6s. 5d. to King, in exoneration of Thos de Moston, late approver of the Dee mills, 26 March 1390 (ibid., p. 252).

Honford, Geoffrey son of John de

Sir John de Hyde and others accused of maliciously indicting him and his brothers Ric. and John, who had served on an indictment jury of the 1353 trailbaston sessions, so that they had been bound over in 200 marks; order to respite the proceedings against them, 1 Sept. 1354 (*B.P.R.*, iii. 176). In the year 1359–60 it was stated that John de Hyde, lord of a moiety of Matley, had killed 'Geoff. de Honford', who had left three coheiresses in wardship (SC6 802/17, m.5). Wm son of John de Hide, John son of Wm de Hide and Hugh Frenshie (see **Hugh Frenshegh**) were indicted for his death, whereupon Sir John de Hide agreed a fine of 200 marks for their pardon, 24 Nov. 1360 (*B.P.R.*, iii. 398–99; *ChRR*, p. 258). On 13 Jan. 1361 the keeping of his Cheshire lands, together with the wardship and marriage of his daughter and heiress, Katherine, were granted to **Robt de Legh**, junior (*ChRR*, p. 288).

Hulpeston, William de (Helpeston)

Master-mason of Cheshire, North Wales and Flintshire, 1361/*c.* 1374

Mason in charge of building the 12 chapels of Vale Royal abbey, he was to be paid 200 marks a year until £860 had been received (less the 500 marks granted for the works when B.P. was in Chester), 5 June 1359 (*B.P.R.*, iii. 344–45). On 24 Aug. 1359 it was ordered that the above money was to be paid to the abbot, as Wm could not find security to perform the agreement for the work specified (ibid., 361–63). Appointed surveyor of the murage of the city of Chester, receiving 4d a day from the keepers of the murage, 11 Nov. 1361 (ibid., 425–26). Order to admit him to the office of master-mason and surveyor of Cheshire, Flintshire and North Wales, at the customary wages and fee, 4 Dec. 1361 (ibid., 428; *ChRR*, p. 230). Paid wages of 6d a day in 1361–62, increased to 8d a day by 1369–70 (SC6 772/3, m.1d; 772/5, m.1d). Vale Royal abbey ordered to carry out their agreement with him over the new work of the chapels, 19 May 1362 (*B.P.R.*, iii. 445). Held 13 acres of land in Handbridge, formerly held by **Sir John de Delves**, from 1362 to at least 1374 (SC6 786/1, m.1; 787/7, m.1). Gift of 40s. 0d. granted him by B.P. on the advice of Sir John de Delves, for his trouble and expense in B.P.'s service, 12 Oct. 1365 (*B.P.R.*, iii. 483). With four other men, he was ordered to conscript masons and workmen in Cheshire and Flintshire for the works at Vale Royal, 3 March 1368 (*ChRR*, p. 230). Still acting as master-mason and surveyor, 1373–74 (SC6 772/9, m.3). It appears that John Harvey is mistaken in thinking that he died in 1375 (see p. 77, n.3), since Hulpeston was granted a royal pardon on 20 Sept. 1377 (*ChRR*, p. 230).

Hyde, John de (knight)

A middle-rank landowner in east Cheshire and retainer of the prince. He served at Crécy and Poitiers. The prince's necessary tolerance of his appallingly oppressive behaviour illustrates the irresolvable dilemma which the government faced in attempting to wage a major foreign war in the generation following the Black Death. He was married twice, first to Margaret Davenport, and secondly to a lady called Alice.

He was found guilty in the 1353 trailbaston sessions of mutilating his servant, John Scott, with **Adam de Mottram's** connivance, in 1350, and of having taken bribes from men not to be recruited as archers in B.P.'s forces (CHES 29/65, m.3d). B.P. ordered that he be pardoned the £90 fine imposed for the above offences, 10 Sept. 1353 (*B.P.R.*, iii. 116). With others he was accused of having maliciously indicted Ric. de Hondeford, and John and **Geoffrey** his brothers, who had served on the indictment jury at the trailbaston sessions, with the result that they had been bound over in 200 marks; order to respite all proceedings against them, 1 Sept. 1354 (ibid., 176). Granted 4 oaks for timber in Lyme wood, Macclesfield forest, 2 March 1355 (ibid., 195). With **Robt son of Robt de Legh** appointed leader of the archers of Macclesfield hundred, to be at Plymouth by three weeks from Midsummer for the Poitiers expedition, 26 June 1355 (ibid., 204). On 30 June 1355, he was given sole charge of those archers (ibid., 205). Granted general pardon for offences committed before 8 May 1357, in return for good service at Poitiers, 19 July 1357 (ibid., 267). Order not to amerce him for non-appearance before the forest-eyre justices, as he was in London on B.P.'s business; his lands were to be seized, if they had been perambulated, and kept until B.P. and council should give orders about them, 4 Oct. 1357 (ibid., 280). For his fine of £66 13s. 4d. imposed on him in the 1357 forest eyre, in respect of land in Norbury, (pledges, John Fitton, Hamo de Mascy, Wm de Dounes, Ad. de Mottrum, John son of Hen. de Honford, and John de Clyf) see CHES 33/6, m.41d. 'John de Hide' was one of the panel for the jury to inquire between Wm Dounes and Adam de Mottram, on behalf of Wm Soty and the tenants of Bollington, 24 May 1359 (ibid., 338). On 11 July 1359 he went to see B.P. at Princes Risborough, to ask for pardon of part of his fine (?forest eyre), and to be excused the first payment, otherwise he would not be able to go overseas with the prince (ibid., 352–53). As 'prince's bachelor' retained for war from the previous feast of St Peter's Chains for 6 months, with 2 esquires, for £6 13s. 4d. for the half year, 16 Aug. 1359 (ibid., 356). In 1359–60 it was stated that 'John de Hyde', lord of a moiety of Matley, had killed Geoff. de Honford (SC6 802/17, m.5). He was pardoned £40 of his fine imposed in the forest eyre, and it was ordered that the remainder be superseded, 30 Sept. 1359 (*B.P.R.*, iii. 368–69). John de Drokenfeld and John de Holyngworth to go overseas with B.P. in the company of him and Sir John Danyel (see **John Danyers**), 8 Oct. 1359 (ibid., 370). Wm son of John de Hide, John son of Wm de Hide and **Hugh Frenshie** were indicted for 'Geoff. son of John de Honford's' death, whereupon 'Sir John de Hide' agreed a fine of 200 marks for their pardon, 24 Nov. 1360; execution of the fine, even if overdue, was only to be made at B.P.'s order; letters of pardon issued 12 Dec. 1360; charter of pardon 6 Oct. 1361 (ibid., 398–99; *ChRR*, p. 258). Granted 12 oaks for timber from Lyme wood, Macclesfield forest, as gift from B.P., 24 Nov. 1360 (*B.P.R.*, iii. 399). Pardoned all his felonies and trespasses in Cheshire, including forest offences, 24 Nov. 1360; pardon issued under the Chester exchequer seal, 12 Dec. 1360 (ibid., 399; *ChRR*, p. 258). Thos de Crue claimed that he and his brother had served with him at Crécy, 23 March

1361 (*B.P.R.*, iii. 413). Order to discharge his recog. for 200 marks, as he had given B.P. satisfaction, 26 July 1362 (ibid., 450). With Ric. son of Ric. de Mascy of Sale, John de Hyde and Alice (his wife) agreed a fine for half the manor of Godley, one-sixth of the manor of Newton, one-quarter of the manor of Matley, land in Stockport, Mottram in Longdendale and Baguley, 38 Edward III (*D.K.R. 28*, p. 63).

Iorwerth, Dafydd ab

'D. ap I. ap Dafydd' petitioned that the sheriff of Flint had seized his goods for the arrears of his account as bailiff of Coleshill cymyd, to the impoverishment of his family, 18 Nov. 1352 (*B.P.R.*, iii. 82–83). 'D. ap I. ap Phil', chosen as archer, had gone away after receiving his cloth and wages; order to arrest him and others (named), 5 Sept. 1355 (ibid., 215).

John's son, William (fisherman)

Caught a sturgeon in the River Dee at Puddington in June 1362, and claimed the customary reward for a royal fish (*B.P.R.*, iv. 47; **9.7; 31.4, 5**).

Jonet, William

Bailiff and approver of the manor of Shotwick, 1350–51 (*ChAcc*, p. 160). Accounted as reeve of the manor of Shotwick, 1351–52 to 1371–72 (SC6 783/17, m.7; 784/2, m.11d; 784/4, m.3; 784/5, m.16; 784/7, m.10; 784/10, m.8d; 785/1, m.11; 785/3, m.4; 785/5, m.9; 785/8, m.6; 785/9, m.3; 786/1, m.11; 786/3, m.12; 786/5, m.7d; 786/6, m.7d; 786/7, m.9d; 786/8, m.11; 786/10, m.3; 787/2, m.3; 787/4, m.2d) [the account for 1369–70 is missing]. 'Wm Jonet de Salghton' (?Saughall) was imprisoned in Chester castle during 1355–56 (SC6 784/7, m.2). Paid 6s. 8d. for catching and selling the fish from 'Tolls' fishery in Shotwick manor, 1360–61 (SC6 785/8, m.6). With 12 others, took Shotwick manor on a 6-year lease, 1363–69 (SC6 786/3, m.12). Fined for fraud as reeve of Shotwick, 1363–64 (ibid.). After the end of the 6-year lease of the whole manor, he and his associates leased the cockshots in Shotwick park, 1370–71 (SC6 787/2, m.3). In 1370–71 he was fined £1 for concealing various items in his account (SC6 787/2, m.3). His reeve's account for 1371–72 was terminated on 24 June 1372, and Richard Champeney replaced him (SC6 787/4, m.2d). Two 'animals' and one mare belonging to him were taken as waif in Frodsham manor, 1371–72 (SC6 787/4, m.3).

Kelshale, Stephen de (citizen of Chester)

Acted, with Wm Huxley, as sheriff of the city of Chester, 1351–52 (SC6 783/17, m.1). Appointed with the chamberlain and Alan de Whetelee to audit the accounts of Roger Skiret, the groom of Adam Lorymer of Buckingham, of the sums with which he had traded on Adam's behalf, 30 April 1353 (*B.P.R.*, iii. 103). Reference to the import of wine in a ship belonging to Stephen de

Kelshale, citizen of Chester, 1353–54 (*ChAcc*, p. 207). He purchased half a sack of the Frodsham demesne wool, 1358–59 (SC6 785/4, m.8). With Thos de Hokenhull, Ad. de Moldeworth, Ric. de Prestlond, Thos son of Ad. de Kelshale, and Wm Teverton, he made a recog. for £40 to B.P., 10 Aug. 1357 (*ChRR*, p. 267). Reference to 'John, late cook to Stephen de K.', 15 Aug. 1357 (*B.P.R.*, iii. 274).

Kenworthay, Richard de

Acted as reeve of Macclesfield borough, 1361/62, (SC6 803/5, m.2d; SC6 803/7, m.2d). Listed as holding one piece and 10 perches of land in Sutton, next to Macclesfield mill, 'de novo', 1383/84 (SC11 898, m.2).

Kyngeslegh, Adam de (clerk)

A general clerk-administrator in the earldom's government, he used the escheatorship (which he held at various times between 1361 and 1397) to develop secular interests. He married, had children, and became wealthy enough for his heirs to be accepted as gentry (See Bennett, *Community, Class*, p. 149; J.L.C. Bruell, 'An Edition of the Cartulary of John of Macclesfield', London M.A. thesis (1969), items 314, 315, 118 et al.). Receiver of the lordship of Denbigh, 1365/1370. Sheriff of Flint and *rhaglaw* of Englefield in 1383.

B.P. made him a gift of two oaks for timber from Lyme wood, 13 September 1358 (*B.P.R.*, iii. 315). With **Henry Torfot**, **Peter de Northlegh**, and John de Kyngeslegh (his brother) leased the agistment and pannage of Delamere forest, 1359–65 (six-year lease) and 1365–72 (seven-year lease), (SC6 785/3, m.1; 785/5, m.2d; 785/8, m.3; 785/9, m.1d; 786/1, m.4; 786/3, m.4d; 786/5, m.2d; 786/6, m.3; 786/7, m.3; 786/8, m.3; 786/10, m.2d; 787/2, m.2; 787/4, m.2). Appointed escheator of Cheshire, and steward of the courts of the demesne manors and towns of the earldom there (except for Chester and Macclesfield), at a fee of £10 a year, 4 December 1361; acting continuously until 23 April 1365; reappointed 3 March 1383; again, 26 July 1386; again, 10 Aug. 1391; again 9 Feb. 1392; his appointment as escheator was cancelled 22 March 1392; re-appointed again on 30 Nov. 1395, and again on 6 Dec. 1397 (*B.P.R.*, iii. 428; *ChRR*, pp. 272–73; 318; SC6 785/9, m.7; 786/1, m.5; 786/3, m.6; 786/5, m.4). Commissioned with **John de Delves** (lieutenant) and **Richard de Whitelegh** (county sheriff) to take St Werburgh's Abbey, Chester, into B.P.'s custody, 16 March 1362 (*B.P.R.*, iii. 440). Paid money on behalf of the chamberlain to the parker of Macclesfield, 1362–63 (SC6 803/7, m.5). He was sold three pieces of land in le Mulnefeld, near Macclesfield, which had escheated to B.P. on the death of Roger de Bosdon, bastard, 11 March 1363 (*ChRR*, p. 272). Ordered by B.P. to collect revenue from the receiver of Denbigh, the chamberlain of North Wales, and the receiver of Dolforwyn and Montgomery, and bring it to London, if the receiver of Denbigh is unable to do so, 1 Oct. 1363 (*B.P.R.*, iii. 462). Repaid the £6 12s. 8d. which he spent on handing over some people who had been indicted in Staffs., 17 April 1364 (ibid., 467). Acted as justice of labourers in Macclesfield hundred, with **Robt de Legh** and **John Davenport**, *c*. 1364/65 (ibid., 486). Sold the multure of Whaley mill, Whitsun to Michaelmas 1364, when the mill could not be leased because it was undergoing major repairs (SC6 803/9, m.1). With others, leased Whaley mill, 1364–65 (SC6 803/10, m.1). With the lieutenant (John de Delves) and chamberlain, he was responsible for letting the tenements in Kingsmarsh to the term-tenants, thus producing the rental used in the account for 1364–65 (SC6 786/5, m.2). Appointed receiver of the lordship of Denbigh, 31 May 1365; still acting in 1370–71 (*B.P.R.*, iii. 480; SC6 772/7, m.5). Petitioned B.P.'s council for repayment of money he spent on arraying the men-at-arms and archers, whose array was subsequently countermanded, 8 July 1365 (*B.P.R.*, iii. 482). Appointed bailiff-manager of the lordship of Longdendale, 25 March 1366, and accounted for one year (SC6 803/12; 803/13). Bought a colt for £5 from the stock of Macclesfield manor, 1366–67 (SC6 803/13, m.5). With others, leased the mills of Macclesfield, ten-year term, 1366–76 [lease granted by B.P. for the two water-mills and the windmill, 8 Sept. 1363 – account for final year missing] (*ChRR*, p. 272; SC6 803/13, m.1; 803/15, m.1; 804/1, m.1; 804/2, m.4; 804/4, m.2; 804/5, m.2; 804/6, m.2; 804/7, m.1). Paid 6s. 8d. to pasture cows in Midgley, next to the river Dane, 1367–68 (SC6 803/15, m.3). Paid 16s. 8d. to pasture 500 of his ewes in the same place, 1368–69 (SC6 804/1, m.2d). Accounted as parker of Macclesfield, 1369–70, and with Reginald de Dounes, 1370–71 (SC6 804/2, m.2; 804/3, m.2). With John Davenport leased the herbage and focage of Macclesfield park, for four years at £10 a year, 1369–73 (SC6 804/2, m.2; 804/4, m.4A; 804/5, m.4). Pastured 700 ewes at B.P.'s pasture at Midgley, for £1 3s. 4d., 1369–70 (SC6 804/2, m.3). Continued to pasture ewes there 1371–76 (SC6 804/4, m.3; 804/5, m.3; 804/6, m.3; 804/7, m.4; 804/8, m.5). Held one messuage near Macclesfield mill, and the lands late of Eleanor Oldhed, 1383/84 (SC11 898, m.1d, 3). Appointed sheriff of Flint and *rhaglaw* of Englefield, 30 Sept. 1383 (*ChRR*, p. 272). With Sir Thos de Arderne and others, appointed a joint-justice to hold the three Hundred courts after the eyre of Macclesfield, 24 Feb. 1386; like appointment, this time with **Sir Robt de Legh** and others, 23 Sept. 1396 (*ChRR*, pp, 6, 291). With Ranulf le Fleccher, gave sureties that Roger le Fleccher of Swettenham should not escape from Chester castle, 23 Feb. 1399 (ibid., p. 273). Acted as a feoffee for the enfeoffment and re-enfeoffment of the manor of Bosley to John de Macclesfield, 20 Aug. 1402 (ibid., pp. 312–13).

Lacy, Peter de (clerk)

Receiver-general of the Black Prince from 1346 to 1371, and also keeper of his great wardrobe from 1347 (Tout, v. 436, 438–39). He also served as keeper of the king's privy seal from 1367 to 1371, and was dismissed from that post (together with those in the prince's service) as a result of the demand by the 1371 parliament that clerical ministers be replaced by laymen (Booth, *Financial Administration*, pp. 66–67).

Lancaster, Henry, duke of d. 1361

For his career, see K. Fowler, *The King's Lieutenant: Henry of Grosmont, First Duke of Lancaster, 1310–1361* (1969). Fowler tells us that Lancaster was in France in the spring of 1353, but does not comment on Knighton's story that he came with the prince to Cheshire in the late summer/early autumn of that year.

Henry held substantial properties in Cheshire, including the baronies of Halton and Dunham, and it is in connection with this that he features in records relating to the county. **Roger Le Strange of Knockin** was one of the duke's feoffees for the lands in Cheshire he had acquired from Sir Hamo Mascy of Dunham in 1347 (Somerville, *Duchy of Lancaster*, i. 39). The Lestrange family had first acquired an interest in the Lancaster lands through Alice Lacy's marriage to Ebulo Lestrange in 1322, and Roger Lestrange had been compelled to give back in 1355, to the duke of Lancaster, the Cheshire property which his family had acquired as a result of the marriage (ibid., 34). A condition of the 1355 surrender was that Lestrange was to receive the property back after the duke's death, and he was in possession of it by Jan. 1362. Consequently, he is mentioned in connection with fines for it in the forests of Wirral and Delamere, presumably because the pardons granted the duke did not apply to him (**45.14**; *B.P.R.*, iii. 211–12, 221, 438–39).

Most of the other references in the Register refer to routine matters, such as the grant of protections when he was going abroad, in 1354, 1355 and 1356 (ibid., 181, 210–211, 225). His close connection with royal policy, and blood relationship to the royal family, explains the favourable treatment the prince gave him in respect of his Cheshire properties. He was permitted to be absent from the 1353 trailbaston sessions, and was pardoned £30 of his share of the resultant common fine (ibid., 172). His baronial serjeanties of the peace were restored to him, as were other franchises, although there seemed to be some doubt about his avowries of Halton (ibid., 210). After both he and the **earl of Arundel** had complained that they were being assessed unreasonably to the common fines of Wirral, Delamere and Macclesfield forests, following the 1357 forest eyres, both were pardoned their fines in 1360 (ibid., 364, 389).

Naturally, he used his influence in Cheshire for his tenants and associates. A pardon for John Baret of his indictment in the trailbaston sessions was granted 'out of respect for Henry, duke of Lancaster' on 10 September 1353. Baret was bedell of Eddisbury hundred in 1352, and was found guilty of converting property to his own use (ibid., 116, *Cheshire History*, 13 (1984), p. 27). The pardon was extended in 1354 to eight others, from Lancashire (*B.P.R.*, iii. 154). The duke induced the prince to accept a fine of £20 from Hugh de Burwes, who had left Chester without permission during the trailbaston sessions (ibid., 126). Exactions in the county court against John de Artonstall (parker of Ringway) and John de Oldefeld were cancelled at Lancaster's request in March 1354, as he claimed they were going overseas with him (ibid., 151).

The only sign of conflict between the prince's and duke's interests in Cheshire came as a result of the duke's extensive liberties, particularly in the barony of Halton. Originally, it had been planned to hold pleas of *quo warranto* during the 1353 general eyre, but when the eyre was abandoned, the investigations into liberties were postponed. They seem to have been resumed seriously in 1357, when Henry claimed to be lord of Halton, and 'constable and marshal of Chester' (CHES 34/1; Somerville, *Duchy of Lancaster*, i. 38–39). The sticking point was the duke's private avowries, but in the end an amicable settlement was arranged by agreement between the princely and ducal councils, whereby they were surrendered for the duke's life, in return for financial compensation (*B.P.R.*, iv. 281–82). An example of how the duke's authority might be abused by his officials occurred in 1354, when Laurence de Mobberley accused Henry's steward in Cheshire, Sir John de Legh, of influencing an assize of *novel disseisin* (*B.P.R.*, iii. 143).

Legh, Isabel de (widow of Sir John de Legh) d. 1369

Her husband was Sir John Legh of Booths, the elder brother of **Robert Legh of Adlington** (the elder) (*EC*, ii. 105). They held half the manor of Torkington, and Sir John Legh died in 1355. When Isabel died, in 1369, her I.P.M. said that this property was held of Sir Thos Arderne by knight service (CHES 3/29 Ed. III/1). **James de Legh** was their son, and inherited the Booths estates (Ormerod, i. 499).

Legh, James de d. 1370

The son and heir of Sir John and **Isabel de Legh**. Appointed one of the commissioners to arrest the boats which had been making an unlawful ferry at the broken Warrington bridge, 12 Oct. 1365 (*B.P.R.*, iii. 483). Bought 20 oxen from the stock-keeper of Macclesfield manor, 1366–67 (SC6 803/13, m.5).

Legh, Robert de (of Adlington, the elder) d. 1370

It is not always possible to distinguish the father (died 1370) and son (died 1382) of this name, successive lords of Adlington, particularly in the 1360s, when both were active in administration. A third 'Robert de Legh' was born in 1362. The offices used as the Legh power-base were those of steward (or deputy, in Chandos's time) of Macclesfield manor, riding forester, justice of labourers in Macclesfield hundred, and justice of the three Hundreds after the eyre.

On 27 Jan. 1346, Edward III granted Queen Isabella's petition that Legh, the principal keeper of her forest of Macclesfield, be excused from the earl of Lancaster's service, (*C.P.R., 1346–48*, p. 451). Bailiff of Macclesfield manor upon its transfer to B.P. from his grandmother, Michaelmas to 27 Dec. 1347 (SC6 1297/3, m.1). Deputy steward of Macclesfield manor, 1350, 1351, 20 March 1355, 1356/57, 1361/62, 1362/63, 1363/64 (SC2 252/2, m.3d; 252/3, m.3d; *B.P.R.*, iii. 198–99; SC2 252/8, m.4d; 252/13, m.4d; 252/14, m.3; 252/15, m.2). As deputy steward of Macclesfield, with Robt Newenham, took fines for offences against the labour legislation, 1350–51 (SC6 802/6). Riding forester of Macclesfield, 1350–51, 18 July 1352 (ibid. and *B.P.R.*, iii. 66). 'Robt son of Ellen de Leghe, riding forester', was to pay a fine of £20, a favourable rate because of his good service, for his mother's alienation of the manor of Adlington without licence 18 July 1352 (*B.P.R.*, iii. 66). Thos de Venables accused him of maintaining people, when he was 'bailiff of Macclesfield', who were debtors of the late Ellen Ardene (widow of Sir John Ardene – Robt's son married her daughter), thus preventing Thos, her executor, from paying part of John de Legh's fine for the death of Peter de Ardene; order to sue Robt for the money, 20 Nov. 1352. Thos petitioned again 14 Feb. 1353, complaining that Robt was preventing him from suing for the money in the eyre of the hundred (ibid., 53, 90; Ormerod, iii. 661). Robt and Sir John de Legh were ordered to protect **Robt de Foxwist**, 20 Apr. 1352 (*B.P.R.*, iii. 62). Acted as deputy bailiff and keeper of Macclesfield forest to Sir Thos de Ferrers, justiciar of Chester, 24 Aug. 1352 (ibid., 74). After he bought the wardship of Richard son of Robt de Eton from Sir Robt de Holland, the ward sued Sir Robt for waste; order to the sheriff to make up a panel to inquire into this allegation from the most substantial men of Macclesfield hundred who were not connected to either party or to Legh, 21 Apr. 1353 (ibid., 102). Acting as deputy to **Sir John de Chandos**, as keeper of Macclesfield forest, 10 Aug. 1353, 2 March 1355, 29 June 1360, 13 July 1360, 16 Feb. 1361 (ibid., 112, 194–95, 386, 391, 406). Ordered to arrest and imprison David de Olton, who had behaved threateningly towards Chester Abbey, 14 Feb. 1354; order repeated 6 July 1354 (ibid., 144, 170). Acted as justice to hold the three Hundred courts held after the Macclesfield eyre (either alone, or with others), 1355, 1356, 1358, 1359, 1360, 1361, 1362, 1363 (SC2 252/6, m.6; 252/7, m.7; 252/9, m.3; 252/10, m.7; 252/11, m.7d; 252/12, m.4d; 252/13, m.8; 252/14, m.7). As deputy keeper of Macclesfield forest, he gave the B.P. to understand that the Coombs of the forest could be enclosed cheaply; order to enclose them, 2 March 1355 (*B.P.R.*, iii. 194–95). Ordered, as deputy steward and forester of Macclesfield, to ensure that the forest was well kept, and to supervise the activities of the foresters, 2 July 1355 (ibid., 207). Reference to an affray in Macclesfield town between Robt de Legh the elder and **Adam de Mottram**, in which **Robt Legh** the younger, **John de Cotton**, Wm del Dounes, and John de Northleye were involved, 13 July 1357 (ibid., 258). On 7 February 1359, he received the fealty of the freeholders of Longdendale lordship to the B.P., in court there (SC6 802/15, m.1). On 30 Sept. 1359 he was pardoned the £20 fine imposed upon him in the Macclesfield forest eyre (*B.P.R.*, iii. 368). With **John Davenport** of 'Wheltrough' assigned justice of labourers for Macclesfield hundred, 1360/61 (SC2 252/12, m.8). With his men he assisted **Adam de Kyngeslegh** to hand over some people indicted in Staffs., 17 Apr. 1364 (*B.P.R.*, iii. 467). With John Davenport and Adam de Kyngeslegh acted as justice of labourers in Macclesfield hundred, before 21 Nov. 1365 (ibid., 486). After his death his widow, Maud (his second wife), claimed in 1371 her dower against the younger Robt of land in Northwich and Legh by Lymm (*D.K.R. 28*, p.67).

Legh, Robert de (of Adlington, the younger) died 9 Nov. 1382

After a military career as a retainer of the prince, during which he served at Poitiers, he took over his father's dominant position in Macclesfield hundred in the 1370s.

'Robt de Legh' made a recog. to B.P. that the 71 archers led by **Sir John Hyde**, presumably at the Crécy-Calais campaign, should not claim a reward granted by the prince, 25 Nov. 1350 (*ChRR*, p. 288). 'Robt son of Robt de Legh', also called 'Robt de Legh le filz', retained by B P. in war, to be paid 66s. 8d. as his half-year's fee, 21 May 1355 (*B.P.R.*, iii. 200). Appointed with Sir John de Hide to be joint leader of the archers of Macclesfield hundred, 26 June 1355; Hide was given the sole command four days later (ibid., 204, 205). However, Legh does appear to have taken a contingent of archers on the Poitiers campaign, since the B.P.'s controller in Gascony paid 'Robt de Legh', with 108 archers, wages on 30 June 1356 (Morgan, *War and Society*, p. 111). Pardoned for his involvement in the affray between his father and **Adam Mottram** in Macclesfield, 13 July 1357 (*B.P.R.*, iii. 258). On 19 Dec. 1358 he made a recog. indemnifying the chamberlain for money due to two archers who had served under him in Gascony (*ChRR*, p. 288). Appointed leader of the archers of Macclesfield hundred for the B.P.'s abortive Rheims expedition, 1 March 1359 (*B.P.R.*, iii. 331). Made a recog. for debt owed to Sir Thos de Arden, 14 April 1359 – his wife was Maud, daughter of Sir John de Ardene – (Ormerod, iii. 661; *ChRR*, p. 288). He and three others were pardoned their indictments for wounding Adam de Mottram in court before the steward of Macclesfield (presumably Legh's father who was acting as deputy steward round about those years), 10 June 1359 (*B.P.R.*, iii. 347). Order to pay him, as one of the B.P.'s 'esquires', his five marks war fee for six months, in connection with the Rheims expedition, 16 Aug. 1359 (ibid., 357). He stated that three archers in the group he was leading were too ill to travel abroad, and obtained their release, 19 Oct. 1359 (ibid., 373). A week later, he and Sir Ralph de Modberlegh obtained release for two more archers (ibid., 374). With two others made a recog. for debt to B.P. (*ChRR*, p. 288). With **Adam de Kyngeslegh**, he took for rent land in Rainow (part of Macclesfield manor) formerly belonging to Peter Arden, 1360/61 (SC2 155/87, m.1d). On 13 Jan. 1361, B.P. granted him the wardship and marriage of Katherine, daughter and heiress of **Geoffrey de Honford** – his mother was Sybil de Honford – (*ChRR*, p. 288; Ormerod, iii. 661). He was chosen to serve on the grand assize to try the writ of right between John de Leycestre and Hugh de Chaderton over the lands of Sir Ralph de Modburlegh, 21 Feb. 1361 (*B.P.R.*, iii. 408). Acted as riding forester of Macclesfield, following his father's death, 1371–76 (SC6 802/6; 804/4, m.2d; 804/5, m.2d; 804/6, m.2d; 804/7, m.1d; 804/8, m.1). Steward of Macclesfield manor, 1371–72 (SC6 804/5, m.2d). With Wm Dounes he leased the herbage of Lyme Handley, 1372–76 (SC6 804/5, m.2; 804/6, m.2; 804/7, m.1; 804/8, m.1). Princess Joan of Wales leased him and Wm del Dounes her part of Bollington, with the watermill, for 12 years at 8 marks a year (*ChRR*, p. 288). He was referred to as 'late bailiff' (that is, steward) of

Macclesfield on 20 Sept. 1382 (ibid.) He died 9 November 1382 (*EC*, ii. 250).

Lepers of St Giles, Hospital of (Boughton)

For the history of this hospital, see *V.C.H.*, iii. 178–79.

Granted 66s. 8d. from B.P. among his charitable donations from the revenue of the trailbaston sessions, 10 Sept. 1353 (*B.P.R.*, iii. 115). The hospital was to have its charters exemplified, quit of the fee of the seal, 4 Oct. 1353 (ibid., 125). Dispute with St Werburgh's Abbey over the hospital's claim that its chartered right to levy alms from victuals brought for sale in Chester applied to the abbey's tenants, 7 Oct. 1353; the abbey complained about this again 19 Feb. 1354 (ibid., 125–26, 146). Another dispute, this time between the hospital and Ric. son of John Braaz of Chester, over land in the city and in Claverton, 20 Feb. 1359 (ibid., 330).

Mareschall, Richard le (of Ince) (clerk)

He made a recog. for 70s. 0d. for having a lease of the lands which used to belong to **John de Elton** of Ince, 6 June 1358 (*ChRR*, p. 325).

Mascy, Richard de (of Tatton, knight) d. 1370.

Ormerod's pedigree of the Mascy family of Tatton does not really help to dispel the fear that the references given below refer to more than one person. Richard Mascy of Tatton, who married the heiress, Alice de Haydok, died in 1370. He was a Cheshire retainer of the prince, who served at Poitiers. Keeper of the avowries from 1357.

It may have been he who was unsuccessfully appealed of having raped Joan Ashley of Ashley, which is not far from Tatton, in May 1350 (CHES 29/65, m.2). He purchased the tithes of Tatton (Rostherne parish) from John de Cravene, rector, before 20 Oct. 1353 (*B.P.R.*, iii. 126–27). He was to be bound over to keep the peace at the suggestion of Wm de Walkden, 15 Dec. 1353 (ibid., 139). He offered to make a fine with B.P.'s council for unspecified misdeeds, 7 March 1354 (ibid., 151). On 25 June 1355 it was stated he is to be paid 5 marks for his war fee for 'this year', (ibid., 204). He served at Poitiers and, on 13 July 1357, was granted the keepership of the Cheshire avowries, during good behaviour, for his good service there (ibid., 258; *ChRR*, p. 328). He is recorded as keeper in 1360–61 and 1369–70 (SC6 772/1, m.2, 772/5, m.2) as well as the year of this account. With his brother, John de Mascy (parson of Sefton), and two others he made a recog. to B.P. for the £10 farm of the avowries on 10 Aug. 1357 (*ChRR*, p. 328). On 13 Feb. 1359 he was called 'leader of the archers of Nantwich hundred in the late war' (*B.P.R.*, iii. 328). He complained on 3 June 1359 that the wages of 12 of the archers who had been with him in Gascony were in arrears, (although it appears that there had only been eight of them); also, he protested that the lease of the avowries had been set at 20s. 0d. above the issues of the office (ibid., 343–44; Morgan, *War and Society*, p. 110). Order to pay him, as one of the B.P.'s esquires, his war fee of 5 marks, for six months, as part of the preparations for the Rheims expedition, 16 Aug. 1359 (*B.P.R.*, iii. 357). On 19 Oct. 1359, he reported that two of the archers in his band were too ill to travel abroad with the prince's army (ibid., 372). He was accused, with his brother John, of using armed force against **Sir Wm de Carynton**, in connection with a land dispute which Sir Wm had won against **Jordan de Bowedon**; order to arrest them and others 'of their covin', if the allegations could be substantiated, 21 Aug. 1361 (ibid., 455). On 15 Dec. 1361, Richard and his brother, with Wm de Maynwaring and John de Leycestre, made a recog. for £20 to B.P. (*ChRR*, p. 328). With his brother and ten others he made a recog. for £1,000 to B.P. and the constable of Chester castle, **Thos de Warrewyk**, that John de Leycester and four others should not escape from prison, [. . . . .] 1362 (ibid.); this was apparently superseded by another recog., for £1,066 13s. 4d., made on 13 January 1363 by Richard, his brother and twelve others, which recog. was presumably forfeited since on 25 April 1363 it was said to be payable at the rate of £100 a year, when a third recog. was withdrawn (*B.P.R.*, iii. 455). On 20 May 1362 he was called leader of the prince's archers on his last expedition into France (*ChRR*, p. 328). On 31 May 1363 the B.P. pardoned £5 of the fine he had made at Chester for the trespass committed by him and others, as a gift to compensate for the horse he had lost in B.P.'s service (*B.P.R.*, iii. 457). Retained by B.P. for life, with two esquires in war time and one in peace time, at a fee of 50 marks a year, 1 March 1365 (ibid., 477). With Edward de Mascy, made a recog. to the chamberlain for £20 which Richard had received from John Worth, being John's annuity, 26 July 1367 (*ChRR*, p. 329).

Mascy, Robert de (of Sale)

Chosen to be a member of the grand assize in the writ of right between John de Leycestre and Hugh de Chaderton, over the lands which used to belong to Sir Ralph de Modburlegh in Cheshire, 21 Feb. 1361 (*B.P.R.*, iii. 408). John de Huxlegh made a recog. to 'Robt son of Wm de Mascy of Sale' for 20 marks, 9 June 1362 (*ChRR*, p. 257). (This is either a mistake for 'Robt son of Richard', or this Robt is another man, the son of an otherwise unrecorded Wm Mascy of Sale, see Ormerod, i. 565).

Maurdyn, Alan de

Master plumber of the principality of Wales and the earldom of Chester from 1353.

Retained by B.P. as master-plumber in Cheshire and Flintshire, and North and South Wales, at 6d. a day plus robe (or 10s. 0d. a year); the chamberlains of Chester, North Wales and South Wales are to pay his wages when in their respective bailiwicks, 14 Sept. 1353 (*B.P.R.*, iii. 119, 489). He had been replaced by 1373–74 (SC6 772/9, m.3).

Merton (Marton), Stephen de d. 1361

He succeeded his father, also called Stephen, to the manors of Gayton, Lach (in Rudheath), and the island of Earl's Eye, during the time of the Black Death (CHES 3/23 Ed. III/8). His fine of £20 for offences in Wirral forest to be reduced to £10, 24 March 1351 (*B.P.R.*, iii. 12). Fined 40s. 0d. for forest offences, 18 July 1351 (ibid., 38). Order to cease demanding rent for his property in Rudheath, which he claimed as appurtenant to his manor of Lach in Rudheath, until the right to it should be decided, 30 Jan. 1353; a further order to stop demanding this rent followed 8 July 1356 (ibid., 86, 229).

Found guilty in the 1353 trailbaston sessions of misusing the liberty of waif and stray in his manor of Gayton to steal other men's animals (pledges for his fine: **Ranulf Roter** and Richard Scott) (CHES 29/65, m.3). After he complained that his manor of Lach (Dennis) had been seized by B.P.'s officials, order to stop; after a further complaint of his that the B.P. had two mills on his land, and was quarrying stone there without permission, order to inquire, 1 July 1355 (*B.P.R.*, iii. 208). Leased one acre of land from B.P. near the Dee mills (on the south side) for five years, [. .] Oct. 1355 (*ChRR*, p. 342). Sold a piece of land between the Dee and Chester quarry to John Spicer, where he was to build a hermitage, before 9 Sept. 1358 (ibid., p. 439). On 22 Jan. 1359 he made a recog. for £100 to **Wm son of John de Stanelegh** – Ellen de Stanelegh married Stephen's son, John – (ibid., p. 342). Acquired licence from B.P. to grant part of his estates to his son and daughter-in-law, and entailed the rest upon them, with remainder to his five daughters, 6 Aug. 1359 (ibid., p. 342; W. Fergusson Irvine, 'The Early Stanleys', *T.H.S.L.C.*, 105 (1953), pp. 45–68). Appointed member of the grand assize to try the writ of right between John de Leycestre and Hugh de Chaderton, concerning the lands which used to belong to Sir Ralph de Modburlegh, 21 Feb. 1361 (*B.P.R.*, iii. 408). He died not long before 29 Oct. 1361, leaving a twelve-year-old daughter, Joan, as his heiress (CHES 3/35 Ed. III/11). His widow, Margery, sued Ellen (widow of John de Merton, her son) for her dower in Gayton and Lach Malbank in Rudheath, 36 Edw. III (*D.K.R. 28*, p. 61, Ormerod, ii. 178).

Mottrum, Adam de

Hereditary gaoler and manorial rent-collector of Macclesfield, in his wife's right, from before 1347 until after 1374. An active 'entrepreneur' in seizing administrative opportunities, he led a group of archers to the battle of Poitiers. His career illustrates the possibilities open to a man from a relatively humble background, and also the dangers of the quest for social advancement, at a time when the government was pressing for both cash and military support, in a society that was becoming increasingly divided.

Earwaker knows little of the family of Mottram (of Mottram St Andrew), but suggests that Adam was a member of that family (*EC*, ii. 348). Gaoler of Macclesfield and collector of revenue within the forest, Sept.–Dec. 1347, in right of his wife, Ellen – daughter of 'John le Gaolar' (SC6 1297/3; SC6 802/13, m.1; Ormerod, iii. 693). Leased Shrigley mill (Macclesfield manor), 1347–49 (SC6 802/2, m.1; 802/4, m.1). Accused, in the 1353 trailbaston sessions, of conniving, in 1350, in **Sir John de Hyde's** abduction from Macclesfield gaol of his servant, John Scott, who was subsequently mutilated and sent to Adam's house to recover (CHES 29/65, m.3d). Leased the mills of Macclesfield, March–Mich. 1351, and 1352–59 (SC6 802/7, m.1; 802/9, m.1; 802/11, m.1; 802/15, m.4; CHES 2/36, m.2d). Parker of Macclesfield in 1351 (SC6 802/7, m.2). Continued to account as gaoler/collector, March 1351 to Mich. 1355; in the latter year, **John de Somerford** and his wife, Sigreda [called 'Tille', possibly mistakenly, in the Black Prince's Register] made good their claim to have the office in alternate years to Adam; Somerford's wife was Ellen de Mottrum's sister (*B.P.R.*, iii. 199. See below). On 21 Jan. 1352 he performed homage and swore fealty to the B.P. in London for the office which he was said to hold in grand serjeanty, in his wife's right (ibid., 54). Leased the common oven of Macclesfield borough for seven years, at 30s. 0d. a year; it was to be put in repair before he took it over, when he would keep it in repair, 4 Feb. 1352; the lease was issued under the Chester exchequer seal on 16 June 1352 [the calendar mistakenly calls this a lease of the profits of the *farm* – should be oven, i.e. *furni*] (ibid., 56; *ChRR*, p. 355). Sued in ejectment by **Robt de Foxwyst** for two carucates of land in Sutton (Macclesfield manor); Foxwyst appears to have lost the case, and thus had to solicit the B.P.'s support to overturn the verdict; Mottram then refused to let Foxwyst have the 100s. 0d. awarded to him for crops growing on the land, and was ordered to do so, 8 Feb. 1352 (*B.P.R.*, iii. 57). In the 1353 trailbaston sessions, which opened on 20 August, Adam was accused of a notable series of crimes of oppression and extortion, both as gaoler and rent-collector, plus housebreaking and abduction; the jury found him not guilty of most of the crimes, but convicted him of taking more money from prisoners in his custody than he should have done, and of converting a heriot colt of Macclesfield manor to his own use; he agreed a fine with the justices of £40 (*Cheshire History*, 13 (1984), pp. 27–28). On 18 Feb. 1354 he was accused of assaulting Richard Janny, deputy-forester to Robt Foxwyst in Macclesfield forest (*B.P.R.*, iii. 145). He complained that **Thos Fitoun** of Gawsworth was claiming land from him on the grounds of a transfer made outside the halmote of Macclesfield, whereas, in Adam's contention, it was 'ancient demesne of the forest' and so should be conveyed within the halmote, 11 May 1354; a further petition, from Adam and his son, John, is dated 20 March 1355, which resulted in an order to stay proceedings in the matter; an inquiry was finally ordered on 26 June 1355; the inquiry was cancelled 13 July 1357, just after a grant to Adam of a reward for good service in France (ibid., 160, 198–99, 204, 259). The B.P. granted him letters of protection until he should have paid the £40 fine owed from 1353, 11 May 1354 (ibid., 161). The

B.P.'s officials asked him for advice in inquiries being undertaken on two contentious matters: (1) the case of a bondman who became a burgess of Macclesfield; (2) concealment of an escheat, for lack of heirs, of the lands of John Mayowe's son, 13 May 1354 (ibid., 162–63). On 3 March 1355, he was arrested for the unacceptable level of arrears on his account for 1353–54, and imprisoned in Chester castle (SC6 802/9, m.1d). It was probably as a result of this that Adam's brother-in-law, John Somerford, petitioned the B.P. for a moiety of the office of gaoler and forest collector, 20 March 1355; Adam counter-petitioned a week later, claiming that the office was too poor to be divided (*B.P.R.*, iii. 199). John was successful, and until 1365 they shared the office – Adam held it in 1356–57 [by deputy, Robt del Clyff], 1358–59 [by two deputies, Nicholas de Neuton and Jordan de Davenport], 1360–61 [by deputy, Nicholas Neuton, who died before the audit], 1362–63 [by deputy, Thos del Wodehouses], 1364–65 [same deputy] (SC6 802/13, m.1; 802/15, m.4; 803/3, m.4; 803/7, m.1; 803/10, m.1). His release from prison in 1355 may have been expedited by the fact that he led a contingent of archers on the Poitiers campaign, which left for France in September 1355; on 30 June 1356, he was paid wages for the 127 archers serving under him (Morgan, *War and Society*, p. 111). His presence in France did not prevent him from strict treatment at the audit in the early summer of 1356 of his account for 1354–55; he left a remainder of just over £36, after which a note is written on the account to the effect that he had set out to Gascony from Cheshire before the audit, in obedience to the prince, who had granted him letters of protection for his goods; consequently, execution of the arrears was to be made from his lands; on 1 Oct 1356, John de Tidrington (vicar of Sandbach) was granted Adam's lands in le Shydeyord (Sutton, Macclesfield manor) by B.P. for three years, for the £10 due from Adam's account for 29 Edw. III (1354–55) (SC6 802/11, m.2d; SC6 784/5, m.1, m.2, m.6; *ChRR*, p. 470). On his return from France, he was granted a general pardon, for good service in Gascony, 9 July 1357 (*B.P.R.*, iii. 258; *ChRR*, p. 355). He acted as executor of Thos de Foxwyst, 1356/57, (SC2 252/8, m.3). Reference to an affray in Macclesfield town between Adam and **Robt de Legh, the elder**, deputy steward and forester of Macclesfield, in which Legh's son and others were involved, and for which they received pardons, 13 July 1357 (*B.P.R.*, iii. 258; *ChRR*, p. 355). Order to discharge him for a deodand charged upon his account, 16 July 1357 (*B.P.R.*, iii. 259). He claimed that when the B.P. had been in Macclesfield, presumably in 1353, his officers had taken from Adam 10 oxen (worth 10 marks), three cows (24s. 0d.), three bullocks (18s. 0d.), oats and vetch (100s. 0d.), 22 cartloads of hay (22s. 0d.), capons and hens (one mark), and he had had little allowance for them; order to inquire, 18 July 1357; order repeated, 10 July 1358 (ibid., 265, 305). He was allowed to pay the arrears of his account, plus the arrears of his £40 fine from 1353 (over and above the £10 10s. 7d. which the B.P. owed him for war wages in Gascony) by £4 instalments, starting at Easter 1358, 22 July 1357 (ibid., 269). On 5 May 1358, he was arrested again, this time for arrears on his account for 1356–57; he claimed that as the account covered the financial year he was serving in France, in the prince's company, his deputy, Robt Clyff should be held responsible for the arrears; furthermore, he said that Clyff had already been arrested on that account at Macclesfield, by writ of **Robt de Legh** (deputy steward), and it was agreed that Clyff be conveyed to Chester the following day to answer the charges (SC6 802/13, m.1d). On 14 Sept. 1358, he was acting as Wm Soty's attorney (*B.P.R.*, iii. 316). There was a complaint from the tenants of Bollington (Macclesfield manor) that Wm de Soty had leased his part of the township to Wm de Dounes and Adam. They had been encouraging Soty to sue the tenants in the county court, so that the one-third held by him might be converted from tenure in ancient demesne to tenure by knight service. The tenants requested that the suit be tried in the Macclesfield halmote, 18 April 1359. They further alleged, on 24 May 1359, that, following an order that the inquiry should, indeed, be held in the halmote, Adam and Dounes had broken up the proceedings, because they could not pack the jury. The tenants requested that the inquiry be allowed to continue. It was possibly in relation to this dispute that Adam was attacked and wounded in the halmote, in the presence of the steward (**Robt de Legh the elder**), by the steward's son (**Robt de Legh the younger**, together with Hamo Fitton, John de Northwell, and **John de Coton**, who were pardoned their indictments resulting from this on 10 June 1359 (ibid., 335, 337, 347). On 3 June 1359, Adam was permitted to pay £8 14s. 0d. of the £45 arrears on his 1356–57 account by instalments, which sum he claimed to have lost through Robt Clyff's fault (ibid., 342). On 6 Dec. 1364, he made a recog. to B.P. for £10, part of John de Seynesbury's £80 fine for the death of Robt de Cliderou (*ChRR*, p. 355). He was given licence by B.P., for a fine of 26s. 8d., to purchase John and Sigereda Somerford's moiety of the office of gaoler and rent-collector on 25 April 1366, which purchase was subsequently effected by final concord (*ChRR*, p. 355; SC6 786/6, m.5d). He was arrested a third time for arrears, on his account for 1366–67 (again, a deputy was running the bailiwick for him), probably in March 1368, when the audit of that year's accounts took place (SC6 803/13, m.1d; 786/7, m.1). He took a lease of the township and mills of Bollington, for ten years, at £5 6s. 8d. a year, from Michaelmas 1369; he still had the lease in 1374–75 (SC6 804/2, m.3; 804/7, m.1). In 50 Edw III, Cecily Leper – the widow of Jordan le Leper, and daughter and heiress of Thos son of Roger de Mottrum, coheiress to the manor of Mottram St Andrew, and Adam de Mottrum's cousin – quitclaimed to Adam all her right in any lands in Mottram; this quitclaim does not appear to have taken effect (*D.K.R. 28*, p. 70; Ormerod, iii. 693).

Mulyngton, Hugh de

Stewart-Brown suggested, in *ChAcc*, p. 206, that this man is the same as 'Hugh Page'. In fact, the version of the Divers Ministers' accounts in the Eaton Hall Charters 321 m.3 makes it clear that Hugh Page served as chamberlain of Middlewich that year, with

'Hugh de Myllyngton' as catchpoll. Furthermore, both men leased the town in 1367 (see below).

Catchpoll of Middlewich, 1352–54 (SC6 784/2, m.2; 784/3, m.2; *ChAcc*, p. 206). 'Hugh de Millington' embarked in Sept. 1355 in the retinue of Sir Ralph Mobberley as a mounted archer in the Poitiers campaign (Morgan, *War and Society*, p. 151). On 24 May 1357, B.P. assigned him a plot in Rudheath to take turves; he was to receive a suitable reward for serving as catchpoll of Middlewich, which office, he complained, he had been forced to occupy for six years without payment (*B.P.R.*, iii. 240). In fact, he did not account as catchpoll in 1354–55, and in the following three years, 1355–58, the town was leased and the names of the town officers are not recorded (SC6 784/5, m.2; 784/7, m.1d; 784/10, m.1d; 785/1, m.2). Chamberlain of Middlewich, 1361–62 (SC6 785/9, m.1d). With Thos Swettenham, Hugh Page, and 9 others, accounted as lessee of Middlewich town, on a three-year lease at £62 13s. 4d. a year, 1367–68; the recog. for the lease was made by Swettenham on 1 Oct. 1367, the lease granted 22 Oct. (SC6 786/8, m.1; (*ChRR*, p. 461).

Munshull, Richard de (the younger) died 13 Jan. 1364

One of the panel to inquire into waste in the lands of Howel ap Oweyn, 10 June 1353 (*B.P.R.*, iii. 106–7). Claimed that he was unable to pay his share of the common fine of Delamere without ruining his family; order to survey his lands, set aside sufficient for the Munshull family's sustenance, and settle the rest so the fine could be paid, 14 July 1360 (ibid., 389). The sheriff had already made extents of his two manors of Aston juxta Mondrum and Church Minshull at Nantwich on 2 June 1360 (CHES 3/34 Ed. III/3). Died on 13 Jan. 1364, and it was not until 16 April 1364 that the writ of *diem clausit extremum* issued (*B.P.R.*, iii. 467). The I.P.M., held on 8 July, found that he had held the manor of Aston juxta Mondrum in chief of B.P., and the manor of Church Minshull from John son of John Lovell; his heiress was Joan, daughter of his brother, Hen. de Munshull (ibid., 470).

Neuton, Nicholas de died c. 1361

Deputy of **Adam de Mottrum** as gaoler and forest collector, (with Jordan de Davenport) 1358–59, (alone) 1360–61 (SC6 802/15, m.4). At the audit of the latter account, which took place in May 1362, he was dead, and his account was rendered by the brothers Richard and Peter de Neuton, his executors (SC6 803/3, m.4; 785/8, m.5).

Neuton, Richard de

Ormerod's pedigree of the Newtons of Newton in Longdendale is not particularly convincing, but suggests that the Neutons referred to here were not of that family. (Ormerod, iii. 859).

Nevill, Robert de (knight)

Granted life-annuity of 100 marks by B.P., for good service at Poitiers, until he should be provided with land to that value elsewhere, 8 Aug. 1358 (*B.P.R.*, iii. 306; *ChRR*, p. 360). On 17 April 1359 he assigned his annuity to John Pecche, citizen of London, for the terms of Michaelmas 1358 and Easter 1359 (ibid., 334). 'Robt son of Sire de Nevill' appointed his brother Alexander, archdeacon of Cornwall, general attorney, 28 Feb. 1366 (*ChRR*, p. 360).

Northlegh, Peter de

'Peter son of Ranulf de Northley' requested a pardon for Roger de Court, for his trespass in Delamere forest, 1 May 1357 (*B.P.R.*, iii. 238). He received a life grant of pasture in Delamere for 12 great beasts a year, and 12 swine in pannage-time (Mich. – Martinmas), by order of B.P. from Gascony, 1 May 1357 (ibid.) He was granted, further, three oaks fit for timber from Delamere for the repair of Our Lady's chapel in Tarvin, and two additional oaks; this grant replaced that of 1 May, 9 Sept. 1358 (ibid., 308). With **Hen. Torfot** and others leased the agistment and pannage of Delamere forest, Xmas 1359 to Xmas 1365 (six-year lease), Xmas 1365 to Xmas 1372 (seven-year lease), (SC6 785/5, m.2d; 785/8, m.3, 3d; 785/9, m.1d; 786/1, m.4; 786/3, m.4d; 786/5, m.2d; 786/6, m.3; 786/7, m.3; 786/8, m.3; 786/10, m.2d; 787/2, m.2, 2d; 787/4, m.2). Amerced 6s. 8d. for taking a growing oak from Delamere, for which he also paid 13s. 4d., 1363–64 (SC6 786/3, m.4d).

Oselcok, Thomas

Catchpoll of Macclesfield borough, 1353–55 (SC6 802/9, m.2; 802/11, m.3). Reeve of Macclesfield borough, 1360–62 (SC6 803/3, m.1; 803/5, m.2d). In the 1369–70 borough account there is a 'new rent' of 6d. for [John] Heppal's and [Thos] Oselcok's shop (SC6 804/2, m.1d).

Parker, Richard le

With Adam le Parker and 17 others made a recog. to B.P. for £220 a year, for a lease of the office of sheriff of Cheshire to Adam for two years, 24 April 1335 (*ChRR*, p. 375). With Adam le Parker and Thos de Clive made a recog. to Thos Ferrers and Wm de Lynford of £17 for the lease of one-quarter of Middlewich, 20 Oct. 1344 (ibid.) Together with Wm Hamelyn and Hugh de Blakenhale, mainpernors of Adam le Parker (dead), imprisoned in Chester castle, for a debt of over £36; on petition, they are to be allowed to pay the debt by annual instalments of £6, 17 May 1351 (*B.P.R.*, iii. 20).

Parker, Thomas le (of Denbigh)

Order to the chamberlain of North Wales that Thomas, as a member of the

Caernarfon castle garrison, be paid ½d. a day in addition to his garrison wages to make and repair the artillery in those parts, 8 Dec. 1354 (*B.P.R.*, iii. 489). Order to pay him his wages of 3d. a day, plus travel expenses into North Wales, as B.P.'s artiller in Cheshire and North Wales, 1 Dec. 1360 (ibid., 402).

Pekton, Richard de

John son of Hen. de Honford, John de Dokenfeld, and Thos de Stathum made a recog. to B.P. for £10, for the wardship and marriage of 'Ric., son and heir of John de Pecton', 16 Dec. 1362 (*ChRR*, p. 216).

Penbrugg, John de (yeoman of the Prince's chamber)

Granted Guy de Provence's former lands in Little Saughall (Shotwick manor) by B.P., recently held by the late Wm de Stafford; also granted the office of riding-forester of Wirral, at pleasure, for 6d. a day, 20 Dec. 1359 (*B.P.R.*, iii. 379; *ChRR*, p. 377). On 16 Mar. 1362, B.P. granted him, for good service, the wardship and marriage of Cecily, daughter and heiress of Thos Doun (*B.P.R.*, iii. 440). Penbrugg's lands in Little Saughall were granted to Reginald Hokere on 12 Oct. 1375 (*ChRR*, p. 186).

Peter's son, John (Peresson; Pierson)

Bailiff of Drakelow manor, 1361–64, and Michaelmas 1364 to 23 April 1365 (SC6 785/9, m.2d; 786/1, m.2d; 786/3, m.3d; 786/5, m.1d). Leased the turbary ('flaghtes') and pasture of Rudheath (Drakelow manor), for £2 a year, 1362–65 (SC6 786/1, m.3; 786/3, m.3d; 786/5, m.2).

Pierresson, Alan (Pierissone; Peressone; Peter's son).

Catchpoll of Macclesfield borough, 1358–63 (SC6 802/15, m.2; 802/17, m.2d; 803/3, m.1; 803/5, m.2d; 803/7, m.2d). Leased the stallage, etc., of Macclesfield for £3 13s. 4d. a year, (five-year lease) 1369–74; 1374–76 (SC6 804/2, m.1d; 804/4, m.1; 804/5, m.1; 804/6, m.1d; 804/7, m.2d; 804/8, m.3).

Poker, William le d. 1365

Succeeded his brother, Thos, as hereditary bailiff ('poker') of Macclesfield hundred, held of the earl by grand serjeanty, 20 Feb. 1359 (*B.P.R.*, iii. 329–30). Accounted 1360–64 (SC6 803/3, m.1; 803/5, m.2; 803/7, m.2; 803/9, m.2). At the audit of his 1363–64 account in Jan. 1365, he was imprisoned on account of his large arrears (SC6 803/9, m.2). He died 22 April 1365; his sisters Margery and Margaret (wife of Ric. Ward of Somerford) received their brother's bailiwick on 9 June, for which they were charged a relief of £4 13s. 4d. (one year's value) (SC6 786/5, m.5).

Porter, John le (gate-keeper of Chester castle)

Order to pay him 30s. 0d. a year, as long as he remains porter of Chester castle, as a gift of B.P., 13 Sept. 1353 (*B.P.R.*, iii. 117). 'J. le P., citizen of Chester' made a recog. for 7 marks to Simon de Bradgate, 11 Aug. 1361 (*ChRR*, p. 386). With Roger Wyot, made a recog. for 8 marks to Robt son of Ric. de Salghton, 23 Aug. 1362 (ibid.) On 25 June 1367, with David son of Madog de Caldecott, made a recog. for £10 to John de Beston (rector of Alderley) and four others (ibid.) In the I.P.M of Ric. Done of Crowton, *c.* 1391, a 'John Porter' held land of Ric. in Chester (ibid., p. 153).

Pygot, William

A member of the panel from which the inquiry into the dispute between Wm Soty and the tenants of Bollington (Macclesfield manor) was to be drawn; the inquiry was disrupted by the calculated misbehaviour of Wm Dounes and **Adam de Mottrum**, 24 May 1359 (*B.P.R.*, iii. 338).

Pyrye, Hugh de

Order to deliver to him three oaks in Peckforton park, 13 July 1357 (*B.P.R.*, iii. 258). Bailiff-itinerant in Cheshire and Flintshire, at 40s. 0d. a year, from 11 March to Mich. 1362 (SC6 772/3, m.2d; *ChRR*, p. 383).

Roter, Nichola le (widow of Ranulf le Roter)

Her husband was killed on 4 July 1362, and the I.P.M. which followed on 23 July found that he had held property in Kingsley, Norley, Acton (Weaverham parish), Weaverham, Bradley (Frodsham parish), Frodsham and Heswall (CHES 3/36 Ed. III/13). He had taken a ten-year lease of the manor of Frodsham, for £80 a year, from Michaelmas 1361 (SC6 785/9, m.5). After his death, Nichola took over the lease for the year 1362–63 (SC6 786/1, m.4d). She then petitioned B.P.'s council for the lease to be terminated; this was granted on condition that she pay £5 a year for the remaining eight years (1363–71) to compensate B.P. for the loss he might otherwise incur. On 9 Feb. 1365, she petitioned for her discharge from this sum, as she claimed the manor was yielding over £80 a year (*B.P.R.*, iii. 474). For a discussion of the basis of this claim see Booth, 'Farming for Profit', pp. 86–87. With **Hen. Torfot** and Thos son of John de Frodsham she made a recog. to B.P. for 20 marks, for part of Ranulf Roter's fine of £40, 15 Sept. 1363 (*ChRR*, p. 411). Her son, also called Ranulf, was of full age at his father's death, and it may be he that this fine refers to – possibly for the homicide of Wm Harding, or for assisting Wm de Bunbury with the killing of **Robt de Frodesham** in self defence – imposed 24 May 1363 (*B.P.R.*, iii. 486; CHES 29/67, m.115d). She leased Mickledale (Frodsham manor), for 13s. 4d., 1363–64 (SC6 786/3, m.5).

Roter, Ranulf le (the elder) oc. 4 July 1362

Attorney, and then steward of the abbot of Chester. Farmer of the manor of Frodsham, 1360 to 1362.

According to Ormerod, Ranulf was a member of a younger branch of the Thorntons of Th.-le-Moors, and was, therefore, a cousin of **Sir Peter de Thorneton** (Ormerod, ii. 17). He contracted a marriage in 1340 with Alice, the ten-year-old daughter of **William de Stanlegh (the elder)** (W.F. Irvine, 'The Early Stanleys', *T.H.S.L.C.*, 105 (1953), pp. 56–59). In 1349/50 his mother, Emma, leased him all her lands in Kingsley, Newton and Crowton for her life, at an annual rent of £4 4s. 0d. (*D.K.R. 28*, p. 51). Husband of **Nichola le Roter** (q.v.). He paid 8s. 0d. for recovering money in court before the justiciar of Chester, 1351–52 (SC6 783/17, m.3). In 1353–54 he was said to hold lands in Anderton of Sir John St Pierre (*ChRR*, p. 424). With Thos de Dutton and Hen. Beston respectively bought the marriages of Elizabeth, Maud and Beatrice, three of the daughters and heiresses of Sir Peter de Thornton, together with the keeping of their lands; Ranulf paid 90 marks, 28 Nov. 1356 (*B.P.R.*, iii. 231; SC6 784/10, m.6). With Ric. del Shagh and three others made a recog. to B.P. for £60, 16 Dec. 1356 (*ChRR*, p. 410). Acted as attorney of the abbot of Chester in the 1353 trailbaston sessions (*Cheshire History*, 11 (1983) p. 41). With Ric. Scott acted as a pledge for **Stephen Merton's** fine for misusing the liberty of waif and stray in his manor of Gayton, 1353 trailbaston sessions (ibid., p. 43). On 1 June 1359, he stated that he had bought the marriage of Hen., son and heir of Roger de Praers, on the understanding that the B.P. would grant him the heir's lands, at a suitable rent, on the death of the current holder; as a result he asked that the manors of Duddon and Eaton by Congleton be extended and delivered to him; order followed to let him have them for what others were prepared to pay (*B.P.R.*, iii. 341). On 29 Nov. 1360, he made a recog. for 100 marks to B.P. for the fine imposed upon Sir Reginald de Grey of Ruthin, for unlicensed alienations of property within the manors of Rushton and Eaton by Tarporley by Grey and his ancestors (*ChRR*, p. 204). With **Hen. Torfot** and John Fog, he bought all the livestock of Frodsham manor for £125 15s. 3d., 1360–61 (prior to the manor being let to him from Mich. 1361) (SC6 785/8, m.7). On 28 Nov. 1360, Wm de Stanley, the younger (master forester of Wirral) complained that Roter, steward of the abbot of Chester, with his armed gang, had threatened him on being challenged for offences committed in Wirral forest; after being pursued, Roter then took refuge in one of the abbot's manors. Roter and his men were acquitted of this charge, by order 21 Feb. 1361 (*B.P.R.*, iii. 401, 410). Took a ten-year lease of Frodsham manor, from Michaelmas 1361, for £80 a year (SC6 785/9, m.5). At the county court of 2 Aug. 1362, the coroner of Eddisbury hundred, and the townships of Kingsley, Norley, Crowton, and Acton, presented that Robt son of Robt de Neuton, John le Chylde, Ranulf de Tyldeslegh, and Hugh de Tyldeslegh had feloniously killed Ranulf le Roter the elder, at Kingsley, on Mon. 4 July 1362 (CHES 29/67, m.118d). For subsequent events, see **Nichola Roter**.

Salisbury, William de Monte Acuto (Montagu), earl of d. 1397

His father had made his fortune as one of the engineers of Edward III's coup d'etat in 1330. He was granted the Montalt inheritance by the king in 1337, and had received possession of it in 1338 (*C.Chart. R., 1327–41*, p. 432; *C.P.R., 1338–40*, p. 114). As a result of this grant, William inherited the lordships of Mold and Hawarden, and the manors of Great Neston, Lea Newbold, and Bosley (in Cheshire), together with the office of hereditary steward of Chester (*B.P.R.*, iii. 454). He did not receive the knight's fees of Hawarden lordship, or the advowsons of Hawarden and of Holy Trinity, Chester, until 1361, following Queen Isabella's death (ibid., 419). In addition, the elder William Montagu had been given the lordship of Denbigh in 1331, part of the property of the fallen Roger Mortimer (*C. Chart. R., 1327–41*, p. 210). The younger William, having succeeded his father in 1344, leased the lordship from the prince during his minority, but lost it in 1354, after a legal judgement heavily influenced by the personal intervention of Edward III in favour of the young Roger Mortimer (R.R. Davies, *Lordship and Society in the March of Wales, 1282–1400* (1978), pp. 50–51). On 14 July 1360, he established that he had overpaid £42 10s. 6¾d. when he had been lessee of two-thirds of the lordship (the remainder being in dower) from Mich. 1344 to 20 Oct. 1347, and it was ordered that the sum should be allowed to him from his fine for a trespass in Macclesfield forest (*B.P.R.*, iii. 390; **42.1**). He fought at Crécy, and was with the prince on the Poitiers campaign, and letters of protection were issued by the chamberlain in his favour on 28 May 1356 (*B.P.R.*, iii. 226).

Some of the references to him in the Cheshire records concern the operation of forest law in his estates in the county. On 18 May 1351, he complained to the prince's council that tenants from Macclesfield forest were grazing their livestock on the property of his tenants in Bosley (ibid., 23). The community of Wirral forest claimed in July 1352 that Salisbury and the abbots of Chester and Whalley, together with their tenants, should contribute to a common fine for the amercements before John de Macclesfield in the forest sessions; the prince disagreed (ibid., 68–69). Respite was granted him on 11 Sept. 1358 for forest offences in Bosley, allegedly committed in Queen Isabella's time (i.e. before 1347). On the same day an order was issued to replevy to him his manor of Gt Neston, its park and franchises, which he had not claimed at the forest eyre (ibid., 312). He is listed among the Wirral landlords who were bound to pay puture to the Wirral foresters, 1 Dec. 1361 (ibid., 434).

Another group of references concern jurisdictional problems between Cheshire and his lordships of Mold and Hawarden. Hawarden manor, a marcher lordship tenurially tied to Cheshire, had been included in the 1353 common fine of 5,000 marks, and on 20 Feb. 1354 he complained that his tenants there had been assessed unreasonably (ibid., 146). On 23 Feb. following, Salisbury made a *cydfod* with the prince, to arrange the extradition of criminals between Flintshire and the lordships of Mold and Hawarden (ibid., 149). This was followed by the complaint of an accessory to a homicide, who said that he should not be punished in Flintshire when the crime had been committed on Salisbury's territory (ibid., 180).

There are also references to grants of the Montagu lands in Cheshire to feoffees, as part of family settlements. In 1348/49 he and his first wife, Joan, were granted a licence to alienate the honour of Hawarden, and the manors of Mold, Gt Neston, Bosley and Lea to feoffees (*D.K.R. 28*, p. 49). This marriage was annulled in 1349, and Joan subsequently married the Black Prince (*D.N.B.*, xxxviii. 214). In September 1358, he was granted another licence allowing him to enfeoff Sir John Wingfield, Ric. de Acton, and Walter de Guppehey with Gt Neston, Bosley and Moldsdale, and a further rearrangement took place in 1362, whereby Hawarden, Bosley and Neston were entailed on Montagu and his second wife, Elizabeth, and their heirs male (*B.P.R.*, iii. 311–12, 454). It may be that the grants of Lea Newbold to Sir John Wingfield in 1351, and to Sir Ric. de Aketon, in 1351/52, were also connected with such rearrangements (*B.P.R.*, iii. 54; *D.K.R. 28*, p. 49).

Sancto Petro (St Pierre), John de (knight) born *c.* 1308

> The family had become involved in Cheshire affairs when Sir Urian St Pierre took part in the Barons' Wars on the side of the Lord Edward, and was responsible for retaking Beeston castle in 1265. Edward rewarded Urian with the marriage of his ward, Idony, the heiress to a quarter of the barony of Malpas. Sir John St Pierre was his grandson, and succeeded not only to the quarter of Malpas barony, but other properties throughout Cheshire, together with a pourparty of the master-serjeanty of the peace of the county. Idony's claim came from her father, David 'the clerk', who was illegitimate, and had set aside the claims of the legitimate heir, his uncle Philip, the ancestor of the Egerton family. It was through his second marriage, to Isabella Egerton, that Sir John Delves was able to revive the Egerton claim, and successfully manipulate the Cheshire judicial system to get possession of part of the St Pierre estates which, since 1353, had been in the hands of the Black Prince. (Booth, *Financial Administration*, pp. 130–32; Ormerod, ii. 598–99, iii. 522).

With Thos Blaston, chamberlain of Chester, he was appointed to lead the Cheshire levies back to the county, Jan. 1329 (*C.P.R., 1327–30*, p. 347). He was in the king's service, in the company of the future earl of Salisbury, *c.* 1332 (*C.C.R., 1330–33*, p. 510). Late in 1332, he was pardoned all his trespasses in Cheshire (*C.P.R., 1330–34*, p. 375). In Aug. 1347, he was at war overseas, in the company of the earl of Lancaster (*B.P.R.*, i. 118). On 2 July 1351, the prince made him a gift of 100 marks, upon the marriage of his son, Urian, to the daughter of Sir Golford Gistels (*B.P.R.*, iii. 33). In 1352, he became involved in a violent dispute with members of the Maisterson family of Nantwich, in which the bishop of Waterford played a part. The bishop was Roger Cradock, O.F.M., whose pontificate covered the years 1350 to 1361. He was likely to have been a relative of **David Cradok**, whose family also had property in the Nantwich area (E.B. Fryde, D.E. Greenway, S. Porter and I. Roy, *Handbook of British Chronology*, 3rd ed. (1986), p. 376; Bennett, *Community, Class*, p. 141.) Although the details of this episode have yet to be worked out, it was clearly serious since it was referred to the prince's council, and the parties on both sides had to acquire charters of pardon as a result (*B.P.R.*, iii. 61, 67–69, 71; iv. 102).

On 7 April 1353, St Pierre sold the life-interest in his Cheshire property to the Black Prince, in return for £1,000, and the office of keeper of Beaumaris castle, together with lands in Anglesey worth over £110 a year (*B.P.R.*, iii. 96–97, 123–24). It is not clear why St Pierre made this arrangement with the prince, whereas the prince's motivation was obviously financial (Booth, *Financial Administration*, pp. 130–32). A comprehensive policy of asset-stripping, particularly of the estate's woodland, followed, and part of the principal St Pierre residence, the manor-house at Peckforton, was dismantled and removed to the top of Eddisbury Hill, for use by the master-forester of Delamere (*B.P.R.*, iii. 166).

St Pierre went to live in Beaumaris, and many of the subsequent references to him in Cheshire result from disputes with the county officials arising out of differing interpretations of the agreement between the prince and himself. For example, over wardships and tenurial questions: Nov. 1353 (*B.P.R.*, iii. 135), May 1354 (ibid., 160–61), July 1355 (ibid., 207–8, 220), Nov. 1355 (ibid., 219, 220), Oct. 1359 (ibid., 370), Aug. 1362 (ibid., 452), May 1365 (ibid., 479); over grants of property made by Sir John before his agreement with the prince: Sept. 1353 (ibid., 122), Oct. 1353 (ibid., 125), Nov. 1353 (ibid., 133).

In 1363, **Sir John Delves** claimed a portion of the St Pierre property, through Isabel, his wife, with the prince's agreement. The consequent law-suit was decided in Delves's favour, and six surviving letters written by St Pierre from Beaumaris make it clear that he felt that sharp practice had brought about an unjust conclusion (Booth, *Financial Administration*, pp. 131–32). Ormerod's pedigree of the barons of Malpas is not one of his best, and it is not known when St Pierre died, or what subsequently happened about the estates, apart from the fact that at least some of them appear to have returned to his descendants.

Shareshull, William de (knight, chief justice of the King's Bench) *c.* 1289/1370

For his biography, see B.H. Putnam, *The Place in Legal History of Sir William Shareshill* (1950). A native of Staffordshire, like John Delves, he was a childhood friend of Sir Roger Hillary, a justice of the court of Common Pleas (G.O. Sayles, *Select Cases in the Court of King's Bench*, Selden Soc., 82 (1965), pp. lxvi–lxx), who acted as co-justice with him over the trailbaston sessions of 1353. He was also an associate of the elder William Montagu (earl of Salisbury) in the 1320s. From 1333 to 1361 he was a member of the king's council, and from 1338 served as the most important legal specialist member of the Black Prince's council, while being a puisne justice of the court of Common Pleas. He was dismissed from his official positions as a result of Edward III's purge in 1340, spent 1340/41 in exile in Wales, and was reinstated subsequently, being appointed chief baron of the Exchequer in 1344, when he may have played a part in the reorganisation of the Black Prince's financial administration which resulted in the setting up of the prince's own exchequer in 1343/44. In the period following the Black Death, he was responsible for the labour legislation of 1349/51, and the 1352 statute of treasons. He became chief justice of the court of King's Bench in 1350, from which he retired in 1361, and he appears to have left the prince's council round about the same time. For an analysis of Shareshull's legislative policies after 1349, see G.L. Harriss, *King, Parliament and Public Finance in Medieval England to 1369* (1975), pp. 342–43.

The major details of his involvement with Cheshire and the rest of the Black Prince's English and Welsh estates are given here:

He was in Cheshire in 1346, with Peter Gildesburgh, to raise the mise levied on the county in that year. He held general eyres in North and South Wales in 1346/47, and was present at the Chester county court in 1347 (Putnam, *Place*, p. 67). In Dec. 1347, he held sessions to bring about the 'recovery' of Rudheath and Kingsmarsh, which proved to be a major addition to the Black Prince's land revenue in the county (SC6 783/17, m.6). In 1348, he held pleas of *quo warranto* for North Wales at which **John Delves** acted as the prince's attorney: it may have been Shareshull's observation of his performance in this role which resulted in Delves's transfer from the **earl of Arundel**'s to the prince's service (*Record of Caernarvon*, p. 151). He was appointed by the prince, with Sir Roger Hillary, to hold a general eyre in Cheshire on 19 Aug. 1353, for which sessions of trailbaston were substituted in return for a common fine of 5,000 marks payable by the county community (Booth, 'Taxation and Public Order: Cheshire in 1353', *Northern History*, xii (1976), pp. 16–31). Shareshull went on to hold financially-profitable trailbastons in Cornwall and Devon in 1354/55, and in Cornwall again in 1358/59 (Putnam, *Place*, p. 39). He came out of retirement to serve as justice in eyre for the prince in the lordship of Denbigh in 1362 (ibid., p. 40; *B.P.R.*, iii. 440, 448–49). In 1364, he was requested to act once again, as justice to hear cases in error in Denbigh lordship, but appears not to have agreed to participate (ibid., 463).

He had landed wealth in Staffordshire valued at £40 a year in 1337 (R.H. Hilton, 'Lord and Peasant in Staffordshire', *Nth Staffs. Jnl. of Field Studies*, 10 (1970), pp. 1–20). In 1357, however, he increased his wealth very greatly through his marriage to Dionisia, the widow of Sir Hugh Cokesey (Putnam, *Place*, p. 7).

Shryggelegh, Robert de

Lease of the herbage and focage of Lyme Handley and Harrop (Macclesfield manor) granted to him and Wm del Dounes, for six years, at £10 a year, 3 July

1352 (*ChRR*, p. 156). Acting in 1353–54 – second year of 6-year lease, 1354–57; again in 1358–59 – with Wm Dounes; lease of Lyme Handley only, 1359–64; three-year lease, 1365–67 (term not completed) (SC6 802/9, m.1; 802/11, m.1; 802/13, m.1; 802/15, m.4; 803/3, m.4; 803/7, m.1; 803/9, m.1d; 803/12, m.1; 803/13, m.1). Leased the coal-mines of Macclesfield forest, 1358–59 (SC6 802/15, m.4). Approved three acres of land in Pott Shrigley (Macclesfield manor), 1360–61 (SC6 803/3, m.4).

Somerford, John de

He and his wife, Sigreda, successfully claimed the right to hold the office of gaoler of Macclesfield and collector of revenue within the forest, alternately with **Adam de Mottrum**, in 1355 (*B.P.R.*, iii. 199). He accounted for the office in 1355–56, 1357–58, 1359–60 [by deputy, **Robt Worth**], 1361–62 [same deputy], 1363–64 [same deputy] (SC6 802/13, m.1d; 802/15, m.4d; 802/17, m.1; 803/5, m.1; 803/9, m.1). Ordered to go to Chester castle to help clear up the dispute over Adam de Mottrum's account for 1356–57, audited in the spring of 1358 (SC6 802/13, m.1d). On 25 April 1365, Adam was granted licence by the B.P. to purchase the Somerfords' moiety of the bailiwick (*ChRR*, p. 355).

Soule, Henry

With **Wm le Fleccher**, catchpoll of Middlewich, 1361–63; with Hamo the clerk, 1363–64 (SC6 785/9, m.1d; 786/1, m.1d; 786/3, m.2). 'Bailiff' – presumably this means catchpoll – of Middlewich, with Wm Busshell, 1365–66 (SC6 786/6, m.1).

Spridlyngton, William de (clerk, bishop of St Asaph) died 9 April 1382

> Member of the prince's council. Auditor of the prince's ministers' accounts, 1350 to 1361. Assessor of the duchy of Cornwall, 1356 and 1371. Bishop of St Asaph, 1376 to 1382.

Auditor of the Cheshire accounts, 1350–61 (*ChAcc*, p. 203; SC6 783/17, m.3; 784/3, m.1; 784/7, m.1; 784/10, m.1; 785/7, m.7; 785/8, m.8). Leased B.P.'s manor of Little Weldon in 1351 (*B.P.R.*, iv. 18). Gift of £10 paid him by B.P. through the chamberlain, 17 July 1352 (*B.P.R.*, iii. 69) With Nich. Pynnok (auditor 1349–54) presented **Thos le Yonge** to Sir John Wingfield (B.P.'s business-manager, 1351/61), as escheator of Cheshire, Flintshire and Maccles-field, and steward of the lands of the earldom of Chester in Cheshire, 1 Oct. 1352 (ibid., 78). He and Pynnok persuaded Sir John Wingfield to make an ordinance that the chamberlain pay the costs of the clerks writing the accounts within the chamberlain's bailiwick, 23 Oct. 1352 (ibid., 79). With Nich. Pynnok and Thos Hockele appointed to audit all officials (except central and household) of B.P. in England, Wales, Cornwall and the earldom of Chester, 11 Sept. 1353 (ibid., 117). Gift to him from B.P. of £20 out of the receipts of that year's trailbaston sessions, in recognition of his hard work and to repay 'certain secret costs',

14 Sept. 1353 (ibid., 118). On 16 Sept. 1353 he was ordered, together with the lieutenant and chamberlain, to survey the B.P.'s escheats in Flintshire, find out their greatest value since the conquest (of Wales), and sell them to their local communities as profitably as possible, 16 Sept. 1353 (ibid., 121). Together with Delves and **Burnham**, he and Pynnok were the recipients of detailed instructions concerning the administration of the B.P.'s estates in Cheshire, 26 Jan. 1355 (ibid., 187–88). Acted as assessor and arrentor in the assessions of the duchy of Cornwall, Feb.–March 1356, April–May 1364, June 1371 (Duchy of Cornwall Office, Assession Rolls). It was ordered that he was to be present, together with Burnham when the escheator, Thos le Yonge, took the I.P.M. of **Sir Peter de Thornton**; he and Burnham were to inquire, themselves, into that part of Thornton's inheritance which belonged to the prince, 27 May 1356 (*B.P.R.*, iii. 225–26). Notification that B.P. had pardoned him the 66s. 8d. owed for the book called *Catholicon*, bought from the effects of the late bishop of St Asaph, 14 Oct. 1359 (ibid., 371). Acting as member of B.P.'s council in 1360 (ibid., 388). With Delves, Burnham and Sir Ric. de Stoke commissioned to deliver to the widowed countess of March her dower of Denbigh lordship, 24 Aug. 1360 (ibid., 392).

The B.P. first requested that he be elected bishop of St Asaph in 1357, but the chapter chose **Llywelyn ap Madog ab Elis** instead, and the local clergy were clearly anxious to have a Welshman in the see. Similarly, the prince's attempt to foist Alexander Dalby on the diocese of Bangor in 1366 was thwarted, after the pope had ordered an inquiry into the candidate's proficiency in Welsh. Spridlyngton did become dean of St Asaph – although the date of his appointment does not survive, he was in post by 11 June 1375. The prince finally succeeded in having him provided to the see on 4 Feb. 1376, and he thus became the first English bishop of St Asaph (*Fasti*, xi (1965) pp. 37, 40; *Cal. Papal Registers: Petitions*, i. 48; *Cal. Papal Registers: Papal Letters*, iv. 25; *FMA(2)*, p. x).

Appointed one of B.P.'s executors, he served as one of eleven commissioners to make a valor of the prince's property in 1376 (Booth, *Financial Administration*, p. 173).

Stafford, John de

Order to inquire into the rights he and his wife, Isabel, claim in the manors of Stockport, Poynton and Woodford, for Isabel's life; escheator was not to collect revenue there until the matter was resolved, 11 Sept. 1353 (*B.P.R.*, iii. 116). He complained that he was being penalised for that part of Isabel's manor of Poynton in Macclesfield forest for offences committed when Sir John Ardern was life-tenant of the property, and for which Sir John had had a pardon, 24 Nov. 1358 (ibid., 325–26). According to the account of the descent of this property in Ormerod, iii. 792–96, Isabel was the widow of Robt de Eton, former rector of Alderley, second son of Joan, the heiress of Sir Ric. de Stockport. Eton resigned his benefice in 1332, on succeeding to his mother's property (*EC*, i. 338–40). Stafford was, therefore, her second husband, and after his death she married Thos Stathum in 1361/62. Sir John de Arderne of Aldford was her mother-in-law, Joan's, second husband, and at his death in 1349 he was in possession of Stockport, Poynton and Woodford (CHES 3/23 Ed. III/12).

Stafford, Richard de (knight) (Destafford) died *c*. 1380

> For a brief biography of this younger brother of Ralph, earl of Stafford, see Margaret Sharp in Tout, v. 390. Stafford survived the prince, and died some time before 22 Aug. 1380 (*ChRR*, p. 241).

Stafford was a military retainer, friend, councillor and administrator/adviser of the Black Prince throughout the latter's adult life. He was one of the commissioners appointed in 1343 to take possession of the principality of Wales on Edward's behalf. In 1345 he served on a commission of oyer and terminer in the lordship of Denbigh, and wrote that year to the B.P.'s council about the disturbances in North Wales following the murder of Hen. Shaldford, the prince's attorney, on 14 Feb. 1345 (*Cal. Anc. Corr. Concerning Wales*, pp. 229–30). He was appointed steward of all the prince's lands in England and Wales, for an annual fee of 100 marks, in 1347. This was the now somewhat old-fashioned system whereby a layman held office jointly with a cleric, who specialised in finance (Peter Gildesburgh). It was superseded by Feb. 1351, if not earlier, when Sir John Wingfield took on the new post of manager of the prince's business (*ChAcc*, p. 129). Despite his displacement from the stewardship, Stafford continued to serve in a high place on the prince's council, and visited Cheshire in this capacity in Nov. 1351, Feb. 1352, with the state visit of Aug.–Sept. 1353, again in 1357, and 1358 (*B.P.R.*, iii. 53, 58, 117, 265, 269, 299). On 16 Feb. 1361, he was appointed a justice to hear errors in the lordship of Denbigh, with **John Delves** and Wm Banastre (ibid., 406). In the early 1360s, he was also acting for the B.P. as one of the feoffees of the St Pierre inheritance (ibid., 443).

His other major involvement with the affairs of the earldom was as co-justice with **Sir Ric. Wiluhby** and John Delves to hold the Cheshire forest eyre of 1357 (which was originally to be held in 1353) (ibid., 276; CHES 33/6). This proved to be a long-drawn out affair, and the last session held by the justices occurred after May 1359, although the business was not finally cleared up until near the end of 1361 (*B.P.R.*, iii. 338, 432, 435).

He received some patronage from the prince in Cheshire and Flintshire. On 1 Oct. 1358, he was given a life-grant of 200 marks a year of land and rent, which comprised the town of Northwich (£66) and the lordship of Hopedale (£60), together with £7 6s. 8d. from the rent of Kingsmarsh (*B.P.R.*, iii. 323–24; *ChRR*, p. 441). This grant was confirmed by the king in Oct. 1359 (*C.P.R., 1358–61*, p. 303).

Stanlegh (Stanley) William de (the elder) (master-forester of Wirral) *c.* 1310 – Apr. 1360

> For the biographies of the elder William (also called 'William son of John') and his son (1337/98) see the meticulous account of W. Fergusson Irvine, 'The Early Stanleys', *T.H.S.L.C.*, 105 (1953), pp. 56–59. Stanley's younger daughter, Ellen, married John, the son of Stephen de Merton (lord of Gayton in Wirral) in 1359. John de Merton died without issue in 1361.

He received forest ordinances, as master-forester of Wirral, 24 March 1351, part of the tightening up of forest law that was to bear fruit in the 1357 forest eyre (*B.P.R.*, iii. 15–16). On 11 Apr. 1351, he was ordered not to interfere with the abbot and convent of Chester in Wirral forest (ibid., 17). He complained that John Domville was depriving him of puture in his two townships (presumably Brimstage and Oxton) in Wirral forest, 14 July 1351 (ibid., 34). Order to pay him the fee of 30s. 0d. a year, granted him by B.P. for keeping Shotwick park, 18 July 1351 (ibid., 37). Entry **45.15** presumably refers to payment to his son of the same fee. He and John Lasselles, his riding forester, were paid 20s. 0d. expenses for travelling to London to speak to B.P. about Wirral forest, 18 July 1351 (ibid., 38). In Sept. 1351, men of Brimstage and Oxton (see Domville, above), and others in the forest were attempting to deny, through legal action, his right to puture in the forest; B.P. ordered Hen. de Motlowe and John de la Pole to plead on Stanley's behalf (ibid., 42). On 26 Nov. 1351, Sir Thos Ferrers (justiciar of Chester) was ordered not to proceed in this plea unless either Sir John Wingfield or **Sir Ric. Stafford** were present (ibid., 54).

Burnham was ordered to give him a copy of the estreat called *vide* for the revenue to be levied in his bailiwick, so he could keep it as a warrant, 22 July 1352 (ibid., 67). He was ordered, as keeper, to deliver two does to Wm Stafford, yeoman of B.P.'s chamber, as a gift from the prince, 4 Oct. 1352 (ibid., 78). On 19 Apr. 1353, he was paid 66s. 8d., gift from B.P., for his expenses in coming from Chester to London on business connected with Wirral forest (*B.P.R.*, iv. 86). Ref. to Robt de Pulle having made a fine before Ferrers, on behalf of the whole community of Wirral (except for Stanley and Lasselles), for a default before the riding foresters, 24 Apr. 1353 (*B.P.R.*, iii. 102).

He and his under-foresters were accused at the 1353 trailbaston sessions of numerous corrupt and oppressive practices in Wirral (Booth, 'Taxation and Public Order: Cheshire in 1353', *Northern History*, xii (1976), pp. 26, 30). In Nov. 1355 he was in prison for being an accessory to the death of Ric. de Bechyngton, when he petitioned for release (*B.P.R.*, iii. 254). Two years later, in July 1357, Roger de Bechynton and Thos de Hokenhull petitioned B.P., complaining that they had been maliciously imprisoned in Chester and ruined by the enmity of (unnamed) persons connected with the affair of Wm de Stanley, because they refused to go along with their malicious proposals (ibid.)

Stanley forfeited his bailiwick, as a result of the Bechyngton homicide, and it was returned to him 17 Aug. 1357 following his acquittal; a further order to return it followed 13 Sept. and 30 Nov. (ibid., 275, 279, 283). Before he received it back, Delves and Burnham were ordered to make an inventory of the game in Wirral forest, to prevent Stanley making trouble for the man who had had custody of the forest following the seizure, (John Doune) 28 Aug. 1357 (ibid., 276–77, 357, 372). He sought a warrant to allow him to buy timber and firewood in Wirral forest, as he had none of his own, 8 Feb. 1359 (ibid., 327). He was dead by 27 Apr. 1360, when the writ of *diem clausit extremum* was issued (ibid., 380).

His son, William Stanley the younger, sued an *ouster-le-main* on 21 June 1360, following his father's death, as he was of age, and had done homage and sworn fealty to B.P. on that day for one-third of the manor of Storeton and the bailiwick of the forestership of Wirral, held for one-eighth of a knight's fee (ibid., 385).

Stokes, Richard de (clerk)

He acted as auditor of the accounts of the earldom of Chester, 1359–60, 1361–69, 1370–71, 1372–73, 1373–74 (SC6 785/9, m.4; 786/1, m.1; 786/3, m.1; 786/5, m.1; 786/6, m.1; 786/7, m.1; 786/8, m.1; 786/10, m.1; 787/2, m.1; 787/5, m.1; 787/7, m.1).

On 24 Aug. 1360, he was appointed by advice and ordinance of Sir John Wingfield, together with **Delves** (steward of Denbigh), **Spridlyngton** and **Burnham** to assign and deliver to the countess of March (widow of Roger, earl of March) her dower of the lordship of Denbigh, which was in the prince's hands because of the minority of Edmund Mortimer (*B.P.R.*, iii. 392).

With **Peter Lacy**, John Henxteworth and Wm Spridlyngton, he was made a remainderman in the enfeoffment of the St Pierre lands to Thos de Delves, Thos de Budenhale, and Hen. de Coton (clerks), 2 Apr. 1365 (ibid., 477). After the prince's death he was appointed a baron of the king's exchequer, Oct. 1377 (*C.P.R., 1377–81*, p. 31). As such, he was commissioned, together with Robt Grafton, as auditor of Wales and the earldom of Chester, and surveyor of wardships, 5 Feb. 1378 (ibid., p. 109).

Strange (Strangee), Roger le (knight)

This is clearly Sir Roger Lestrange of Knockin (Salop), who had been compelled to restore to **Duke Henry of Lancaster** in 1355 the lands that his family had acquired in Cheshire through the marriage of Alice Lacy, widow of Earl Thomas of Lancaster, to Ebulo Lestrange in 1322 (Somerville, *Duchy of Lancaster*, i. 34, 39). A condition of the surrender was that Lestrange was to receive the property back again after the duke's death, and he was in possession of it by Jan. 1362. (*B.P.R.*, iii. 211–12). This land was part of the Mascy barony of Dunham (Ormerod, i. 526–29), which included the manors of Bidston, Moreton, and Saughall Massie (in Wirral forest), and Kelsall (in Delamere forest). The pardon to Duke Henry of his shares of the common fines of the two forests following the 1357 forest eyre presumably did not apply to Lestrange, and that is the reason he had to be granted atterminations of the fines (**45.14**). See p. lxviii for his lordship of Maelor Saesneg (Flints.)

Stretton, Hugh de

With Hen. de Molynton (vicar of Backford) and two others, made a recog. to Queen Isabella for 10 marks, 9 July 1354 (*ChRR*, p. 457). Sheriff of Chester city, with **Henry Doune**, 1361–62 (SC6 785/9, m.1).

Stretton, William de (knight)

Reference to him receiving a £10 annuity from the B.P. on 13 Dec. 1352 (*B.P.R.*, iii. 85).

Swetenham, Thomas de (clerk of the escheator)

Acted as deputy to **Thos le Yong**, as steward of Middlewich, 1360–61 (SC6 785/8, m.4). Acted as escheator of Cheshire, Mich. – 4 Dec. 1361 (when he was succeeded by **Adam de Kyngesley**), following the death of Thos Young; Swetenham rendered Young's last account, that for 1360–61, on 12 May 1362 as 'Young's clerk' (SC6 785/8, m.8; 785/9, m.7). He bought four oxen from the stock of Macclesfield manor, 1360–61 (SC6 803/13, m.5). 'Thos Swettenham of Middlewich', with **Hugh Mulyngton** and 10 others took a lease of Middlewich, for three years, at £62 13s. 4d. a year, 1367–70 (SC6 786/8, m.1; 787/2, m.1 – the account for 1369–70 is missing). Swetenham made a recog. for the lease on 1 Oct. 1367, and the lease proper was granted by letters of the B.P. dated 22 Oct. following (*ChRR*, p. 461).

Swynerton, Thomas de (knight) d. 1361

> The Swynertons were a wealthy Staffordshire family, of sub-baronial status (Morgan, *War and Society*, p. 55).

Thomas's father, Sir Roger de Swynerton, had been given the two Cheshire manors of Great and Little Barrow by Edward III in 1334, following the forfeiture of Hugh Despenser, earl of Winchester. Roger was succeeded by his son, Robert, who died in 1349 when his brother, Thomas, inherited the property (Ormerod, ii. 340). B.P. made a gift to him of six oaks from Delamere forest, 10 March 1353 (*B.P.R.*, iii. 95). On 22 May 1355, Thos complained that he and his tenants were being prevented from taking wood and underwood in Barrow park; order to inquire (ibid., 200–1). His liberties in Barrow not to be investigated until his return to England, 29 June 1355 (ibid., 206). On 28 Nov. 1356 he paid a £40 fine so that his sister Philippa, widow of **Sir Peter de Thornton**, might remarry freely (ibid., 232). He petitioned B.P. to have his charters allowed in the forest eyre (1357), or before the B.P.'s great council; he was not able to attend in person, as he had to guard the French king; order to try his claims in the eyre, and send the results to B.P. and his council, 5 Sept. 1357 (ibid., 278). On 12 May 1358, he informed the prince that his manor of Barrow had been seized; lieutenant ordered to be at London, quinzaine of Trinity following, to explain the reasons for the seizure to the prince and council (ibid., 300–1). Order to allow him to work the manor of Barrow, providing he gave security for the issues in case the B.P. had a right to them, 17 June 1358; order to deliver the manor to him, 30 June 1358 (ibid., 302). Further order to **Delves** and **Burnham** to give reasons why the manor had been seized, 1 July 1359 (ibid., 350). Letters of protection to him, as he was going overseas with the king to war, 21 Oct. 1359 (ibid., 373). On 14 July 1360, ordered to delay collecting the penalty imposed upon him in the forest eyre on account of Barrow manor until the following Michaelmas (ibid., 389). Order to delay the trial of the business between him and the prince in the county court until the quinzaine of Hilary 1361, 13 Oct. 1360 (ibid., 394). A further order to delay all the business against him relating to Barrow in the Delamere forest eyre until after Easter 1361, 9 Nov. 1360 (ibid., 395).

Taillour, Hugh le

His undated appointment as bailiff of Kingsmarsh appears in the Recognizance Roll for 1354/55 (*ChRR*, p. 466). He acted as bailiff of Kingsmarsh (under the bailiff of Drakelow), 1354–55, 1357–60, 1361–62 (SC6 784/5, m.12; 785/1, m.9; *ChAcc*, p. 246; SC6 785/5, m.5; 785/9, m.2d). No bailiff of Kingsmarsh is named in the accounts for 1355–57 or 1360–61, so it is probable that Hugh was acting in those years also. He accounted separately as bailiff of Kingsmarsh, 1362–63 (SC6 786/1, m.3d).

Tappetrassh, William

Acted with Roger Page as 'bailiff' of Middlewich, 1351–52 (SC6 783/17, m.1d). Chamberlain of Middlewich, 1352–53 and 1360–61 (SC6 784/2, m.2; 785/8, m.3d).

Thorneton, Peter de (knight) died 9 May 1356

According to the pedigree in Ormerod, ii. 17, Sir Peter Thorneton was a cousin of **Ranulf Roter** (of Kingsley). He was married twice, the second time to Philippa Swynnerton, and had an extensive estate, consisting of the two manors of Thornton-le-Moors and Helsby, together with property in the area round Kingsley, and also in Wirral (*B.P.R.*, iii. 229; SC6 784/7, m.6). Despite his two marriages, he did not manage to father a male heir, and at his death in 1356 had had eight daughters. As he was a tenant of the earldom by military service, the

financial consequences of this situation greatly interested the prince's administrators. Of the eight daughters one, Mary, died without issue, and may have
predeceased her father. Another, Katherine, forfeited her share of the property,
for an unknown offence, not long after her father's death. Three, Ellen (the
mother of **Peter de Dutton 45.3**), Margaret, and Emma (the mother of **Matthew
de Weverham 45.3**) were already of age, and married, by 1356. That left the
prospects of the three others, Elizabeth, Maud and Beatrice, which were
profitably marketable.

Nineteen days after Thorneton's death, **Spridlyngton** (chief auditor) and **Burnham** were ordered to report on the current value of the inheritance and its value
before the Black Death, and the price that could be got for it, since people were
already sounding out the prince's council with offers. In particular, the value of
the wardships and marriages of the three younger daughters was to be stated.
They were both told to be present at the inquisition post mortem, since it was
suspected that plans were being made to falsify the ages of the two eldest heirs.
Letters of *diem clausit extremum* were sent to the escheator that same day, 27
May 1356 (*B.P.R.*, iii. 225–26). In fact, the complications of dealing with this
inheritance were very great, and it was not for over five years that the details
were sorted out.

First, on 4 June 1356, the manors of Thornton-le-Moors and Helsby were
delivered to the widow since she had held them jointly with her husband. Later
in the year she paid £40 for a licence to marry, – she subsequently married Sir
Thos de Dutton (*B.P.R.*, iii. 229, 231). By 28 Nov. 1356, the wardships of the
three younger girls had been sold – Maud (to Hen. de Beeston, for 85 marks:
Henry married her himself); Elizabeth (to Thos de Dutton for £86 13s. 4d.: she
was married to Hamo Fitton); Beatrice (to **Ranulf Roter** for 90 marks: she was
married to Thos de Sainsbury). Dutton also bought the land forfeited by
Katherine, for £100 (except for the Chester property, which was bought by **John
Delves**) (ibid., 231–32, 306). The prince's officials also made profit from the
underwood growing on the lands of the wards.

The importance of such investments in heritable land for prominent members of
the county community is illustrated by the tussle for the possession of Maud de
Thorneton. In Feb. 1358, Hen. Beeston claimed that while he was negotiating
the purchase of her wardship and marriage, associates of Thos de Dutton (who
had her in his temporary guardianship, presumably as county sheriff) caused her
to be affianced and contracted to Hugh, son of Geoff. de Dutton; Henry
managed to conclude the deal, and get possession of his new ward, whom he
then married himself (*B.P.R.*, iii. 297). On 1 December 1361, the business was
concluded when the county officials were ordered to partition the lands of Sir
Peter de Thorneton between the heirs (ibid., 426).

Thressk, Thomas de

Acted as attorney of **Wm, earl of Salisbury**, in his capacity of free tenant in Wirral and contributor to the puture of the foresters there, 1 Dec. 1361 (*B.P.R.*, iii. 433–34). A feoffee of Wm, earl of Salisbury, for the regrant of Hawarden manor, the stewardship of Chester, and Bosley and Neston manors, to the earl and his wife, 5 Feb. 1363 (ibid., 454).

Tieu, John le (Tewe; Tuwe)

Received grants, as 'B.P.'s servant', for good service in Gascony, of a general pardon, a licence to practise all trades in Middlewich, and exemption from assizes and juries, 18 May 1357 (*B.P.R.* iii. 239–40). Order to inquire into his complaint that he had suffered various wrongs, presumably in Cheshire, while he was in B.P.'s service in Gascony, 8 June 1357 (ibid., 249–50). Order to inquire into another complaint, this time that the burgesses of Middlewich were preventing him from enjoying the franchises granted in the town, 15 Aug. 1357 (ibid., 274). He submitted a further petition to the B.P., which does not survive, and which resulted in a third order to inquire on 28 Feb. 1358 (ibid., 298). Accounted as lieutenant of **Sir John Chandos**, as steward and bailiff of Longdendale lordship, 3 April 1359 – 26 Mar. 1361 (SC6 802/15, m.1d; 802/17, m.5; 803/3, m.4d).

Torfot, Henry died *c.* 1380

Bailiff of the manor of Frodsham, from 1349 to 1380.

He leased various pieces of the demesnes of Frodsham in the arrentation roll made *c.* 1346 (SC11 896). Accounted as bailiff of the manor of Frodsham, 1349–52 (SC6 801/14, m.1; *ChAcc*, pp. 159–60; SC6 783/17, m.8). With Wm Weston and two others, leased the fisheries of Were and Warthe (Frodsham manor), 1351–52 (SC6 783/17, m.8). Leased the greater part of the manor jointly with **Robt son of Ric. de Frodesham**, seven-year lease, 1352–59 (SC6 784/2, m.11; 784/4, m.2; 784/5, m.13; 784/7, m.2; 784/10, m.2; 785/1, m.2; 785/3, m.2). Accounted as bailiff of the part of Frodsham manor that was not leased, 1355–59 (SC6 784/7, m.9; 784/10, m.8; 785/1, m.10; 785/4, m.8). With **Peter de Northlegh** and two others leased the agistment and pannage of Delamere forest, Xmas 1359 to Xmas 1365 [six-year lease]; 1365–72 [seven-year lease] (SC6 785/5, m.2d; 785/8, m.3, 3d; 785/9, m.1d; 786/1, m.4; 786/3, m.4d; 786/5, m.2d; 786/6, m.3; 786/7, m.3; 786/8, m.3; 786/10, m.2d; 787/2, m.2, 2d; 787/4, m.2). He and six others (including **Ranulf le Roter**) made a recog. of £192 to B.P. for the lease of the same, 10 Jan. 1360 (*ChRR*, p. 473). Accounted again as bailiff of entire manor of Frodsham, 1359–60 (SC6 785/7, m.7). With Ranulf le Roter and John Fog, he bought all the livestock of Frodsham manor, 1360–61 (SC6 785/8, m.7). [The heading for the 1360–61 account is missing]. From 1361–62 Ranulf Roter leased the manor; 1362–63 his widow, **Nichola Roter**. Henry accounted as bailiff of the residue of the manor during these two financial years (SC6 785/9, m.6; 786/1, m.11) – the statement in this account (**5.2**) that he was joint-lessee with Roter appears to be a mistake. In 1362–63 he was fined £10 for neglecting to repair Holpool Gutter in Frodsham manor (SC6 786/1, m.10). Accounted as bailiff of entire manor of Frodsham, 1363–69; [account missing 1369–70]; 1370–74 (SC6 786/5, m.3; 786/6, m.2d; 786/7, m.4; 786/8, m.4; 786/10, m.4; 787/2, m.4; 787/4, m.3; 787/5, m.3; 787/7, m.3). With Thomas John's son, he approved 15⅓ acres of land in Wabmore, as freehold of Frodsham manor (SC6 786/3, m.5). In 1364–65 he bought the 'cropps' of three oaks from Delamere forest (SC6 786/5, m.2). On 9 Feb. 1365, he petitioned B.P. to be allowed to act as hereditary bailiff of Frodsham manor, complaining that he was being prevented from taking the dues called 'pelf'; he was instructed to make his claim in the county court, so that its judgement could be certified to B.P.'s council (*B.P.R.*, iii. 474–75). 20 Mar. 1365, he paid a 26s. 8d. fine for a burgage in Frodsham, with other properties (for 8s. 7d. a year rent) (*ChRR*, p. 473). Henry continued to account as bailiff until 1379–80 (this account being rendered by his executor, Ric. Torfot) Sharp, *Contributions*, Appendix, p. 177.

Tranemol, John de

Accounted as sheriff of Chester city, with Hen. Walsh, 1360–61 (SC6 785/8, m.1). He bought the sturgeon that had been caught off Puddington in 1362 (**9.7**).

Tranemol, Margaret de

B.P. granted her, a 'poor woman', a halfpenny a day for life, in his charitable grants made near the end of his first visit to Cheshire, 20 Sept. 1353 (*B.P.R.*, iii. 122).

Trussell, Warin (knight) died *c.* 1365

He was the brother of '**Sir Wm Trussell the uncle**', and uncle of '**Sir Wm Trussell the son**' (Ormerod, iii. 227). The manor of Willaston (Wirral) had been settled by Maud Trussel on Warin, her third son, in 1316/17 (ibid., 229). Ordered to pay 5 marks of the 10-mark fine imposed upon him for offences in Wirral forest, 24 Mar. 1351 (*B.P.R.*, iii. 11–13). On 18 July that year there is a reference to his 40s. 0d. fine in Wirral forest (ibid., 37). After representations by friends of 'Sir Wm Trussell and Sir Warin (his uncle)', the justices of the Cheshire forest eyre were ordered to examine their charter of franchises relating to the Cheshire forests, 13 [April] 1359 (ibid., 334). He complained that he had been fined £60 16s. 0d. for enclosing Willaston manor in Wirral forest, despite the licence to enclose granted to Sir Oliver de Burdeaux and Maud, his (second) wife – whose heir Warin is; order to examine his charter and, if it should not acquit him of the fine, B.P. pardoned him £60 of it 'by grace' and ordered that that sum be discharged in the common fine of Wirral forest, 10 June 1359; the order was repeated on 14 July following, with the addition that the sum, if pardoned, should be deducted from the community of Wirral's total fine, and that the property of Sir Warin seized for non-payment of the fine, or its true value, should be restored to him (ibid., 348, 353–54). Willaston manor was taken into B.P.'s hand on Sir Warin's death on supposition that it was held in chief; as it was found to have been held by him jointly with Maud, his wife, from Sir Thos Arden, by grand serjeanty, order to restore it to Maud, 7 July 1365 (ibid., 481).

Trussell, William ('the son'; of Warmingham; knight) died 12 Feb. 1380

The Trussell family had been involved in Cheshire administration since the early fourteenth century, when Sir Wm de Trussell had been justiciar of Chester, 1301/6, (Sharp, *Contributions*, Appendix, p. 5). There are two men of this name mentioned in the account: Sir Wm Trussell, lord of Warmingham (also called Sir Wm Trussell 'the son'), and Sir Wm Trussell of Kibblestone (normally called **Sir Wm Trussell 'the uncle'** – the ref. dated 14 July 1360, below, appears to refer to the son, rather than the uncle, however). The latter was the uncle of the former, and was the brother of **Sir Warin Trussell**. At his death on 12 Feb. 1380, Sir Wm Trussell the son held the manors of Warmingham, Ashton (by Kelsall) and North Rode (Ormerod, iii. 227; **8.9; 42.2**). His father, Sir John Trussell of Kibblestone (Staffs.) had entailed his manor of Warmingham upon him in 1337, and had been granted a licence to enclose and cultivate his wastes in Ashton (Delamere forest) and North Rode (Macclesfield forest) in 1336, and it may have been a confirmation of this charter that was being relied on in the 1363 law-suit from the Macclesfield forest eyre referred to in **42.2** (*ChRR*, p. 476; E163/4/47, m.15). 'Sir Wm son of John Trussell' was granted, with David de Calvylegh, the wardship and marriage of Ellen, sister and co-heiress of Ralph de Calvylegh, together with half Ralph's lands, 17 March 1352 (*ChRR*, p. 476).

He served on the Poitiers campaign as a knight bachelor of the prince, and was granted a £40 annuity from the Chester exchequer, for good service at the battle, on 16 Nov. 1363, (confirmed by the king on 15 Dec. following), together with a further 40 marks on 26 Aug. 1366 (Duchy of Cornwall Office, Henxteworth's *Jornale*, ff 3v, 4v; *B.P.R.*, iii. 461; *ChRR*, p. 476; *C.P.R., 1367–70*, pp. 45–46).

In May 1354, it appears that he had had part of the St Pierre inheritance in his hands, for the life of **Sir John St Pierre's** (unnamed) wife, who had recently died (*B.P.R.*, iii. 157). In March 1355, complaints were made to B.P.'s council that Wm's tenants of Ashton in Delamere forest had been abusing their rights of pasture in the forest, presumably granted by the 1336 charter (ibid., 195). On 9 Nov. 1355, he was granted letters of protection since he was in Gascony on the king's service, in the prince's company (ibid., 217). He and his uncle, Sir Warin Trussell, had not shown their charter relating to properties in the Cheshire forests to the prince's council by Apr. 1359 (presumably following the 1357 forest eyres), (ibid., 334). On 8 July 1359, 'Wm Trussell, the prince's bachelor' was granted a respite for the £80 owed by him for offences against the forest law in Cheshire (ibid., 352). The prince's council was to be given a copy of the forest eyre rolls which related to his property at its Midsummer meeting in 1360, so that the charters concerning his franchises could be determined (ibid., 384). On 14 July 1360, the chamberlain was ordered to respite the money owed by 'the prince's bachelor, Sir Wm Trussell of Cubblesdon' for his manors of Ashton and North Rode, until his claims before the justices of the forest were decided (ibid., 391). On 6 Feb. 1377, he acquired licence to purchase the reversion of some property of Thos Bradford in the vicinity of Chester, together with the serjeanty of the East Gate of the city (*ChRR*, p. 477).

Sir Wm Trussell the uncle's main sphere of operation was in Flintshire and North Wales (see the Biographical Note, p. 195). In May 1359, the justices of the forest eyre were instructed to allow 'Sir Wm Trussell of Cublesdon, the uncle' to make his claims in the eyre, if he should want to. It is not clear which property that could refer to, since the manor of Willaston (in Wirral forest) appears to have been held by **Sir Warin Trussell**, the other uncle of Sir Wm T. of Warmingham (Ormerod, ii. 544).

Wakebrugg, William de

Retained by B.P. as serjeant pleader in the counties of Chester and Flint, and elsewhere, from Mich. 1353, at £5 a year; order to pay him his fee for the previous year, and then annually, 13 Nov. 1354 (*B.P.R.*, iii. 180). Order to pay him, and Wm. Banastre, £8 for their labour in the recent (1357) Cheshire forest eyres out of the eyres' issues, 8 July 1358 (ibid., 304).

Walker, Hugh le

Reference to his tenure of property in Hope town, 14 Sept. 1358 (*ChRR*, p. 67; *B.P.R.*, iii. 316).

Warrewik, John de d. 1360

A Wirral landowner, lieutenant of the sheriff of Anglesey and constable of Beaumaris castle.

Between 1326 and 1351, he was involved in 11 recognizances, probably concerned with leases of tithes of St John's and St Peter's churches, Chester (*ChRR*, p. 509). He appears as constable of Beaumaris and sheriff of Anglesey in the 1343 fealty roll (D.L. Evans, 'Some Notes on the History of the Principality of Wales in the Time of the Black Prince [1343–1376]', *Trans. Hon. Soc. Cymmrodorion*, 1925–26, p. 32). 'John de Werwyk' to pay £20 of the £40 fine imposed on him for offences in Wirral forest, 24 March 1351 (*B.P.R.*, iii.

12). Complaint that the imprisonment of him and others, for hunting in Wirral forest, was against their immemorial customs, 18 May 1351 (ibid., 25). On 3 June 1351, as part of a general 'sounding out' exercise, he was asked whether he would be prepared to pay his £20 fine for trespasses in Wirral forest (ibid., 30). On 18 July following, a fine of 10 marks imposed on him for trespasses in Wirral forest (ibid., 38). Ref. to him as former lieutenant of **Wm Trussell** of Kibblestone, as sheriff of Anglesey and constable of Beaumaris castle, 23 July 1351 (ibid., 39). Petition by several (unnamed) men, who had been found to be villeins at John's suit rather than avowrymen, for reversal of the proceedings; order to inquire, 27 Jan. 1355 (ibid., 188–89). Complaint by him that his property in Upton and Frankby had been seized by the escheator as held in chief; order to inquire 7 July 1359 (ibid., 351–52). A *sicut alias* writ of *diem clausit extremum* issued on the death of 'John de Warrewik the father', 9 May 1360; new writ issued 15 Feb. 1362, followed by a *sicut alias*, 8 July following (ibid., 438, 447, 381). Order concerning the lands of Margery, his widow, 1 Oct. 1363 (ibid., 462).

Warrewik, Thomas de died 7 March 1364

Constable of Chester castle, from 1325 to 1364 (with interruptions).

He was first granted the office of constable of Chester castle on 10 May 1325 by Edward III when he was still earl of Chester; after his accession, the king confirmed the appointment on 16 May 1328; it was extended for Thomas's life in 1344 (*C.P.R., 1340–43*, p. 8; SC6 784/7, m.2). Thomas lost the office subsequently. In the 1342–43 receiver's account, Ric. de Merton appears as constable of Chester castle; he could have been Warwick's (resident) under-constable, or there may have been another, unrecorded hiatus in Warwick's tenure of the office (*ChAcc*, p. 118). He had certainly been dismissed before Midsummer 1348, since Ric. de Fouleshurst held the constableship at that date at farm for £40 a year. Thos Garlek succeeded him at Mich. 1348 (ibid., 121–22). It was next held by **Ric. Doune**, who accounted as lessee of the office in 1351–52, but he forfeited it for maladministration and extortion on 16 Aug. 1353 (SC6 783/17, m.1; *B.P.R.*, iii. 194). Thos de Bradegate, who had fought on the Crécy campaign, was appointed by B.P. orally 20 Aug. 1353 (SC6 784/2, m.1). The office of constable of Chester castle for life was restored to Thos by the B.P., in accordance with his father's previous grant, at 12d a day, by letters dated 26 June 1355, which took effect from the Xmas following (*B.P.R.*, iii. 205; SC6 784/7, m.2). On 7 June 1356, it was ordered that he be paid his wages from the date of the grant of the office, despite the fact that he did not come to Chester until long afterwards; this was in response to the king's wish, expressed to the lieutenant and chamberlain in letters under the secret seal, 7 June 1356 (*B.P.R.*, iii. 227). Ordered to guard Master Benet ab Iorwerth in Chester castle with maximum security, 6 Feb. 1358 (ibid., 291). He forfeited the office on 6 April 1359 because of Master Benet's escape; he was restored a second time, on 26 Oct. 1359 (to hold at B.P.'s pleasure, at 12d. a day) (ibid., 374–75). References to him acting as constable, 17 May and 22 June 1362 (ibid., 446–47). Died 7 March 1364 (SC6 786/3, m.3).

Wasteneys, William died *c.* 1357

Recipient of general pardon, 28 June 1349 (*ChRR*, p. 510). Order to levy the debts owed the abbot of Chester by him, and others of Macclesfield hundred, 11 April 1351 (*B.P.R.*, iii. 18). Charged 13s. 4d. for having the sheriff's aid, in the county sheriff's account 1351–52 (SC6 783/17, m.3). With **John de Wetenhale** of Dorfold, Wm de Wetenhale of Alpraham, and **Alex. Deneys**, made a recog. to Sir John de Chorleton, junior, for £10, 26 Sept. 1352 (*ChRR*, p. 144). On 23 April 1354, with Thos de Venables, made a recog. for £20 to B.P. (ibid., p. 510). In 1355, with Edmund de Cotton, made a recog. to Thos de Ardene for £1,000 (ibid.) Inquiry in 1355/56 found that Cecily, widow of Wm de Wasteneys (this Wm's father), gave the manor of Elton to Sir John de Ardene to gain support in the quarrel between herself and **Peter de Thorneton** (*D.K.R. 28*, p. 57). Wm was charged a fine of £10 in the 1354–55 escheator's account for this alienation (SC6 784/5, m.7). On 4 June 1356, order to impose a lenient fine for what was only a technical offence, (*B.P.R.*, iii. 227). Wm was killed in 1356 (or early 1357), and **John de Elton**'s father was indicted of the death (ibid., 235–36). Writ of *diem clausit extremum* issued after his death, 15 March 1357 (ibid., 237). Order to inquire into Sir Thos Arden's claims in Wm's lands, 28 May 1357 (ibid., 243). On 16 June 1357 Katherine, Wm's widow, and 6 others made a recog. to B.P. for £12 odd to have a meadow in Elton moss which used to belong to Wm (*ChRR*, p. 510). She claimed that Wm's lands in Elton had been re-enfeoffed to her husband and herself in tail, and that they should not, therefore, have been seized on the ground that the heir is a minor; order to inquire 16 July 1357 (*B.P.R.*, iii. 260). Wardship of John, son and heir of Wm. de W. granted to Ric. de Sutton, king's yeoman, to be held until the heir's majority, quit of what is due to the B.P. in respect of Delamere forest, 5 Sept. 1358 (ibid., 307; *ChRR*, p. 459). Sutton granted licence to dig turves anywhere on the moor in the Wasteneys' lands, by B.P.'s special grace, 28 Aug 1359 (*B.P.R.*, iii. 364). Sutton had granted Katherine 2 marks a year for the keep of her son, and the B.P. granted it to Sutton, 19 Oct. 1359 (ibid., 372–73). Complaint by Sutton that he was still being distrained to pay part of the common fine of Delamere forest; order to repay him, and respite the fine until the heir's majority, 1 June 1360 (ibid., 382). Further complaint by Sutton, this time that extortions and trespasses had been committed against him in the Wasteneys' lands; order to inquire at the next visit of the auditors to Cheshire, 20 May 1361 (ibid., 418).

Wetenhale, John de (of Dorfold) died *c.* 1361

It is particularly difficult to relate the information provided by the record evidence to the pedigree of the Wettenhall family given in Ormerod, ii. 195.

Ormerod identifies four branches of the family in the 14th century: the Wetenhales of Cholmondeston (iii. 367), of Nantwich (iii. 479), of Wettenhall (ii. 195, iii. 479), and of Dorfold (ii. 195). None of the linkages inspires much confidence, and there is little correspondence with the list of no fewer than 17 members of the family who appeared as supporters of **Sir John St Pierre** in 1351 in his feud with the Maistressons (*B.P.R.*, iii. 61). Of these, four were called Thomas, three William, three Peter, three Ranulf, and two John. They fall into eight family groups (either as brothers, or as fathers and sons) but with no geographical locations given for them. One of the groups was John Wettenhall of Dorfold and his brothers, Peter and Thomas. It is likely that it was this Thomas who achieved fame in the wider world, as seneschal of the Rouergue, in the principality of Aquitaine, between 1364 and 1369 (Morgan, *War and Society*, p. 134; Bennett, *Community, Class*, p. 180).

It is not possible to be sure of the identity of the John de Wetenhale mentioned in **15**, or the Ranulf son of John de Wetenhale referred to in **12.8**. The latter was possibly a member of another branch of the family, the Wettenhalls of Church Minshull, apparently unnoticed by Ormerod. It may have been Ranulf's father (John) who leased the hundred of Nantwich for three years, for £20, with Matt. de Fouleshurst, on 2 Dec. 1357 (*B.P.R.*, iii. 285). Again, it could have been this John who acted as the pledge of **Alex. Deneys** in **15**. With such a superfluity of Wettenhalls, and the difficulty of making the information in the Black Prince's Register correspond with Ormerod's jejune pedigrees, this must be conjectural at the moment.

John de Wetenhale of Dorfold was the second son of Sir John de Wetenhale, the younger, lord of Wettenhall, who died in 21 Edward III (Ormerod, ii. 195). His father appears to have settled the manor of Dorfold on him. John leased the Grosvenor bailiwick in the forest of Delamere in 1351–52 (SC6 783/17, m.1d). The wardship and marriage of Ric., the heir of Ric. Grosvenor, had been bought from the B.P. by Peter de Wetenhale (presumably John's brother). After Peter's death, John acted as his executor, and had sold the wardship to Robt de Pulle by 16 Feb. 1353 (*B.P.R.*, iii. 92). On 3 Mar. 1361, the escheator was ordered to hand the wardship of the heir of 'John de Wetenhale' to John Pecche of London, who had purchased it from the B.P. (ibid., 412). An inquiry was held 4 May 1361, after John of Dorfold's death, into whether he had enfeoffed certain of his lands to **Ranulf de Becheton** (parson of Woodchurch) and **Wm de Blaken** (chaplain) in order to re-enfeoff them to himself and Agnes, his wife, and to their son, Thomas. (The order to inquire was repeated 21 Dec. 1361). The charter cited in **16.2** must refer to this transaction. On the same day, Thos de Wetenhale was allowed to hold all the lands seized on account of the minority of Ric., son and heir of John de Wetenhale of Dorfold, until their future was decided (ibid., 416–17, 437; *D.K.R. 28.* p. 61). This suggests that this Thos (also described as the prince's yeoman), in whose interest the charters of pardon and licence to alienate were granted, was not the son of John, (as suggested in

Morgan, *War and Society*, p. 134), since that Thos had, presumably, pre-deceased his father. Possibly he was John's younger brother. On 20 Oct. 1361, it was stated that 'the prince's yeoman, Thos de Wetenhale,' had made a recog. for £40 to B.P. for the lands of John de W., and its execution was to be postponed (*B.P.R.*, iii. 424–25). There followed an order to withdraw this recog. (which had been made by Thos, together with Wm Munshull and Wm de Wetenhale of Alpraham), since the inquiry had been held by then, 24 Aug. 1362 (ibid., 451).

Weverham, Matthew de 1342 to *c.* 1398

Born round about Lady Day 1342; Sir Matthew de Chetulton was his godfather (Ormerod, ii. 115). Accused by **Wm de Stanley** of being one of a group of armed men under **Ranulf le Roter** who had threatened him when exercising his office in Wirral forest; order to inquire 28 Nov. 1360 (*B.P.R.*, iii. 401). Thos de Frodesham allowed to pay by instalments the £18 6s. 8d. in arrears of the £23 owed for the marriage of Matthew, 1 Dec. 1361 (ibid., 427). Order to deliver to 'Matthew son of Ric. de Weverham' his lands as he had come of age, 24 Oct. 1363 (ibid., 460). Dead in or before 1398, leaving three daughters and a widow, Beatrice (daughter of John de Ardene) whom he had married in 1374 (*ChRR*, p. 511). In Ormerod, ii. 116, it is stated that Matthew was the son of Hugh de Weverham, which must be incorrect.

Whetelegh, Alan de

With **Stephen de Kelshale** appointed auditor of the accounts in dispute between Adam Lorymer of Buckingham and Roger Skiret, his groom, who had been trading on Adam's behalf, 30 April 1353 (*B.P.R.*, iii. 103). Petitioned B.P. for the return of 9 shops in Chester, bought from Ric. Wade, 18 March 1354 (ibid., 154). Accounted as mayor of Chester, 1360–64 (SC6 785/5, m.4; 785/9, m.2; 786/1, m.2; 786/3, m.3). When mayor, acted as escheator of the city of Chester, 13 Nov. 1360, 14, 21 Feb., 7 July, 1 Dec. 1361 (*B.P.R.*, iii. 396, 405, 408–9, 421, 426).

Whitelegh, Richard de

Sheriff of Cheshire, 1361 to 1367.

Granted pardon on 2 Dec. 1357 for acquiring land in Antrobus from the duke of Lancaster, on account of his long and good service under the sheriffs of Cheshire; order to make out letters of pardon 15 Feb. 1358 (*B.P.R.*, iii. 285, 292–93; *ChRR*, p. 522). His appointment as keeper of the duke of Lancaster's franchises in Cheshire, which had been seized into B.P.'s hands, cancelled 28 Feb. 1359 (*B.P.R.*, iii. 331). Appointed sheriff of Cheshire, at B.P.'s pleasure, at £20 a year, 4 Dec. 1361 (ibid., 428). Accounted as sheriff, 1361–67 (SC6 785/9, m.4d; 786/1, m.9; 786/3, m.11; 786/5, m.6d; 786/6, m.6d; 786/7, m.5). On 12 Oct. 1365, commissioned as sheriff, with three others, to arrest those people of

Lancashire making a ferry across the Mersey by the destroyed Warrington bridge (*ChRR*, p. 522).

Wilaston, Robert de

With his wife, Margery, sued by Adam de Praers for land in Cheshire; Adam claimed that they were unlawfully delaying the trial of the suit, 28 Nov. 1353 (*B.P.R.*, iii. 134).

Wiluhby (Willughby) Richard de (knight, justice of the Common Pleas) d. 1362

A landowner with property in Notts. and Derbys., he had served on the Irish bench in the 1320s, from which he was dismissed in 1327. He was appointed a puisne justice of the Common Pleas 6 Mar. 1328, and transferred to the King's Bench 15 Dec. 1330, where he served as chief justice from 1338 to 1340. Like **Wm Shareshull** he fell victim to the 1340 purge, after which he was re-appointed puisne justice of the Common Pleas on 9 Oct. 1341, in which office he served until his retirement in 1357 (*D.N.B.*, lxii. 40–41; G.O. Sayles, ed., *Select Cases in the Court of King's Bench*, Selden Soc., 82 (1965), pp. xvi–xvii).

He clearly acted as a legal specialist member of the prince's council in the 1350s, although much less prominently than Shareshull. It was originally intended that he should hold a forest eyre for Cheshire on 19 Aug. 1353, alongside the general eyre to be held by Shareshull and Hillary (*B.P.R.*, iii. 111). However, this eyre was postponed as part of the agreement between the prince and the magnates of Cheshire, which preceded the grant of the common fine of 5,000 marks, on the grounds that ten years had not elapsed since the last forest eyre (in 1347) (ibid., 112). A reference dated 28 Nov. 1353 confirms that the preliminary investigations which formed part of the 1353 forest eyre had been held before the postponement was granted (ibid., 133). On 3 Dec. 1353, Wiluhby was granted £33 6s. 8d., out of the proceeds of the trailbaston sessions, by B.P. for his expenses in coming to, and returning from, Cheshire (ibid., 136).

On 22 Aug. 1357, notification was given that the postponed forest eyre was to be held eight days before Mich. 1357, by ordinance of the prince's council made when **John Delves** was previously in London; the justices were to be Wiluhby, Delves and **Sir Ric. Stafford** (ibid., 275; CHES 33/6). Considerable opposition from the forest communities was anticipated, and on 16 Sept. 1357, Wingfield informed the justices that he had been told that a confederacy of Cheshire people had been planned to pervert the inquiries in the eyre, and they were told to postpone the session if it should prove necessary (*B.P.R.*, iii. 278). The eyre continued to hold sessions through 1358 and into 1359, and the last order to the justices was dated 26 May 1359, when they were told to receive the claims of **Sir Wm Trussell** of Kibblestone 'at their next sessions' (ibid., 338). Most of the references to the eyre up to that date concern petitions of landowners in connection with privileges they claimed within the forest, negotiations of fines by individuals and communities, and complaints of injustice (ibid., 283, 285–87, 291, 294, 298, 312, 315, 335–38). The last business to be cleared up following the eyre was the set of claims by **Wm de Stanlegh, the younger** in connection with his office of master forester of Wirral, determined on 5 Dec. 1361 (ibid., 432, 435).

Worth, Robert (of Tytherington)

With Hugh de Foxwist, pledged **Robt de Foxwyst's** fine of £40; referred to on 7 July 1354 (*B.P.R.*, iii. 172). Accounted as deputy to **John de Somerford**, as gaoler of Macclesfield and collector of revenue within the forest, 1359–60, 1361–62, 1363–64 (SC6 802/17, m.1; 803/5, m.1; 803/9, m.1). As Somerford's deputy, fined 13s. 4d. for non-payment of arrears on the account for 1363–64, and gaoled for over £40 arrears when that account was audited in Jan. 1365 (SC6 803/9, m.1d). He was probably the younger brother of **Thos Worth**.

Worth, Thomas de died *c.* 1362

Acted as forester in Macclesfield forest, 24 March 1351; did homage and fealty for his office, 25 Oct. following (*B.P.R.*, iii. 15, 43). Dead by 24 Aug. 1362 (ibid., 451–52). Katherine, his widow, sued Wm de Hulm (her grandson – see Ormerod, iii. 700) and his wife for her dower in Macclesfield and other places, 1362/63 (*D.K.R. 28*, pp. 61–62). **Robt Worth** was probably his younger brother (Ormerod, iii. 700).

Wyrlegh, Hugh de

Appointed rider of Delamere and Mondrum, at 3d. a day, 29 April 1362; order to pay his wages 14 May (*B.P.R.*, iii. 443; *ChRR*, p. 545). Acted with others to sell wind-fallen oaks for the B.P. in Delamere forest, 1361–62 (SC6 785/9, m.1). Referred to as 'late rider', 1364–65 (SC6 786/5, m.2d).

Yong, Thomas le (yeoman) died *c.* 1361

Escheator of Cheshire and Flintshire, 1352/61, sheriff of Cheshire 1359/61.

He was appointed escheator of Cheshire and Flintshire, and steward of the demesne manors and towns of Cheshire (except for Chester and Macclesfield) on 1 Oct. 1352. His wages, of 2d. a day for the escheatry, and 40s. 0d. a year for the stewardship, were surprisingly low. (*B.P.R.*, iii. 78). As steward, he witnessed the hoeing of the corn of Drakelow manor in 1353–54 (SC6 784/4, m.1). His fee was increased to 10 marks a year, backdated from Mich. 1356, and then to £10 a year from 1357–58, 21 July 1357 (*B.P.R.*, iii. 268). He accounted as steward and manager of the lordship of Longdendale, 1357–58, and together with **Robert Legh** (the elder) received the fealty of the freeholders of the lordship in 1359 (SC6 785/7, m.9d; 802/15, m.1). He was appointed, in addition, sheriff of Cheshire, at the usual fee (i.e. £20 a year) on 1 Oct. 1359 (*B.P.R.*, iii. 369). On 16 July 1360, B.P. gave him three oaks from Macclesfield forest (ibid., 391).

His sheriff's account for 1360–61 was audited on 11 May 1362, his escheator's account the following day, when his clerk represented him; it appears that he had died not long before 20 Oct. 1361, the date of the last order addressed to him in the Register (SC6 785/8, mm.5, 8; *B.P.R.*, iii. 424).

FLINTSHIRE

Balle, Reginald

One of bailiffs of Hope, 1349–50 (*FMA (2)*, p. 29). Keeper of park of Llwydcoed, 1349–50 (ibid., p. 27). Mayor of the borough and constable of the castle of Hope, 1352–53 (ibid., p. 97), 1361–62 (SC6 1186/21, m.1), 1362–63 (U.C.N.W. Bodrhyddan 562). With another, leased agistment of Estyn (Rusty) forest for 3 years at 60s. p.a., payable to **Ric. de Stafford**, knt., 16 Aug. 1359 (*ChRR*, p. 209). With 7 others, made recog. to Stafford for £344 10s., to be void if he and his fellows were removed from the lease of Hope town, held of Stafford as lord of Hope and Hopedale, 16 Jan. 1368 (*ChRR*, pp. 19–20). The Balles were a prominent family in the town (U.C.N.W. Bodrhyddan MSS and Bodrhyddan Add. MSS).

Birchover, Ithel de died *c.* 1371

Burgess of Flint. Farmed pleas and perquisites of the Flint courts at £5 p.a., 1349–50 (*FMA (2)*, p. 37); do., 1350–51 (ibid., p. 61); do. for 6 years at £6 6s. 8d. p.a. 6 Oct. 1357 (*ChRR*, p. 37). Bailiff of Flint, 1355–56 (SC6 1186/13). One of those commissioned to take wid. of Ithel ap Cynwrig Sais into safe custody, 11 May 1365 (*B.P.R.*, iii. 478). Appointed escheator of Flintshire during pleasure, 30 Sept. 1365 (*ChRR*, p. 37). Succeeded as escheator by s. John, 1368–69 (SC6 1187/11). Dead by 1371 when exors. were being sued (CHES 30/11, m.16). His name suggests that he was partly Welsh.

Bleddyn ap Gwenllian ferch Bleddyn ap Madog

Of Ystrad Alun. May have been s. of **Dafydd ab Ithel Fychan**. In 1349 Madog ab Ieuaf ap Hwfa conveyed a messuage and lands in Llys-y-coed and lands in nine other townships to Dafydd and Bleddyn with remainder to the heirs of Bleddyn and in default to Bleddyn and Tudur ab Ithel Fychan (U.C.N.W. Mostyn 2173). This may have been a means of ensuring that Dafydd's lands passed to his s. who was illegitimate in the eyes of the law since Dafydd was a cleric. Bleddyn ap Dafydd ab Ithel Fychan made fine for acquiring 10 acres in Dolfechlas without licence, 15 Mar. 1361 (CHES 30/10, m.2d).

Cynwrig ap Bleddyn ap Madog

Clerk. Of stock of Edwin (P.C. Bartrum, *Welsh Genealogies A.D. 300–1400*, Edwin 8). Quit of suit to county, hundred and tourn while receiver of issues of escheat lands in Englefield, 14 Sept. 1358 (*B.P.R.*, iii. 317). Granted 5 acres in Rhuddlan by the prince, 22 Aug. 1359 (*ChRR*, p. 315). Executor of will of bro. Ithel, late portionary rector of Northop, 2 Mar. 1383 (CHES 30/13, m.3). Sued over lands in Gronant and claimed 1369 grant from Black Prince, 28 Mar. 1390 (CHES 30/14, m. 3). Order to conduct him from Chester castle, where he was

then confined, to Rhuddlan castle, 27 May 1390 (*ChRR*, p. 315). See also
B.P.R., iii. 310, 315.

Cynwrig ap Roppert ab Iorwerth

Of stock of Ednywain Bendew (Bartrum, Ednywain Bendew 3). Farmed
Caerwys with Ednyfed ab Ieuan for 6 years at 24 marks p.a. and to maintain
millpond at own expense, 10 Aug. 1358 (*ChRR*, p. 409). The grant was renewed
for 3 years at the same farm, 30 Sept. 1364 (ibid.) and for 3 years at £16 6s. 8d.
p.a., 30 Sept. 1367 (ibid.). Steward of Caerwys with Heilin Goch during
pleasure, 1 Oct. 1380 (ibid.). Farmed offices of sheriff of Flintshire and
constable of Flint for 3 years at £46 13s. 4d. p.a. and raglotry of Englefield for 3
years at £64 p.a. and 20 marks p.a. for maintenance of justiciar and chamberlain,
with proviso that he appoint an Englishman as deputy-constable, 30 Sept. 1360
(ibid.), and appointed on same day to investigate breaches of Statute of
Labourers. Coroner of Englefield, 1375 (CHES 30/11, m. 39).

Dafydd ab Ithel Fychan d. 1368

Of the stock of Edwin (Bartrum, Edwin 16). One of the sons of Ithel Fychan of
Halkyn. A cleric: rector of Cilcain, 1345 (U.C.N.W. Mostyn 2472) and of 3 parts
of the portionary church of Northop where he had succeeded his bro. Ithel
Person by 1347 (CHES 30/8, m.57d). He had at least 2 ss., **Bleddyn** (q.v.) and
Dafydd, known as Dafydd Whitmore. First appears as witness to a deed, 1330
(U.C.N.W. Mostyn 2490). Involved in the activities of his bro. Cynwrig Sais and
amerced 100 marks, 26 Nov. 1341 (CHES 30/8, m. 4, *FMA (2)*, pp. 11–12). With
his bros. quitclaimed interest in Gronant marsh to prince, 16 Feb. 1349 (CHES
30/8, m.5d; *FMA (2)*, pp. xxxiv–xxxv). With bros. petitioned the prince against
Rhys ap Roppert, 20 Nov. 1352 (*B.P.R.*, iii. 80). Accused of illegal occupation
of escheat lands and acquitted, 25 July 1356 (CHES 30/9, m. 24). With co-rector
Cynwrig ab Ithel summoned to answer the prince about presentation of clerk to
free chapel of Flint which was in his gift, 11 Mar. 1359 (CHES 30/9, m.41;
B.P.R., iii. 324). Exor. of Thos Geffray, 1343 (CHES 30/8, m.16) and of bro.
Ithel Person, 1350 (CHES 30/8, m.83). Acquired lands in Englefield, 1330/49
(U.C.N.W. Mostyn 2003–4, 2154–55, 2169–73, 2198–2200, 2565, 3238, 3322)
and witness to many deeds to which bros. were parties. Dead by 18 Sept. 1368
(CHES 30/8, m.4).

Dafydd ab Ithel Person

Nephew of **Dafydd ab Ithel Fychan** and son of Ithel Person ab Ithel
Fychan, portionary rector of Northop (d. 1341). Member of inquisition which
found that men of Maelor Saesneg, Hope and Hopedale owed one-third of the
mise of 1,000 marks due from the whole county community, 28 Sept. 1349
(CHES 30/8, m.77). Made fine of 10 marks for acquiring land without licence,

1349–50 (*FMA (2)*, p. 24). Coroner of Englefield, 1350 (CHES 30/8, m.83d); had ceased to be coroner by 1356 (CHES 30/9, m.23d). Bound over to keep the peace towards Ieuan le Taillour of Caerwys, 20 June 1351 (CHES 30/8, m.85). Action brought against him by cousin Einion ab Ieuan ab Ithel over fostering his son and over land, 25 July 1356 (CHES 30/9, m.24d). Involved with s. Rhys Wyn in affray at Rhuddlan, 22 Oct. 1369 (CHES 25/24, m.6d). Plaintiff in action over detention of horse, 26 Sept. 1373 (CHES 30/11, m.26). Still living 1388 (*ChRR*, p. 25). Pledge on various occasions.

Ithel ap Bleddyn ab Ithel Anwyl

Of stock of Edwin (Bartrum, Edwin 12). Keeper of wood of Ewloe, 1349–50 (*FMA (2)*, p. 26). Farmed coal mines in lands of manor of Ewloe and lands formerly of his father there at £5 6s. 8d. p.a., 1350–51 (ibid., p. 59). Farmed coal mines in Ewloe for 1 year at 10 marks p.a., 30 Sept. 1354 (*ChRR*, p. 260). Farmed coal mine on lands which he holds of prince in Ewloe at 4 marks p.a. for as long as it can be worked, 8 Sept. 1358 (ibid.) Farmed other coal mines in Ewloe for 6 years at 6 marks p.a., 28 Sept. 1358 (ibid.) Farm renewed for a further 6 years, 1 Oct. 1364 (ibid.) Farmed manor of Ewloe with Thos Peytevyn, knt. 1367 (ibid.) Bailiff, with Ieuan Bongam, of township of Coleshill from 1350–51 (*FMA (2)*, p 50); still bailiff, 1366–67 (SC6 1187/8). Escheator [of Englefield] in Flintshire during pleasure, 3 Dec. 1357 (*B.P.R.*, iii. 288). With his wife Gwenhwyfar, made fine of 20 marks for acquiring 10 carucates in Northop, Wepre, etc. without licence, 16 May 1354 (ibid., 165). Sued over lands in Northop, 13 Sept. 1372 (CHES 30/11, m.20). Granted protection by the king on his departure to the coast to stay there for the defence of the realm, 27 Sept. 1386 (*ChRR*, p. 260).

Llywelyn ap Madog ab Elis d. 1375

Bishop of St. Asaph, 1357/75. Son of Madog ab Elis of Llangar, one of barons of Edeirnion in Merioneth and a descendant of Madog ap Maredudd of Powys (d. 1160). One of the few remaining members of the native Welsh aristocracy (A.D. Carr, 'The barons of Edeyrnion, 1282–1485' in *Jnl. Mer. Hist. & Rec. Soc.* iv (1964), pp. 294–95). Llywelyn was dean of St. Asaph, 1357, when he was elected bishop (*Fasti*, xi. 43). Chamberlain of Chester ordered to deliver mitres, vestments, etc. of his predecessor to him, 5 July 1358 (*B.P.R.*, iii. 303–4). Lieutenant-justiciar ordered to deliver two consecrated rings of his predecessor and a load of lead to him, 9 Sept. 1358 (ibid., 310). Complained that the sheriff was forcing his tenants to attend the tourn, 4 Feb. 1364 (ibid., 473). Made fine of £100 for licence to make a will, 16 May 1366 (*ChRR*, p. 9). Involved in action over advowson of Northop, 5 June, 18 Sept., 18 Dec. 1368 (CHES 30/11, mm.1, 4, 5). Appeared at sessions to answer writ of *quo warranto*, 9 Sept. 1370 (CHES 30/11, m.12). Dead by 24 Nov. 1375 (*Fasti*, xi. 37). Left instructions for his burial in the choir of his cathedral next to the high altar on the gospel side (will, 18 Jan.

1373 in Browne Willis, *Survey of the Cathedral Church of St Asaph* (1720), pp. 53–54).

Stoke, John de

Burgess of Rhuddlan. Bailiff of Rhuddlan, 1349–50, 1350–51, 1351–52 (*FMA (2)*, pp. 25, 52, 82). One of farmers of half pleas and perquisites of town, 15 June 1351 (*ChRR*, p. 452). Farmed pleas and perquisites of courts of Rhuddlan for 4 years at £12 p.a., 30 Sept. 1353 (ibid.) With wife Alice, petitioned prince concerning lands of John le Mercer of Chester who d. without heirs, 10 Feb. 1355 (*B.P.R.*, iii. 189). Granted the lands of John le Mercer and reversion of the dower of his wid. Agnes at fine of £50, 14 July 1357 (*ChRR*, p. 452) and lieutenant-justiciar and chamberlain ordered to deliver the lands to him (*B.P.R.*, iii. 270). Pleas and perquisites of Rhuddlan courts farmed by him and others for 4 years at £12 p.a., 30 Sept. 1357 (*ChRR*, p. 403). With the whole commonalty of the town of Rhuddlan, farmed the town for 6 years at 20 marks p.a., 20 Oct. 1367 (ibid., p. 452).

Trussell, William (knight) ('the uncle'; of Kibblestone; knight)

Known as 'the uncle' to distinguish him from his nephew, also Sir William (Ormerod, iii. 229). Granted townships of Cleifiog and Llanllibio (Anglesey) for life, 3 Jan. 1334 (*C.C.R., 1333–1337*, p. 196) and described as 'king's yeoman'. Given custody of Beaumaris castle, 18 Nov. 1333 (*C.P.R., 1330–1334*, p. 480). Sheriff of Anglesey, 4 Feb. 1334 (*C.F.R., 1327–1337*, p. 386) and for life, 1 Oct. 1334 (ibid., 420). Constable of Beaumaris for life (ibid.). Payment of Anglesey arrears respited because he was going abroad in the king's company, 22 June 1338 (*C.C.R., 1337–1339*, p. 514). Allowed to nominate a competent sub-sheriff during his absence, 19 Dec. 1337 (ibid., p. 222). Ceased to be sheriff, relinquished townships and granted Ewloe at £7 6s. 7d. p.a., 10 Mar. 1350 (*FMA (2)*, pp. 36–37). Permitted to pay off Anglesey and Beaumaris arrears over the next 2 years, 23 July 1351 (*B.P.R.*, iii. 39). See also *B.P.R.*, iii. 67, 85, 338; other references are prob. to his nephew, **Sir William Trussell the son.**

William (Gwilym) ap Llywelyn

Appointed *rhaglaw* of Mallaen and Maenordeilo commotes in Carmarthenshire by the prince at the request of Sir John Chandos, 1361 (*B.P.R.*, iii. 404). Probably William ap Llywelyn Ddu or William ap Llywelyn Fychan, constable of Maenordeilo, 1353–55, and of Mallaen and Maenordeilo, 1361. Also bedell of Mallaen, 1326–28, 1332–33, 1335, and constable of Mallaen, 1335–38, 1352–54, 1355–57 (R.A. Griffiths, *The Principality of Wales in the Later Middle Ages: the Structure and Personnel of Government I: South Wales, 1277–1536* (1972), pp. 386, 380, 381, 388).

APPENDIX 1

List of the Accounts of the Chamberlains of Chester, 1301 to 1374

This list begins with the published accounts, and starts with the name of the chamberlain and the period of each account. Then, after *a.*, follows the reference number of the unpublished account. In the case of SC6 accounts, the original class (as witnessed by the ink-stamps) is given in bold, in square brackets. The reference to the published version of the Cheshire portion of that account follows after *b.i.*, and the Flintshire portion after *b.ii.* Major corrections and omissions from the Cheshire portions in *ChAcc* are indicated in *b.i.* (preceded by *CORR*), where appropriate. From 1360 onwards, there follows a simple list of the remaining unpublished accounts which survive up to 1374, the last one for the Black Prince's time. All documents are in the form of rolls sewn chancerywise, unless otherwise stated.

1. Account of William de Meltone, chamberlain of Chester, 7 February to Mich. 1301.

    a. National Library of Wales, Wynnstay MS 86.
    b. *Cheshire in the Pipe Rolls*, pp. 189–220.

This is the only complete transcript of a chamberlain's account hitherto published. There is no translation.

2. Account of William de Melton, chamberlain of Chester, 1301–2.

    a. SC6 771/1 [**Treasury of the Exchequer**] 9 mm.

This account runs from the *morrow* of Michaelmas (30 September) 1301 to Michaelmas (29 September) 1302.

    b. i. *ChAcc*, pp. 1–14.

CORR. p. 13. The 'Sum Total of the said purchases' . . . (£1,014 6s. 8¼d.) should read £1,104 6s. 8¼d. (*FMA(1)*, p. 20, mistakenly prints this sum as '£1,114 6s. 8¼d').

This translation is reasonably full, although it omits the Flintshire receipts. Later *ChAcc* accounts generally have considerable omissions.

    b. ii. *FMA(1)*, pp. 3–20.

3. Account of William de Melton, chamberlain of Chester, 1302–3.

    a. SC6 771/2 [**Q.R.**] 8 mm.
    b. i. *ChAcc*, pp. 15–27.

CORR. p. 24. 'carrying the letters of Sir William de Bliburg, the Prince's chancellor *of* Chester . . .' should read 'carrying the letters of William de Bliburg, the prince's chancellor, *from* Chester . . .'.

This includes Flintshire receipts as well as the Cheshire material, but omits Flintshire expenses.

> b. ii. *FMA(1)*, pp. 21–37.

4. File of particulars of receipt of the chamberlain's account relating to Cheshire, 31st year, 1302–3.

> a. SC6 771/3 [**Q.R.**]

A file of nine pieces of parchment of varying sizes, tied in the corner.

> b. i. *ChAcc*, pp. 27–37.

CORR. p. 27. 'Trespasses and Escapes' should read 'Frithmote and Escapes'.

5. Account of William de Melton, chamberlain of Chester, 1303–4.

> a. SC6 771/4 [**Q.R.**] 7 mm.

For the file of particulars of expenses and liveries relating to this account, see SC6 1268/4; for the account of works at Macclesfield manor and Chester castle, E101 486/15.

> b. i. *ChAcc*, pp. 38–46.

From this account onwards, Stewart-Brown normally omitted items which had already appeared in previous accounts, if the sums of money remained the same.

CORR. p. 39. A marginal note next to 'Wines of prisage sold' reads 'Custom of hides and wool: Nothing this year'.

> b. ii. *FMA(1)*, pp. 38–49.

6. File of particulars of receipt of the chamberlain's account relating to Cheshire, 32nd year, 1303–4.

> a. SC6 771/5 [**Q.R.**] 14 pieces.
> b. i. *ChAcc*, pp. 46–75.

7. Account of Hugh de Leominster, chamberlain of Chester, 1305–6.

> a. SC6 771/6 [**Q.R.**] 7 mm.

The expenses side is missing.

> b. i. *ChAcc*, pp. 76–77.
> b. ii. *FMA(1)*, pp. 50–61.

8. Account of Stephen de Chesthunte, chamberlain of Chester, 18 December 1312 – Michaelmas 1313.

> a. SC6 771/7 **[W.R.]** 3mm.

There are blanks in the places for sums of money in this account, which suggests that it is an incomplete draft. The first part of the account is missing.

> b. i. *ChAcc*, pp. 78–82.

CORR, p. 79. The sum '43s. 10s. 3d.' should read '£43 10s. 3d.'

> b. ii. *FMA(1)*, pp. 62–67.

9. Account of William (*not* Walter) de Folborn, chamberlain of Chester, [9] June–Michaelmas 1315 (*not* 1315–16, as in *ChAcc*, p. 83).

> a. SC6 771/8 **[W.R.]** 4 mm.

This is an incomplete account for part of a year, and was probably not audited. The dorse is blank. It cannot be for the whole of 1315–16, as Stewart-Brown maintained, since the chamberlain's fee covers the period from 9 June to Michaelmas in the 8th year of Edward II (i.e. 1315). Furthermore, the sum charged to John de Thornham for the manor of Frodsham (p. 83) corresponds to that in his manorial account, which runs from June to Michaelmas 1315 (SC6 801/12).

> b. i. *ChAcc*, pp. 83–88.
> b. ii. *FMA(1)*, pp. 68–73.

10. Account of Richard de Sancto Edmundo, chamberlain of Chester, 26 May – Michaelmas 1320.

> a. SC6 771/9 **[Q.R.]** 4 mm.

This is another part-year account, probably unaudited. The dorse is blank.

> b. i. *ChAcc*, pp. 89–94.
> b. ii. *FMA(1)*, pp. 74–80.

11. Claims of Master William de Esington, former chamberlain of Chester, upon his account, Michaelmas 1325–21 December 1326.

a.   SC6 771/10 **[Q.R.]** 2 mm.

There is a summary version of the account for this period (SC6 1268/4/2, m.7).

b.   i.   *ChAcc*, pp. 95–99.
b.   ii. *FMA(1)*, pp. 81–83.

12.   Account of John Paynel, chamberlain of Chester, 17 December 1326 – 13 March 1328.

a.   SC6 771/11 **[Q.R.]** 4 mm.

This is a draft account, and mm.3 and 4 have been struck through. The enrolled version appears on the foreign membranes of the Pipe Roll (E372/174, rot. 44). The dorse is blank.

b.   i.   *ChAcc*, pp. 100–6.

The missing section of the first part of this account, p. 101, can be found in the enrolled version.

b.   ii. *FMA(1)*, pp. 84–92.

13.   Account of Thomas de Blaston, chamberlain of Chester, Michaelmas–29 November 1328.

a.   SC6 771/12 **[Q.R.]** 2 mm.

Another draft account. For the enrolled version, see E372/174, rot. 47., which also gives Blaston's account from 7 (!) March–Michaelmas 1328. There is also an account of the works done by Master Richard de Legh, carpenter, as 'surveyor of works in Cheshire and Flintshire' for the latter period (E101/487/5).

b.   i.   *ChAcc*, pp. 107–8.

CORR. p. 108. The wages of 30s. 0d. paid to Master Richard de Legh, carpenter, are omitted. Also, the foot of the account is omitted, in which it is stated that Blaston made a livery of £400 to Richard de Bury, treasurer of the King's Wardrobe. The enrolled account has a sum of £328 6s. 8d. allowed to Sir Oliver Ingham, when he was seneschal of Gascony.

b.   ii. *FMA(2)*, pp. 1–4.

14.   Accounts of John Paynel, chamberlain of Chester, 1331–32; 17 September – Michaelmas 1335; 1335–36.

a.   SC6 771/13 **[Treasury of the Exchequer]** 3 mm.

The first of the three accounts is dated wrongly, as 1334–35, by *ChAcc*, p. 109 (but correctly in *FMA(2)*, p. 5). In the second and third of the accounts Paynel is called 'receiver of the issues of the chamberlainship of Chester . . .'. This is just a periphrasis for 'chamberlain', and is not the same as the distinct office of 'receiver in Cheshire and Flintshire' that Brunham held in 1342–43 (see account 15). There is a later analysis of these accounts in C260/53/27. There are two chamberlain's accounts on the Pipe Roll for the period between 1328 and 1331, viz. that of Simon de Ruggeley, 23 October–Xmas 1330 (E372/176, rot. 50), and that of John Paynel, Xmas 1330–Michaelmas 1331 (E372/177, rot. 41).

    b. i. *ChAcc*, pp. 109–10 (1331–32), p. 111 (17 September–Michaelmas 1335), pp. 111–13 (1335–36).

Virtually all the information in the single foot of these three accounts has been omitted in the edition.

CORR. p. 109. The date 'eighth year of the said King' (i.e. Edward III) can also be read '*fifth* year . . .'. The unpublished foot of the account (771/13, m.3) makes it clear that 'fifth year' is the correct reading.

 p. 110. Before 'In money delivered to Master John de Brunham . . .' insert 'Expenses in the castles, Shotwick park, etc., £149 7s. 3d.'
 p. 113. Before the payment to 'Sir Hugh de Frenes . . .', insert a payment to 'William de Clynton, justiciar of Chester, Michaelmas–1 November 1335, £8 10s. 9¼d.'
 '£95 13s. 4d. delivered to Sir William de Hoo . . .' should read '£995 13s. 4d.' There are also several other liveries of money, including £733 5s. 1d. to Master John Brunham, treasurer of the earl of Chester.

    b. ii. *FMA(2)*, pp. 5–6 (1331–32), pp. 7–8 (17 September–Michaelmas 1335), pp. 8–10 (1335–36).

15. Account of John de Brunham the younger, receiver in Cheshire and Flintshire, 1342–43.

   a. SC6 771/14 **[Q.R.]** 1 m.

Sir Henry and Sir Thomas Ferrers farmed the justiciarship of Chester, for the last time in its history, from 1336 to 1346. The farm was £1,200 a year until 15 March 1341, when the office was seized into the king's hands. It was restored to Sir Henry on 31 March 1342, but at the higher farm of £1,333 6s. 8d. a year. The farm was paid directly to the prince's wardrobe (SC6 1268/3). Brunham is here accounting not as chamberlain, but as the prince's receiver of those revenues excluded from the restored farm, principally the profits of Hugh de Berwick's sessions of oyer and terminer held while the justiciarship was in the king's hands in 1341.

b.   i. *ChAcc*, pp. 114–18.

CORR. p. 114. 'The younger' is omitted from Brunham's name.

Before 'Receipts . . .' insert 'Arrears of the last account, £28 13s. 3½d.' struck through 'because below in the foot'. Similarly, insert in p. 117 'Livery of money: to Peter de Gildesburgh . . 56s. 0d., . . . £120 6s. 8d. . . ., £116 0s. 0d.' also struck through 'because below in the foot'. See Booth, *Financial Administration*, pp. 25–29, for the significance of this change in accounting practice.

b.   ii. *FMA(2)*, pp. 11–14.

16.   Account of (Master) John de Brunham (the younger), chamberlain of Chester, 1347–48.

a.   SC6 771/15 **[Q.R.]** 6 mm.

Although this account is in a good state of repair, it is incomplete, lacking heading and several sum totals, as well as liveries and final balance. It is probably an unaudited draft. The younger Brunham's full name is given in the Frodsham manorial account for 1346–47 (SC6 801/13, m.1).

b.   i. *ChAcc*, pp. 119–27.
b.   ii. *FMA(2)*, pp. 15–23.

17.   Account of Master John de Brunham the younger, chamberlain of Chester, 1349–50.

a.   SC6 771/16 **[W.R.]** 4 mm.

The beginning of this account has suffered considerable damage. Although it has sum totals, it lacks the auditors' note 'probatur', and is probably a preliminary draft.

b.   i. *ChAcc*, pp. 128–31.

CORR. p. 128. Insert a marginal note at the foot of the page (in the original it follows the Flintshire receipts) – 'The abovesaid receipt of the counties of Chester and Flint, £1,018 11s. 8¾d.' The fact that this note was never written in 'text', as a sum total of receipts, confirms that this account is a preliminary draft.

p. 129. 'Hugh de Byntre Huntyngdon' should read 'Hugh de Huntyngdon' (as in *FMA(2)*, p. 27).

Insert a note to the sum £83 6s. 8d. (Ferrers' expenses in repairing the Dee bridge) – 'Inquire by the auditors, because the bridge is not yet finished'.

p. 130. For 'John de Wynggefeld, steward of the lands of Sir Thomas de Ferrers, . . .' read 'John de Wynggefeld, steward of the *lord's* lands . . .'

b.   ii. *FMA(2)*, pp. 24–28.

18.   Account of Master John de Brunham the younger, chamberlain of Chester, 1350–51.

a.   SC6 771/17 **[Q.R.]** 8 mm.
b.   i. *ChAcc*, pp. 159–70.

CORR. p. 160. For '10s.' received of the 'said Richard [Doun] . . . for the issues of his bailiwick [of Delamere] . . .' read '£5'.

Insert before the last line 'For £18 14s. 0d. received from Thomas de Wilton, bailiff and approver of the manor of Drakelow'.

p. 165. before 'EXPENSES AND DELIVERIES' insert the 'Sum Total of the Receipts, £1,990 16s. 1½d.'

p. 166. For '225 days' worked by Nicholas de Eccleston, carpenter, read '125 days'.

Insert among the 'FEES AND WAGES NEWLY CONSTITUTED' the wages of Hugh de Huntyngdon, mason in Cheshire, Flintshire and North Wales, at 6d. a day (1350–51), £4 6s. 6d., 'and no more, because the chamberlain of North Wales is charged for 192 days of his wages when he was employed in those parts.'

p. 167. Insert before the works at Frodsham 'To workmen working on the enclosure of Shotwyk park, which had largely fallen down on account of old age, £6 0s. 10d.'

p. 169. Before '36s. 0d. allowed for a quarry bought of Stephen de Merton . . .', insert 'To clerks writing and duplicating account rolls, etc., of which one part remains in the treasury at Chester, and the other part at Westminster, 6s. 8d.'

b.   ii. *FMA(2)*, pp. 49–56.

19.   Account of Master John de Brunham the younger, chamberlain of Chester, 1353–54.

a.   SC6 771/18 **[W.R.]** 9 mm.

Most of m.1 is missing, including all the arrears and part of the receipts.

b. i. *ChAcc*, pp. 206–19.

CORR. p. 210. Before 'FINES FOR THE PEACE BROKEN' insert 'ISSUES OF THE [ESCHEATRY] OF CHESHIRE: £20 11s. 8d. received from Thomas le Yonge, escheator of Cheshire, for the issues of his bailiwick this year, and £5 from the same on 6 March, in money delivered on the account for issues this year'.

p. 212. 'Of the £851 7s. 9d. atterminated to John de Chorleton' is followed by the names of 26 other people who were also fined in the 1353 trailbaston sessions.

p. 214. After 'Item to Thomas le Belward and his fellow porters . . . 6d.' insert 'COST OF PARCHMENT AND OTHER NECESSARIES: . . . Paid by ordinance of the auditors, for the expenses of three clerks writing and duplicating this account, and the ministers' accounts of Cheshire and Flintshire, and Macclesfield, from 14 January to 18 March 1354, nine weeks and two days, 53s. 4d.'

p. 217. Footnote 1. *Pace* Stewart-Brown's statement, it appears that Gregory, provost of Killala, had been provided to the see of Down by the pope at Avignon on 29 January 1353. This provision was annulled on 31 May 1354, and it is unlikely that Gregory ever had possession of the bishopric (*Handbook of British Chronology*, 3rd ed. (1986), p. 347).

p. 218. For '£2,291 8s. 10¾d. . . .' read '£2,191 8s. 10¾d.'

b. ii. (There are no further published extracts from the Flintshire portions of the accounts).

20. Account of Master (!) John de Brunham the younger, chamberlain of Chester, 1354–55.

a. SC6 771/19 **[W.R.]** 7 mm.
b. i. *ChAcc*, pp. 220–31.

CORR. p. 220. Before 'And for 9s. 8¼d. received of William Jonet . . .' insert '£12 4s. 11¾d. from Thomas le Yonge, escheator of Cheshire and Flintshire, arrears; £4 13s. 6d. from Richard le Bruyn, mayor and escheator of Chester, arrears; £16 19s. 8d. from William Dyseworth, bailiff of Drakelow, arrears'.

p. 223. For 'Sum, £244 15s. ¾d.' read 'Sum, £264 15s. 0¾d.'

p. 227. After '26s. 8d. received of Geoffrey de Werberton the younger' seven fines are omitted.

Richard de Wylughby is called 'justice assigned to hear and determine divers felonies and trespasses at Chester on Monday after the Nativity of the Blessed Virgin Mary, 27 Edward III (9 September 1353)'.

p. 228. Before 'EXPENSES AND DELIVERIES' insert '19 dozen, 11 ells of white, 4 dozen of green cloth, for archers going to war, sold this year, £17 6s. 8d.'.

Before 'EXPENSES AND DELIVERIES' insert 'Sum Total of Receipts, £3,686 3s. 4¼d.'

p. 229. After 'To Philip de Raby . . . £4 11s. 4d.' insert 'To Nicholas de Eccleston, carpenter, £6 1s. 8d. and a robe, 10s. 0d.' and 'To Hugh de Huntyndon, mason, Michaelmas to Lady Day, 177 days, £4 8s. 6d.'

p. 230. In the expenses of placing palings on Peckforton park ditch, for '286 perches' read '1,286 perches', and follow with 'by the greater hundred, namely at 2½d. a perch . . .'.

p. 231. For 'SUM TOTAL of the expenses, £1,029 5s. 4d.' read 'SUM TOTAL . . . £719 5s. 4d.' A detailed foot of the account follows, all of which is omitted. Near the end, m.4d, appear the following RESPITES:

£60 which he paid to divers knights and others retained with the prince for war, in part-payment of their fees: Ralph de Modberlegh, knight, £11 13s. 4d.; John Danyers, knight, £23 6s. 8d.; William de Caryngton, £6 13s. 4d.; Hamo de Mascy of Puddington, £5; John Danyers, £5; Thomas Stathum, £5; Robert le Bruyn, 66s. 8d.; by letters of 21 May 1355.

£11 13s. 4d. which he paid to John Griffyn, knight, retained with the lord for war, half his fee for one year; by letters of 25 June 1355.

£6 13s. 4d. which he paid to Richard Mascy and Hamo de Assheleght, retained with the lord for war, half their fee for one year; by letters of 25 June 1355.

£186 4s. 0d. which he paid to divers knights and others leading 300 archers of Cheshire, and 100 archers of Flint, (being the wages of the said leaders for eight days, of the rest for 21 days), from Cheshire to Plymouth, each knight taking 2s. 0d. a day, each esquire 12d., each Cheshire archer 6d., each Flintshire archer 3d.; by letters of 26 June 1355, (*B.P.R.*, iii. 204).

£77 6s. 0d. which he paid for 1,000 ells of cloth, – 500 ells of green, 500 ells of white, – for the said archers; by letters of 26 June.

Sum of respites, £341 16s. 8d.
Clear remainder, £350 15s. 6¾d.

21. View of the account of Master John de Brunham the younger, chamberlain of Chester, Michaelmas 1356 – 23 June 1357.

    a. SC6 771/20 [**W.R.**] 2 mm.
    b. i. *ChAcc*, pp. 232–36.

CORR. p. 234. After '27s. 6d. received of Thomas Starky', insert '50s. 0d. from Hugh Burghes; 50s. 0d. from Richard Hogh'.

p. 235. After the wages of John de Tychemerssh appear those of Master John de Brunham (£13 6s. 8d.) and Nicholas de Eccleston, carpenter (60s. 0d., plus a 10s. 0d. robe).

p. 236. After the expenses paid to Thomas de Pulle, for making palings for Peckforton park, insert 'Paid for the carriage of thirteen couple of mill-stones, from Anglesey to Chester for the Dee Mills, 10s. 8d.'.

22. Account of [Master John de Brunham the younger], chamberlain of Chester, 1356–57.

    a. SC6 771/21 [**W.R.**] 6 mm.

Most of m.1 and part of m.2 are missing, as are the dates normally found at the head of both the receipts and expenses sections. A comparison of the sums, and the names of the officials charged in the Macclesfield section, shows that they correspond with the Macclesfield Ministers' accounts for 1356–57 (SC6 802/13) and not 1357–58, as Stewart-Brown thought (*ChAcc*, p. 237). Also, at the end of this account it is stated that the chamberlain answers 'in the great roll of debts of the 31st year', that is 1356–57 (*ChAcc*, p. 242).

    b. i. *ChAcc*, pp. 237–43.

CORR, p. 239. Eleven fines are omitted from 'ATTERMINATIONS OF FINES BEFORE WILLIAM DE SHARESHULL . . .'.

p. 240. Before '15s. 0d. received of Richard, son and heir of Simon de Becheton . . .' insert 'ISSUES OF THE ST PIERRE LANDS: Adam de Praers, receiver, £135 6s. 7½d.; Ralph de Brunham, receiver, £132 4s. 0d.'.

p. 241. For 'the lord Chamberlain's letters . . .' read 'the lord's letters to the chamberlain . . .'.

p. 242. For '*Regard* of Robert de Houghton and Richard le Stalker . . .' read '*Reward* of Robert de Houghton and Richard le Stalker . . .'.

For 'One *letter* bag . . .' read 'One *leather* bag . . .'.

For 'Paid John Alcok, the lord's *storekeeper* at Macclesfield . . .' read 'Paid John Alcok, the lord's *stock-keeper* at Macclesfield . . .'.

Following 'And he owes £278 23¼d. . . .' the unpublished account goes on to give liveries of money, by twelve indentures, to Peter de Lacy, which total £1,899 11s. 11d.

23.   Account of Master John de Brunham the younger, chamberlain of Chester, 1358–59.

       a.   SC6 771/22 **[W.R.]** 7 mm.
       b.   i. *ChAcc*, pp. 244–57.

CORR. p. 245. For '£99 10s. 6d. received of Robert de Bredon . . .' read '£199 10s. 6d.'.

p. 246. Before '£17 17s. 3¾d. received of the said William . . .' insert '£5 0s. 0d. from William de Dyseworth, bailiff of Rudheath'.

For '£94 13s. 4d. received of Adam de Mottrum . . .' read '£84 13s. 4d.'

p. 250. The editor has omitted here 24 'OLD ATTERMINATIONS OF DIVERS MEN OF CHESTER AND CHESHIRE', eleven 'NEW ATTERMINATIONS OF DIVERS MEN OF THE COUNTY OF CHESTER', four 'ATTERMINATIONS OF FINES FOR THE PEACE BROKEN' (in addition to the one which he published), and one 'ATTERMINATION OF A FINE BEFORE SHARESHULL'.

Insert before the fee for Matthew de Fouleshurst's charter the 16s. 4d. fee for Stephen de Merton's charter for licence to tallage.

p. 251. Before 'EXPENSES AND DELIVERIES', insert 'ISSUES OF THE ST PIERRE LANDS: Robert de Houghton, keeper and receiver, £276 17s. 5½d.', and follow it with 'SUM TOTAL OF RECEIPTS (of both counties): £3, 281 9s. 7¾d.'.

p. 252. For '£99 17s. 3¼d.' (the sum of works) read '£199 17s. 3¼d.'.

p. 255. Follow 'To John de Delves for arduous affairs outside his bailiwick

. . .' with '. . . for three weeks, in going to South Wales from Chester, staying and returning, at 5s. 0d. a day . . .'.

p. 256. (Nearly all of the foot of this account is omitted. The liveries by the chamberlain to Peter de Lacy total £2,233 3s. 1¾d. The final balance is £564 10s. 2¾d., the respites £99 5s. 8d, the clear remainder £465 4s. 6½d.)

24. Account of Master John de Brunham the younger, chamberlain of Chester, 1359–60.

 a. SC6 771/23 **[W.R.]** 5 mm.

Much of m.1 is missing.

  b. i. *ChAcc*, pp. 258–76.

CORR. p. 264. For '£40 received of Richard del Wodehouses . . .' read '40s. 0d.'

p. 266. For '100s. 0d. received of William Gerard . . . for licence to *entail* certain of his lands' read 'for licence to *tallage* certain of his lands . . .'.

Insert after Gerard's instalment a deleted fine of Sir Reginald de Grey, cancelled 'because in the escheator's account'.

p. 268. Before 'SUM TOTAL of the receipts, £3,449 11s. 8½d.', insert 'FOREIGN RECEIPT: £160 from John de Wodhull, chamberlain of South Wales, in aid of a certain payment of £2,000 to be made to Richard, earl of Arundel, to whom the prince is bound for a loan'.

p. 269. Sir Bartholomew de Burgherssh's fee should read '£60'.

Follow 'William de Stanlegh, forester of the forest of Wyrhale, for the custody of Schotewyke park . . .' with 'from Michaelmas 1359 to [14] April 1360, on which day he died, 16s. 5d.'

p. 275. In the respite of £6 6s. 11½d. for Peter de Dutton and Matthew de Weverham, it should read '41s. 8d. for divers vills in Delamere forest for the 33rd (*not* 34th) year' when this phrase occurs the first time.

25. Account of Master John de Brunham the younger, chamberlain of Chester, 1360–61.

  SC6 772/1 **[W.R.]**

The heading and arrears are missing.

SC6 772/2 [**W.R.**]

The heading and arrears missing. In this copy, the sums of money have been added in a different hand and ink-colour, although there are some blanks where sums should have been. This version also has the note *probatur* after the sums, and may be the prewritten copy actually used at the audit.

26. Account of Master John de Brunham the younger, chamberlain of Chester, 1361–62.

SC6 772/3 [**W.R.**]

The account edited in the present volume. This is a duplicate version.

SC6 772/4 [**W.R.**]

27. Account of Master John de Brunham the younger, chamberlain of Chester, 1369–70.

SC6 772/5 [**W.R.**]

The heading is missing, as well as the arrears and all the issues up to and including the manor and hundred of Macclesfield.

28. Account of Robert de Parys, chamberlain of Chester, 1370–71.

SC6 772/6 [**Q.R.**]

This is a duplicate account, since one of the respites is granted 'ut in compoto suo originali'. Thus, 772/7 may be the original.

SC6 772/7 [**W.R.**]

29. Account of Robert de Parys, chamberlain of Chester, 1372–73.

SC6 772/8 [**W.R.**]

This is an original account. Much of the first part is missing, or illegible.

30. Account of Robert de Parys, chamberlain of Chester, Mich. 1373 to 17 July 1374.

SC6 772/9 [**Q.R.**]

This is a duplicate account, which was audited in January 1375. It was handed over by the Black Prince's auditors after his death. Presumably, therefore, this was the copy made for the prince's exchequer at Westminster. On m.2 it is stated that the ancient alms are allowed 'per acquietanciam super compotum originalem liberatam'.

31. Account of John de Wodehous, chamberlain of Chester, 17 July to Mich.
1374.

SC6 772/10 [Q.R.]

This is a duplicate account, and at the end cf the dorse appears the original title of the roll, which appeared on the outside when it was rolled up: [D]UPLICATIO COMPOTI JOHANNIS DE WODEHOUS CAMERARII CESTRIE DE ULTIMA PARTE ANNI XLVIII.

APPENDIX 2

List of dates of audit of the accounts of the earldom of Chester, 1349 to 1374

The chamberlains' accounts (Chamb) do not normally give the date at which they were audited. The dates in this list have been derived, therefore, from references in the divers ministers' accounts (Cheshire) (DM), the Macclesfield ministers' accounts (Macc), and the St Pierre receivers' accounts (SP).

Account	Date of Audit	Reference
1349–50 (DM)	February 1351	*ChAcc*, p. 132
1350/March 1351 (Macc)	June 1352	SC6 802/6, m.1
1350–51 (Chamb)	June 1352	*ChAcc*, p. 159
1351–52 (DM)	Oct., Nov. 1352	SC6 783/17, m.3
1352–53 (DM)	November 1353	SC6 784/2, m.5
1353–54 (DM)	January 1355	SC6 784/3, m.1
1353–54 (Macc)	Feb., Mar. 1355	SC6 802/9, mm.1d, 2d
1353–54 (SP)	Mar. 1355	SC6 783/1, m.1
1354–55 (DM)	May to July 1356	SC6 784/5, mm.1, 2, 6
1354–55 (SP)	June 1356	SC6 783/2, m.1
1355–56 (DM)	June 1357	SC6 784/7, m.1
1355–56 (SP)	June 1357	SC6 783/4, m.1
1356/Feb. 1357 (SP)	June 1357	SC6 783/4, m.1
1356–57 (DM)	April 1358	SC6 784/10, m.1
1356–57 (Macc)	May 1358	SC6 802/13, m.1
1357–58 (DM)	May 1359	SC6 785/1, m.3
1360–61 (DM)	May 1362	SC6 785/8, m.5
1361–62 (DM)	March 1363	SC6 785/9, m.4
1362–63 (DM)	October 1363	SC6 786/2, m.1
1362–63 (Macc)	November 1363	SC6 803/7, m.1d

Account	Date of Audit	Reference
1363–64 (DM)	January 1365	SC6 786/3, m.1
1363–64 (Macc)	January 1365	SC6 803/9, m.1d
1364–65 (DM)	January 1366	SC6 786/5, m.1
1365–66 (DM)	March 1367	SC6 786/6, m.1
1366–67 (DM)	March 1368	SC6 786/7, m.1
1366–67 (Macc)	March 1368	SC6 803/13, m.1
1367–68 (DM)	February 1369	SC6 786/8, m.1
1368–69 (DM)	March 1370	SC6 786/10, m.1
1370–71 (DM)	April 1372	SC6 787/2, m.1
1372–73 (DM)	April 1374	SC6 787/5, m.1
1373–74 (DM)	January 1375	SC6 787/7, m.1

APPENDIX 3

Cheshire's 'Great Rebellion of 1353': its Genesis and Diaspora.

When the research relating to the Cheshire portion of this chamberlain's account was begun in 1968, it was quite clear that one of the main avenues of investigation must be the causes and effects of the rebellion of 1353. The rising was well-established in the literature and was mentioned by articles and monographs on fourteenth-century Cheshire history in the journals and publications of regional learned societies, and had found its way into the Oxford History of England. Those who had written about this momentous event included names who commanded the highest authority in the study of medieval history.

It has been recounted elsewhere how, during the course of the research mentioned above, the researcher came, eventually, to what was, for him, the surprising conclusion that the evidence for the Cheshire rising of 1353 was not just weak or ambiguous, but non-existent.[1] It may be impossible to prove a negative, but it is hard to envisage a rising being followed by sessions of trailbaston, as in Cheshire in August 1353, in which there is no hint of any planned, large-scale attempt to overthrow, or even oppose lawfully-constituted authority.[2] The pleas of the sessions of trailbaston held during the prince's 1353 visit are now published, and those who still cherish the notion of a rebellion in that year can judge the evidence for themselves.[3]

The process whereby the myth of the 1353 rebellion was created, grew in the telling, and became dispersed throughout the academic literature, is both fascinating and provides a salutary lesson. The principal texts are set out below. They demonstrate that the route by which the 'great rebellion' found its way into academic acceptance was through H.J. Hewitt's 1929 monograph (**6 (a)**), which took over the misinterpretation by G.P.R. James (**4**) and R.P. Dunn-Pattison (**5**) of Knighton's chronicle's account of the events of 1353 (**1, 2**). Since 1957 it has been known that Knighton was writing his chronicle some forty years after

---

1 Booth, 'Taxation and Public Order'.
2 If there had been an uprising or rebellion in Cheshire in 1353, we should have expected to find in the trailbaston roll the sort of evidence that the court of King's Bench examined at Wigan in 1323, when it was clearing up the aftermath of the Banastre revolt of 1315 (G.H. Tupling, *South Lancashire in the Reign of Edward II*, Chet. Soc., 3rd ser. i (1949)). For a close parallel to what happened in Cheshire, examine the outbreak of disorder that occurred in the Winchester district in 1249, which provoked the personal intervention of King Henry III (F. Pollock and F.W. Maitland, *The History of English Law*, 2nd ed. (1898). ii. 655).
3 The pleas are published in calendar form in *Cheshire History*, 11 (1983), pp. 39–51; 12 (1983), pp. 24–28; 13 (1984), pp. 22–28; 14 (1984), pp. 23–26; 16 (1985), pp. 21–25.

1353;[4] moreover, the mistakes of detail committed either by the chronicler, or his source – presumably a Leicester abbey chronicle – in recounting the events in question, mean that no definite reliance can be placed on the details he gives of the prince's visit to Cheshire.

The records of the prince's own administration – both at the centre, and in Chester – tell us that the holding of a general eyre for Cheshire was announced on 26 June 1353. It was the result of 'grievous clamours and complaints' which had reached the prince of 'wrongs, excesses and misdeeds' which needed his presence in the county to put right.[5] The prince had intended to visit Cheshire for some time, and it is clear that he, or his officials in London, had actively solicited these 'grievous clamours', since by letters dated 18 April 1353, those who wished to complain of misbehaviour by the Cheshire officials had been invited to address his council in person.[6] A planned 'state visit' to Cheshire and North Wales, in which the prince would do justice to his subjects there and raise money for his military ventures, was modified to a visit to Cheshire alone, presumably because of the nature of the complaints that the prince and his council were receiving in the late spring of 1353.

The 26 June letters tell us that the prince planned that two distinct courts would be held in Chester on Monday after the Assumption (19 August). One was the general eyre, of which the justices were to be Sir William Shareshull and Sir Roger Hillary. The other was the forest eyre, to be presided over by Sir Richard Willoughby and unnamed associates. The two justices in eyre were commissioned by letters under the Chester exchequer seal dated 3 July, in which they were told to do justice in accordance with the laws and customs of Cheshire. In addition, they were to be guided by a special ordinance which had been made for them, by current statutes, and the 'articles of the eyre'.[7] Neither the ordinance nor the text of the articles has come down to us. After the commission, the record continues with the instructions to the sheriff to proclaim the general eyre, and summon the large body of people who would be obliged to attend.[8] The prince arrived in Chester about 10 August with his 'great council', including Sir John Wingfield, Sir Richard de Stafford, Sir Bartholomew Burg-herssh the younger, Sir Edmund de Wauncy (steward of the household), Sir Nigel Loring (chamberlain of the household) and Sir John Chandos.[9] A

4 V.H. Galbraith, 'The Chronicle of Henry Knighton' in *Fritz Saxl: A Volume of Memorial Essays from his Friends in England* (1957), pp. 136–48.
5 *B.P.R.*, iii. 111.
6 For the prince's plan to visit Cheshire in 135⁻, see ibid., 11. For the letters of 18 April, ibid., 100.
7 CHES 29/65, m.1 (the single membrane of the plea roll of the general eyre).
8 Ibid.
9 For those present, see *B.P.R.*, iii. 112ff., together with the list of witnesses to the prince's charter of 10 September 1353, executed before his return to London (C53/162, m.11). Charters granted either under the prince's privy seal, or his Chester exchequer seal, and which contain

banquet, to which several of the prince's Cheshire subjects were invited, was held at Chester castle on Thursday 15 August, the feast of the Assumption.[10]

On the following Monday, 19 August, the general eyre sat at Chester, in the shire hall in the castle, under the presidency of Shareshull and Hillary. Its plea roll tells us that the legal advisers of the community of Cheshire argued that the eyre would be contrary to the customs of the county, and offered a fine of 5,000 marks payable at the Chester exchequer within four years, whereupon the prince accepted the fine and granted a postponement of the eyre for thirty years.[11] The letters cancelling the general eyre are, however, dated 18 August 1353, that of the day previous to the holding of the eyre.[12] On 19 August, further letters were issued cancelling the forest eyre, on the grounds that the legal period had not elapsed since the last one had been held, in 1347.[13] It was on 19 August, also, that new letters were issued by the prince, commissioning Shareshull and Hillary as justices of trailbaston, followed by an order to the county sheriff, and the city officers, to summon those persons who ought to come to the court to attend on 20 August.[14]

Clearly, although Knighton has recorded the main elements of these events, he has made some important errors of detail, apart from the slip of putting Dieulacres for Vale Royal, which was spotted by Sir Joshua Barnes (3). He says that the justices in eyre sat for a considerable time, when they only met for a single day. The fine was 5,000 marks, and not 5,060. Knighton does not distinguish between the two eyres, and seems to suggest that Willoughby was Shareshull's senior justice for the general eyre. He does not mention Hillary at all. Furthermore, he or his source may have confused the earl of Stafford with his brother, Sir Richard de Stafford, whom we know was present. Although there is no reason to doubt that the prince's military household performed the job of protecting the two justices as they presided over their trailbaston sessions – for about three weeks – *magno tempore* indeed – it would be rash to accept Knighton's view that there was an element of trickery on the prince's part, in

---

lists of witnesses, are very rare indeed. Consequently, there is no reason to suppose that the witnesses named were not present, as may have been the case with a royal charter granted under the great seal of England.

10   The list of guests from Macclesfield hundred to be invited to dine with the prince, which was sent to Robert Legh the elder on 10 August, does not survive (*B.P.R.*, iii. 112).

11   CHES 29/65, m.1. The phrase following the names of the justices in the plea roll has been written over an erasure, and now appears as 'justiciariis domini Comitis Cestrie'. This neutral expression very likely replaced some phrase such as 'justiciariis itinerantibus apud Cestriam', following the agreement of the prince and his leading Cheshire subjects. It enabled the community to argue, after the thirty-year period was up, that the eyre had not been held.

12   CHES 29/65, m.1; *B.P.R.*, iii. 112.

13   *B.P.R.*, iii. 113. Sir Richard de Stafford is named as co-justice with Willoughby.

14   CHES 29/65, m.2. The commission and the heading to the plea roll calls them justices of oyer and terminer, but the semi-official name 'justices of trailbaston' was used in the prince's order of 10 September 1353 to pay various sums out of the proceeds of the sessions (*B.P.R.*, iii. 115).

substituting the trailbaston commission when the community felt that they had discharged their liability after the 5,000-mark common fine was agreed. Of course, as was pointed out some time ago, there is no need to cast doubts on Knighton's account of a 'rising' in Cheshire, since he does not say, or even imply, that such an event occurred.[15]

The business of the visit was formally concluded on 10 September 1353 when the prince, probably at a session of his great council, granted a charter of liberties to the county.[16] In it, he rehearsed the summons of the general eyre, and its postponement in return for the common fine. This is followed in the charter with an explanation of the reason for holding the sessions of trailbaston, which repeats that it was because of *diversas et plures querelas horribiles* that the prince had been impelled to come to Cheshire at that particular time, so that he could put an end to such evils, and find out what was behind them. The charter then follows with other grants which are not relevant to the argument here.

There are two points to be made about the myth of the great rebellion. The first is that Hewitt only used the calendared version of the charter of 1353, which a copyist's error caused to be wrongly dated 10 September 1346 (20 Edward III).[17] This is the reason why he mistakenly held that there were two attempts to hold a general eyre in Cheshire – although he thought the first occurred in 1347 (possibly because that was the year an actual *forest* eyre was held) – and two fines of 5,000 marks to buy them off (**6(a.)(iv).**). This amazing duplication was accepted both by Barraclough (**7**), and by T.B. Pugh (**9**), probably because it fitted in well with the notion of the Black Prince's greed for money.

The second point is that while the myth clearly grew in the telling, as Barnes's 'insolence or riot' became James's 'rising, general revolt, rebellion', then Dunn-Pattison's 'open revolt', and Barraclough's 'great rebellion', it also changed its character, all without the benefit of any apparent contact with contemporary original sources. It can be seen that there are, in fact, two different stories. One tells of a riot, rising or rebellion, which was put down by armed force and a general eyre, one of the main tasks of which was to unmask and punish the ringleaders: thus Barnes (**3**), James (**4**), Dunn-Pattison (**5**). This tale lost favour in the 1920s, but has surfaced more recently in some of the crop

15 Booth, 'Taxation and Public Order', p. 21.
16 CHES 2/36, m.4; C53/162, m.11; *C. Chart. R., 1341–1417*, p. 313.
17 The calendared copy is taken from an *inspeximus* and confirmation issued by Richard II in 1389. When the date was transcribed at the end of this copy, it was given as '20 Edward III (England) and 14 (France)'. This must be wrong, since Edward's French regnal year should be thirteen years less than his English one, and not six, as here. Although the copy made of the 1353 charter for the recognizance roll is damaged, more than enough survives to show that the *inspeximus* of 1389 is a copy of it. Consequently, in the 1389 copy it is the English regnal year that was transcribed incorrectly, and it should have read '27 Edward III (England)'. Unfortunately, both the person producing the calendar, and those using it as a source for Cheshire history, did not note the discrepancy, and accepted 1346 as the date for the original charter.

of books which were published, in 1976 and after, to celebrate the six-hundredth anniversary of the Black Prince's death.[18] Hewitt's story, though, puts the elements the other way round; to him the eyre provoked the rebellion, partly because of the bad weather and near-famine conditions England was experiencing, partly because of the prince's heavy fiscal exactions in Cheshire and his infringement of the community's liberties, but also because Hewitt wrongly believed it was the second general eyre and common fine to be inflicted on Cheshire within six years (**6 (a)**). Although he had modified his view by 1958, when he wrote that it was but a 'threatened rising' which had provoked the prince's armed intervention (**6 (b)**), by 1967 he felt that the mere proclamation of the eyre, in July 1353, had caused the rebellion, which had to be quelled by the 'overwhelming, organised force' of the prince, the duke of Lancaster and the others, when they arrived in Cheshire in early August (**6 (c)**). This also seems to have been Barraclough's line, when he spoke of the abuse of powers by the absentee earl causing the rebellion, with the suggestion that either the announcement, or the actual beginning of the eyre had brought it about (**7**).

All this might be thought to be labouring a point of very small significance. However, whether a rebellion did or did not take place is of considerable moment to the history of fourteenth-century Cheshire. Also, the story of the career of the great rebellion of 1353 shows how, despite every historian's genuflection in the direction of the critical method applied to the use of original sources, it is very difficult to dislodge a convenient myth from the calendar, particularly if it has the endorsement of writers of unimpeachable reputation. In 1980, Michael Prestwich could only bring himself to say that the notion that a rising took place in Cheshire in 1353 was exaggerated, and there was, after all, considerable disorder in the county.(**10**)[19] This view appears to imply that a rebellion is but the extreme development of any outbreak of disorder; as if, in an

18   Barbara Emerson in *The Black Prince* (1976), p. 81, wrote of an attack on the prince's officials leading to an 'insurrection' in Cheshire, which provoked armed intervention. This led to the fine of 5,000 marks to be paid in lieu of an eyre but then, so she says, the eyre sat again. Presumably this second session is a mistake for the trailbaston sessions. Hubert Cole's *Black Prince* (1976), p. 84, tells of a 'revolt' in Cheshire, followed by the prince's visit, during which judicial sessions were held to deal with the ringleaders. Similarly, John Harvey, in *The Black Prince and his Age* (1976), p. 93, tells us that a 'serious revolt' had to be put down by the prince in person, and that the 5,000-mark fine was a punishment for those who had taken part in it. Michael Packe's posthumous *King Edward III* (1983), p. 206 blames the prince for stirring up a 'serious rebellion' in Cheshire through his harsh exactions, which required military intervention and the punishment, through the trailbaston court, of those involved in the rising. Richard Barber, in *Edward, Prince of Wales and Aquitaine: a Biography of the Black Prince* (1978), p. 106, properly dismisses the notion of a rebellion in Cheshire, but then he had read *Northern History* (see next note).

19   Prestwich cites Richard Barber's book (see previous note) in his select bibliography to Chapters 8 and 10, but not Booth, 'Taxation and Public Order', which Barber himself had cited as his grounds for stating that there was no revolt in Cheshire in 1353.

area where violent crime (rape, personal assault, robbery, burglary) are allowed to grow unchecked, then what will happen is that the leading criminals will, sooner or later, set themselves up to overthrow lawfully constituted authority. What is true above all is that the opinion of anyone, on any historical matter, is only as good as the sources on which that opinion is based. Perhaps we can now lay the Cheshire rising of 1353 to rest; it may be that evidence as yet unknown will bring it back to life, but until that most unlikely event should happen, it is best not spoken of.

TEXTS[20]

1. Knighton's account of the events of 1353 in Cheshire (text).

Chronicon Henrici Knighton . . ., ed. J.R. Lumby, Rolls Series, ii. (1985), pp. 75–76.

Anno gratiae MCCCLIII sederunt justiciarii apud Cestriam super le Eyre magno tempore; et in defensionem eorum ne compatriotae eos nocerent assistebant prope in patria princeps Walliae, Henricus dux Lancastriae, comes Warwych, comes Stafford, pro timore patriae. Justiciarii, dominus Ricardus de Wylughby, dominus Willelmus de Scharshull. . . .

Jam redeamus ad ea quae facta sunt apud Cestriam priusquam ulterius procedamus de Scotis. Illi de patria Cestriae videntes enormitatem delictorum suorum, et se non posse pro tempore in judicio pro fortitudine adversa contendere, finem fecerunt cum principe Walliae domino suo pro v. mille marcis et lx. solvendis infra iiij. annos proxime sequentes, et fecerunt securitatem qualem princeps petere voluerit, ea quidem conditione quod le Eyre non transiret super eos. Cumque se crederent esse quietos et liberatos in toto, justiciarii sederunt de novo super Traylbastons, et levaverunt pecuniam ultra mensuram, et multae terrae et tenementa seisita in manus principis, et fines multas fecerunt quasi sine numero. Et in redeundo venit princeps per abbathiam de Dewleucres, et vidit ibi miram structuram fabricae ecclesiae quam inceperat rex bonus Edwardus, et contulit eis de mera eleemosyna sua in subventionem operis praedicti v[c]. marcas. Homo credebat sub tali summa ipsum decimasse perquisitum suum de comitatu Cestriae.

2. Knighton's account of the events of 1353 in Cheshire (translation).

In the year of Grace 1353, justices in eyre sat at Chester for a considerable time.

---

20 Brackets are used thus in Appendix 3:
    [   ] Square brackets enclose editorial matter inserted.
    ⟨   ⟩ Angle brackets are used to enclose footnotes/endnotes in the extracts quoted, which are inserted in the texts in the positions to which they relate.

In order to defend them from harm by their fellow-countrymen, there waited nearby in the county the prince of Wales, Henry duke of Lancaster, the earl of Warwick, the earl of Stafford, for fear of the county. The justices were Sir Richard de Wylughby, Sir William de Scharshull. [There follows an account of the failed attempt to conclude an agreement between the English and Scots at Newcastle-upon-Tyne. As part of the agreement, the Scots demanded pardons for the crimes which they had committed since King David II was captured (at Neville's Cross in 1346), for which they were prepared to offer security to him. Otherwise, they threatened to choose another king].

Now let us return to the events which happened at Chester before we proceed further with the Scots. Those people of the land of Chester, seeing the enormity of their crimes and that they were not able, in the circumstances, to withstand judgement because of the strength of the forces ranged against them, made a fine with the prince of Wales, their lord, for 5,060 marks, payable within the four years next following. And they gave such security as the prince desired to have, on condition that the eyre should not be imposed upon them. But when they believed that they were quit and entirely discharged, the justices sat anew upon Traylbastons, and levied untold amounts of money. Many lands and tenements were seized into the prince's hands, and people made many – almost numberless – fines. On his journey back, the prince passed the abbey of Dewleucres, and saw there the wonderful example of ecclesiastical architecture that had been started by good King Edward. He conferred on the abbey, as an act of pure charity, 500 marks in aid of the said work. It was believed that this sum represented his tithe of the profits he had made from the county of Chester.

[The chronicle continues with an account of the session of the royal council at London, which ordered that the lords of the North of England, together with others who had claims to land in Scotland, should cross into Scotland with King David].

3.   A seventeenth-century account of the troubles of 1353.

Sir Joshua Barnes, *The History of . . . Edward IIId, . . . together with That of Edward . . . the Black-Prince* (1688), p. 468.

About this time ⟨Knighton p2606 n 12 & Dugdale 1 Vol. p. 161⟩ the Cheshire-Men had committed some great Insolence or Riot against the Servants of the Prince of Wales (on what Occasion I have not found) which were Officers under the Prince, as he was Duke of Chester. Wherefore the King being extreamly incensed against them, and resolving to make them submit to Law or to the Sword, sends forth Sir Richard Willoughby and Sir William Shareshull, his Justices Itinerant to sit in Eyre at Chester. At the same time ordering sufficient Forces under the Leading of his son the Prince attended with Henry Duke of Lancaster and the Earls of Warwick and Stafford, to go thither to prevent any Violence or Insurrection of the People. But when the Cheshire men knew in their Consciences, that they were in fault, and saw plainly, there was little Contending in Battle as in Law, against such Force and such Right, they compounded with the Prince of Wales, their Lord, for 5,060 Marks, to be paid within four Years thence to come, and gave him such security as the Prince himself desired, on Condition, that the Justices should no longer continue their Circuit of Eyre upon them. However because they would not according to their Duty submit to, but capitulate with their Prince, when they thought themselves quit and wholly free; the Justices came and sat again upon the Inquisition of Traillebaston, and leavied vast Summs of Money, and seised many Landes and Tenements into the Hands of the Prince, and raised Fines without number. After which the Prince passing upon his return thro' the Abby of ⟨Vid. Sir Rich. Baker in Ed. I titulo, Works of Piety done in his Time Unde Corrigo Deaulencros in Vale Royal⟩ Vale-Royal, and seeing there a wonderful Structure of the Fabrick of a Church, which the good King Edward his Great Grandfather had begun, of his meer Princely Good-will gave toward the Promotion of the said pious Work 500 Marks, which Summ was esteemed a Tenth of his whole Perquisites in Cheshire.

4. 'Two-Horsemen James' takes up the reins.

G.P.R. James, *A History of the Life of Edward the Black Prince*, ii (2nd ed., 1839), pp. 105–6.

While these events were taking place in France the domestic affairs of England proceeded without any event of great importance. The people, in the tranquillity of peace, began to recover from their weariness of war; and various tumults in different parts of the country announced that repose had brought about that accumulation of animal power which must always have some object whereon to expend itself. The most serious of these disturbances was a rising in Cheshire; and the scarcity which at this time ⟨Knighton, col. 2606⟩ affected both England and France rendered the distress of the people so great, and their condition so desperate, that active measures of coercion were necessary to suppress general revolt, while other means were employed to relieve absolute want.

The Black Prince, under whose jurisdiction as Earl of Chester the county of Cheshire had been placed, marched directly thither at the head of a considerable force, while the justices in Eyre were sent to take cognisance of the promoters of rebellion. ⟨Barnes⟩ The tumults were thus soon brought to a conclusion; and some severe fines were levied upon the estates of those who had fomented the spirit of discontent.

George Payne Rainsford James lived from 180? to 1860 (S.M. Ellis, *The Solitary Horseman: or, the Life and Adventures of G.P.R. James* (1927)). He wrote over 90 books, mostly historical romances or popular histories. He was appointed historiographer-royal to King William IV, probably on the strength of his biography of the Black Prince, in which the Cheshire rising of 1353 first appeared. He was known as 'Two-Horsemen James' because of the alleged frequency with which he used either two such, or a solitary horseman, as a scene-setting device. His fellow writer of romances, W. Harrison Ainsworth, wrote to James and told him that he thought that he (James) was 'Currer Bell', the pseudonymous author of *Jane Eyre*. It is now difficult to get hold of a copy of any of his books.

5.   Dunn-Pattison puts a socio-economic gloss on the rising.

R.P. Dunn-Pattison, *The Black Prince* (1910), pp. 127–28.

For the next two years we have little or no record of the Prince's doings, till, in the year 1353, we find him reaping the consequences of the Statute of Labourers. From the commencement of December, 1352, to the middle of March, 1353, the country was visited by an extraordinary hard frost. The bitter cold was ended by a furious hurricane, which did untold damage to buildings and trees. This was followed, from March to July, by a severe drought. Famine ruled the land, and the peasantry, irritated by the attempted regulation of wages, in many places broke out in discontent. In Cheshire they rose in open revolt, and attacked the servants of the Prince who were entrusted with supervising his interests. In the preceding year the men of Buckingham had set on the Prince's servants; but the insurrection in Cheshire was much more serious. Accordingly, in addition to sending Sir Richard Willoughby and Sir William Shareshull, the itinerant justices, to sit in Eyre at Chester, the King was obliged to despatch the Prince, the Duke of Lancaster, and the Earls of Stafford and Warwick, with a strong force, to restore order and support the judges. Against such an imposing array the men of Cheshire could do nothing, and were glad to compound with the Prince their lord for five thousand marks. On his return from the north, the Prince, with that pious generosity which was a great cause of his continual financial embarrassments, devoted a tenth of the fine to the completion of the Abbey of Vale Royal, begun by his great-grandfather. There can be but little doubt that the Prince's extravagance was the real cause of the revolt in Cheshire. His agents had to screw every penny they could out of the unfortunate peasantry, and this at a time of scarcity, when the social relations between lord and peasant had been strained by the Statute of Labourers.

6.   The 1353 rebellion survives the impact of historical research, and enters respectable, academic literature.

(**a**.) H.J. Hewitt, *Mediaeval Cheshire: An Economic and Social History of Cheshire in the Reigns of the Three Edwards*, Chet. Soc., new ser. 88 (1929).

(**i**). p. xiv (Sources and Bibliography/I. Original Authorities/A. Unpublished)

T.R. Book 179 (The Register of the Black Prince). – It has recently been calendared, but is not yet printed. This contains instructions to the justice and chamberlain respecting the administration of the earldom, petitions, inquisitions, and other documents. The material is detailed, covers many aspects of administration and is particularly useful for the light it throws on estate management and on the circumstances which led to the rising of 1353.

(ii). p. xvii (Sources and Bibliography/II. Original Authorities/B. Published).

Knighton: *Chronicon* (ed. J.R. Lumby, Rolls Series, 1895) gives a rather obscure account of events in Cheshire in 1353.

(iii). p. 12 (Chapter II: The Land).

Already customs are not identical with the liberty granted by the charter, [i.e. the Magna Carta of Cheshire, in respect of payments for forest assarts in the 1350s] and a further departure both from the charter and the customs arises in the practice of requiring licences to enclose and cultivate land in the forest. Since this practice involved an infringement of what was deemed to be an ancient right, it was bitterly contested by the men of the county, and indeed formed one of the causes of the rising of 1353. ⟨*Vide infra*, 17⟩.

(iv). pp. 17–18 (Same Chapter).

Enough has been written to illustrate one aspect of the Black Prince's policy with regard to his earldom of Chester. That the continued pursuit of such a policy [the exaction of forest-eyre fines in 1347 and the 1350s] in a region so turbulent as Cheshire should lead to an outbreak of violence, was natural enough. In many parts of England shortage of food and the attempt to regulate wages had caused discontent. To these grievances were added in Cheshire the heavy fines made before the justices and the infringement of ancient customs. Already in 1347 the commonalty had declared that the eyre itself was 'harmful to the laws and customs of the county' and had offered to make a fine of 5000 marks on condition that the eyre should cease and certain liberties be granted. The prince had accepted the fine and granted a respite of the eyre for thirty years. ⟨*Calendar of Charter Rolls (1341–1417)*, 313–15. The commonalty made a recognisance for the payment of the sum stated, but the *Chamberlains' Accounts* contain no indication that payment had begun before the question rose again in 1353⟩. Another eyre was, however, held at Chester in 1353 and this appears to have been the immediate cause of the rising. The proceedings were protracted and it was necessary to protect the justices. The Black Prince, the duke of Lancaster, and the earls of Warwick and Stafford therefore marched into the county with their men. Against this display of force the men of Cheshire were powerless. They agreed, therefore, to make a fine of [p. 18] 5000 marks on condition that they should be exempt from the eyre. A second time the fine was accepted, and when the whole affair appeared to be closed, the justices sat again and seized lands and tenements and levied very many big fines. ⟨*Chronicon Henrici Knighton*, (Rolls Series, 1895), Vo. II, 75. Knighton refers to the 'enormous offences' of the men of Cheshire, but does not indicate any particular offence . . .⟩.

(**v**). p. 152 (Chapter IX: The Population).

The general lawlessness of the county has already been illustrated in connection with the safety of communications. . . . It was not the cause of the rebellions of 1353 and 1393. It is, however, closely connected with all these movements [i.e. the two mentioned, and the peasant risings in Vale Royal and Wirral] for, although they sprang from specific causes, the magnitude and bitterness were in each case increased by the lawlessness of the participants.

(**b**.) H.J. Hewitt, *The Black Prince's Expedition of 1355–1357* (1958), p. 16.

Not until 1353 did he [the Black Prince] visit his earldom of Chester and then the occasion was a threatened rising which he quelled by a display of force, followed by very heavy fines. ⟨Hewitt, *Mediaeval Cheshire*, 15–19⟩.

(**c**.) H.J. Hewitt, *Cheshire Under the Three Edwards* (1967).

(**i**). p. 18.

But worse was to follow [after the 1347 forest eyre, and the resultant forest-eyre fines]. In July 1353, proclamation was made throughout the county that another eyre was to be held. Enraged by the events of the preceding years and fearful of the lengths to which the next eyre might go, the men of Cheshire rose in revolt. No information has been found about incidents, but the fact that the Prince, paying his first visit to his earldom, was accompanied by the Duke of Lancaster and the Earls of Warwick and Stafford and their men, probably indicates that overwhelming, organised force was available and the men of Cheshire were powerless. A fine of 5,000 marks was made on condition that they should be exempt from the eyre for thirty years.

(**ii**). p. 107.

The government of a county so prone to disorder presented serious difficulties. . . . The rising of 1353 was suppressed by a display of force and, a little later, the Prince forbade all assemblies of armed men.

7.   An historian of international stature pronounces: the 'Great Rebellion' is born.

Geoffrey Barraclough, 'The Earldom and County Palatine of Chester', *T.H.S.L.C.*, 103 (1951), p. 41.

Hence, although it may be true that Cheshire 'increased in productivity under the vigilant care' of the Black Prince's ministers, ⟨P. Shaw, 'The Black Prince', *History*, XXIV, 1939, 10⟩ its increased wealth was drained off to pay for the prince's prodigal expenditure, and ever harsher means, including the abuse of legal procedure, were taken to extract more and more revenue. The fines exacted in 1347, 1353 and 1357 exceeded in magnitude anything Cheshire had ever known; ⟨H.J. Hewitt, *Mediaeval Cheshire*, 16–19; Stewart-Brown, *Chester County Court Rolls*, xxx–xxxi; Cf W. Fergusson Irvine, TRANSACTIONS, vol. CI, 1950, 39–45. Details of the extortions are recorded in *Cheshire Chamberlains' Accounts*, 1301–1360 (Rec. Soc., LIX, 1910).⟩ and the abuse of his powers by the absentee earl aroused deep-seated resentment throughout the county. The outcome was the great rebellion of 1353. ⟨Cf Hewitt, *op. cit.*, pp. 12, 17, 152 . . . .⟩.

8.   The final accolade: *The Oxford History of England.*

May McKisack, *The Fourteenth Century: 1307–1399*, The Oxford History of England, V (1959), pp. 203–4.

It did not make for good order in the land that, the clergy apart, almost the whole male population of fighting age should have been not only armed, but trained in the use of arms. . . . Doubtless, the ordinary man needed no official encouragement to carry a knife in his belt when he went abroad; but it was a more serious matter that the able-bodied men of the village, trained to act as a military unit, could without difficulty organize themselves in defiance of the law. It may well have been the experience gained by the country folk in the *posse* which made it necessary for the Black Prince himself, with Lancaster and other lords, to take armed forces into Cheshire to suppress the rising of 1353; ⟨H.J. Hewitt, *Medieval Cheshire* (1929), p. 17.⟩ . . . .

9.   A Migration of the Cheshire rebellion to the Welsh March.

T.B. Pugh, ed., *The Marcher Lordships of South Wales, 1415–1536: Select Documents*, Board of Celtic Studies, University of Wales. History and Law Series no. xx (1963), p. 38.

[Footnote two].
Even more was paid in the county-palatine of Chester to buy off eyres held by the justices of the Forest in 1347 and 1353. In return for a fine of 5,000 marks in 1347, the Black Prince granted that there would be a respite from the eyre for

thirty years. The holding of an eyre in 1353 led to a rebellion, and another fine of 5,000 marks was exacted (H.J. Hewitt, *Medieval Cheshire* (Chetham Society, New Series, Vol. 88, 1929), pp. 17–18).

10.   A reluctant convert.

Michael Prestwich, *The Three Edwards: War and State in England, 1272–1377* (1980), p. 278.

Cheshire also caused the prince's officials frequent problems. While suggestions that an actual rising took place there in 1353 are an exaggeration, there was considerable disorder in the county. A general eyre might have settled matters, but the prince, in need of money for the wars, accepted 5,000 marks in lieu from the local communities. Forest fines were threatened later, and again fines were paid in order to avoid the visitations of the justices.

INDEX

References to sections/entries in text/translation are in bold type: references to pages in ordinary type.

biog. = biographical note   par. = parish   s. = son of   wid. = widow of   w. = wife of
d. = daughter of   b. = brother of

abedywes *see ebediw*
accounting practice Chapter II
  allowances and exonerations xxxvi
  analysis of expenditure lvi–lix
  analysis of revenue xlix–lvi
  arrears, treatment of xxvii–xxviii, lxv, 53
    (n. 5), 122–23, 128, 130, 148, 157, 162–63,
    166, 190, 195
  clerks, use of xxix
  control of building works xxxv
  debts, great roll of xxxvii
  form of accounts xxvii
  money, liveries of xxxvi, lix
  originals and duplicates xxix–xxxii
  particulars and vouchers xxxiv–xxxv
  prest xxxv, lviii–lix
  respites xxxvii
  See also audit and auditors of accounts
Acton (Ches.) **45.4**, 118, 167–68
Acton, Alan de 118
Acton, Alice de 118
Acton, Richard de 118
  See also Aketon
Acton, Robert de **2.4**, **5.12**, 13 (n. 1), **45.4**, 118
  (biog.)
Acton, Robert s. Thomas de 118
ad quod dampnum, inquisition of 140
Adamesone, John, of Chester 43 (n. 1)
Adam's son, Adam 139
Adlington (Ches.) xliii–xliv, lxi, 19 (n. 1),
  155–57
Adynet, John **23.10**
Adynet, William 148
agistment and pannage xxv, 129–30, 152, 165,
  181, 192
Ainsworth, W. Harrison 220
Aketon, Richard de, knight 170
Alan's son, Richard 139
Alcok, John **6.7**, 118–19 (biog.), 206
Aldecroft, John de 45 (n. 5)
Alderley, Nether (Ches.) 35 (n. 3), 122
Alderley parish (Ches.) 167, 175
Aldrington, Thomas de 129
ale, brewing of lxxix
Aleyn, Richard, of Nantwich **12.11**

alms,
  of earls of Chester **28**, **48.2**, **48.3**, 208
  of Black Prince 182, 217–20
  See also tenure of land
Alpraham (Ches.) **12.13**, 122–23, 186
Alvanley (Ches.) 43 (n. 4)
Amory, Roger d' (Dammary), justiciar of
  Chester 120
ancient demesne 33 (n. 3), 161, 163
Anderton (Ches.) 139, 168
Anglesey, county of lxxiii, 171, 184–85, 195, 205
annuities, grants and payment of 75 (n. 4), **30.1**,
  30.2, **30.12**, **30.13**, **30.14**, 119, 127–28, 133,
  138, 142, 147, 159, 165, 178, 183
Antrobus (Ches.) 37 (n. 1), 188
Apelton, Thomas de (of Chester) 43 (n. 1)
Apelton, William de **29.8**, 77 (n. 2), 119
Aquitaine (France), principality of lvi, lx, 133,
  135, 187
  See also Gascony
Arden, Thomas de xlvi, 186
Ardene, Ellen wid. of John de, knight 156
Ardene (Arden), Peter de 156–57
Ardern (Arderne), John de, of Aldford, knight
  174–75, 186
Arderne, Maud de lxii, 157
Arderne (Arden), Thomas de, knight 153, 155,
  157, 183, 186
arian medi lxix, lxxiv, lxxix
arian sir lxvii
Arthull (Ches.) 147
Artonstall, John de, parker of Ringway 154
Arundel, Richard Fitz Alan, earl of xxvi, lii, **4.1**,
  9 (n. 1), **8.2**, 17 (n. 2), **30.2**, 79 (n. 2), 119
  (biog.), 134, 154, 172, 207
Ashley (Ches.) 158
Ashley (Asshelegh), Hamo de 126, 204
Ashley, Joan 158
Ashton (Ches.) 37 (n. 4), 41 (n. 2), 45 (n. 4),
  121, 183–84
Assheton (Asshton), Master John de, clerk,
  prebendary of St John's, Chester **45.12**,
  108–9, 109 (n. 3), 119–20 (biog.)
Assheton, Robert s. Robert de 132
Asshewell (Assewell), Simon de, clerk of the

225

Blount, John, of Chester 123, 140
Bollington (Ches.) lxiv, 124, 146, 150, 157, 163, 167
  tenants of 150
Bongam, Ieuan **19.5**, 194
Booth, P.H.W. xxi
Bordeaux (France) 130
boroughs
  Flint **23.3**, **23.10**, 192
  Frodsham (Ches.) 182
  Hope (Flints.) 120, 126, 192
  Macclesfield (Ches.) **6.2**, 103 (n. 2)
  Rhuddlan (Flints.) 195
Boseden, Thomas de 144
Bosedon (Bosdon), Roger de, 148, 152
Bosley (Ches.) 19 (n. 2), 136, 153, 169–70, 181
Bostok, David de 43 (n. 4), **13.8**, 45 (n. 1), 121 (biog.), 145
Bostok, William de 43 (n. 4). 45 (nn. 1,2), 121
Boudon, John s. John de **13.11**, 45 (nn. 3,4), 121 (biog.)
Boudon (Bowedon), Jordan de 41 (n. 2), **13.10**, 45 (nn. 3,4), 121 (biog.), 126, 159
Boughton, lepers of St Giles of **28.11**, 73 (n. 3), 158 (biog.)
boundaries, confirmation of (Flint borough) **23.3**, 61 (n. 1)
Bowere, John le 142
Boyd, W.K. xvii
Boydell, Elizabeth wid. Ralph 131
Boydell, Robert 132
Boydell, William 132
Braas (?Brace), William, attorney **30.15**, 85 (n. 1), 121–22 (biog.)
Braaz, Richard s. John, of Chester 158
Bradegate, Thomas, constable of Chester castle 139, 145, 185
Bradford (Ches.) **28.8**
Bradford, Thomas de 184
Bradgate, Simon de 145, 167
Bradley manor (Frodsham par., Ches.) 33 (n. 4), 132, 146, 167
Bradwall (Ches.) lxi, 140
Bredon, Robert de **4.4**, 120, 122 (biog.), 206
Breghton (Broghton), Nicholas de **9.5**
Brerton, William de, knight 43 (n. 4)
Brescy, John 136
Bret, Richard le, of Davenham 121
Brimstage (Ches.) 176
Brindley (Ches.) **18**
Brittany, Joan, duchess of 136
Broadbottom (Ches.) 127
Broghton *see* Breghton

Brokesmouth, Henry 43 (n. 4)
Bromfield and Yale, lordship of xlviii, lxxiii, 119, 125
Bromlegh, John de **12.12**, 35 (n. 2), 122 (biog.), 139
Brontë, Charlotte ('Currer Bell') 220
Broxton hundred (Ches.) 148
Brugge, Nicholas del **5.7**
Brundelegh, John de, of Wistaston 148
Brunham, Master John de, the elder 124 (biog.), 200
Brunham (Burnham), Master John de, the younger, chamberlain of Chester xxiv, xxxii–xxxiv, xxxvi–xxxvii, xliii, lii, **9.6**, **28.10**, **29.3**, 75 (n. 3), 123, 124–26 (biog.), 131–33, 136, 151, 153, 174, 176–77, 180, 200–8
Brunham, Ralph de 120, 205
Bruyn, Ranulf le 140
Bruyn, Richard le, mayor of Chester 203
Bruyn, Robert le 204
Buckingham 151, 188, 220
Budenhale, Thomas de 141, 177
building work xxxiv, lvii–lviii, **34**
  castles 197, 200
  Frodsham manor 202
  in forests **8**
  lead smelted for **49.1**
  Macclesfield park lodge **34.5**
  Shotwick park 202
  Vale Royal 77 (n. 3), **35**, 149, 217–20
Bulkylegh, William de, of Tarporley 43 (n. 3)
Bulkylegh (Bilkylegh), William s. William de, of Alpraham **12.13**, 35 (n. 3), 122–23 (biog.)
Bunbury (Ches.) lxi, 141, 148
Bunbury, William s. John de 43 (n. 4), 145, 167
Burdeaux, Oliver de, knight 182
Burgherssh, Bartholomew de, the elder, knight xxv
Burgherssh, Bartholomew de, the younger, knight, justiciar of Chester **29.1**, **29.2**, 75 (nn. 1,2), 123–24 (biog.), 135, 207, 213
Burghes, Hugh 205
Burton, Richard de 122
Burton in Wirral (Ches.) xl, 87 (n. 3)
Burwes, Hugh de 154
Bury, Richard de *see* Sancto Edmundo
business-managers of the Black Prince *see* John de Wingfield and John de Delves
Busshell, William, catchpoll of Middlewich 173
Butley (Ches.) 19 (n. 3)
Byntre, John de, knight 57 (n. 2), 123, 138
Byrchore *see* Birchover

Shore, Henry del **14.2**
Shotwick, Castle (Ches.) xxviii–xxix, xxxv (n. 36), xl, **2.9**, **5.1**, **45.15**, 120, 126, 151, 176, 200, 202, 207
Shotwick, Church **31.6**
Shrigley *see* Pott Shrigley
Shropshire xlvii, 35 (n. 3), 122, 134, 137, 143
Shryggelegh, Robert de **14.1**, 172–73 (biog.)
Shutlingsloe hill (Ches.) xli
Shydeyord (Shideyord), le (Macclesfield, Ches.) 31 (n. 3), 162
Skiret, Roger 151, 188
socage 132
Somerford (Ches.) 166
Somerford, John de **6.1**, 13 (n. 2), 161–63, 173 (biog.), 190
Somerford, Sigreda (?Tille) w. John de 161, 163, 173
Sonky, Thomas le, bailiff of Rhuddlan **3.4**, **19.9**
Soty, William lxiii–lxiv, 124, 146, 150, 163, 167
Soule, Henry, catchpoll of Middlewich **5.8**, 173 (biog.)
Southwark (London) 135
Spark, Maud 145
Speed, John xlv
Spicer, John 160
Spridlyngton, William de, auditor, bishop of St Asaph xxvi, xxix, **45.13**, **50.4**, 173–74 (biog.), 177, 180
Stafford, Hugh de Stafford, earl of 146
Stafford, Isabel w. John de 174
Stafford, John de **8.3**, 17 (n. 3), 174–75 (biog.)
Stafford, Ralph de Stafford, earl of 175, 214, 217–18, 220–22
Stafford (Destafford), Richard de, knight xliii, lxxix, **5.11**, 11 (n. 6), 15 (n. 3), 95 (n. 1), 122, 175 (biog.), 176, 189, 192, 213–14
Stafford, William de 166, 176
Staffordshire liv, 152, 156, 171–72, 178
Stalker, Richard le 206
stallage 166
Stanlegh, Alice de 168
Stanlegh (Stanelegh), Ellen de 33 (n. 3), 160, 176
Stanlegh (Stanelegh), William de, the elder lxiii, **12.9**, 33 (n. 3), 130, 160, 168, 176–77. (biog.), 207
Stanlegh, William de, the younger 86 (n. a), **45.15**, 143, 168, 177, 190
Stanlow (Ches.), abbot and convent of 73 (n. 4)
stannaries (Devon) 124
Stanthorne (Ches.) 130
Starky, John 128
Starky, Thomas 128, 205

Stathum, Thomas de 133, 166, 175, 204
steward of Chester 169
Stewart-Brown, R. xvii–xxii, xlvi
Stile, Henry 145
Stockport (Ches.) lxii, 151, 174–75
Stockport, Joan heiress of Richard de, knight 175
Stoke, Alice w. John de 59 (n. 2), 195
Stoke (Stokes), John de **23.1**, **23.2**, 59 (n. 2), **45.11**, 195 (biog.)
Stoke, John de xlviii (n. 40)
Stoke, Richard de, knight 174
Stokes, Richard de, auditor xxvii, xlvi, 177 (biog.)
Stone Dunham *see* Dunham on the Hill
Storeton (Ches.) **45.7**, 120, 177
Strange, Ebulo le 154, 177
Strange (Lestraunge, Le Strangee), Roger le, knight lxviii, **45.14**, 111 (n. 1), 119, 154, 177–78 (biog.)
strays, payment for lxxix
See also waif and stray
Strech, Robert 43 (n. 3)
Stretton, Hugh de, sheriff of Chester city **4.2**, 178 (biog.)
Stretton, William de, knight **30.1**, 79 (n. 1), 178 (biog.)
stud, Black Prince's at Macclesfield 118, 129
sturgeon xlviii, **9.7**, **31.4–31.6**, 151, 182
subsidy *see* taxation
Sumpter, David le, of Minshull 43 (n. 4)
Surrey, earl of *see* Warenne
Sutton (Macclesfield, Ches.) 143, 152, 161–62
Sutton, John de, knight 140
Sutton, Richard de, king's yeoman 186
Swan, William 141
Swetenham, Thomas de **17.1**, 53 (n. 3), 164, 178 (biog.)
Swettenham (Ches.) 153
Swynemore, John de 148
Swynemore, Reginald de 148
Swynerton, Robert de, knight 178
Swynerton, Roger de, knight 178
Swynerton, Thomas de, knight **45.1**, 178–79 (biog.)

Tabbelegh, Adam de 132–33
Tabley, Over (Ches.)132
Taillour, Hugh le **5.10**, 179 (biog.)
tailor of the Black Prince's chamber **30.1**
Tait, James xx
Talar Goch lead-mine (Flints.) lxxviii
tallage **12.9**, **12.10**, 206–7
tanners of Chester **13.1**, 41 (n. 1), 49 (n. 3), **16.1**

Index 247

Wovere, David de 141
wrecks, payments for lxxix
Wychough (Ches.) 141
Wyot, Roger 167
Wyrlegh, Hugh de **30.18**, 85 (n. 4), 131, 190 (biog.)
Wystanesfeld (Whistansfeld), William **14.2**, 49 (n. 2)

Yate, William s. William del, of Congleton 51 (n. 1), 137
Yekheth, Thomas de 37 (n. 4)
Yong (Yonge), Thomas le **2.6**, **2.7**, 3 (n. 6), **17.3**, 53 (n. 3), 120, 173–74, 178, 190–91 (biog.), 203
Ystrad Alun (Flints.) 192

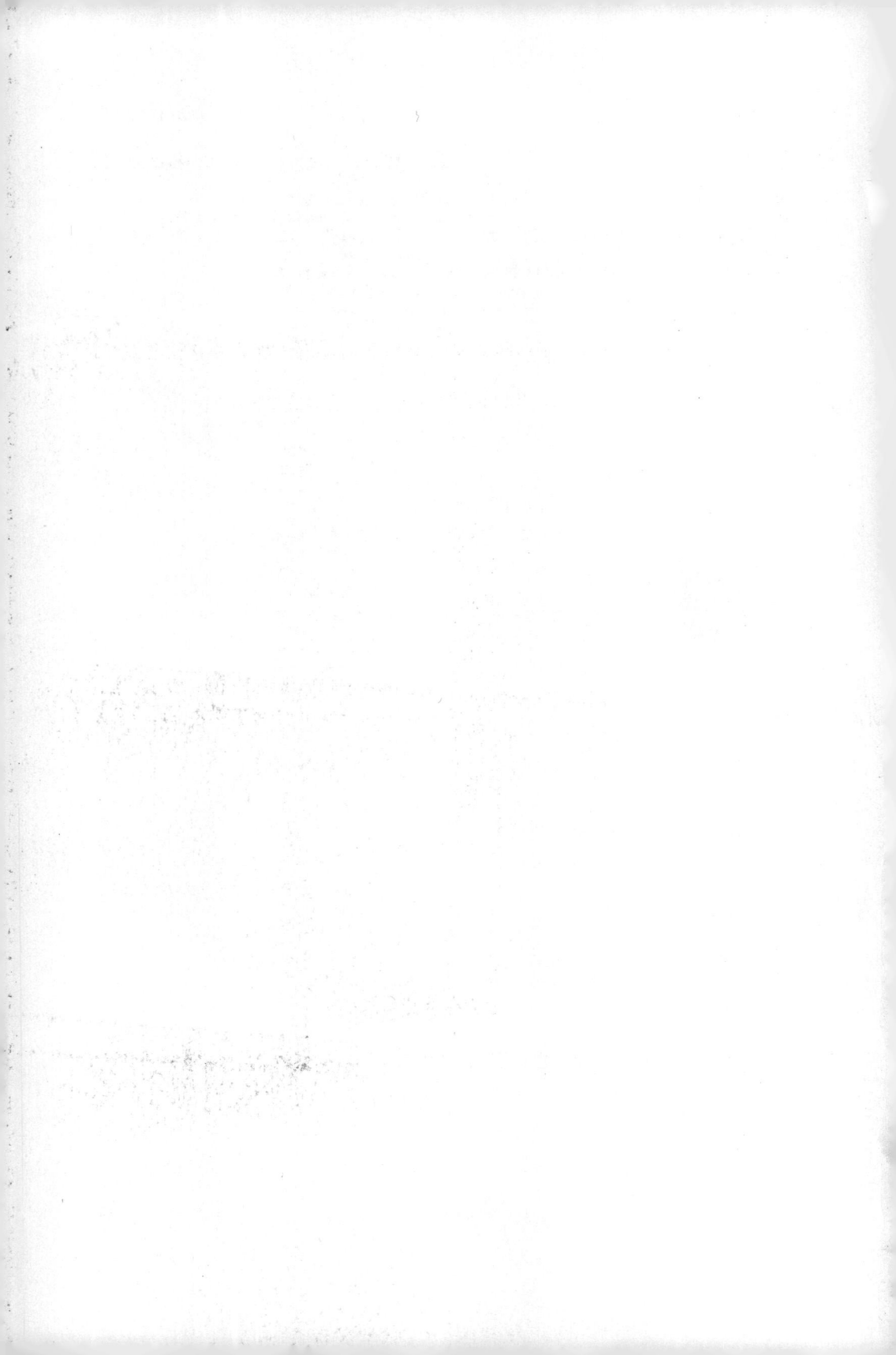